Tyra

Tyra

Through Blood, Sweat, and Tears

Elizabeth Ellen Ostring

RESOURCE *Publications* · Eugene, Oregon

TYRA
Through Blood, Sweat, and Tears

Copyright © 2021 Elizabeth Ellen Ostring. All rights reserved. Except for brief quotations in critical publications or reviews, no part of this book may be reproduced in any manner without prior written permission from the publisher. Write: Permissions, Wipf and Stock Publishers, 199 W. 8th Ave., Suite 3, Eugene, OR 97401.

Resource Publications
An Imprint of Wipf and Stock Publishers
199 W. 8th Ave., Suite 3
Eugene, OR 97401

www.wipfandstock.com

PAPERBACK ISBN: 978-1-7252-8793-8
HARDCOVER ISBN: 978-1-7252-8794-5
EBOOK ISBN: 978-1-7252-8795-2

02/11/21

Dedicated to my grandchildren

Andrew, Matthew, Samuela, and Nathanael,

With love,

So they will understand.

I believe in Christianity as I believe that the Sun has risen,
not only because I see it, but because by it I see everything else.

C.S. LEWIS *IS THEOLOGY POETRY?*

The greatest argument in favor of the gospel
is a loving and lovable Christian.

E.G. WHITE *MINISTRY OF HEALING*

Contents

List of Illustrations | ix
List of Main Characters | xi
Glossary of Swedish Terms | xiii
Author's Note | xix

Part One: Questions | 1
    Chapter 1: A Finnish Christmas | 3
    Chapter 2: In the Finnish, Who Are We? | 20
    Chapter 3: Summer Lightning | 37
    Chapter 4: A Finnish War | 54
    Chapter 5: What's in a Name? | 70
    Chapter 6: Work | 87
    Chapter 7: Karl | 102

Part Two: Blood, Sweat, and Tears | 125
    Chapter 8: The Funeral | 127
    Chapter 9: Axel | 143
    Chapter 10: Nykarleby | 159
    Chapter 11: News | 178
    Chapter 12: Another War, Again, and Again | 197
    Chapter 13: Fugitive | 216
    Chapter 14: The Unthinkable | 238

Part Three: Love | 267
    Chapter 15: Kiruna | 269
    Chapter 16: Exploring | 284

Chapter 17: Takla's Letters | 299

Chapter 18: Voyage | 312

Chapter 19: Ape Land Battles | 329

Chapter 20: Choices | 341

Chapter 21: Home | 355

Bibliography | 369

List of Illustrations

Group 1, between Parts One and Two

1. Anna Lall on her wedding day, 1900.
2. Johan Rådman, Anna Lall's father.
3. Anders Lall, husband of Anna, and Tyra's father.
4. Confirmation Class, Tyra 3rd from L, front row.
5. Collage of Tyra, her cousins and friends. Algot is on the L of top L photo.
6. Tyra's work reference.
7. Tyra aged about 20.
8. Tyra.
9. Tyra.
10. Karl Rådman.
11. Finnish Funeral Hearse.
12. Axel Östring in army dress uniform.
13. Elna Marie Hendriksson Östring, 1905–1932.
14. Östring family, L-R, Edit, Mor Anna, Johan, AnniAstrid, and Erik.
15. Östring family, back L Axel. R Elna. Front L Mor Anna, and R Father Emil Hendricksson Östring.
16. Östring family home, Sorvich.

Group 2, Between Parts Two and Three

17. Tyra and Axel, Wedding Day, July 2, 1931.
18. Tyra and Axel's house, on right, in Brännon.
19. Tyra with farm horse and unidentified rider.
20. Anna Lall's baptismal certificate.
21. Nils aged about two.
22. Finnish soldiers.
23. Tyra and Nils with family cow.
24. Tyra and Nils with family pet.
25. Erik Östring.
26. Kiruna Mine and Town, circa 1955.
27. Östring's house, (note snow) Kiruna
28. Tuullovaara Mine.
29. Roland in Kiruna.
30. Nils and Erik in Kiruna, 1953.
31. Nils and Roland in Kiruna.
32. Nils (facing camera) in Tuulovaara mine.
33. With Finnish friends in Kiruna. Back Row, Nils second L, Axel far R. Front row, Tyra has Roland, wearing dog-shirt, sitting on her knee.
34. Family group, Kiruna, L to R, Nils, Tyra, Axel, Roland.
35. Axel, circa 1955, when the family left for Australia.
36. Death Notice of Anna Lall, December 30, 1955.
37. Nils with family's first car.
38. Axel and Tyra at Roland's wedding, 1972. The young man to Tyra's L was the best man, Dr. Keith Powers.
39. Grave of Tyra and Axel, Mullumbimby, NSW, Australia.

List of Main Characters

Anna Lall, wife of Anders Lall
Anders Lall
Tyra Lall, their only child

Karl Rådman, Anna Lall's brother
Lisa Rådman, Karl's wife
Algot & Hjalmar Rådman, their two sons

Pastor Virtanen—fictitious, representative character
Reverend Svenson (later Lindgren)—fictitious, representative character
Reverend Urho Järvinen—fictitious, representative character.

Lukas Larson (later Lukas Tobelius)—fictitious neighbor of the Lall family in Vasa. His story is typical of the painful events surrounding the Finnish Wars.
Elin Larson, his wife
Tobbe, Erik, & Jan Larson, their sons

Rolf Nilsson—fictitious neighbor of the Rådman family in Oxkangar. His tragedy was a real event experienced by relatives of the Östring family.
Sonja Nilsson his wife (later Sonja Rolfholm)

Axel Östring, married Tyra Lall
Elna Östring, Axel's sister
Erik Östring, Axel's half-brother
Emil Johan (John) Östring, Axel's half-brother
Anna Östring (Mor Anna), Axel's stepmother
Nils Axel & Sven Anders Roland, Tyra and Axel's sons

Takla & Karl Höglund, neighbors of Tyra and Axel in Nykarleby.
Harry Nylund, Takla's brother and Tyra's Australian neighbor
June Nylund, his wife

Edit Söderholm, Mullumbimby friend of Tyra's

Glossary of Swedish Terms

Åbo	Swedish for the historical name of Turku, city in Finland
Diet	Finnish parliament
Far	father
Fika	approximately morning or afternoon coffee.
Fru	Mrs
Fröken	Miss
Griser	doughnuts
Häst	horse, *kvinnlig* häst—mare
Helsingfors	Swedish for Helsinki
Herr	Mr., or teacher
Knäckerbröd	traditional rye crisp bread.
Kossa	cow
Mor	mother
Morbor	uncle, literally mother's brother
Mormor	grandmother, literally mother's mother.
Morfar	grandfather, literally mother's father
Nikolaistad	Name of the Finnish city of Vaasa under the rule of Tsar Nikolai I of Russia, and his successors
Oxkangar	an island, now attached to the mainland by a bridge, off the north coast of Finland.
Pepparkakor	ginger nut biscuits

Glossary of Swedish Terms

Rådhusgatan	literally "red house street", where the Lall family lived
Skriftskola	confirmation class
Sisu	a Finnish term meaning fortitude, stamina, and dependability
Suomi	Finnish for Finland
Tammerfors	Swedish for the Finnish city of Tampere
Vasa	Swedish for Vaasa
Yah	(transliteration of Swedish ja) yes

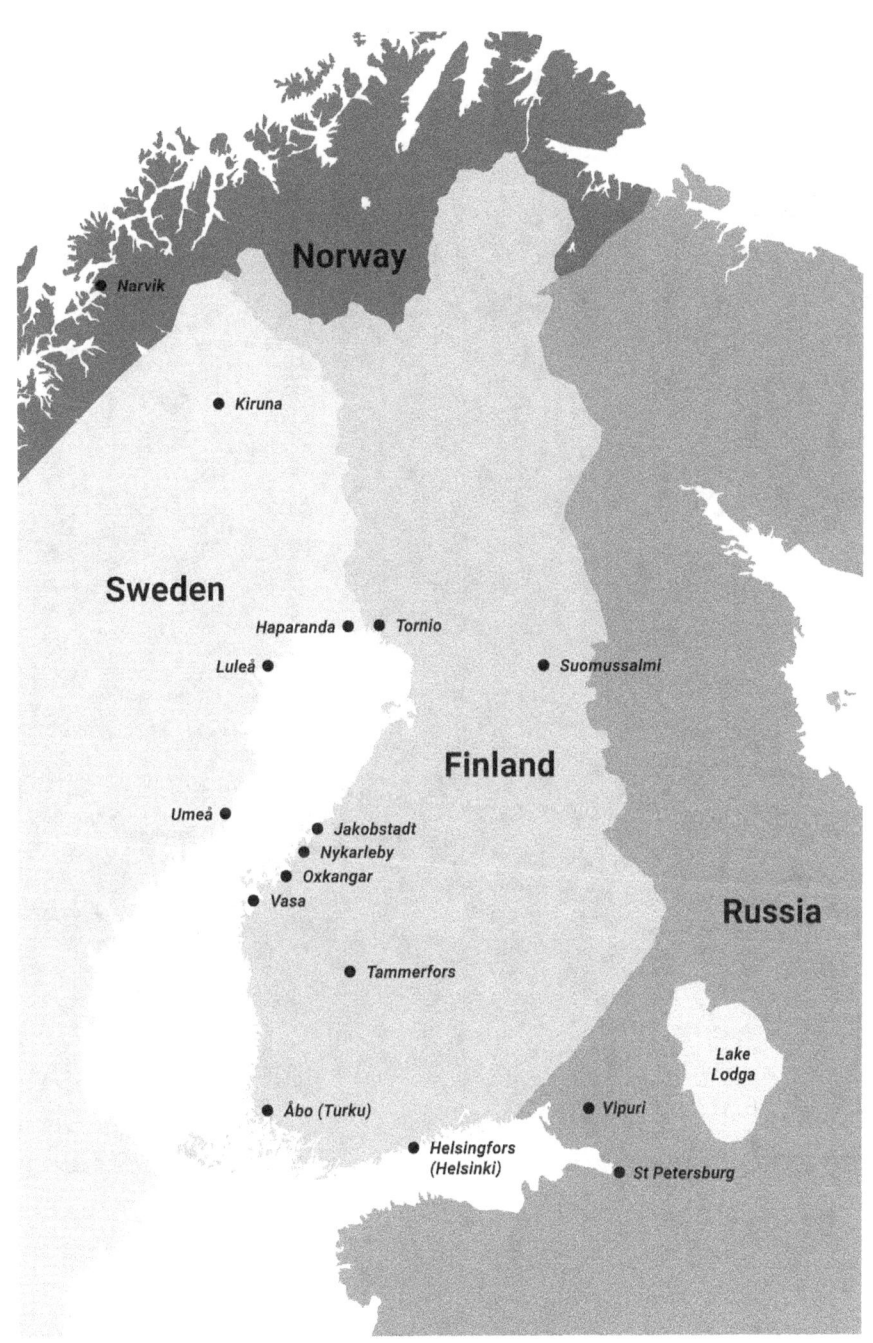

Map of Finland and Sweden

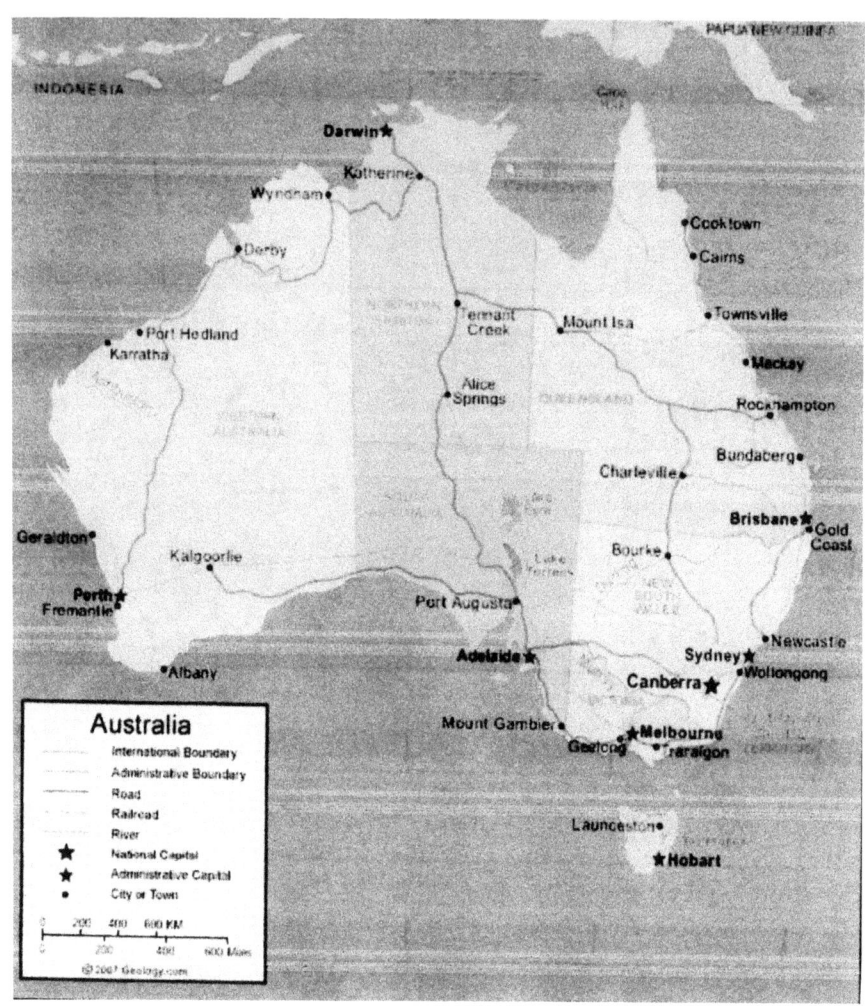

Map of Australia

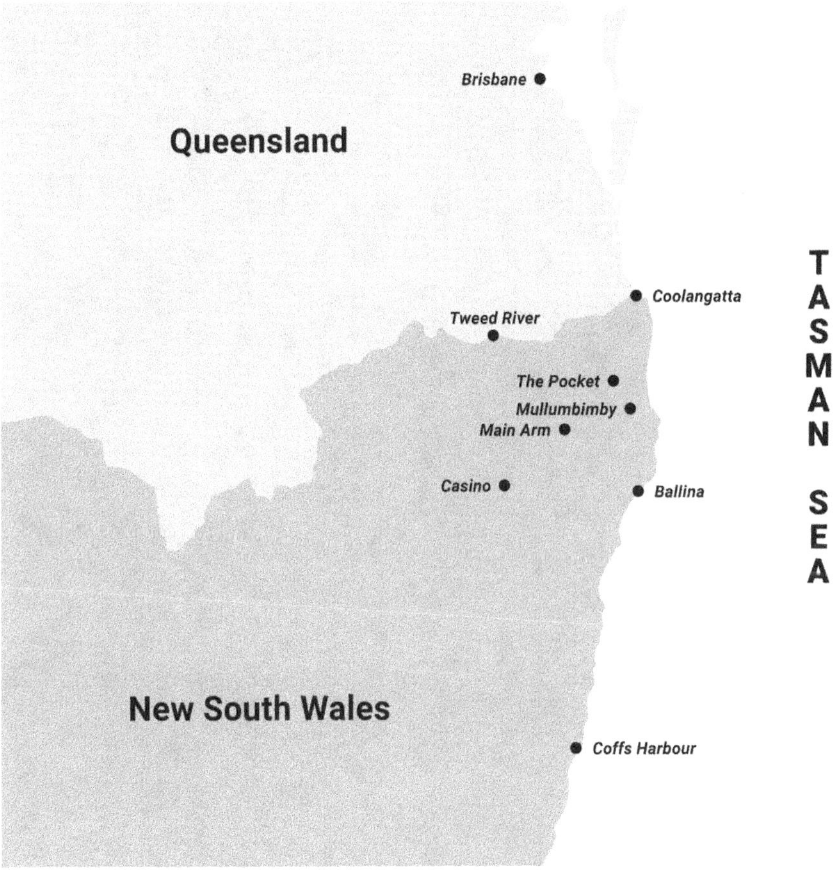

Map of New South Wales and Queensland, Australia

Author's Note

SET PRIMARILY IN THE traumatic times of Finland's infancy as an independent nation, this is the true story of one woman's struggle with life and her gradual faith development. Christianity is often presented as achievement. But learning to utterly trust God and appreciate His leading despite disheartening circumstances, no matter how bad, is surely the most important Christian task. Sometimes this account may appear critical of certain Christians, but persistent reading will show that these eventually enriched Tyra's life. Many people contributed to Tyra's faith development: her parents; members of the Lutheran church; her husband and brother-in-law; a young unnamed Adventist minister; members of the small Adventist fellowship in Nykarleby, Finland; the Mullumbimby Adventist church in Australia, and so on. Importantly, ultimately Tyra herself powerfully impacted the lives and faith of others.

The subtitle, "blood, swear, and tears," has been traced to a sermon, based on Luke 22:44, by Welsh preacher Christmas Evans (25 December 1766—1838), translated by J. Davis in 1837, and immortalized by Winston Churchill in his famous 1940 war speech.[1] It epitomizes the religious and conflict themes of the book.

All main events, notably the most dramatic, are historically factual, but expressed through my imagination. Occasionally real events from the experience of others during Tyra's lifetime have been used to indicate problems as Tyra would have experienced life, for example, the barn fire. I became aware of the story of my mother-in-law only after her death, and discovered few primary documents exist except limited family photographs and a recently discovered treasure trove of 370 letters exchanged between Axel and Tyra while he was at the frontline during Finland's Continuation War. Therefore, oral history from her family

1. The Phrase Finder: article "Blood, Sweat, and Tears"

was my main source, to which I have added educated imagination. The book is thus in the form of a novel, not a biography. Her extended family strongly requested that I write her life as "story" and not as an academic treatise (which, knowing me, they feared I might!). I have been researching material for this book for 36 years, visiting all the places Tyra lived, and reading as widely as I could (see bibliography) on the history of her country although there is remarkably little about Finnish history available in English. I hope her story will encourage others to make sense of the traumatic events of their lives, and like Tyra, finally know how great, and good, God truly is.

I have not tried to capture idiomatic speech, to avoid alienating the reader. However, I indicate the characters are not speaking English by using a few Swedish words: Mor (mother), Far (father), Yah (yes) are the most common. Swedish is used instead of Finnish for place names, the norm for Tyra, her family, and many Finnish people during Tyra's life in Finland.

I would like to express special appreciation to my sister-in-law, Ethel Östring for her significant help with information and photographs, and translation of the wartime letters that brought the story together, to Carole Ferch-Johnson, Kathryn Lewis, and Ardis Stenbakken for their advice and critical review of the manuscript, and Sam Ryan for helping with the maps. I am very appreciative of the assistance of the staff at Wipf and Stock, Publishers, and all those who have in any way encouraged me in this project. To my husband Dr. Roland Ostring, for his patient acceptance of my preoccupation with his family's story, most of which he did not know himself until I began my research, I give my very special love.

Part One

Questions

Chapter 1

A Finnish Christmas

CHRISTMAS DAY, TIME OF joy and festivity; day when the Nordic winter darkness begins to recede; day celebrating the birth of the Son of God who came to bless the human family. But on this Christmas Day, in the Grand Duchy of Finland, all was not joyful. Powerful forces were at work in the land, forces that shattered the country and the lives of the people in it. Slowly, very slowly, Finland and its people rose from the ashes of conflict to begin new life.

The Nikolaistad Central Lutheran church was full, because State and Church declared it should be. All citizens must attend church at Christmas. After a hurried reading of the biblical story of the Wise Men, the young relief minister, in stilted, bookish Swedish, gave a long scolding harangue to the congregants, urging them to be better citizens. His concept of a better citizen included "our great Finnish language" and "attaining national autonomy", suggesting he spent a good deal of his time at seminary attending political meetings rather than theological classes. For twenty years a fervent spirit of nationalism had engulfed Finland. The parson's words were tedious, nothing novel. No one cared what he meant, least of all Anders Lall, Tyra Maria's father, who so often recalled this day that it became part of Tyra's own memories, the beginning of her awareness of the complexities of life. But Anders admitted he longed for a shaft of celestial wisdom to relieve the humdrum tedium of his life. An audible sigh of relief, like a ripple of spring breeze, swept through the congregation when the minister finally sat down and children filed into the church.

Part One: Questions

The hands of Anna, Tyra's mother, tensely clasped inside her squirrel fur muff, relaxed as the children's choir entered. Anders' heavy breathing and hard set shoulders clearly announced the sermon displeased him. Did she hear him murmur under his breath, "What about Jesus?" Furtively, Anna glanced at her husband, and to her relief met his twinkling eye. Of course, he would not smile at her. That would be so unmanly, so un-Finnish. But she did feel a soft pressure on her arm as he uncrossed his legs and his well-worn sealskin trousers creaked slightly.

It was unusual to have children singing in church. Such a solemn and sacred duty was normally reserved for men. The male choirs of Finland were excellent, their deep, sonorous tones rousing patriotic fervor. But the local school teacher had conferred with the relief minister, and they agreed that in keeping with the new Finnish concept of gender equality, it was suitable that a mixed children's choir perform for the annual Christmas program. The children sang the wonderful *Julvisa*, written by Österbotten poet Zacharias Topelius, of whom the congregation was very proud. How splendid, they thought, that someone from their own northern neighborhood had become nationally famous through his poetry and historical writings. Even better, the renowned Finnish composer, Jean Sibelius, had written the music for this beautiful Christmas song. Anna wondered what those illustrious men would think of the morning's sermon. Sibelius was very patriotic, but he was a Swedish Finn, like all members of the congregation, not like the young firebrand parson from the south. But innocently unaware of their parents' discomfort from the sermon, the children sang earnestly:

> Give me no splendor, no gold, no pomp, at blessed Christmastide
> Give me God's glory and angel hosts and peace on earth so wide!

Their breaths made faint puffs of vapor in the cold air. Despite the deacon's dedicated, early morning stoking with large bundles of well-dried birch wood, the potbellied stoves in the church merely succeeded in removing the ache from the cold. But everyone was warmly dressed, and not concerned about the icy temperature. Anna's and Anders' hearts swelled with parental pride as they watched Tyra, their seven-year-old daughter, solemnly singing the familiar song.

The children filed out to change their robes, walking stiffly in single file, self-conscious about the importance of their performance. But one small boy was so enraptured with his accomplishment that he remained steadfastly gazing ahead as his companions left the church. Suddenly he realized he was alone, and raced after his friends, the sleeves of his gown flapping wildly, causing a crescendo of muffled coughs and giggles from the congregation. Unfazed by this minor procedural hitch, with commendable dignity, the minister stood and announced the final hymn. To the pleasant surprise of the congregation, after the nationalistic severity of his sermon, it was the Swedish version of the national anthem, *Vårt Land*.

> Our land, our land, our fatherland,
> Sound loud, O name of worth!
> No mount that meets the heaven's band,
> No hidden vale, no wave-washed strand,
> Is loved, as is our native North,
> Our own forefathers' earth.
>
> Thy blossom in the bud laid low,
> Yet ripened shall upspring.
> See! From our love once more shall grow
> Thy light, thy joy, thy hope, thy glow!
> And clearer yet one day shall ring
> The song our land shall sing.

The majestic notes of the organ ceased, and the minister intoned a prayer of blessing over the congregation. Suddenly, the beautiful stained glass window at the front of the church glowed with color as a shaft of the newly risen sun glanced across it. The congregation, encouraged by this sign of celestial blessing, rose and filed out into the snowy cold.

The young parson, warmly clad in voluminous robes, stood shaking hands as he smiled benignly at each person. The sun, low on the horizon, made long, blue, distorted shadows across the frozen landscape as people walked down the snow on the path beneath the gaunt black branches of birch trees. Occasionally a pat of snow fell from the trees, making a soft thud beside the exiting congregants.

"Good morning, Herr Lall, isn't it?" enthused Pastor Virtanen, thrusting his hand out to shake Anders'. "How good to see *you* here."

Anders, noting the emphasis on *you*, nodded curtly, and used both hands to ram his sheepskin hat on his head. Anna quickly grasped the minister's proffered hand. "And good morning to you, Fru Lall," smiled the pastor, as unfazed by Anders' gruff behavior as he had been by the choirboy's delayed departure, "and a special greeting to our young Fröken who sang so beautifully." Dropping Anna's hand rather hurriedly, he bent to offer his to Tyra, who, frightened at this unexpected attention, bobbed a quick curtsy.

The Lall family's heavy boots crunched down the frozen path. It was only a few blocks to their home on Rådhusgatan in central Nikolaistad, but in the bitter cold it seemed much further. Close by loomed the large, imposing, well-lit bulk of the central police station, a guiding landmark. As soon as she thought they were out of earshot of the priest, Tyra asked excitedly, "Mor, Far, did I sing well? Did you laugh at Lars when he forgot to come out?" She was tenderly reassured.

Anders, despite chafing at the sermon he had endured, looked at his attractive wife with pride. The new, short, Russian-style, white fleece sheepskin jacket he had recently bought, richly embroidered with colored wool, looked very well over the voluminous red and black striped skirt she was wearing. He had watched her weave that skirt on her loom and knew it was made of the finest wool he could obtain. He also knew she had woven her layers of red wool petticoats, and knitted the thick red stockings that peeked mischievously above her boots. Best of all he liked her hat, a ruffled, puffy ball of scarlet felt, trimmed with her own crocheted white lace, sensibly covering her whole head for warmth, but allowing tendrils of her thick dark hair to escape. Under his own dark sheepskin coat he proudly wore one of Anna's colorfully patterned pullovers. Tyra Maria, away from the restraint of church, skipped happily in her new black boots, twirling her layers of red skirt and petticoats, also made by her mother, while waving her long blue wool scarf like a flag. Her black plaits streamed behind her.

The family turned the corner and the usually reserved Anders exploded with pent up anger. "That ridiculous young colt!" he growled. "How dare he come from some peasant village down by Helsingfors and blast us about Finland for the Finnish, and the beauties of a common language! Who's he working for? The church, or some non-existent independent government of Finland? He couldn't even crack a smile when that cute young kid forgot what he was doing!"

"Pastor Virtanen was just doing his best, husband," said Anna consolingly. She was a very devout woman. "They all talk and behave serious like that. It's to encourage us to be good citizens."

"You mean you go to church every week to listen to humorless people like him rave? He didn't inspire me to make my appearance more often than the demanded Christmas and Easter visits! I'm a pretty good citizen without his encouragement! Doesn't he know the history of his country? He couldn't even speak good Swedish! I'm perfectly happy for him to use Finnish in personal conversation, but it's not the language of educated people, and certainly not what we speak up here, so there's no point using it in a church where no one understands! And surely, it's supposed to be Christmas. Why didn't he talk about Jesus Christ and the Christmas story instead of all that inflammatory political stuff? Or have we all stopped being Christians and become mere Finns instead?"

Anna was aghast at her husband's attitude, but she did not show it. "The regular pastor is more traditional, and gives nice general talks. You like him, surely," offered Anna, as soothingly as she could muster. "I don't think he's comfortable with this Finland for the Finnish stuff. When he gets back, come and hear him."

It was most unfortunate, Anna thought, that on one of the rare times Anders attended church this young firebrand should be speaking. The Reverend Svenson was a wise man. He accepted without protest Anders' muttered explanations about essential deliveries on Sundays as a reason for his irregular church attendance, and as long as Anders' church tax was paid up, and he attended on Christmas and Easter, he made no complaint. Anna was worried that Pastor Virtanen seemed to know of Anders' irregular attendance, but she was sure Reverend Svenson's wisdom would prevent trouble.

"When I was a child," continued Anders angrily, "church was all about how good the Tsar was to us. That's when I lost interest! Bah! You know those Tsars were *not* good to us, at least, not in my lifetime! How come they don't talk about God there? We don't go to church to hear about the government!"

"Well, Tsar Nikolai did rebuild our city," said Anna, apologetically. "We should be grateful."

"Yah, he only did that so he could change its name in his own honor!" retorted Anders. "What sort of a person uses a terrible tragedy just to get veneration for himself?"

Suddenly Tyra slipped on an icy patch of snow. Before she fell, Anders' strong arms grabbed her. He swept her to his shoulders, his anger melting in a rush of protective fatherly love. While she giggled and buried her face in his warm furry hat, he carried her the last few meters home.

As the family removed their heavy boots in the front porch of their home, the door opened and they were engulfed in clouds of warmth, appetizing smells, and squeals of delight. They quickly entered the comfort of their snug house.

"Algot! Hjalmar!" cried Tyra, greeting her cousins racing to meet her. "So you *are* alright, after all?"

"Come and play with our new tops," coaxed Algot, the elder boy.

"I thought..." began Anna with a puzzled frown, watching the children run off.

"Yah, yah, the boys did seem tired and a bit unwell this morning, but it was just the excitement from last night," smiled Anna's sister-in-law, Lisa Rådman.

"It wasn't us who were sick, it was Far!" blurted out Algot cheekily, stopping to listen to his mother. "He was the one who had a bad headache and couldn't get out of bed! Me and Hjalmar were fine!"

"Hush!" said his mother crossly. "Enough of your impertinence!"

"You didn't miss much not coming," muttered Anders irritably, as he hung his coat on the rack inside the door, and threw his hat on the shelf above.

Anna rolled her eyes, raised her eyebrows, and her sister laughed. "We got a lecture on being properly Finnish!" explained Anna. "The minister was very patriotic, but clearly rather against being a Swedish-speaking Finn."

"It was a dreadful service!" exploded Anders.

"Not keen on the religious stuff, eh?" sneered Karl, Algot's father, coming from the dining room without hearing what had been said. He gave Anders a hearty slap on the shoulder. Karl had carefully informed his local minister in Oxkanger that the family would be away at Christmas, and believed it was unlikely his absence from church in Nikolaistad would be reported.

"Religion's fine. It's the politics that drives me nuts," growled Anders. "But let's get into the spirit of Christmas, and don't let that sermon spoil our lives."

"Far! Far!" yelled Hjalmar, racing up the hallway. "Come! Quick! Tyra's top doesn't spin right! You must fix it!"

"What a calamity!" laughed Karl. He followed Hjalmar to investigate the disaster of a non-spinning top. Anders watched his wife and sister-in-law enter the kitchen, smiled happily at the vision of the table groaning with food and decorations, and decided he too would investigate his daughter's top-spinning problem.

What fun they'd had last night, during the traditional Christmas Eve festivities, Anders remembered, as he strode across the dining room. Good weather and a waxing moon had allowed the Rådman family to travel 40 kilometers from Oxkangar to Nikolaistad by horse drawn sleigh in convoy with three other families, to join the Lall family for Christmas festivities. Although Anna, with Tyra's help, had decorated the tree with rosy apples, a few colored glass balls from the shop, lots of *pepparkakor* shapes (the crisp and spicy ginger nut cookies Anders loved), a traditional straw yule goat, and numerous candles, it now groaned under the added collection of Lisa's decorations. Sitting proudly in the center of the table was a large *ljustaken* (candelabrum), which Anders had made from discarded scraps of iron found along the roads he daily travelled. Anders' father was a blacksmith, and from him he had learned rudimentary metalworking skills. Tyra decorated it with colored paper from school, and Anna inserted twelve candles that burned brightly. On the sideboard, groaning with as much food as the table, shone the Rådman *ljustaken* which Karl had skilfully carved from birch wood.

Karl agreed to act as *Jultomten*, the traditional horned goat creature who gave out Christmas gifts, the *julklappar*. Karl had found a most impressive set of goat horns to attach to his usual sheepskin hooded jacket. He made a birch-bark mask, authentically painted by Lisa, and the huge flowing beard beneath the mask had taken months of summer wool gathering. The children shrieked with delight as he handed out the gifts, carefully pretending they had no idea of his identity, while giggling and whispering that of course they knew it was Algot's and Hjalmar's Far. Neither of their mothers made a murmur of protest at the foolish but traditional lumps of carefully straw-wrapped birch wood they received from the *Jultomten*. "How good for the fire!" the women laughed, adding conspiratorially, "Men don't have much originality! Will one ever think up something worthwhile for Christmas!"

Karl and Lisa had brought three large, beautifully crafted wooden tops for the children, which performed perfectly on Christmas Eve. Anna made knitted hats as her gifts, the boys' striped blue and white, Tyra's red and white. Anders found a set of wooden toy soldiers for his nephews, and, indulging his fancy, he bought Tyra a large rag doll with lovely yellow wool hair, a bright blue dress, and real leather shoes. Privately, Anders presented Anna with a necklace of pretty red beads, but of course no Finn would allow such romantic foolishness to be made public.

The evening's food was magnificent, and on reflection Anders suspected his over-indulgence had not improved his interest in the parson's political sermonizing. After three courses of all his favorite foods, plus dessert, his stomach was still groaning next morning. The first course was herring baked in Anna's delicious white pepper sauce, boiled potatoes, platters of sliced hard-boiled eggs, and the egg and anchovy mixture called *gubbröra*, that Anders especially enjoyed. This was followed by by the Christmas ham, which Anna had boiled, basted with egg, mustard, and breadcrumbs, and then baked. Platters piled with pickled cucumbers, beetroot, slices of cheese, and crisp rye bread accompanied the ham. Next came Anders' favorite, *lutfisk*, with potato and cheese casserole, mashed peas, and mushrooms in white sauce. *Lutfisk* is a bland, jelly-like dish made by soaking fish in a strong lye solution, but its time-consuming preparation made it special for Christmas. Finally, there was barely room for dessert, the traditional sweet rice porridge flavored with cinnamon, but how could he disappoint the women and all their effort? Karl brought bottles of potato *brännvin,* and to be polite Anders drank half a small glass. But he did not like the effects of alcohol, and often scolded his wife's brother for drinking too much. He was pleased Anna did not drink any. Well, in a few minutes he would be eating all the leftovers from last night's feast. He determined this time he would eat more frugally, to avoid another dose of complaining stomach.

"What's the problem with the top?" Anders asked, bursting into the bedroom. The children, looking very glum, were perched along the edge of the bed Anders, Anna, and Tyra shared in winter. In the corner, an untidy pile of quilts indicated the bedding Lisa had brought for the Rådman family. Anders was pleased Anna used her own hand woven linen sheets and the blankets his parents gave for wedding presents.

"A bit of a prank, that's all," grinned Karl. "Algot's idea of a joke. At least that's what he says."

Anders raised his eyebrows quizzically. "How so?"

"Far, it's fine, truly. Algot didn't mean anything," said Tyra hurriedly. She was very fond of her cousin, and eager to avoid his getting into trouble. Peacemaking was always her aim. She did not understand why Algot thought that doing nasty things to people was funny. She knew he really liked her, so why did he try to make her sad? But she also knew his father was very stern, and if she complained about Algot's behavior he was likely to be severely punished. She certainly did not want that when Christmas was supposed to be a special time.

"He did so!" declared Hjalmar, angrily. "He tied that dirty piece of string around her top, and made it stop spinning. And then he was going to cut the point right off but I stopped him!"

"Mr. Goodie Goodie!" sneered Algot, giving his brother a shove.

"He's a bad boy!" insisted Hjalmar. "He'll go to hell. I know he will!"

"It's alright, Far, honestly," insisted Tyra. "Algot only meant fun. He didn't do anything to hurt me."

"He's admitted his crime," said Karl, "and said a very sincere sorry. I don't think he'll get up to any more mischief. If he does, he sure knows what I'll do to him. He won't be sitting down comfortably for quite a while!"

"I know he's sorry, and won't do it again." Tyra tried to smile encouragingly at her father and uncle.

"But he's a big boy, and he should know better," persisted Hjalmar, undeterred by his brother's shove. "It's not funny spoiling someone else's top!"

"I suppose he *is* a big boy," laughed Anders. "Five going on almost six is very big when you're barely four, isn't it?"

"Yah!" pouted Hjalmar.

"Far, can I show you how good the tops really are?" suggested Tyra, earnestly, placatingly. The children jumped from the bed, and spun their tops. They made a healthy buzzing noise, and most satisfyingly, Tyra's spun the longest.

"I think we can safely declare Tyra's top is now working perfectly," announced Karl, and everyone cheered.

"I still think Algot's mean!" insisted Hjalmar.

"Come, let's eat," said Anders.

Tyra picked up her new doll, carried it to the dining room, and settled it under the Christmas tree. It flopped unhealthily, until she propped it against the trunk of the tree. "You can have all the *pepparkakor* you like, Molly," she told the doll cheerfully. "Just make sure you leave some for us!"

When the family settled around the table, Anders lifted a heavy book from the shelf above the sideboard. "We'll begin with this," he said.

"You're kidding! You're not really going to read *that*, are you?" guffawed Karl. "I thought you'd had enough sermonizing at church!"

"Didn't get much from church, so thought I'd read this," responded Anders firmly. "Karl, no making fun of me. It's my house, and it's Christmas, remember. Start behaving like a Finn!"

There was a moment's tense silence. Lisa coughed nervously and Anna smoothed imaginary wrinkles on the tablecloth.

Karl grinned. "Go ahead with your pious reading! I can tell our parson I went to church, if you do," he sneered. Anna and Lisa frowned, and shuffled uneasily. Tyra's lower lip trembled. How could Morbor Karl speak so rudely to her father, her hero?

"I like the Christmas story," said Anders. "I'll read my favorite bit. It isn't long." He took some time to find the passage, and the children fidgeted noisily. "Here it is," he announced, and taking a deep breath, carefully intoned the familiar story.

> And there were in the same country shepherds abiding in the field, keeping watch over their flock by night. And, lo, the angel of the Lord came upon them, and the glory of the Lord shone round about them: and they were sore afraid. And the angel said unto them, "Fear not: for behold, I bring you good tidings of great joy, which will be to all people. For unto you is born this day in the city of David a Savior, which is Christ the Lord. And this shall be the sign unto you; Ye shall find the babe wrapped in swaddling cloths, lying in a manger." And suddenly there was with the angel a multitude of the heavenly host praising God and saying, "Glory to God in the highest, and on earth peace, goodwill toward men."[1]

Anders laid the Bible aside, and took a deep breath. There was a solemn hush.

"I like the presents story best," said Hjalmar suddenly, and everyone, except Anders, laughed.

"Yah, we read that story in church. The baby was a king, so of course people brought him presents," responded Anders earnestly. "But fancy being a shepherd, and seeing all those angels! Now that really is something!" He shook his head in wonder, grinned mischievously at his small nephew, then turned to his daughter. "Now, what's your favorite story, Tyra?"

After a thoughtful few moments Tyra replied, "I like the cow one."

"The cow one?" said her aunt, puzzled, and both her cousins tittered.

Tyra looked down, mortified that she had said something very, very foolish.

"Of course, dear," said her mother kindly. "You mean the one where the baby was born in the barn because there was no room anywhere else, and his mother put him in the cow food box." Tyra looked up, and nodded gratefully.

"I like that one too," said Anders, encouragingly. "Why, that's where the shepherds went after they'd seen the angels."

"I'm starving!" declared Karl rudely, reaching for the plate of *lutfisk*. "I didn't get breakfast this morning."

---

1. Luke 2:8–14 KJV. Anders, of course, would have read from the Swedish Bible.

"And who's fault was that?" said Anna sarcastically. "But, brother, please behave yourself!"

"He can say the blessing," declared his wife saucily, and Karl, without bowing his head, mumbled something no one heard.

"We've put all the food on the table, and you can choose what you like," directed Anna. Immediately the children began calling for their favorite dish. Anna and Lisa were kept busy filling their plates, while the men piled their own.

Eating is a very serious Finnish occupation, and as the candles in the *ljustaken* flickered brightly the family munched their meal in silence, except for requests for a desired platter, clinking cutlery, crackling *knäckerbröd*, the crunch of strong champing jaws, and a few suppressed giggles from the children. When rice porridge at last was served, Karl asked, "Anyone want some of my *brännvin*?"

"No," said Anna firmly. "Put it away, I insist. I've prepared coffee." She turned to the children. "Today you can cut *pepparkakor* off the Christmas tree." There were immediate cries of "I want a star!" "I want a heart!" and, "I want a reindeer!"

"You can have whatever figure you like," said Lisa, as the children chose their favorite shapes.

"Why does everyone make a fuss about that ginger stuff?" grumbled Karl. When he got no response, he added, "There's always the stable to enjoy real men's stuff." Holding up his bottle he turned to his brother-in-law. "Coming out with me, Anders?"

"No way. I suffered enough from your evil potion last night. I'll stick with Anna's coffee and *pepparkakor,* thank you very much."

Karl shrugged. "I always did think you were a bit of a girl!"

"Karl, how dare you!" cried Anna, her eyes blazing. "I've never seen that *brännvin* stuff improve you, so leave my husband alone!" What Karl said under his breath was inaudible.

After the meal, Algot announced he wanted to make a snowman. "Great idea!" everyone agreed.

While mothers found layers of warm clothes and bundled up children, fathers located strong lanterns. The watery sun had long set, a soft bluish glow on the horizon was all that was left of where it had been. The moon was at its zenith, casting a silver glow over the city, but without lanterns making a snowman was difficult.

"Auntie, have you got an old hat and scarf for the snowman?" asked Algot.

"What about that red hat that's too small for me?" offered Tyra. Anna nodded approval.

"You can have my scarf," said Hjalmar generously, unwinding his from his neck. "I don't like it one little bit!"

"Certainly not!" frowned Lisa. "If you take that off you can't make the snowman!" Hjalmar quickly rewound his scarf, and pulled his jacket collar up round his ears.

"And who's being wicked now?" sneered Algot.

"Here's an old rag I use for the horses. Will that do for a scarf?" said Anders, offering a ragged piece of once-red cloth.

"Hurray!" shouted the boys, "Great!"

"Thank you, Far," said Tyra. The bickering of her uncle and cousins bothered her. Christmas was not supposed to be like that.

It was a serious business making a snowman. Shovels were gathered from the stable, gloves became wet and needed replacing by hovering mothers, and before the old hat and rag-scarf could adorn the mound of shaped snow, small pieces of birch wood must be found for the snowman's eyes, mouth, and nose.

"He needs a *pepparkakor* so he won't be hungry," announced Tyra, generously.

"Perhaps he could have Molly to keep him company," teased Morbror Karl, but Tyra frowned in horror. A few minutes later she came out triumphantly bearing a round piece of ginger nut which she stuck in the snowman's mouth.

"He's welcome to that!" shrugged Algot. "No one likes those plain old round ones!"

"But he does!" declared Tyra staunchly. "And they taste the same as the fancy shapes."

"Children, come inside! It's too cold for you to be out there any longer!" called Anna. "You can play snowman tomorrow."

"I agree," laughed a gruff voice on the snowy pathway. "Can I come in too?"

"Why, it's Lukas Larson!" exclaimed Karl. "Where d'you hide these days!"

"He's our neighbor now," replied Anders, adding hospitably, "Come on in, come on in! Bring your family over too. It's Christmas, you know."

"We've got plenty of coffee and *pepparkakor*," added Anna. "Do bring Elin, and your boys."

"I'll do just that," declared the shape, and a few minutes later Lukas, with wife and three boys, Tobbe, Erik, and Jan, were divesting warm coats and wraps, and joining the family around the table. While Lisa stoked the wood stove and filled the largest kettle with water for coffee, Anna carried platters of gingerbread, crackling *knäckerbröd,* cheese, and the remains of the Christmas ham. Karl surprised them by offering to bring in armfuls of well-dried birch wood for the fire, but he made more trips to the stable than necessary, and his voice became steadily more raucous with each trip.

"Who'd like to come to my sauna?" asked Lukas, when the coffee pot was empty and the platters seriously depleted. "It's all stoked up and ready to go!"

"You men go, while we do the dishes," suggested Anna.

"Can we come too?" pled Algot, and his brother quickly joined his entreaties.

"Why not!" boomed Karl, now obviously drunk, and slapping Lukas heavily on the shoulder. He knocked Hjalmar over with a massive thwack that was intended to be comradely. "You're men, aren't you?" Hjalmar started crying. Algot turned angrily and hit his father hard on the legs, but fortunately Karl did not notice who had struck him.

"What about Tyra?" asked Algot. Despite his attack on her spinning top, she was his special friend. "She isn't a man, but she's as good as a boy, and if I dress her up I could make her look like one!"

"Yah, and Tyra's mother should come too!" Karl leered. Anders quickly stepped between his wife and brother-in-law.

Tyra looked uncertainly at her mother. "Am I allowed to go?"

"Anders, are you going?" asked Anna softly. "Someone needs to keep an eye on Karl."

"Of course," replied her husband. "I'll watch Tyra and the boys."

"I'll stay and help with the dishes," offered Elin. "It'll be nice to talk with you both."

Once more thick jackets, boots, scarves, and hats were bundled on, and a laughing procession headed to the Larson sauna. Soon shouts and giggles indicated a good time was being had by all.

"A sauna's just what Karl needs to sober him up!" declared Lisa angrily, when the women were on their own. "I don't know where he stashes his *brännvin* because if I did I'd tip it all out on the street! I hate the stuff!"

"Yah, he was rather boisterous," returned Anna.

"Boisterous! Is that all you call it? I don't know why he does it!" continued Lisa, almost in tears. "Normally he's the best of men, but when he gets that demon inside him, I never know what he'll do. Goodness gracious, he was even making a pass at you, Anna, his own sister!"

"Come and help me carry water from the well," requested Anna of Elin. "You know where it is, of course!"

By the time the neighbors had carried water inside, Lisa had regained her poise, poured hot water from the pot on the stove into a large wooden bowl, and was elbow-deep in suds washing Christmas dinner plates.

"While you're here, you must see Elin's embroidery, Lisa," encouraged Anna. "She does beautiful work."

"Nothing as good as your spinning," smiled Elin deferentially.

"Oh, Lisa does beautiful embroidery too," explained Anna, "so she'll appreciate your work."

"How long are you staying?" asked Elin. "Could we perhaps do something together?"

"Weather permitting, we hope to leave in a week, after the new year."

"Elin also makes wonderful rag carpets," said Anna. "It's a pity you can't see what she does, Lisa."

Elin laid down the plate she was drying. "Maybe you can! That's why I was asking how long you were here. I've just bought the mesh for a new rag carpet, and I've been saving scraps of cloth for months. I'm sure I have enough to complete it. Why don't we get together over this holiday time, and start making a rug together?"

"What a great idea!" chimed Anna and Lisa together. "Even if we don't finish it, we could get things well along the way for you," added Lisa.

A burst of yells and squeals announced the sauna bathers were rolling in the snow. The women looked with satisfaction at their pile of clean dishes, glad they had finished before the men and children returned. Soon Anders and Lukas trooped in looking happy, rosy, and flushed, pushing ahead of them a quiet troop of children. Karl staggered at the rear, looked around him in a daze, and slumped on a chair. "I'm slaughtered!" he exclaimed.

"They'll sleep well tonight!" laughed Lukas. "Karl especially!"

Suddenly, through the clear night air the church clock chimed. Everyone counted. "Eight o'clock!" declared Algot triumphantly. "Yippee! Mor always makes me go to bed at seven!"

While the children unsuccessfully pled for more time out of bed, their parents made plans to get together over the holidays, and said farewells into the frosty night.

The holiday week sped by. Anders and a sober Karl took the children, sometimes accompanied by Lukas Larson's boys, for rides in the sleigh. The lanterns and bells on the sleigh made excursions seem like fairy rides. The men spent hours in the stable, and after much hammering and childish laughter the children emerged with a miniature sleigh that gave Molly many a giddy ride.

Anna, Lisa, and Elin began work on the new rag carpet, and by the end of the week it was almost complete. Often they found Tyra silently watching them as they worked, and then suddenly Algot would burst into the room and loudly demand where his cousin was hiding. "It's no fun without her!" he would exclaim, pouncing on her. "She's got to come with us! She stops all the fights!"

Evenings were spent reading. The children loved listening to stories, a favorite being the little boy whose mother made him a beautiful cap, but the princess wanted it. Tyra, Algot, and Hjalmar always brought out the caps Anna had made when they read that story, and proudly declared they wouldn't let some old princes take their caps either! Anders spent many hours reading *The Duchess of Finland*, a long romantic historical novel written by their favorite Zacharias Topelius. Although the children could not understand much of it, they enjoyed the deep sonorous tones of Anders, who often stopped and explained a passage. Lisa and Anna sat nearby, knitting, and Karl puffed contentedly on his pipe.

The entire family attended church on Sunday, even Karl. Stars twinkled brightly as they crunched along the footpaths, the children pretending to skate on the snow, Anna and Lisa ready to catch them if they fell. To Anna's relief, this time Pastor Virtanen refrained from political admonition, and although he had nothing spiritual to offer his congregation, he did confine himself to expansive and encouraging admonition for the New Year.

"1914 will be a year of new possibilities!" he declared pompously. "Humanity is making steady progress towards improvement in all aspects of life. Here in Finland"—at that Anna felt Anders stiffen beside her, but she need not have worried, and Tyra looked up sharply at her father—"we are learning new ways to improve our lives, every year. Everyone wants to be a good and responsible citizen. Finns care about their families, and their neighbors. They are learning to live the way God wants them to live."

As the pastor droned on, Anna's mind switched off. She watched with delight as the freshly-risen sun brought the church's stained glass window to life. Quietly she directed Tyra's attention to the beautiful sight, and was rewarded with a sunny smile of appreciation.

When the service was over, and they filed out in dignified solemnity, Anders politely shook the parson's proffered hand.

"I see you have all your family with you today, Herr Lall," said Pastor Virtanen somewhat diffidently, remembering Anders brusque manner on Christmas Day. "I wish you all the very best for 1914. Would you like to introduce your family?"

Anders politely named his in-laws, who stood stiff and impassive.

"A good year to all of you," repeated Pastor Virtanen, a benign smile across his youthful face while he absent-mindedly gazed over their heads at the next person coming towards him.

"Nice weather," said Anders, nodding courteously, but looking steadfastly ahead. He was down the church steps before he adjusted his hat.

Perhaps the parson, darkly silhouetted on the church steps against the surrounding snow, and congratulating himself on his fine morning's performance, might have preached differently had he known what was to befall his unexciting congregants in futures for which he was so confidently predicting meaningless pleasantries. What if he had known that one boy listening to his platitudinous words would be a murderer? What words of encouragement might he have uttered had he realized many of the men seated impassively before him, whose rough provincial hands he so patronizingly shook, would be slaughtered in horrific wars, wars fought on a brutal international scale, and even worse, cruel, vicious civil strife that tore the Finland he professed to love so well into bitter tribal factions? And what would he have said, or done, had he known that the church he so blithely represented, through careless record-keeping, and a partisan spirit, would be the trigger for sending an innocent young woman to the other side of the world? Perhaps, had he known, he might not have skipped his classes in pastoral care to attend the exciting political rallies of Helsinki University.

But he knew none of this; only time would unfold the tragedies.

His parishioners were content to fulfill their church attendance duty and get on with their humdrum lives. He knew they were uninspired by his patriotic fervor, and he was uninspired by the blandness of their lives, but fortunately he was heading back to the excitement of what they ignorantly called Helsingfors, and he could leave them to their spiritual fates under the insipid preaching of Pastor Svenson.

Three days later the Rådman family returned to the farm at Oxkangar. Anna and Lisa packed plenty of sustaining food: nourishing rye bread, two big rounds of fresh cheese. The Lall cow donated a large bottle of still-warm milk, kept under the piles of quilts to stop it from freezing. Anna offered a large bag of *pepparkakor* to keep Algot and Hjalmar happy. Anders ensured the lanterns were trimmed and burning brightly.

"Send a letter when you get home!" called Anna as the sleigh slid off, bells jingling, lamps swaying.

"Thank you for everything!" called Lisa. "I'll write!"

"I'll write too," called Tyra. "I'll tell you how Molly is, and how my top is spinning, and about all the fun we're having!"

"Come and see us when school finishes!" yelled Algot, as the sleigh rounded the corner and disappeared from sight. "And bring your top! Then we'll really have some fun!"

"And remember, we live in the best country in the world!" shouted Tyra, having the final word.

Chapter 2

In the Finnish, Who Are We?

EXCITEMENT RIPPLED THROUGH NIKOLAISTAD. The ice of winter had given way to long, warm summer days. Midsummer celebrations burst forth in city parks and gardens. Of special interest was the arrival of a band billed to play rousing summer dance music and works from celebrated national composer, Sibelius. Anna, Anders, and Tyra joined the crowds to hear the stirring music. Everyone knew this music was defiantly nationalistic, and as the first bars broke on the crowd their hearts thrilled with patriotic fervor and the desire to throw off the yoke of Russian governance.

Daaar—imp! Daaar—imp! Thus began the famous *Finlandia*.

Standing in the crowd Tyra felt the power of the stirring music. At school she had been told it was not good music, and loyal Russian citizens should not listen to it, but the mood of the crowd convinced her the teacher was wrong. When the notes softened to a prayer-like melody, excitement filled her heart, and she noticed many people, even her strong and steady father, were blowing their noses very hard. Something was happening in her country, something she did not understand, but felt proud of.

Next afternoon Tyra burst into the kitchen. "Mor! Mor!" she cried, "We've done it!"

"Done what?" said Anna vaguely. The smiling face of Tobbe Larson reminded her.

"We've done it, Mor! We've cleaned the stable. Tobbe's such a help. And you know what? He really likes horses! Möja likes him too!" Tyra was so excited about the horses she dearly loved that she did not notice the strain on her mother's face. "You know, Mor, Tobbe says he really likes helping me clean the stable. Isn't that kind of him to say so?"

Tobbe, eldest son of Lukas Larson, was a quiet, dependable boy. His father was proud that from an early age his son displayed the essential Finnish character trait of *sisu*, that tough mix of stamina and bravery. If Tobbe said he would do something, he would. But you couldn't push him. Anna knew it was love for the draught horse Möja that motivated his willingness to help clean the stable, but she suspected he was also rather fond of Tyra.

Anna had never been interested in her husband's draught horses, but Tyra was. Anders was proud of his strong Belgian team, renowned as largest and most powerful of pulling horses. Tyra, like her father, loved them. As a tiny child she frightened her mother by fearlessly wandering around the great legs of these essential beasts. Ander insisted they were gentle animals, that they would never hurt their child, but their hooves were huge, with great feathered fetlocks. Anna realized Möja was the lifeblood of the family, that their existence depended on her faithful pulling, but she was afraid of her. When Anna went into the barn the horses ignored her, but for Anders and Tyra they clearly had a deep affection. Whether or not they had apple or carrot treats to offer, both horses would nuzzle them, whinnying softly their appreciation. Once Anna asked Anders how his favorite horse had received her ridiculous name. A horse called strawberry? But he grinned, patted Möja's warm chestnut flank, and said, "Isn't it obvious she's as sweet as one?" Anders, it seemed, had a fixation on food names for his horses, because he named Möja's daughter Kanel, meaning cinnamon. It was a very apt name. Möja might be sweet, but Kanel was spicy.

"Everything's ready for tomorrow!" declared Tyra. "Far will be so pleased. Tobbe rubbed down Möja while I did Kanel. Möja missed me, but she behaved beautifully for Tobbe. And Mor, do you have everything ready for tomorrow?"

Tyra was surprised her mother responded vaguely, as though her thoughts were far away. Didn't she remember that they were going to Oxkangar, the yearly visit to her cousins' farm that Tyra enjoyed so much? An only child, Tyra's cousins were very important to her. She knew her mother appreciated Möja, and was glad Anders chose to take her to Oxkangar, not skittish Kanel. But why was her mother not interested?

"It smells nice in here," said Tobbe, suddenly. "I like new bread."

Anna laughed. Tobbe was very polite, as always, but his gentle hint was irresistible. "Just wait a moment, Tobbe," she replied, "and I'll get you some. I need to get this batch in the oven, and then I'll help you."

"Thanks Mor!" smiled Tyra, settling herself on a chair while she patted another for Tobbe. The new bread was worth waiting for, but again she noticed her mother's anxious expression, the loss of her usual cheerfulness. Something really was bothering her mother.

Anna finished kneading the dough, covered it with a towel, and set it near the warm stove to rise. She retrieved a newly made loaf, and deftly cut two thick slices. "I have some butter for you," she smiled, as she handed the still-warm pieces to Tyra and Tobbe.

"Ah, Fru Lall," said Tobbe seriously, "this bread is good!"

"My mor always makes good bread," said Tyra loyally. "You should come more often. I'm sure she'd give you some. If you helped me clean the stable every day, Mor would give you bread every day!"

"My mor said Tyra could come and play with my brothers this afternoon," said Tobbe, chewing his last bite. "May she?"

"Yah, that's fine. Make sure she's home by five," replied Anna, again a distant expression in her eyes.

Tyra confided to Tobbe as they walked down the path to his home, "I don't like it! Something's bothering Mor. She's not behaving normally."

"Yah," said Tobbe, "my mor didn't look too happy either, when I think about it."

Earlier that afternoon Anna had heard heavy, hurried footsteps running down the path, someone in a big hurry. She looked up from kneading dough, just as Anders burst into the kitchen.

"Look at this!" he exclaimed urgently, tossing a newspaper on her spotlessly scrubbed pinewood table. Before she could say a reproving word, he was gone.

But bread needed her attention. The newspaper could wait. On the farm where she grew up bread making was an autumn activity, no hardship at that time of the year working beside warm stoves. But in the city, whenever Anders brought her cheap flour she made as many loaves as possible to last through winter. Summer bread making was hot, heavy work, and she brushed a trickle of perspiration from her face.

She punched down the dough, deftly cut it into four portions. Quickly, the result of much practice, each portion was rolled into a sausage, formed into a ring, placed on a tray, allowed to rise, and then set in the heated oven. Already a good number of ring loaves were threaded on the wooden poles hanging across the ceiling, promising plenty of food in the coming months. Anna planned to make two more batches of bread that day, but a break to discover Anders' news was welcome. She picked up the newspaper.

GERMANY DECLARES WAR ON RUSSIA

"Oh, no!" she cried, as she read the headline, and sank on a chair. The paper dropped from her hands, its cheap ink making more dirty smudges on her once spotless table.

People are never content, she thought angrily, endlessly trying to get more. A month earlier papers carried the tragic news that Archduke Franz Ferdinand of Austria-Hungry was assassinated while visiting the Bosnian city of Sarajevo. Those people in Bosnia and Serbia seemed intent on fighting, themselves or their Austrian rulers, she thought. But why should Russia get involved? The so-called brotherhood of Slavs was ridiculous, an excuse to mind other peoples' business! Those Balkan countries weren't part of Russia, and never had been. So why had Russia provoked Germany by mobilizing its army? War with Russia meant *them*, the non-Slavic people of Finland, the people of Nikolaistad. Why should they be involved with a dispute half a continent away? Russia must hope to regain prestige and lands it lost in previous wars. But, as fear clutched her heart, she realized this war could mean Anders, her Anders, Tyra's father, might be sent to war. Oh, never!

But all she could do was get on with her work. She stood up, poured water, sugar, flour, and starter yeast mixture into her wooden mixing bowl, and leaving it to work, measured out flour. Being part of Russia had meant trouble for Finnish people for at least 20 years. And all the talk about Finnish independence was another version of trouble. Where would it all end?

She pulled four loaves from the oven, and turning to the new dough pushing hard against the covering towel, began working it. She was placing the last four loaves in the oven, looking forward to a chance to relax after a hard afternoon, when she heard Anders talking to Lukas Larson as they walked up the cobble path from the stable. As they came into the kitchen both were frowning and serious.

"Can you stay for coffee?" she asked.

"Thank you," said Lukas.

Anders confirmed Anna's suspicion. "We've been talking about that war," he said, sitting down heavily. "Everyone is."

"Then you need coffee and warm bread," responded Anna, as she picked up the kettle, filled it from the bucket, and placed it on the center of the stove. "I've been busy all afternoon and the water isn't hot. But I have fresh bread."

"That will be great," returned Anders. "Waiting for the water to boil will be good. Give us a chance to talk!"

"Being part of Russia is just a liability," exploded Lukas, bitterly, as he sat down. "I'd like to be independent like that young parson was ranting about in church a few months ago, but we aren't a united country. Independence would merely cause another heap of trouble."

"It was a sad day for Finland when Tsar Alexander died. That son of his has done nothing but try to make us Russians ever since." Anders sat on his favorite chair, pulled off his heavy boots, and revealed bright blue socks hand-knitted by Anna.

"Frankly, we Finns have spent centuries grumbling about our overlords, yet never doing anything about it. Up north here we happily bought the Swedish idea that we were eastern Sweden. Down south they're much too close to that snobbish St Petersburg to be comfortable with things Swedish. But it was that Bobrikov who caused the trouble," observed Lukas, angrily spitting out the name Bobrikov. "He must've been doing what the Tsar wanted, but who knows. If he'd had his way Finland would have disappeared. We were a Grand Duchy after Russia won that war against Sweden a hundred years ago, but he tried to change everything. I used to think we were better off with Russians than Swedes. To the Swedes we were just the eastern part of their country, but the Russians did give us the dignity of being a Grand Duchy."

"Well, it was the Tsar who signed that manifesto saying Russia could overrule anything our diet voted. He has to take final responsibility. Even when half a million Finns signed that petition and Father George Capone and his followers walked with it all the way to the Winter Palace in St. Petersburg, that pigheaded young ruler wouldn't even admit the delegation into his high and mighty house! Talk about bad-mannered!" Anders scraped his chair angrily.

"He was crazy!" declared Lukas. "Bobrikov, I mean. Or perhaps it was, like you say, the Tsar. Just like that, they abolished Finnish and Swedish and everyone had to speak and write in Russian in government! You don't need to talk to Finns in Russian to make them understand! Do you know how many people emigrated after he took over? It was thousands, I know that much!"

"Perhaps that was the point," returned Anders grimly. "We weren't meant to understand, and those who didn't could simply get out."

"I signed that petition," said Anna, quietly.

"And yah, half a million . . ."

"You what?" broke in Anders, sitting forward. "*You* signed that petition! You never told me!"

There was a stunned silence. Lukas chewed his bread. Anna smiled.

"You never asked me!" she replied, her eyes sparkling. "You told me you had that long delivery the day they came for signatures. You said before you left how you wished you could sign. When that nice young man came, I thought, hey, I'm A. Lall the same as my husband is. So I told him I was sure my husband wanted to sign, and I took the form into the bedroom, signed it there, and brought it out. The young man was very happy, and he never asked who signed it! He told me he and his friends had skied all the way from Helsingfors to get people to sign!"

"Quite a woman you've got," remarked Lukas, his mouth full of bread. "Hope she doesn't get you into trouble. Maybe I better go home and ask Elin what she's been doing that I didn't know about!"

"My Anna's no trouble. She's got a hotline to heaven. She must've known what they were going to do in just a few years, all that women's suffrage and liberation! But why didn't you tell me?"

Anna looked demurely at the floor. "I confess at the time I thought I'd done something dangerous, and it was best you didn't know. Then as things got better, and after all the trouble women were accepted and the Tsar gave us the right to both vote and govern Finland, I just forgot about it."

"Yah, things did improve for a while, but not before Russia got some swift kicks," said Lukas. "Just think! Remember how Bobrikov abolished the Finnish army? According to him we were Russians, there was just a Russian army, and the Finnish army was officially disbanded." Lukas picked up a small piece of paper and began tearing strips off it, screwing them into balls. "Then he calls us up to serve in that precious Russian army and you know what happened!"

Unexpectedly Anders laughed. "He said there was no Finnish army, and by our great Tsar's ticklish toes, there wasn't! There really truly wasn't! What did you do to get out of call up?"

"Let me see, 1902, wasn't it? Well, of course I was still on the family farm in Oxkangar. It's not too hard to hide on a farm. Actually my brothers and I just went fishing. Honestly! The recruitment officers were pretty lazy, and you could be sure they only came in the afternoon. So we did all the farm chores in the morning, then disappeared out to sea. It was great fun. We did well fishing, and I made good money. I even thought of giving the Russian recruitment officer a thank you fish, but it didn't take me long to throw that idea away!"

"Lucky you. We were just married, and the last thing I wanted was to go into the army. It was trickier to hide in town. I did all my deliveries down back roads. Anna was wonderful. I don't know how she did it, but she developed a network of information, so I always knew where some officer might be lurking. They wouldn't listen when half a million signed the petition not to abolish our language. But that gave us the perfect tool not to understand the call up. All we had to do was work out what language the recruitment officers spoke. I never met one who could speak Russian, Finnish, and Swedish. It was hilarious watching them try to make themselves understood by people who simply would not, chose not, to understand!"

"It was pretty impressive. Half a million men signed that petition. Sorry Anna, but it was mostly men, wasn't it?"

Tipping her head rather saucily, and opening her eyes wide, Anna nodded. "Remember, I'm your equal now!" she smiled. "I wonder if any other women signed? There was nothing to stop us, you know!"

"Most definitely you're an equal," agreed her husband. "But I'm not sure how many others are your equal! May I gently remind your equal self that the kettle has just boiled?"

Anna laughed merrily, and rose to perform her hostess duties.

"Yah, well, equal or not, that petition got ignored, but there was no ignoring the fact that less than half those called up for the army reported for duty. Bobrikov abolished the Finnish army. He sure did." Lukas hit the table hard with his clenched fists, and then threw back his head and laughed cynically.

"Well, he and Russia paid for their folly, that they did."

"What was the Imperial Court thinking? Not only did they want to abolish our Grand Duchy, but they insisted on running everything over there in the Far East as well."

"Oh that? I think Japan was a pretty slippery customer," observed Anders. "They thought they owned Manchuria and Korea and could just parcel it out how they liked. Both sides were disgustingly greedy and wanted everything. Russia was just the unlucky loser."

"They deserved to lose!" declared Anna, defiantly tossing her head as she placed a steaming cup of coffee in front of Lukas. "Remember those reports of what Russian soldiers did in Manchuria, looting and raping women? The Japanese were bad. But Russians are supposed to be Christians. They were a disgrace!"

"Good woman, not in war! In war anything goes. Now, remember this. There are just two things in war: the enemy and winning. How you get rid of the enemy and win doesn't matter."

"Lukas Larson you make war sound despicable! Most men talk as though it's something noble, but I think you might be telling me the truth!" cried Anna. "Anyway, Russia lost, and I think they deserved to!"

"I don't think that war hurt us Finns much, but it certainly hurt Russian morale, and there's been trouble ever since."

"Yah, come to think of it, it was in the middle of that war that Bobrikov was assassinated, June, 1904." Lukas stretched his long legs, and sipped his coffee.

"We were all so pleased he was gone. But it's worried me ever since. I mean, to assassinate can't be right," said Anna. "God told us not to kill. But I just don't know what you do when you have someone like Bobrikov who won't listen to anyone."

"My good Anna, you're more than a bit naïve," responded Anders gently, as though he were speaking to a child. "Killing is acceptable in war, even in the Bible you love, and Bobrikov must have known he was at war with us."

"Sibelius was very brave when he wrote that march, *In Memoriam*, about the assassinator Eugen Schauman. He could have been accused of treason for that!" Lukas shook his head.

"Sibelius was smart," smiled Anna. "He's been writing political music for decades. He let people think he was simply composing music for himself, and those Russians just accepted what he said! What interests me is what inspired Eugen Schauman, the assassinator. I mean, he sacrificed his own life to get rid of Bobrikov. He really thought he was doing the right thing. They say his mother read him those *Tales of Ensign Stähl* by our very own Johan Ludvig Runeberg. You know, the Runeberg who wrote our national anthem."

"Is that right? Did he do that? Can't say I'm much into poetry myself. But I do like *Vårt Land*. Stirs the soul, it does." To everyone's surprise, Lukas suddenly burst into song.

"Our land, our land, our fatherland,
Sound loud, O name of worth!
No mount that meets the heaven's band,
No hidden vale, no wavewashed strand,
Is loved, as is our native North,
Our own forefathers' earth."

"Man, you stir my soul too," responded Anders, as his friend's baritone solo ended. "Didn't know you could sing! You should join a choir! Anyway, Russia got stirred up about their defeat by the Japanese, and a few other things. They were pretty unhappy. There were demonstrations all over the place, here and in Russia itself." He paused, adding, "Do you remember those strikes? I tried to make a few deliveries that November week, but it was not worth risking my life. Wow, were those socialists angry!" Suddenly he grinned. "Ah, but Anna had a hey day. I did all the repairs she wanted done around the house! Her happiness made up for all the misery everywhere else!"

"That's when they printed that Red Declaration, wasn't it?" asked Anna. The men nodded. "Printing it on red paper was very startling. I thought all those demands were crazy, ridiculous ideas, but then the Tsar agreed to virtually everything. He must've been really scared and really worried. He even gave us women the vote!"

Suddenly they were interrupted. "Hey Mor! Hey Far!" greeted Tyra, coming quietly into the room. "Am I back in time?" her face was strained and white.

Silence greeted her. How long had she been listening, they wondered. This war stuff was not suitable for any child, not even a sensible one like Tyra.

Anna looked at her daughter, then at the old clock. "Yah, you certainly are on time. You have five minutes to spare. Did you have a nice afternoon?"

"Yah, I did." Tyra looked around her familiar kitchen. "But what's wrong? You all look so solemn and worried. What's the matter?"

"Nothing, child," said Anders. "Run and get your toys ready for the farm tomorrow."

"Thanks for the reminder, Tyra. Your parents are busy and I must be going," said Lukas, standing up. "Elin will be wondering where I am. Thanks Anna for the coffee and bread. It was good."

Lukas left, and Tyra walked out, but remained listening outside the door. Anna stayed on her chair, her shoulders drooping wearily. Anders put his arm round her. "This war thing might be alright," he said, reassuringly but unconvincingly. "Just bluff and bluster. The worst we'll have is too many Russian soldiers in town."

"I hope you're right husband. But I'm not fond of soldiers, and as you have often reminded me, we're right in the middle, right between Russia and problems in Europe."

"True, but let's think positively. By the way, I have a little something for you. One of my customers couldn't pay, but he gave me a nice piece of cured bacon, and a bushel of fresh potatoes. I'll get them."

"That would be just great for supper tonight. I've had a busy day, so something nice and easy would be most welcome."

Hastily, Tyra ran from the door as her father came out.

Soon Anna had a large pot of potatoes bubbling on the stove, with bacon sizzling in the frying pan. As a treat she shelled the fresh peas she had bought from the central market. Tyra set the table. Once seated, and grace said, Anders helped himself generously from the potato pot, and drizzled butter over them. The meal proceeded in silence.

"I'll check the horses," said Anders, putting the last piece of potato in his mouth, and pushing away his plate. "I won't be long."

"Horses?" said Anna. "I thought you were taking Möja. Kanel always seems so skittish, and I'm not in the mood for anything exciting at the moment."

"I've decided to take both. Möja will keep Kanel calm. Karl might be able to use both."

"He's not taking any risks," thought Anna, as she watched her husband plod heavily out the door. "Armies have a nasty habit of confiscating horses."

Tyra watched her father go, and took courage to ask again, "Mor, why are you and Far so solemn? What's wrong? I'm a big girl now. I'll be eight in a few days. Tobbe said there's going to be a war. What can I do to help you?"

Anna gasped, but smiled in spite of herself. Her daughter's offer of help was endearing, even if inappropriate. "The dishes, that's what you can help with. I'll talk to you when you've helped with the dishes," she replied.

Obediently Tyra began stacking plates, and carried over the wooden bowl. She watched her mother lather the water with a bar of yellow soap, and wished she could play with the bubbles. She loved the way they reflected colors. Dutifully she wiped the plates dry, trying to guess what Tobbe meant by war, and what made her parents so serious and quiet. She remembered how sad her father was when Möja was sick, and he thought she might die. But Möja was very healthy now, so that couldn't be the problem. She remembered her mother was sad for many days when her mother, Tyra's Mormor, died, but they talked then. So what was the big secret now, that no one wanted to talk about?

"Can you tell me now?" she asked, as the last plate was stacked in the dresser. "When I was over at Tobbe's house his mother was looking sad too. What's wrong with everyone?"

"Get ready for bed, then we can talk."

Obediently Tyra ran off and quickly washed her face and changed her clothes. "Now, will you tell me? I've done everything you asked, and you promised to tell me!" she demanded, a little angrily, as she came back to her mother.

Anna sighed. "There's no putting you off, is there? I'll start by telling you about when you were a baby." Tyra was ready to protest vigorously that she had heard that story many times, but decided if she wanted to find out anything, she better cooperate with her mother.

"Far and I waited a long time to get you," Anna began, and although Tyra knew this she listened patiently. "We waited more than six years, and when I knew you were coming we were very happy." Anna was lost in thought. "Far and I wanted another little girl, or boy, but God never gave us one. So we are very glad we have you."

"That's good," said Tyra. "Were you very old when you had me?"

Anna laughed. "Let's see. I was born in 1882, and I married when I was eighteen. So I must have been twenty-four when you were born."

"Oh, Mor, that's awfully old! Did you get married in a white dress? How old was Far when he married you?"

"Yah, I got married in a white dress, I'll show you a picture I have when I got married. It's in the attic. And Far was the same age as me. We were both very young. But your Far is very hard working, and we managed well. Anyway, let me continue. Once upon a time, more than a hundred years ago . . ."

"What a long time!" broke in Tyra, her eyes wide. "Were you alive then?"

"Yah, it is a long time, and I certainly wasn't alive then!" Anna laughed. "Well, one hundred years ago there was a terrible war between Russia and Sweden. For hundreds and hundreds of years Finland was part of Sweden. People used to call Finland East Sweden."

"Oh, so that's why we talk Swedish even though we live in Finland," said Tyra with sudden understanding. "But we really aren't Swedish, are we? We're ourselves, aren't we?"

"That's right. Well, after that war, in 1809, Finland became part of Russia. The Tsar and a powerful army general called Napoleon signed a treaty that made us part of Russia. At first the Russians treated us well, and they called us the Grand Duchy of Finland."

"But we aren't Russians, are we? My teacher at school says the Russians have been good to us, and one of the Tsars built our city after it burned down. He says we should be very grateful to Russians."

"Perhaps the Russian people are good," replied Anna, bitterly, "but I don't think the government is. Let me tell you about our city. It used to be called Vasa, named after a good king in Sweden. When my mother was a tiny girl, about sixty years ago, the fire happened. Mor told me about great leaping flames, people and animals screaming, running around frantically. It was summer and most of the wells were almost dry, and so was everything else, so the town burned very quickly. Most of the buildings were made of wood, not stone. In just a few hours everything burned up, there was nothing left. Nobody had a home. Only four or five buildings made of stone didn't burn down, but all the other buildings were gone, just ashes."

"What made the fire start?" asked Tyra, wide-eyed.

"It was very sad, just one person caused all that damage. A foolish drunk man went to sleep in another man's barn. He lit his pipe, then let it fall into some dry moss or hay. When the barn caught fire he got scared because he shouldn't have been there, so he ran away. Because he was afraid and ashamed he didn't tell anybody about the fire and he didn't try to put it out, or get anyone to help him. Sparks from the burning barn fell on other buildings, and soon the whole town was burning. By night everything had gone." Anna shook her head sadly.

"All of it gone? That was very bad, but wasn't it good the Tsar helped build it again?"

"Well, I don't know, child. That's what I was trying to explain. You see, for hundreds of years our town was called Vasa, after the kings of Sweden. But the Tsar said we had to change our name to remember him, and how good Russians are because they helped us rebuild our town, so that's why we're called Nikolaistad."

"Well! That's funny. It sounds as though that Tsar was rather selfish. I've noticed Aunt Lisa, and Tobbe's mother always call our town Vasa, and I thought that was very strange. But Mor, I still don't understand, what has this got to do with you and Far being so solemn tonight?"

"Well, I know it's very complicated, but I'm explaining that our town, and our country, isn't really Russian. We're not happy that Russian people make us do what they want, and they don't listen to what we would like to do. We're Finnish people."

Tyra sat still for several minutes, pondering what this new revelation could mean. School always told her how good Russians were, but now her own mother was telling her something else. Who should she believe?

"Mor, my teachers tell me Russia is good. I don't understand. Who's telling me the truth?"

"Listen carefully, and you can decide." Mother and daughter sat pondering.

"Just before you were born, as I started to tell you," Anna began again, "there was lots of trouble here in Finland. Russia was fighting a country called Japan, far, far away, and it didn't win. There were lots of angry people in Russia, some of them did bad things and hurt people. Finally, this trouble made the Tsar scared, and he listened to what people were saying, and did what they wanted him to do. Just after you were born in August 1906 our government was changed. Everyone had the chance to choose who the government would be, women as well as men. Women were even allowed to become part of the government."

"You mean you weren't a real person before that? How awful!" Tyra was horrified.

Anna smiled. "Of course I was a real person! You're a real person when you do what's right. But do you know what? Finland was the first country in the world to allow women to be real people, as you say. Women had the chance to vote, and go to the diet, our parliament. There were nineteen women who went to the diet in the elections the next year."

"Only nineteen? Aren't there lots more ladies in Finland than that!"

"You funny child!" Anna laughed. "Not everyone wants to go to parliament. I certainly wouldn't like that job at all. I much prefer looking after you and Far. But you know, before that not even all the men in our country were what you call real people. There were supposed to be four groups of people in the government and those groups were country farmers, church ministers, city business people like Far, and noble rich people. But in fact it was only people who were very rich that ever got the chance to vote or go to parliament, and they made sure they got all the parliament jobs."

"That doesn't seem fair," declared Tyra, shaking her head. "I always thought governments were special, that they were the people who told us how to be good. Isn't that what the preacher says in church?"

Anna sighed deeply. "I wish that was true, but it isn't, at least, not quite. We all have to learn to do what's right by working out what God wants us to do."

"But God lives in heaven, so how can we ask him? Wouldn't it be much easier to ask the government? Mor, is Finland really the only country in the world where everyone is a real person?"

Anna smiled. "No, it's not. But I don't think there are many countries that allow everyone to vote. When we got the vote in Finland they told us there were only two other countries in the whole world where women could vote. Women in those countries can vote, but they can't be in the government, like we can here in Finland. Those countries are New Zealand and Australia, but they're on the other side of the world. I've never met anyone who's been there. You know, after they made the changes here in Finland, there were ten times more people who were allowed to vote!"

"Ten times! That sounds like a lot more people," nodded Tyra, picking up Molly and fiddling with her hair. "But tell me, I still don't know why you and Far are so worried! Mor, you can't really be worried about all those things that happened such a long time ago!"

Anna looked at her daughter. She was only seven years old, but certainly very perceptive. She hoped Tyra's questioning mind would not get her into trouble with authorities sometime in her life.

"Well, I wanted to explain all that because just when we thought things were getting better, Russia is causing us trouble again. They have decided there's going to be a war with a country called Germany, and that means Russian soldiers will have to fight."

"Where's Germany, Mor?"

"It's a long way from us, across the sea, or over land. You can get there by train or by ship."

"So, who decided to do the fighting? Those people in Germany, or the ones in Russia?"

"I would have to say both of them. They just don't like each other."

"But do people in Finland want to fight anyone? It sounds as though only Russian soldiers want to fight, so they can fight those Germans all by themselves. Far won't have to fight, will he? He's not a Russian, he's a

Finnish man, and he's not even a soldier," concluded Tyra cheerfully. "If Far had to fight, that would be a very bad thing."

"You're right. It would be very bad, very bad indeed. So we'll have to pray Far doesn't have to become a soldier and fight in some war that none of us want. Let's kneel down right now and pray about it."

"I hope God listens," said Tyra, as she obediently knelt. "Sometimes I wonder if he does listen."

"Of course he does!" retorted Anna reproachfully.

As mother and daughter ended their prayer, Anders came in.

Tyra jumped up. "Mor's been telling me about the war," she announced importantly, running to her father.

"She's been what!" cried Anders, horrified.

"She's very perceptive," replied Anna, defensively. "She noticed we were serious and wanted to know why. I tried to put her off, but she just persisted asking why we were sad. I've given her a simple history lesson. I found she has a very Russian view of everything."

"That's the problem with those schools!" exclaimed Anders. "Do you sing the national anthem at school?" he asked sternly.

"The what, Far?"

"Oh, no!" groaned Anders. "Don't tell you don't even know that! You know, *Vårt Land*."

"Of course, Far!" said Tyra proudly, and immediately launched into the first verse. "Don't you remember we sang it in church at Christmas!"

Anders raised his eyebrows, and nodded. "Good! I'm glad you know something. I should read you the story that song comes from."

"You mean it's a story, and not just a song?" Tyra loved stories.

"It is indeed. Now since you're growing up, perhaps we can start tonight, as a special treat to cheer everyone up."

"That sounds like a very good idea, Far." Tyra danced cheerfully around the kitchen.

Anders needed Anna's help to locate the family copy of *The Tales of Ensign Ståhl*, but eventually it was found in a large chest beside their bed.

"You don't think it's too gruesome?" asked Anna anxiously.

"To be honest, I haven't read this since I was at school," said Anders, awkwardly. "If it gets gruesome, I'll improvise, promise!" He grinned cheerfully at his wife. As his deep voice read on and on, Tyra's head drooped lower and lower on Molly's yellow plaits. Gruesome or otherwise, she had no idea what was being read to her.

"She's asleep," whispered Anna. Anders nodded, closed the book, and carried Tyra upstairs to a small couch she used for sleeping during the summer. Anna tucked a quilt over her, and she and Anders walked quietly out of the room.

"Why did you tell her?" Anders demanded angrily when they were alone. "She's far too young to have to worry about war!"

"She asked. Maybe you would've been better at saying no than I was, but I doubt it. I put her off several times, but she was very persistent. When Tyra wants to know something she shows a marked degree of *sisu*!"

"You mean you haven't noticed that? But why did you tell her? Does she understand?"

"Of course."

Anders shrugged, then relaxed. "Perhaps it's better she hears it from us, and not some garbled version from school. Sooner or later she has to learn that all is not well on the Russian front, despite what those teachers might tell her."

"You can talk to her too. You no doubt know a great deal more than I do."

"Hmm," grunted Anders. "I'll leave it to you. You'd give the most unbiased view. You know what you've already told her. I might just confuse her."

"Let's do it together," was Anna's wise suggestion. "And meanwhile, I need to get things ready for tomorrow. Is everything right with the horses?"

"Yah. We should leave early, though, so get your jobs done, and get some sleep."

"I hope I don't have nightmares!"

It was two hours before Anna finished her preparations. Anders was already sound asleep, breathing the deep, heavy, sleep of a hard working man, when she came into the bedroom. She was pulling down her nightdress when a small whisper crossed the room. "Mor?"

"You should be asleep!"

"I can't stop thinking. Our teacher told us we're God's children. Is that right?"

"Yah."

"Does that mean people in Germany aren't God's children because they fight other people?"

Anna suppressed a wry smile. "They're supposed to be God's children. All the people in the world are God's children."

"Really? The teacher made it sound as though only Russians were."

This time Anna could not help smiling. "No, we all belong to God. Only some people don't know it. Or if they do, they certainly don't behave the way God wants them to."

"Then why doesn't somebody tell German people they belong to God? Wouldn't that stop this horrible war thing?"

"I wish it were that simple, my dear child."

"If they knew we were all God's children they wouldn't fight other people! I'm sure I've heard Pastor Svenson say in church that if we are God's children we should love one another."

Anna sat down on her daughter's bed. "You're absolutely right. I wish everyone listened in church the way you've done!"

"I mean, war is killing people, isn't it? And God surely doesn't want us to kill, does he?"

"No he doesn't."

"When I grow up, I'm going to stop people going to war, and tell them they belong to God."

"That's a wonderful idea. But you need to go to sleep, or you'll be too tired to enjoy the ride to Oxkangar."

"I'm praying God will listen to us, and stop that silly war thing!" Very soon Tyra was fast asleep, and Anna crept into her own bed.

Chapter 3

Summer Lightning

Tyra rolled over, and watched the sun shining through chinks in the curtains. But when she looked around the room, she suddenly realized both her parents were missing. With happy relief she remembered their trip to Oxkanga. Seizing her dolls, Molly and Mia, she went in search of parents.

"Good morning, Mor!" she cried, rubbing sleep from her eyes. "I want to bring Mia because you made her, and Molly because Far gave her to me. And can we bring the book Far was reading last night?"

"Yah, good idea! I'll get the book!" said Anna. "Now, run and get dressed, because we're almost ready to go."

"You look tired, Mor," said Tyra. "I'll get dressed quickly and come and help."

"Thank you," said Anna, "but we're nearly ready, so just hurry yourself."

With thoughts of war invading her dreams, Anna had slept fitfully. In northern Finland summer has only one hour of night, and winter only one hour of watery daylight. Heavy curtains allow summer sleep, and Anna and Anders, hard at work carrying water, firewood (to fuel stoves), walking everywhere and doing essential work manually, normally slept easily, resting when opportunity provided. Anna had entered the kitchen as the church clock struck four, and sunlight, pouring in the windows, dazzled her. She was dressed when Anders walked in.

Mentally Anna ticked off supplies for Oxkangar: wide-brimmed hats to keep strong summer sun from their faces; bedding, but not much needed in summer; clothing, rolled into a strong canvas bag; and four new pillows, stacked by the door. Lisa had admired Anna's down pillows at Christmas. This provided Anna with the perfect gift idea for her hostess. It was easier to obtain goods in Nikolaistad than in the country. Only food for the journey was necessary. Farms had liberal supplies of basic food, and Lisa would be insulted if Anna implied farm fare was not good enough. Importantly, the Lall family would work while at the farm, and could eat farm food without feeling any sense of indebtedness.

"What can *I* carry out?" asked Tyra, dressed and ready to go. Anna gave her the pillows.

The church clock was striking five as Anders drove the horses and cart into the street. Lukas Larson waved as they clopped by. "We'll look after the cow!" he called.

"Look Mor!" cried Tyra excitedly. "I've just noticed. We live in Rådhusgatan, right? And now I know why!"

"Do you dear?" said Anna absent-mindedly, still mired in thoughts of war.

"Yah! Look! All the houses in our street are painted red, just like the name says. Isn't that nice!"

"Yah."

"But our house is the nicest. The white paint round our windows is brightest!"

They passed the churchyard, birch trees bright with leaf, grass green beneath. Tyra continued her lively commentary. "Look! There are my birds!"

"Your birds?" asked Anna. "Which do you call your birds? Several different birds are on the grass under the trees."

"Those brown spotty ones with grey heads, busy eating. They sing very softly."

"Those *are* nice birds," agreed Anna. "They're fieldfares, cousins to blackbirds and song thrushes."

"Oh, I never thought of birds having cousins, like I do. Tobbe promised he'd show me lots of birds, even where they have nests. He's told me lots about birds. I like those field-something ones because they're friendly. They're always in families."

Anna nodded, thinking how perceptive her daughter was to note that. But one thing Anna did not like. "Have you noticed fieldfares go away in winter?" she asked.

"Yah, most birds go in winter. But they come back in spring. Tobbe said spring is the best time to look for birds and their nests." After a short pause Tyra asked, "Where do birds go?"

"They fly south, to places where it's warm in winter. It's hard for them to find food in the snow in winter. That's why I put out bread crumbs," answered Anna.

"You mean there are places that don't have ice and snow in winter? Really? Do they have summer all the time? Oh, my, wouldn't that be fun! Can we go there sometime?"

"It must be very busy," answered Anna, thoughtfully. "Winter's when I catch up on my jobs, and do my weaving. I can't imagine having no winter, no time to rest."

"Far works all the time. He doesn't get time to rest when it's cold. He goes to work when it's snowing and really cold."

"Yah, dear." Anna worried about her husband on icy winter roads. He had less work in winter, but his reputation for reliability meant he was always first called to carry goods.

"Mor, do those places that have no winter have spring? Spring is such a pretty time, even better than summer. I wouldn't like to live in a place that didn't have spring."

"I don't know. Perhaps they do have some sort of spring. Anyway, birds like our spring more than their summer!" Anna laughed at this strange thought.

They left city streets and trotted into the country; the horses responded to Anders' tension on the reins and picked up speed. Anders kept them at a steady pace, but both were keen to step out in the fresh morning. Möja calmed Kanel, but Kanel made Möja more lively, and Anders observed, "These horses work well together. I've mainly used them together only for heavy loads, but maybe it would help them to share loads more often."

Suddenly Tyra remembered something important. "Far!" she announced, "Mor brought the book. You can read it to me and Algot and Hjalmar."

But Anders did not respond, temporarily occupied guiding the horses along a badly rutted road. The cart swayed ominously, lurching from one pothole to another, and all his skill was required to keep it from tipping. But soon the surface improved, and he relaxed. "I've told those city hall people many times about this rough stretch of road, but no one listens," Anders grumbled. "They're more interested in city streets than country roads, though farmers pay good taxes just like the rest of us!"

Tyra, contentedly playing with her dolls, jumped up and threw her arms wide. "The road might be naughty, but isn't it lovely in the country?" she observed. "It smells so nice! When I grow up I'm going to live in the country."

"And who will you live with in the country?" asked Anna, absently.

Tyra threw her mother a withering look. "I'll marry a farmer, that's who I'll live with! I won't come out here all by myself! But you and Far can come and live with me, if you like."

Anna laughed at her daughter's declaration of independence, and over the horses' clopping hooves she suspected she heard a chuckle from Anders.

"How about we stop in the country you like so much and have breakfast?" suggested Anders. "I'm sure Mor has some good food."

"Hurray!" shouted Tyra, tossing Mia and Molly unceremoniously to the cart floor. "I'm *really* hungry!"

Anders guided the horses to a grassy patch. While he hitched them to a tree and secured the cart with a sturdy plank, Anna removed a cloth from a wooden bucket and spread fresh rye bread, butter, a round of cheese, and a bottle of milk on a clean red gingham napkin. While Anders ate standing beside the cart, Anna and Tyra remained in the wagon. The fresh morning gave them all a good appetite. When they had finished eating, Tyra's pleas to have a run were granted.

"I need to give the horses a drink and some oats, so don't go far. When I call come at once," Anders admonished.

"Yah, Far," promised Tyra, as she nimbly climbed down from the cart and began looking for flowers. Before Anders finished tending the horses she was back with a bunch of white daisies, brilliant blue cornflowers, and a few pink twin flowers.

"Do you have any water I can put these in, so they'll keep for Algot?" she asked.

Anna promised to find something, and off Tyra raced, returning with yellow buttercups.

"See why I like the country! There are so many flowers, although I couldn't find any red poppies," she said, waving her bouquet as she climbed into the cart. "Now, where's the water you promised?"

"There's a little river down the road," said Anders. "I'll let you use my water pannikin for your flowers if you're good."

The stream was soon found and the battered, much-used pannikin filled. Tyra agreed to let her father take responsibility for the flowers, lest water be spilled on the bedding in the cart. Soon the swaying vehicle, warm sun, and a full tummy lulled her to sleep. Anna pulled a hat over her face, lay down beside her daughter, and submitting to the sway of the horses, let herself relax. For mother and daughter, the last of the journey was lost in dreamland.

Screams of delight from Algot and Hjalmar announced their arrival at the Oxkangar farm, and quickly woke them. The boys raced each other up the path to announce the arrival of their cousin (Algot only just won).

"I've decided to give my flowers to Morfar," whispered Tyra, and Anna nodded approval.

"Yah," she whispered back, "he'll enjoy them more than Algot."

Tyra presented her bouquet to her grandfather, a gnarled old man nodding in a chair thoughtfully placed in the sun beside the kitchen door. His hands were heavily scarred from years of blacksmithing, twisted with arthritis, and he was very deaf. But when he smiled appreciatively as his granddaughter presented her bouquet, he looked positively saintly.

"Very pretty, very pretty," he said, patting her on the shoulder. "Thank you very much. You're a good child."

The old man was no longer able to do heavy work, but he helped his daughter-in-law to peel vegetables and other simple tasks. Once a week she assisted him on a laborious tour of the farm, listening carefully to his advice. Karl brushed his father's ideas aside, but Lisa passed them on so they sounded like the latest modern concept. Karl did not realize it, but it was his father's idea to grow flax, which proved very lucrative. As soon as he took over the management of the farm Karl eliminated his father's blacksmith shop because he thought the work was troublesome. Karl increased food crops, but Lisa respected the old man for what he had done to win his farm from the forest, and for the years of essential blacksmithing he had provided the community. The old man's equipment was still in his workshop, and old timers in the district often used it, paying the dismissive Karl handsomely for the opportunity. Anders himself regularly used the services of his father-in-law when he was courting Anna, and he still reshod his own horses whenever he was on the family farm.

"You've arrived just in time to harvest my last field of flax," announced Karl cheerfully, coming from the barn. "I've left it for the kids. Anders' horse and cart will be good for other jobs. Ah, whoa there! You have two horses with you! Don't trust those army captains with your steeds, eh?"

"Of course not," replied Anders curtly.

Soon the children were competing as to who could get the biggest number of flax bundles. "Remember, I want the roots!" Karl yelled with monotonous regularity. Having the roots meant the length of stalk was maximized, and a better quality of flax ensured. Anna's job was tying the flax into bundles, and Anders' to stook them.

"It's a good crop this year, best ever," said Karl proudly. "Just look at the length of those stalks! All at least a meter. They'll fetch a good price, I'm sure."

"He took one of my bundles!" wailed Hjalmar across the field.

"Did not!" shouted Algot petulantly. "You took one of Tyra's, and I took it back. I won't let you be mean to Tyra!"

"Come, come, come, children," coaxed Anna, walking towards them. "Don't waste time fighting! It doesn't matter who has the most bundles."

"It does!" declared Algot. "Far said whoever got the least number of bundles had to get the ones out of the stink pond. He put a whole lot in there a couple of weeks ago. It smells terrible!"

Anna laughed. "I'm sure he was teasing! He won't let you anywhere near that 'stink pond' as you call it. That's his job, for sure."

Karl, striding up, agreed. "Yah, that's right. That flax has been in the retting pond for a week. It's now ready to come out, and I hope Anders will stay to help me thresh it. This field is shady, so flax here matures later. Now if you kids don't behave, you *will* get some bad jobs!"

"It stinks! It really stinks!" insisted Algot.

"Yah, son," growled Karl impatiently. "That's enough of your cheek! I'll push you in that pond right now if you don't stop your sassiness! We all know retting flax smells. But without that stink we couldn't get the fibers out of the flax stalks, and they'd be useless. After all that stinking we'll have lovely silky flax fibers."

"I won't let him do that!" whispered Hjalmar to his brother in a hoarse whisper. Tyra looked frightened. She was not used to her parents speaking unkindly to her, and wondered if her uncle would carry out his threats.

Anders walked over. "Let's count the bundles for fun," he suggested, breaking the tension. Lisa had the highest count, but the children collectively had gathered double the number she had. A little sleight of hand enabled Anders to make each child's bundle count exactly the same.

"Far will have to push us all in the pond!" declared Algot triumphantly, before Hjalmar clapped his hand over his brother's mouth, and tickled him to keep him from saying anything worse.

Anna and Lisa went to prepare lunch, while the children played chase and hide-in-seek in the tiny sheds dotting the hay fields (ready for use in case of an untimely shower of rain during harvesting). The men stooked the flax and admired their handiwork.

"If the weather stays hot, these bundles should dry in a few days, and then they can go in the pond." Karl screwed his eyes and gazed into the cloudless sky, scanning it for signs of unwanted rain. "Last year we had frequent thunder storms, but thus summer we haven't had any. I hate thunderstorms myself. They always mean trouble."

"I was terrified of them when I was a kid," admitted Anders, "although I never personally saw anything bad happen."

Lisa called them for lunch. The busy morning and long trip gave everyone a healthy appetite for the salmon, potato, and leek soup Lisa had prepared, accompanied by fresh rye bread and Nikolaistad cinnamon buns. After lunch Anders' nodding head reminded the family they were up early, and an afternoon nap was in order. Algot and Hjalmar protested vigorously, but when Tyra admitted she needed a rest, they capitulated, and were soon sound asleep themselves.

"Can we pick the apples yet?" pled Algot, when he woke.

"Far's in the orchard right now," said Lisa. "He's checking them, but I think it's too early. How about you go raspberry hunting instead? You'll find plenty of those." She gave the children a basket, and off they ran. Many raspberries were on the canes that grew along the fence, and tiny wild strawberries hid under hedgerows. Soon the basket was brimming.

Just then Karl and Anders arrived with their pockets full of apples. "The apples generally aren't ready, but we found enough ripe ones for the women to make an apple cake!"

"Beat you!" declared Algot triumphantly. "We've got so many raspberries and strawberries Mor's going to make pancakes for supper."

"I don't mind waiting for apple cake," said Karl. "Pancakes are my favorite food!"

"What food crops have you grown this year?" asked Anders, as the men waited for their supper.

"I grow crops for ourselves, and locally, as you know," responded Karl. "Those two fields of flax get me more money than all my oats, barley and rye. Up north here it's a waste of time trying to grow wheat, with all the massive imports from Russia. I grow enough oats to make a tidy sum at the local market. Lisa's good at telling her friends about my oats, and I sell most of it that way. I've got some bags of rye and barley I hope you'll take back to Vasa and sell for me. Which reminds me, when are you returning?"

"Happy to sell for you. I'm friends with a reputable grain merchant who's always glad to get your crop. Now, to answer your question, I'll stay here till Thursday, and go back with Kanel. I'll come back in three weeks. Möja will do good work for you, I'm sure."

"You really are keeping her out of sight of army requisition, eh?" sneered Karl.

"Of course," said Anders, ignoring his brother's taunt. "My horses are the breed most wanted by the army. They're incredibly powerful and can shift enormous loads. I regularly get offers to buy them!"

"I'm not much into horses, but you know what you're talking about. Myself, I've been doing more fishing lately," said Karl. "Perch and pike are plentiful round the island, and they fetch good prices. I'll try to have a barrel or two when you go back, and you can sell them for me in town."

"The kids might be happy to help with fishing, and I can certainly help sell them. Fish get a good price in town."

"Those kids are a bit small for fishing, more nuisance than they're worth. I don't have the patience you have with kids. No, I'll get Rolf next door to fish with me. He's been encouraging me to go winter ice fishing with him, but I'm not keen. You can spend hours on the ice just getting cold!"

"Speaking of children," said Anna, coming out, "how about sending them to find eggs to make *plattar*?"

"Better go with them or we'll have scrambled eggs instead of pancakes," joked Anders.

The egg-hunting expedition was greeted with great enthusiasm. After much discussion it was agreed Anders would supervise Hjalmar and Tyra, with Karl and Algot working together. Algot pled earnestly to go with his uncle, but Karl insisted three children were too much for any man to manage. He had a dozen egg boxes in his barn, and all needed checking. His twenty hens were currently enjoying outdoor summer freedom, and most of them were nesting in new places. Old Magnus the rooster strutted with disdainful importance, while his son Mats tried to act the boss by crowing louder every morning.

Soon it was clear that Hjalmar was only interested in roosters, which he chased with ruthless determination. Tyra, however, carefully discovered eight eggs, including two in unsuspected nests under cow feed-boxes, gently placing them in the basket provided. Algot created much wailing and distress when he turned two of his eggs into scrambled splotches on the barn floor, but everyone reassured him that with the two eggs he still had, plus Tyra's, there were still plenty of eggs for their mothers to make *plattar*.

"She's got a gift for hens and eggs," said Karl, watching his niece carry the basket of eggs. "Why don't you get some for her? A nice little sideline for you, with Anna's help."

"What! And have the horses make scrambled eggs!" laughed Anders.

"No, pen off a small portion of stable. Tyra would do you proud. If you agree, I'll get some chicks that you can take back and see how she goes."

"Not sure how she'd cope with turning roosters into dinner. She has a very tender heart."

"Well, if she's squeamish about that, just sell them off as fowls, and let her concentrate on the egg part."

Tyra presented the egg basket proudly to her aunt. "Ten eggs!" exclaimed Lisa. "That's amazing! I never find more than six!"

"We would've had . . ." began Hjalmar, but Karl quickly hushed him. "Since you didn't find any eggs, I don't think you'd better say anything." Hjalmar retired sulkily behind his mother's skirt. Soon his wounded pride recovered sufficiently to suggest they play chase with the roosters while *plattar* was being prepared. Algot enthusiastically agreed, always keen for a game of chase. Tyra trouped out with them, but spent her time soothing the ruffled feathers of the flustered roosters. Finally, the beautiful russet birds with proud, iridescent green and blue tails learned to stay close by her, and the boys chased each other. The roosters followed Tyra into the barn where she found barley, and for the rest of her stay as soon as they saw her, they came running to her side, begging for food.

Next day Tyra celebrated her eighth birthday. There was no party or presents, as was usual in Finland, but Anna and Lisa made a large apple cake. Algot was awestruck. "Are you really eight years old?" Tyra assured him he would soon reach such an exalted age himself. That cheered him, until he realized that when he became eight, Tyra would be ten. "I'll never catch up with you!" he wailed. "Why did you get born first!"

Tyra was sorry to bid her father good bye, but solemnly promised to look after Anna while he was away. Lisa cheered her with the reminder that it was time for pea-picking, and she and the boys could eat all the peas they liked while they worked. Tyra wondered how the dangerously tempting, delicious little green peas she picked could turn into the dull brown mush of standard Finnish pea soup served with monotonous regularity every Thursday lunch. She decided regular pea soup was made from dried-up, death-sick-yellow, rock-hard old peas, boiled till any life in them had vanished, and she should experiment making soup from fresh green peas. She brought her idea to her aunt.

"Why, of course you can!" laughed Lisa, at Tyra's request. "I like fresh pea soup myself. It's much nicer than soup made from dried peas. Let's add a few nettles, and a nice new onion."

The soup experiment was such a success that Tyra fell asleep dreaming how to keep peas fresh and green so their soup could keep its summer taste and not have the dead winter flavor and color she disliked so much.

As Karl predicted, the warm sunny weather quickly dried the flax, and the time to retrieve the bundles from Algot's stink pond arrived. Tyra was happy to wheel barrow loads of smelly flax bundles to trestles beside the barn, and lift them out onto the trestles to dry. The boys adamantly refused to help, so Anna took turns with her daughter till all were transported.

A few days later, just before breakfast, Karl entered the kitchen after his regular barn inspection looking worried. "The sky's very black out there. We're in for a bad thunderstorm. I need help to get the flax trestles into the barn. They're almost dry, and I'd hate to get them wet now." Lisa, Anna, and the children ran to help.

"Wow, those clouds have rolled up from nowhere," exclaimed Lisa as she and Anna carried another trestle into the barn. "It's getting blacker, if that's possible!"

"We've had so much hot weather it just needs an icy north wind to hit the hot air, and then we get this thundery stuff," grumbled Karl.

"The weather's been so good," said Anna cheerfully. "We can't expect it to be perfect all the time."

A sudden burst of brilliant light was instantly followed by a deafening crash of thunder. "Wow! Did you hear that! This storm's coming fast! Get the children inside quickly. Far too; he's sitting by the door. I'll manage the last couple of trestles."

The thunder and crash of pelting rain became deafening. Karl dashed in the kitchen soaked by the downpour, just as another bolt of lightning ripped across the sky, and zigzagged crazily to earth.

"Mor!" exclaimed Tyra, standing by the window. "I can see lightning hitting the ground all around us! Lots of it! I'm scared!"

Karl glanced out. "Great heavens!" he cried, "She's right! I've never seen so much lightning! This is the worst in years. We'll be lucky to get out of this without trouble somewhere." He pealed off his soaked clothes, making rivers on Lisa's kitchen floor.

"These thunderstorms are terrible," said Morfar in his quivering voice. "Used to cause lots of damage. I remember we lost three good cows in one storm, hit by lightning they were, dead, just like that! A neighbor's haystack burnt down and that was . . ."

"Yah, yah, yah," cut in Karl irritably. "Those were your bad old days. We don't have such problems now!"

"Did anyone see the animals?" asked Anna, suddenly.

"Animals? Look at it out there! Never seen such a tempest! I'm not going out in it! I hope those critters can fend for themselves," said Karl, flatly.

"Far!" called Algot, running down the stairs from the bedroom where he'd been glued to the window watching the thunder and lightning. "There's smoke coming out of Herr Rolf's barn! Lots and lots of it!"

"Oh, no!" exclaimed Karl, when he got to the bedroom upstairs. "He's right! The barn's blazing. You'd think the rain would put it out, but it isn't."

Anna climbed the stairs and with Lisa and watched in horror as flames leapt high from the burning barn. Lightning flashed, and thunder boomed across the sky, but the sounds were retreating as the storm moved away.

"It would be a tinder box, just like ours," said Karl, ruefully watching the conflagration. "Full of dry hay. Must've been a direct hit. What a shame. Rolf was so proud of his new barn. This will be a terrible loss. I guess I better do that ice fishing with him after all. He won't have much else to live on this year."

"We'll all have to pitch in and share hay and do whatever we can to help," said Lisa.

"Look! The roof's fallen in!" cried Algot excitedly.

"Yah, it's all gone! So sad. But isn't that his wife, running towards the barn?" said Anna, anxiously. "The weather's terrible. Why would she risk being out in that thunder and lightning? I see her two older boys with her."

"I'll wait till the storm's passed, then go and see what I can do to help," offered Karl. "She might be stupid enough to be out in that tempest, but I don't have to follow her example!"

But something was wrong, and everyone, except Morfar still sipping coffee downstairs, watched the remains of the burning barn apprehensively. The rain was still pelting down when Karl, muttering protestations, left with an old sack thrown over his head.

"I don't like it," said Lisa. "My neighbor and her eldest son have rakes and a crowbar, and they're looking for something in those smoking ruins. I can't see Rolf anywhere."

"Let's get the children something to eat," said Anna. "I don't think they should be watching."

The boys made mild protests about missing the excitement, but since there was now little to watch in the collapsed barn, they agreed food was better. Tyra was very quiet, and ate little.

Two hours later Karl returned, his clothes covered in soot, a nasty burn seared across his right hand, his face ashen grey.

"How are they?" asked Lisa, her eyes wide with fear.

"Terrible!" whispered Karl, hoarsely. "Terrible." He would say no more. Lisa offered food, but he refused everything except a cup of coffee. For an hour he sat hunched in dirty, wet clothes, trembling, shaking his head jerkily, and muttering "Terrible!" The children crept out of the room, out into the watery sunlight. Tyra counted the hens and roosters and found they were safe. She and Algot gave the trembling Möja oats, and the mare stopped shaking and nuzzled them gently. Hjalmar stroked the wet noses of the milk cows, all of whom were accounted for, urgently telling them the storm had gone.

"I think they're fine now," said Tyra. "We should go inside, or our parents will be cross."

But instead of being cross, they found, to their utter astonishment, their father and uncle, head on his arms, sobbing. "Rolf, gone!" he said, before Lisa bustled them from the kitchen and up the stairs. They waited until she returned to the kitchen before creeping back to eavesdrop outside the door. They caught only snippets of Karl's broken words, but learned enough to understand the fearful thing that had happened.

Rolf Nilsson, and his younger brother visiting from Jakobstad, were stooking hay in a far field when the storm rolled up. Like everyone else, it took them by surprise. They were running home when the first bolt of lightning hit the ground in front of them. Frightened, they turned to the nearby shelter of the barn. But unknown to them, lightning had already struck the building. Mounds of smoldering hay created huge amounts of thick smoke, which first obscured their vision, then overpowered them. Rolf's wife hoped when the barn burst into flame, and the roof fell in, they were already unconscious. The bodies of both men were badly burnt. One detail Karl described with paroxysms of sobbing: when Rolf's body was rolled over, three tiny chicks scurried from underneath.

"Were there any animals in the barn?" asked Lisa.

"Amazingly, they were all out in the field, and unscathed."

The children heard footsteps and scurried back up the stairs. There Anna found them, white-faced and very quiet.

"You should go and feed the horses," said Anna.

"We already . . ." began Hjalmar, but Algot kicked him hard, and he closed his mouth quickly.

"Yah, Mor," said Tyra. "Come boys, let's go."

"I don't want to go near that barn!" screamed Algot. "Our hay might be smoking too!"

"We'll just open the doors," said Tyra sensibly, although she too was frightened. "And anyway, we've been in the barn, so we know it isn't burning."

Hjalmar, who loved cows and they him, amused himself and the others by squirting fresh milk into their mouths. Warm and frothy, it was a special stolen treat, and for a few minutes they forget the horrible story they had heard. Lisa saw what they were doing, but wisely refrained from scolding. They were actually doing the cows a good turn, she decided, as she wasn't sure when Karl would remember, or be in a fit state, to milk them.

When Lisa and Anna called everyone for supper that evening Karl did not appear. Lisa pursed her mouth grimly. "I know what he's doing," she said, bitterly.

"Let's feed the children and Morfar," suggested Anna, "and then investigate."

"You don't need to investigate! I know what he's up to! He does this every time he gets upset!" cried Morfar in his high pitched, plaintive voice. "I'm ashamed of him! A disgrace he is, a drunkard! Nice porridge, Lisa."

"I wish my Far was here to read a story," said Tyra wistfully as she dressed for bed. All the adults in the family could read, but only Anders enjoyed it. With everyone so sad and serious, she longed for her father's stable presence.

"He'll be here the day after tomorrow," said Anna consolingly. "Why don't you read the boys some of the story?"

"Please do!" shouted the boys. "That would be fun!"

"Do you think I'm good enough?" asked Tyra nervously.

"Of course you are!" declared Anna. "Your teacher says you're a very good reader."

"Oh, well, I'll try," she agreed and settled down to her new job.

With a sense of accomplishment, Anna descended the stairs to make sure her father was comfortable, and then joined Lisa in the search for Karl. It did not take long. As Lisa expected, he was in the barn sprawled across a broken hay bale, an empty bottle of his potato *brännvin* beside him, an almost empty one clutched in his shaking hand.

"Karl, it's time to come inside," said Lisa calmly.

"Ish terrbull," he slurred, lifting himself on one elbow. "My sheshal friend gone. Ish not fair, ish not right."

"Please stand, Karl," said Anna, "and we'll help you inside."

"An' what makesh you think a man the likesh of me needsh help? No one can help my friend. He'sh dead."

"Yah, yah, take my arm," persisted Anna. "Take Lisa's other arm."

With difficulty the women got Karl to his feet, and dragging rather than leading, got him out of the barn. He refused to part with his bottle, but it dribbled empty as he walked. As he staggered across the yard he started shouting and cursing, and it was all the women could do to keep him upright and walking. Eventually they sat him on a chair in the kitchen. Suddenly he noticed his empty bottle, and began shouting and cursing even more. With lurching effort he staggered to his feet, and threw the bottle forcefully at Lisa. She ducked, just as it smashed on the wall.

"Karl!" squealed Morfar. "How dare you hit a woman!"

"Go see to the children," said Anna to Lisa. "I'll deal with my brother."

White faced, Lisa was only too pleased to go upstairs.

"Brother," began Anna, "it's been a terrible day. You've lost your friend and neighbor. We're all terribly sad."

"It wouldn't've happened if you'll weren't here!" Karl screamed irrationally. "Go home. Leave ush alone!"

"Yah, Brother, when Anders comes. But please, come and rest on the couch."

"It wash you, I know it wash." Without warning Karl swung his fist and hit Anna hard across her left eye and cheek. She gave a cry of shock and pain.

Their old father began sobbing, moaning, "How could my own son do that to his sister!" But without further struggle Karl submitted to being laid on the couch. Anna rolled him on his side, tucked a quilt around him, and went to Lisa and the children.

"Do you have some very cold water?" she asked calmly as she entered the room. With one glance Lisa realized what had happened, and quickly went out with Anna. As she applied cold, wet cloths to the tender, bruised face of her sister-in-law, she wept.

"Don't cry for me, sister," said Anna. "How often does this happen to you? You ducked so expertly when he threw that bottle, it must have happened before!"

"Not often," admitted Lisa, between sobs. "I've tried to hide it. I feel so ashamed. It really upsets your father. It doesn't happen often, only when he's upset and drunk. It's very bad for the boys, especially Algot, who expresses a lot of hate for his father. Truly, Karl's a good husband most of the time. When he's sober he's always very sorry for what he's done, and willing to do anything I ask to make amends. He'll be mortified when he sees you tomorrow, especially since Anders will find out."

"Sister, I'll speak to Anders first."

"Please do, if you can. But what can I do? I've pled with him so many times. He always promises he won't do it again. But he keeps on making that brew of his, and now he hides it from me."

"It's a national disgrace, you know. We try to drown all our sorrows in drink. We women need to stand up to this problem. We have women in government now, surely we can persuade them to do something."

"Maybe," sobbed Lisa, "but I haven't got much faith in governments, and I haven't got any more fight in me."

"Anyway, thank you for the cold pack. It feels better now. Maybe tomorrow there'll be nothing to see!"

"I wish!" smiled Lisa weakly.

Next day Karl was miserably sick. Anna draped her long hair over her eye so her injury was partially disguised, and she and Lisa visited Rolf's widow to offer comfort and assistance.

Two days later when Anders turned Kanel through the farm gate he was bombarded with childish chatter. "The barn burnt down!" "There was lots of thunder and lightning!" "Far has a terrible headache!" "Möja didn't get hurt!" "Tyra found some new nests!" "Herr Rolf's dead!" "I tried to look after Mor, but she got hurt!" "We picked all the apples!" "Tyra carried the stink bundles!" "Algot made scrambled egg on the barn floor!"

"Whoa! Whoa! Whoa!" ordered Anders, laughing and patting the children on their heads as they ran beside him. "Let's get Kanel some oats, then you can tell me everything. Kanel's come long way all by herself, so she's very hungry and thirsty. Now, has the barn really burned down?"

"No, Far," said Tyra. "It wasn't our barn, but Herr Rolf's. It's very sad. He died."

Anders drew the reins back suddenly, and Kanel came to an abrupt halt. Something terrible *had* happened! It was not just childish chatter. He looked up and was confronted with Anna's green and purple eye. "Oh, no!" he groaned. "What *has* been going on here?"

"Husband, can I talk to you? Let's go to the barn, and children, you feed Kanel. Tyra, you know what to do, don't you?"

"Yah, Mor," said Tyra proudly, adding, "and I know you can't because you've been hurt," as she led Kanel away.

Anna quickly shared the tragedy and its consequences with her husband. Anders immediately insisted on hunting for Karl's brewing equipment, found in a "room" made from hay bales. He dragged every piece into the courtyard, then swinging Karl's heavy sledge hammer, smashed it all to pieces. He angrily resisted Anna's pleas to talk to Karl first. "The fool! The idiot!" he muttered with each swing of the hammer. "If that man ever drinks again it won't be without a massive fight from me!"

"Not feeling so good?" Anders boomed, as he entered the kitchen and thrust out his hand to shake Karl's. Still nursing a pounding headache, Karl winced at his guest's heartiness.

"It was terrible," muttered Karl, fearfully. "I've lost my best friend. Sorry about Anna. It was a bit of an accident, you know, and . . ."

"Yah, yah, yah, I know," responded Anders testily. "But cheer up, it won't happen again."

"No, I won't ever do that again." The relief in Karl's voice was strong. "Great."

When Karl took Anders to the drying flax he hoped his brother-in-law would thresh, he stopped dead at the sight of his smashed brewing equipment sprawled across the yard. "Who dared do this!" he bellowed. "This is criminal!"

"I did! Just helping you to not repeat what you did to my wife," responded Anders calmly. "Try reporting me to the police, and I'll do the same to you! But with a head like yours, I wouldn't make it worse by yelling, if I were you. Now, do you want help threshing flax, or not?"

"And just think," Anders told Anna later, "I thought I was bringing you to safety from war troubles! All I've had to contend with is a few soldiers standing around on street corners!" Anna buried her face on her husband's broad shoulder, and finally allowed herself to weep.

Karl did not eat breakfast with the family. "He's too ashamed!" declared Mofar, spooning oats porridge into his mouth. "And so he should be!"

"He might be trying to do something to make amends," suggested Lisa, with a wan smile. "He's always mortified after he's hit me, and I can get him to do anything at those times."

The cart was loaded and the horses dancing to go, when Karl finally emerged from the barn. He presented a small basket to Tyra. "Don't open this till you get home," he said, smiling sheepishly. "I hope it will make your Far happy."

"Oh, I know what it is!" Tyra cried joyfully, as peepings emerged from the basket. "My chickens! Thank you so much!"

"Karl," said Anders, holding his horses' reins firmly, and looking directly into the bright blue eyes of his brother-in-law, "don't be a chicken. Be a man! If I can rein in these horses, you can control yourself!"

Tyra did not look at her chickens until she reached home, but she had a great deal of time to think as the horses plodded to Nikolaistad. The terrible thunderstorm, death of the neighbor, and her beloved uncle hurting her mother left her with serious questions about both the goodness of God who allowed such things, and the country she was supposed to be proud of. The thoughts frightened her and she dared not share them with her parents. Not even with Tobbe.

Chapter 4

A Finnish War

"I THOUGHT YOU SAID there was a war!" complained nine-year-old Tyra irritably, dropping her school bag on the kitchen table. "It's been more than a year, but the only war I can see is everyone is cross and there's not much to eat!"

"There *is* a war, just be grateful it isn't here!" retorted Anna. "Stop complaining and help me get dinner ready."

"I hope it's not barley porridge again," snapped Tyra. But it was.

Newspapers carried photos of terrible battle disasters across Europe, but glowing descriptions of victories by Russian troops. Nikolaistad, a port city, had concentrations of troops ready for defense, but with no active engagement they were bored and often boisterous. Soldiers, first Russian, then Finnish conscripts, lounged everywhere. Waiting, waiting, waiting made tensions rise, tempers flare. The national habit of using alcohol to deal with stress and distress did not help.

Anna and Anders advised Tyra she must not talk to strangers, unless she knew them very well.

"What about Tobbe's family?" asked Tyra, wide-eyed.

"Only about ordinary things. No questions."

"No questions at all? Can I talk to my teachers?"

"Only about school work."

"You mean I can't I talk to anyone! What if I forget?"

"When there's a war, Tyra, you don't forget."

Tyra had her chicks, now hens, to distract her. While summer lasted Tyra and Tobbe daily took the hens to the churchyard to let them run. When winter darkness took over, she brought them into the kitchen after school and let them enjoy the warmth. Anna refrained from complaint because the hens laid well. Tyra rarely brought her less than two eggs.

The Lall and Rådman families had agreed a 1914 Christmas visit to Nikolaistad was not wise. Night travel was now too risky. Anders advised Karl of a price rise for staple grains, and suggested he consider growing more barley, oats and rye. Karl took the advice. He assured the Lalls he had given up alcohol, and they need never fear visiting him. Anders growled, "He'd better!" Anna said, "Thank God for that!" Early in the New Year Lisa wrote that Morfar Rådman had died quietly in his sleep. Anders decided winter night travel was too dangerous for the family to attend the funeral. Tyra asked, "Why did God take Morfar when I'll miss him?" She was quiet and withdrawn for several days. Anna grieved deeply, silently, for her father.

When summer came, Anders persuaded Anna to spend the entire school holidays on the Oxkangar farm. Anna, still grieving, was reluctant to leave Anders, but he assured her he would come out as frequently as he could. He was again glad to get his favorite Möja out of sight from army requisition.

Tyra was delighted to spend time on the farm, and enjoyed all the usual activities with her cousins. But she missed her grandfather, and was disappointed that Morbror Karl no longer grew flax. Lisa was convinced Tyra had a good influence on Algot and Hjalmar, that they were more willing to work when she was around.

When the Lall family returned to Nikolaistad in autumn 1915, Anders one day brought startling news: 2,000 Finnish men had stealthily slipped out of the country and gone to Germany, where they joined the Prussian Jaegar Light Infantry Battalion. They heard many of the men were university students from Helsingfors.

"They're as sick of nothing happening as I am," said Anders. "But those young hotheads will soon discover there's nothing glamorous about war!"

"They sound foolish to me!" declared Anna, kneading bread aggressively to allay her anxieties. "Won't they be called traitors?"

"Exactly. But they say Sibelius has written more music to celebrate their going!"

"What's a traitor?" asked Tyra.

"Someone bad," said Anna shaking her head and wondering what terrible reprisals Russia would take. But, amazingly, nothing happened.

Thus 1915 became 1916.

Tyra normally walked to school with the Larson boys. But Tobbe turned sixteen the year Tyra turned ten, and began work in the paper company where his father was employed. Tobbe's younger brothers were good friends, but clearly indicated they did not want a girl tagging along to school with them. So Anders decided to accompany his daughter each day.

A few days after Tyra's tenth birthday, back on the Oxkangar farm, the weather was dark and ominous. Thunder boomed, lightning flickered around the horizon, and the children ran inside. Anna retrieved her knitting, knowing from experience that rhythmic movements dissipated her anxiety, inevitable after the Rolf Nilsson disaster two years earlier. Algot and Hjalmar, glued to the windows, watched jagged thunderbolts, but Tyra brought her knitting and sat quietly beside her mother.

"Mor, can we be sure that Herr Rolf and his brother are in heaven?" she asked, unexpectedly.

Startled, Anna said, "What makes you ask that?"

"Well, it's so sad what happened to him and his brother. I asked my teacher at school but he just said if they were good they'd go to heaven, and if they were bad and had not confessed all their sins they'd go to hell."

"I'm sure Herr Rolf was a good man."

"His wife says he was. But, when I asked Pastor Svenson he said Herr Rolf probably didn't have time to confess his sins, so he'd be in hell!"

"You asked both your teacher and Pastor Svenson?" Anna was astonished at her daughter's persistence in this matter.

Tyra dropped her knitting and began to weep. Anna waited until she calmed, then suggested she should let God decide whether Herr Rolf and his brother would go to heaven or hell. Since God was always very kind, Anna insisted, and very fair, he would always do the right thing.

"Yah, that's what I decided," agreed Tyra, wiping her eyes. "But I'm not sure how kind God really is. Why would he allow such a terrible thing to happen? And there's something else, Mor. I watched Herr Rolf's barn burn. It was terrible to see, and I still get bad dreams about it. But when it was burned up, it was burned up. Gone! It didn't go on burning forever. I told Pastor Svenson that, and he said it was just a barn, but God could keep hell burning forever. But why would a good God, who's supposed to love us, keep something as bad as hell burning forever?" Tyra burst into sobs again.

"I've never thought of it like that," said Anna, shocked at how much thinking Tyra had done on these frightful subjects. "But you may be right.

Maybe hell doesn't burn forever, like you say! At least, maybe people in it don't."

"I hope so." Tyra smiled weakly through her tears, and re-commenced knitting. "You don't think I'm bad thinking thoughts like that, do you, Mor? Pastor Svenson said if I didn't stop asking bad questions I'd go to hell myself!"

"Of course not! He shouldn't say things like that to you!" Anna straightened her shoulders defiantly.

Just then Algot and Hjalmar raced down the stairs to announce there was no more lightning, but a loud clap of thunder challenged this assertion. Hjalmar watched his aunt and cousin knitting and asked if he could learn, but Algot laughed. "Knitting's for girls!" he insisted.

• • •

"Something's not right," Anders confided to Anna, a few weeks later as they clopped home behind Möja and Kanel. "The papers are full of European war news, but silent about anything Russian. That's ominous."

"What's ominous?" asked Tyra, but neither parent responded.

"Did you get flour for me?" asked Anna.

"I've got all I can, but the army comes first," answered Anders angrily. "Everything's hard to find, especially food from Russia. Wheat flour is impossible to buy."

"Oh, no!" exclaimed Anna.

Karl supplied them with plenty of barley, but plain boiled barley porridge, meal after meal, day after day, week after week, did not satisfy. They longed for a piece of rye bread. Tyra had often complained about the rock hard loaves of dried rye bread that were staple winter fare, loaves so hard they had to be soaked in milk, or coffee, to make them edible. But now after so much barley she longed for rye bread, and promised never to complain about its hardness again. Sometimes Anders brought home a few potatoes, scavenged from farmer clients, and these were a real treat.

That Christmas Anna had no flour to make *pepparkarka*. There was no Christmas ham, no *lutfisk* accompanied by potato and cheese casserole. Anna bought some precious rye bread and that was the center of their celebrations.

As 1917 went from winter to spring food shortages got worse and worse. Tyra stopped complaining about being hungry because she knew her mother could not help. Newspapers stunned everyone by announcing

Tsar Nicholas had abdicated, but the struggle to find food still dominated thoughts. A few weeks later came the horror of bread rationing and detested coupons. Anders persuaded Tyra to give him one of her hens, because they could no longer afford to share barley with it and it had long since stopped laying eggs. But neither Tyra nor Anna could eat any of the tough meat the old bird provided. When Anders asked for her second bird Tyra would not speak to anyone for two days, and spent the time silently stroking her last remaining hen.

"We have to do something," said Anders as he watched his daughter caressing her old bird. "Food in the city is impossible to find. My family in Solv would have us, but it's more dangerous there than in Oxkangar. Solv is only 10 kilometers from here, and Oxkangar four times that distance, but Oxkangar is much more isolated, and best of all close to Sweden if things get really bad. We could get a fishing boat across the Kvarken to Sweden if life gets too tough. In winter you can ski across the Gulf of Bothnia!"

"True, husband, about skiing the Kvarken, but let's wait," advised Anna. "I still have barley, and surely we should get something with those bread coupons. It's only two months till school holidays and we'd be going to Oxkangar anyway."

"I don't want to go to school anymore," said Tyra, but no one heard, and she was too frightened to persist.

Anders conceded to Anna's suggestion. "Alright, we'll wait. But be prepared to leave any time if I get tipped bad information. I'm getting very little work. The port is dead because we aren't exporting to Europe, and there's nothing on the farms for me to bring into the city. Bread coupons might look pretty," he added bitterly, "but I'm not sure I could actually pay for bread. Last week two soldiers hired me to take them somewhere, told me their food rations were halved, and they'd received no pay for weeks. I listened sympathetically, but when we reached their destination they refused to pay anything! I protested, but they threatened to beat me up. I chose to stay in one piece, but that doesn't provide money to feed us. Things are getting ugly. I'll have to sell Kanel."

"Oh, no! There must be a way to keep her!"

"She's valuable, and the army would be glad to have her. I have no choice." Next week Kanel was sold to an army officer, but for not much more than half the price Anders wanted.

By late March the Lall family were indeed back in Oxkangar, glad to have more to eat after months of boiled barley. Anders got local carting work, and helped with odd jobs around the Rådman and other farms. It was great to eat good potatoes, not the half rotten ones available in the city, and fresh nettle greens were sprouting in sheltered, snow-free places around the farm. Karl regularly slaughtered a fowl, a welcome treat for the hungry refugees from the city. They felt energized, happier, and less irritable after one week on the farm.

Then one day newspapers carried the unbelievable news that the Finnish parliament passed a law restricting Russian authority to foreign policy and military matters.

"How can they possibly get away with such nonsense!" protested Karl. "Don't they know how big Russia is and how small we are?" Anders said nothing. With society disintegrating around them, what could anyone say? Fortunately, Tyra was too busy with her cousins and hens to realize what was happening.

Although the Russians did react, and declared the Finnish parliament dissolved, nothing happened. There were hot, angry words, which merely made Finns more anti-Russian and galvanized their desire for national independence. Anders and Anna tried to be discreet about their discussion, but the angry and frequent exclamations, invectives, and expletives from Karl soon alerted his sons and niece that something was dreadfully wrong in their country. Lisa and Karl urged Anders and Anna to stay till the political situation settled, but Anders was anxious to get Karl's bushels of oats, rye and barley to Nikolaistad. Not only did he want to help Karl's finances, but he well knew of the dire shortages in the city, and was keen to do his part to help. His friend the grain merchant was very pleased to purchase the whole cartload for double the usual price, and people were clamoring to buy before Anders could even unload.

Then just a few days after Tyra returned to school the country was stunned by news of the Russian Bolshevik revolution.

"What's going to happen now?" cried Anna fearfully. "Who are those Reds that are supposed to govern us? What have they done with the Tsar?"

"Who knows! All I know is that Reds are against nobility. But who's going to feed all those soldiers hanging around town?" retorted Anders. "They don't show any signs of going back to Russia! Get ready to leave the moment I tell you, and Tyra should not go to school." Tyra made no protest.

"The teacher said we must be loyal to Russia," she said. "But when we asked who we should be loyal to, the Tsar or the new leaders called Bolsheviks, they couldn't tell us. Mor and Far, I'm scared!"

"To be honest, so am I!" admitted Anna.

"As I said, just get ready to leave the moment I tell you," repeated Anders.

The winter night was long, with no prospect for Christmas festivity, when on December 6, 1917, newspapers announced something incomprehensible to both Anders and Anna. "There has been an administrative change in Finland," headlines read. An administrative change? A what? The article under the headlines was just as nebulous. The truth, all the people of Finland slowly realized, was that Finland had declared its total independence from Russia, but in the non-speak of politics in general, and political wartime chaos in particular, no one knew what it portended.

"Mor," said Tyra when she was tucked into bed a few days later, "You told me not to talk about war and things like that. But no one talks about anything now, and it's scary. I used to think we had a good country, but now I don't know!"

"Hush child. No one knows what to talk about. Everything is changing. Why, do you know we don't live in Nikolaistad any more! Our town has its proper Swedish name again, Vasa!"

"Really? That funny name that Lisa and Elin used to call it? But Mor, the Russians won't like that, will they? Is that why they've had all those soldiers here?"

"Dearest child, you don't need to worry about Russia or Russians any more. We're our own country now!"

"You mean, we don't have that song, you know, the one that says, 'Our land, our land, our fatherland...'"

"Oh Tyra, that's the song we *can* sing! We can really sing it now! It's our own national anthem!" answered Anna fervently. "We'll always sing that! At long, long last, our country is free! But we have to wait to see what it means. Let's sing that song right now!"

To the surprise of everyone, Lenin, Russia's new leader, closed his eyes to the rebellion on his doorstep, convinced that the noble proletariat of Finland would rise and gain control without his having to waste his slender resources. What concerned him most was negotiating peace between his beleaguered country and Germany. Therefore, on New Year's Eve, at exactly midnight between 1917 and 1918, Lenin signed formal recognition of Finland's independent sovereignty. There was quiet rejoicing in Finland for three weeks.

"Well, I never expected we'd get out of Russia so easily!" smiled Anders, his voice triumphant.

"Are we really truly not Russians any more?" Tyra wanted to know.

"I think so," replied Anna, uncertainly.

But on January 27, 1918, the whole country discovered the raw brutality of what their independence would cost them. Newspapers carried more incomprehensible news. Red Guards had seized power in southern Finland, ordered all the members of the newly formed Finnish Senate be arrested, but gave enough warning for all of them to escape.

"We've gone mad!" lamented Anders.

"I knew it was too good to be true," sighed Anna.

"You told me there was a war between Germans and Russians. How come we're fighting ourselves now?" accused Tyra. Her parents had no answer.

While newspapers reported that Red guards controlled the more populous southern parts of Finland, in newly renamed Vasa conservative opinions predominated. Strongly bonded to Sweden in language, outlook, and geographic proximity, Ostrobothnians were fiercely nationalistic, and against anything that bound them to Russia. The large number of Russian soldiers stationed in the area were quickly relieved of their arms, and an army which had consisted of about 38,000 soldiers at the declaration of independence rapidly rose to 60,000 fiercely patriotic men. Contacts in both Sweden and Germany provided arms, although never as many as were requested or needed.

As the winter days of 1918 lengthened, and nights grew shorter, Anders arrived home one evening in cheerful mood. "I've got good news," he announced. "My friend the grain merchant has offered me a job transporting for him. He's offered work before, but I preferred my independence. Now, I'm willing to work for anyone so we can eat! And here's more good news: General Mannerheim is the leader of the Whites opposing that Red rebellion down south, and he's set up headquarters right here in Vasa. What's more, he offered my friend the grain merchant the job of supplying his army. My job is to scour the country for all the grain I can find. I haven't much hope of finding grain this time of the year, but they'll pay me for looking!"

"General Mannerheim! Not the Carl Gustav Emil Mannerheim that marched in front of the newly crowned Emperor Nicholas twenty years ago?"

"Yah, that's him. He was in the Russian army for thirty years, and knows how to get things done, how to fight. Remember those Jaegar Battalion soldiers that went to Germany? Well, they've also come back to help, and they're German trained, supposedly the best. Between them and Mannerheim they'll make mincemeat of those Russian-toady Reds down south!"

"Oh, I pray it doesn't come to that!" wailed Anna.

"You mean we're going to have a war right here in our own city?" asked Tyra fearfully. "But war means terrible things like killing, doesn't it?"

"Don't worry child. I'll get you out of the city if there's any fighting," Anders tried to reassure. "But like it or not, there's no chance to avert war. The country is split into two hostile factions. Those Reds talk grandly of class struggle, but if they win we'll be back under Russian domination. We knew a bit about the tsars, but those Bolsheviks, who knows what they'll do to us! Murderers! That's all they are! Who wants to be back under Russia? For me, never! For that I'd be willing to fight, but I'm glad they currently only want young men!"

"Oh, no! Fighting our own people! How terribly, terribly wrong! How dreadful!" Anna wrung her hands despairingly.

"I thought our country was a good country, and we'd never do anything so bad as fight each other! What would God have to say about this? Mor's right, it's dreadful!" exclaimed eleven-year-old Tyra.

And dreadful it was.

As soon as he could arrange the journey in reasonable daylight safety Anders took Tyra and Anna to Oxkangar. He was convinced serious fighting would occur near the middle of Finland, and Oxkangar, on the Bay of Bothnia, would be far from hostilities. Anna wanted to stay with him in Vasa, but bowed to his decision to take her to his idea of safety. The prime beneficiary of the arrangement was Tyra's beloved last hen. She had a wonderful time on the Rådman farm, clucking joyfully, and getting her feathers ruffled by the young birds on the farm. She rarely laid eggs, but she gave Tyra comfort.

Tyra would soon be twelve. Anna and Anders had tried to protect her from war news, but old newspapers were carelessly scattered about the Rådman house. Tyra, an avid reader, quickly learned the terrible atrocities perpetrated by Red Guards in the south. Because most Russian soldiers had been stationed there, Red troops had plenty of weapons. But they lacked trained leaders, and dealt with their emotions with alcohol. Anna had few answers to her daughter's troubled questions. The shocking atrocities perpetrated in the south deeply angered General Mannerheim and Whites in the north, and when they had their chance, they took their revenge in just as brutal ways. It made Anna sick but she remembered with agonizing horror Lukas Larson's angry words: "There are just two things in war: the enemy and winning. How you get rid of the enemy and win doesn't really matter." Tyra became more and more withdrawn, and spent a lot of time at the Nilsson farm with Sonja.

One mid-March day Tyra ran across the fields from the Nilsson home. "Mor!" she cried breathlessly when she found Anna. "Come quick to Fru Nilsson! She's very upset."

"Tyra, if she's upset she won't want someone annoying her," retorted Anna.

"Mor, she does. When I found her crying I asked if I could call you, and she said, yes, get your mor. So Mor, do come."

Anna looked at the clock and the potatoes she was peeling for dinner. The meal could wait a few minutes. She followed her daughter across the fields to the Nilsson's house. Tyra unhesitatingly opened the door, "Fru Nilsson, my Mor has come. Shall I bring her in?"

"Thank you for coming," smiled Sonja Nilsson, her eyes red from weeping. "I feel ridiculous, but after what happened to Rolf, I'm over sensitive to the loss of family and friends."

"What's happened?" asked Anna gently, fearful there had been some mishap with one of Sonja's boys.

"We're at war, right? Bad things happen I know. But I've just received word from my brother in Nykarleby—I come from up there—that one of their close friends has lost a son."

"But—is there fighting around Nykarleby?" said Anna in sudden fright. Nykarleby was a mere 40 kilometers from Oxkangar, much too close for comfort.

"No, no. Young men from there volunteered to fight with General Mannerheim. They were on a train travelling to Tammerfors when Red guards put a bomb under a carriage, and my brother's friend's son was killed, along with several others. He was only seventeen, the same age as my eldest. Tammerfors is the sort of northern capital for those awful Red guards. That's where the fighting will be." Sonja began weeping again.

Anna touched Sonja's hand. "This is very tough on your family, and hard for you because of your own terrible losses. But how good that there are young men prepared to fight for their country, and for what they know is right. I don't understand Red guards fighting something they call class, but I do understand young men wanting to keep us free from Russian control. We've all suffered from Russia." Even as she spoke, the words sounded hollow to Anna's ears, but platitudes were all she could think of to offer.

"Thank you for reminding me of the good those boys were trying to do. It's been so hard to keep the farm together since Rolf died. Karl and Lisa have been very good to me, and I'm grateful. But it's a constant struggle. I get upset by anything these days. It could've been my eldest son on that train, but fortunately he's been able to get out of the army, at least for now, because of my situation."

"Do you plan to go to the funeral?" asked Anna.

Sonja smiled weakly. "That shows how foolish I am! I hardly know this young man well enough to do anything like that, even if I could leave the farm. Worry from war gets me frightened about everything. Now, would you like to have a cup of coffee with me?"

Anna thought about the pile of half-peeled potatoes, and of Lisa and Karl coming home tired and hungry after trying to plough despite a light covering of snow. She was about to refuse the invitation, then decided sometimes things just have to wait. "Yah, thank you," she said.

"I haven't got anything to have with the coffee," Sonja apologized, "nothing except *knäckerbröd*."

"With all the food shortages, *knäckerbröd* sounds wonderful!" smiled Anna.

"Do you think she's better now?" Tyra asked anxiously as mother and daughter walked through gathering dusk back to the Rådman's farm.

"Tyra, this terrible war is making us all hurt. Everyone is sad and miserable. I worry about your Far, and even Möja. More and more people will lose friends and family in the fighting. I pray it won't be someone too close to us. But knowing someone cares about you helps the pain, at least a little bit. Thank you for getting me."

"Morbror Karl told me he will get me more chicks," said Tyra. "That's his way of caring, don't you think?"

"Certainly!"

Two weeks later Anna was walking to the barn to look for eggs when she was overjoyed to see Anders' in his cart trotting down the farm driveway. With undignified joy she ran to meet him, and stopped as he reined in Möja. He climbed down from the box, and gripped her hands in both of his. Suddenly he threw his arms around her and hugged her tight. Such unexpected affectionate behavior made Anna burst into tears.

"Anna, my Anna! How good to see you! Things are improving! There is hope! We have reinforcements!" he exclaimed.

"Reinforcements?"

"Germans have landed down south, and are pushing towards Tammerfors. That's where the Reds have concentrated their forces. Now, I have to tell you something you mightn't like, but I was asked (that means told with no chance of saying no) to billet two soldiers in our house."

"Oh, no!"

"Don't worry, they haven't been a problem. I admit I was shocked how young they were, poor boys, and they've been very anxious to help. The thought of them going to fight is disturbing."

"Sonja Nilsson was distressed about some attack on a train headed for Tammerfors that killed a family friend. He was only seventeen."

"Yah, I heard about that. A cowardly deed. So many fighting in this terrible war are just boys. Tobbe Larson has been conscripted."

"Oh, no!"

"Don't worry, with that Jaegar battalion, German reinforcements, and Mannerheim in charge, things will go well."

But no one rejoiced at what finally happened at Tammerfors, least of all Anders. Intense fighting went on for days, with confused reports. The famous Jaegar troops were indeed there, plus volunteer Swedish soldiers. The bombed destruction of the once proud city was heartbreaking. Finally, on April 6, the thrashed and maimed Reds raised a white flag, and the cruel battles were over. Reports claimed one thousand soldiers on both sides had lost their lives, then came terrible stories of mass executions of unarmed soldiers. More than 10,000 Red prisoners were taken, and heart rending photos of them lined in huge ranks, made to stand in the biting cold for 24 hours in the central square of Tammerfors, found their way into almost every newspaper. These hapless men were gathered into crowded camps where disease and starvation killed large numbers. Like most northern Finns, Anders, Anna, and Tyra did not want Russian control, but when they heard that every Russian, man, woman, and child found in Tammerfors had been summarily shot, even Anders broke down and wept.

"A good way to make more enemies," mumbled Anders, as he awkwardly tried to comfort his women. "They're fools!"

"Reds are calling Whites butchers," said Karl, dry-eyed and angry. "It's crazy!"

"War is just butchery!" declared Anna, sniffing. Tyra was silent.

"I'm glad Germans came to help us," said Lisa. "I'm not too fond of Germans, because they started that European war which still goes on forever. But they've helped us."

"Maybe," said both men.

"You know," said Anders suddenly shaking himself, "in all this bitter, senseless civil war of ours, I'd completely forgotten there was a European war still going on out there. Does any one know what's been happening?"

No one did.

When Spanish 'flu struck later that year, the Finnish concentration camps crowded with Red Guard prisoners and stranded Russian soldiers provided most of its victims in Finland. Altogether it was estimated that nearly 40,000 people lost their lives as a result of the so-called Finnish war of independence, an appalling loss in a total population of only four million.

Late September, Anders finally decided it was safe to bring his wife and daughter back to Vasa. Tyra brought her beloved old hen, but also a basket carrying Karl's gift of another four chicks.

"I'm glad she'll have those chooks to distract her," said Anders as Anna packed their clothes the night before they returned. "I'm not sure how she'll take the news that Tobbe was killed."

"Tobbe! Oh, no! Not Tobbe!"

"Yah, terrible. I only heard yesterday. When Elin and Lukas hadn't heard from him for a month they made enquiries, and after several weeks discovered he'd been killed in one of the early battles around Tammerfors. In the sick mix-up of war, it took time to identify who he was, and then no one saw the urgency to tell his parents. I hadn't seen Lukas for a couple of weeks, then yesterday was shocked to see him walk down the street drunk as a sailor. You remember how anti drink Lukas was. I helped him home, and Elin told me the dreadful news. Lukas had appeared to cope well, but broke down at work, and was induced to share the tragic news about Tobbe with workmates, who foolishly took him out for coffee and laced his drink. With sobs he told me, 'Anders, it's terrible stuff. Once they got some into me, I lost all notion of what I was doing, and was a pawn in their hands! It made me laugh foolishly, and I drank anything they put in front of me!' I told him I totally understood, that once a friend had made me drunk (never told you about that, did I, but that's why I now choose not to drink) and we had a sauna together. But I dread telling Tyra."

"She's going to take it hard, but best she hears from us than someone else."

The golden autumn weather was very pleasant on the return journey to Vasa; the northern countryside was not ravished by war. But as they neared Vasa Tyra cheerfully asked when Tobbe would come home. Anders' efforts to break the news were painfully clumsy, but somehow he did it. Tyra sat silent and white faced through his short but garbled, mangled, and confused speech, and never said a word. When Anders finished, Anna began what sounded, even to her, another babble of noise about the nobility of giving one's life for the good of the country.

Suddenly Tyra turned on her parents angrily and summed up her version of their noble speeches. "I hate it! Do you hear? I hate it! And I hate what you're saying! Why do you pretend everything's alright? Do you think I'm stupid? Why isn't anyone honest about this awful war? Thousands and thousands of people, good people like Tobbe, have died because of this stupid fighting! Stop talking about noble acts! Stop talking about how good our country is! As for that stupid song about the fatherland, I won't ever sing it again! What's noble about being dead? War is a dreadful, beastly, horrible, wicked thing! When I grow up I'll do anything, anything, do you hear, anything, to help men not to go to war! People who start wars must be very, very bad, the most wicked people that ever could be, and ever have been. If there is such an awful place as hell, they should be the first ones sent there!"

"Tyra!" exclaimed a shocked Anna impetuously. "What a wicked thing to say about our national song! You could go to hell for that!"

Tyra's face went white, and contorted with pain. "I'm not wicked," she whispered. "At least, I didn't mean to be! How can you possibly say war is good?"

A stunned, utterly shocked silence followed her anguished murmur, a silence broken by the fluttering feathers of the old hen, who received a liberal but unwanted bath from Tyra's tears. And the gently clopping hooves of Möja.

Suddenly Anders pulled hard on the reins and brought Möja to a surprised standstill. Anna gave a startled cry. To her amazement Anders stood up, and climbed into the cart. He knelt beside Tyra, putting his strong, horse-guiding hands on her shoulders.

"Child," he said, and paused, "you're not wicked. God loves you, and God knows Tobbe was your special friend. He understands how upset you are."

"You mean I won't go to hell for saying that about the song?"

"Of course not! You're right. Those warmongers should get to hell long before you do! Now it was a silly thing to say, I'm sure you'll agree. But we all make mistakes. God knows that. Look, I'm no expert as the priest will tell you, but I do read the Bible sometimes, and it seems Jesus came to help people who've made mistakes. Just be careful you don't tell anyone else you don't like the national anthem!"

"Yah, Far."

Anders gave his daughter a final pat, climbed back to his driving seat, and with a flick of reins got Möja walking again.

Anna sat like stone, horrified by what she had said. Then Anders felt her moving close to Tyra, and something that sounded like "I'm sorry, Far is right," was whispered to his daughter. Tyra was fast asleep on Anna's shoulder when they turned into Rådhusgatan.

But the final Finnish independence story of the year 1918 made the whole family laugh. In October, the newspapers declared that parliament voted the country should have a King! In appreciation for German services rendered during the civil war, German Prince Friedrich Karl of Hesse was invited to become King of Finland, and what's more, he agreed! "That's taking thankfulness a bit far!" chortled Anders, when he shared the gossip. "Germany should just keep out of our affairs!"

"A king!" giggled Anna. "What do we want one of those for! And a German one at that! Surely, after all those people ranting about Finland for the Finnish, we could find a Finnish person for the job!" Then she added mischievously, "Why, we could even have a woman!"

But a month later came the welcome news that Germany was defeated in, for Finns, the generally forgotten European war. Evidently gratitude was no longer necessary, and to the relief of its inhabitants, Finland was saved from having a German sovereign!

"I wonder what we'll do with ourselves next!" speculated Anders, stroking his chin mischievously. "If we don't have a king, maybe we could turn parliament into a circus. That would be more fun!"

"Well, as far as government is concerned, I couldn't care less! They've caused enough trouble to last me the rest of my life!" declared Anna. Then, smoothing the tablecloth, she added wistfully, "I'm hoping next year Karl will grow flax and I can get back into weaving."

Anders looked at his wife in astonishment. After all the horrors and deprivations of war, after everything that had happened, after the nonsense of a German king, how could any woman dream of weaving!

"I know what I want to do!" announced Tyra, looking up from her embroidery. "Go back to school! That's what I want to do. I haven't been since March last year, and that's more than a year ago."

Anna and Anders looked up, shocked. Caught in their own pain, the uncertainty of not knowing where their next meal would come from, or what bizarre thing the great powers of Europe would do to their small country, neither had realized how much war had disrupted their daughter's life. She was right, she should go back to school.

"And Far, do you know what you need to do?" continued Tyra, suddenly smiling.

Anders raised his eyebrows. "I thought I was very busy doing what I need to do," he retorted, grinning, "looking after you and Mor."

"Oh, that's just your ordinary work. But Möja's looking really old and tired. I'm sure she misses Kanel. At least, I do! You need to get another horse and give her a rest."

"You're right," said Anders, thoughtfully. "You really are right! You know, she's a bit old, but I think I'll let Möja have one more foal. I hope she has a filly."

"Do you like girls, Far?"

"Ones like you, I do!"

Chapter 5

What's in a Name?

SCHOOL AND A NEW foal were certainly distractions. Tyra enjoyed learning, but struggled to settle into study. The terrible loss of Tobbe brought the horror of war with devastating pain into her life. What was going to happen next? she wondered. Would somebody decide that the people of Vasa needed to be sent to concentration camps, or executed like those poor people in Tammerfors? Who could she trust, apart from her parents? Could she trust even them?

    The shattering aftermath of the bloody Finnish civil war was a maze of jagged fracture lines of distrust across all relationships and ideologies throughout the country. Finland was supposedly free at last, but at huge cost. There was little to rejoice about in the new country, where food shortages and economic distress still dominated the lives of most people. Once the common enemy was Russia, now the enemy was "others" of their own people. "Red" and "White" did not translate into simple or clearly defined ways. It was not "south" versus "north", not those with money against those without, not even those who supported Russia versus those who did not. One apparent rallying point was language, but this caused another series of painful ruptures. How does a country under the domination of others for almost a millennium demonstrate its individuality? How does such a new country heal into a unity after the appallingly deep scars of a civil war perpetrated in its mere infancy, only weeks after its declared independence? How does it find unity? How does such a damaged country even eat? Finland, reborn in the chaos of European turmoil in general, and the Russian revolution in particular, struggled with these issues, at precisely the same time as Tyra grappled with her own heartaches and burgeoning womanhood. A historian has aptly noted the general Finnish situation: "The awfulness of that climate of uncertainty, the demoralizing effects of not knowing where your allegiance should lie, the inability to make firm plans for a future that none had any way of knowing how to conceptualize, affected all Finns."[1] The pain of this turmoil made the naturally taciturn and stoical Finns even more so, and allowed little opportunity for the youth of the country to find answers to their pain.

Tyra had no idea how to cope with the loss of her friend Tobbe. What can an eleven-year-old girl do, what can she feel, when her friend is killed, killed in a brutal war where families and neighbors tore each other apart? A friend she admired, looked up to, and counted on. Tyra, an only child, was warm hearted and friendly, although naturally of quiet disposition. From a young age she willingly carried responsibility. An excellent student, she made made the most of her school opportunities. But as she returned to school after more than twelve months' absence, the endless questions in her mind were so painful she dared not articulate them to anyone. She became an adolescent at precisely the time her country began its infancy. She withdrew deeply into herself until both her parents were concerned.

She had been saddened by the tragic death of Rolf Nilsson. Whilst neither her parents, her teachers, nor her pastor was able to answer her philosophical and metaphysical questions arising from this, she felt she had some understanding of what had happened. But Tobbe's death? Although six years older, until he left school and went to work he was her main companion. Now, he was dead. But *how* he was dead she did not know, no one knew. In her imagination she saw the frightful photographs in newspapers: the bombed out buildings of Tammerfors, the piles of corpses, the incredibly long rows of prisoners. Apparently newspaper editors conspired to produce copy aimed to primarily to stir the hatred these gruesome portrayals engendered. But what had *really* happened to Tobbe? Was it a bomb, like the one that killed Fru Nilsson's friend? Was he shot and left for dead by an army too distracted to care? Had he fallen and injured himself, and been killed by hungry wolves, or even a bear? Sometimes out on the farm at Oxkangar she heard wolves howling, mournful, scary, creepy sounds. Or was he taken prisoner, mistaken for being on the wrong side, and shot without being able to say goodbye?

---

1. Goss, Glenda Dawn. *Sibelius—A Composer's Life and the Awakening of Finland*, p396

Endlessly, the appalling parade of possibilities ran through her mind. She longed to talk to Elin Larson, but the only time she mentioned Tobbe Fru Larson burst into tears and ran from the room. Tyra never again dared mention the topic. Tobbe's younger brothers never talked about their brother.

Although she struggled with the purpose of life, school did prove a distraction. After some thought, and consultation with her parents and teachers, she decided to repeat her final year in *folkskola* (primary) because she had missed so much time, but she quickly caught up and wished she had been brave enough to go straight into the "learning school" (secondary). But school was different now. Russia was hardly mentioned, history lessons were all about the greatness of the Finnish people. Often what she had previously been taught was in stark contrast to her current lessons, and it was utterly confusing. Fortunately, there were other pupils her age repeating their last year of school, and she had friends. By the time she finished *folkskola* in the spring of 1919 teachers suggested she move to a *gymnasium* rather than the usual learning school. Both Anna and Anders were surprised by this suggestion, and unsure how to advise their daughter. Although both had completed *folkskola* and read well, it never occurred to them that more schooling could be useful, especially not a university education for which a *gymnasium* was preparation.

Apart from school, Tyra had one other other pain-numbing activity—working till she was so tired she fell asleep as soon as her face hit the pillow, with little chance that nightmares about Tobbe's death would start again. She asked Anna to teach her cooking and weaving, and offered to help care for Möja. Anna was more than willing to teach, but with food still scarce and limited, lessons were brief. Weaving was just as difficult because locally grown flax was no longer available, all arable land being used for food crops to lessen massive shortages. Flax imports were non-existent because Finland had yet to establish viable markets. Even the once major exports of wood and wood products to Russia dwindled to trickles because of the huge internal and financial difficulties facing the new Soviet Republics. However, she did have two distracting tasks she really enjoyed: Anders wasted no time in getting Möja in foal, and her beloved chickens. One of Karl's chicks proved to be a rooster. Tyra was delighted with this, enthusiastically moved into the chicken breeding business, and to the surprise of her parents, allowed Anders to sell her surplus roosters for pocket money for the family.

One mid summer evening in 1919 Tyra was helping Anna prepare the meal when Anders burst into the kitchen and triumphantly announced. "I have good news for my women!"

Tyra smiled with delighted pride at being elevated to woman status, despite being rather short and skinny because of food shortages. "What is it, Far?" she asked eagerly.

"Our new government is getting down to business, and trying hard to make us a good, safe country. They've outlawed alcohol!"

Stunned silence followed his announcement, then Tyra asked incredulously, "Really? No alcohol at all? You mean Morbror Karl can't ever get drunk again?"

Anders nodded and smiled broadly.

"But Far, all he has to do is buy some from the shops!"

"Or make another still in his barn," groaned Anna.

"Well, the sale and manufacture of all alcohol is now totally outlawed in this country. Those women in parliament must've been busy!"

Anna smiled in spite of herself. "Glad you give women the credit! If they really can stop drunkenness it would be wonderful. But I'm more than a little skeptical. There are too many people who'll find a way round the law, mark my words."

"I suspect people realized those dreadful atrocities perpetrated on both sides of our frightful war were alcohol related. That might be the real reason for the law,"[2] responded Anders.

Anna was right. Not everyone agreed a ban on alcohol was good, in fact the law was defied from the start.

That year, on their renewed annual visit to Oxkangar, Tyra noticed how tall and plump Algot and Hjalmar were. Although two years younger, Algot was as tall as she was. But after a month on the farm, with freshly dug potatoes, green vegetables, and seemingly limitless bread and chicken, Tyra began to fill out and was significantly taller when she returned to Vasa.

She and her cousins were picking blueberries in the forest one day, a chore they all enjoyed, when Algot startled her with the question, "Are you a White or a Red?"

Tyra stood and brushed away mosquitoes. The damp forest floor that grew blueberries so well bred mosquitoes in zinging abundance. "I'm not sure," she began. "But we're all Whites up here, aren't we? I mean,

---

2. Alcohol was again banned in Finland for a short time at the end of World War II, for explicitly those reasons.

General Mannerheim was in Vasa, wasn't he? He was the leader of the Whites, right? Mor and Far don't talk about him much, but I think he's a good man. Why do you ask?"

"Oh, just that some scrawny boys on a farm down the road are called Reds. They're about the same age as you, but they work like men. Mor says they're orphans, with no parents. When I asked her what happened to their parents she said thousands of kids lost their parents in all the fighting, and most of them live in big buildings called orphanages, but some of the older ones have been sent to work on farms because the country needs food badly. She said many people who normally helped with work on farms got killed in that war."

"That's sad. Did your Mor tell you how many orphans there are?" queried Tyra. "Do you think there'd be more than one hundred?"

Algot shrugged. "When I asked Mor she was vague, the way adults are when they don't want you to know something. But I kept asking and finally she said she'd read there were twenty thousand of them. Twenty thousand! I don't believe her because that's an awful lot of kids! I mean the father of our neighbors, the Nilsson boys, he died, but they didn't go off to some orphanage. Their mother looks after them."

Tyra shook her head in amazement. "Twenty thousand! I can't believe so many children have no parents! Why, that's more than the whole city of Vasa! You must have heard wrong! Have you talked to those boys?"

"Yah, I have," said Algot in a secretive manner, "but don't tell anyone. The first time I talked to them they got yelled at by their farmer for being lazy. He called them useless Reds and other bad names, and they ran away from me. But that farmer is mean to everyone, and Mor doesn't let us go near his farm. Those boys look skinny and underfed, even worse than you!"

"Am I skinny? What's wrong with being skinny?" asked Tyra, tossing her head and laughing. "You both look fat to me!"

Her cousins laughed. Algot said, "You're a bit fatter since you came here. Mor says the way you eat here you'd think you never had any food at home! Sometimes I talk to those boys if I creep up to a fence where they're working and we keep a lookout for the farmer. I've brought them some of Mor's bread, when no one was looking, and they ate it so fast it was weird. But I'm not sure if Mor would allow me to take them bread, so I can't do it too often."

"Do you know what being a Red means, and what being White really is?" asked Hjalmar unexpectedly. He picked up his bucket, half filled with luscious blueberries, and walked to a grassy mound beneath a birch tree. As the sun filtered through the trees it turned the blueberry bushes into beautiful stripes of bright sunny lime green, and rich forest green shade. Hjalmar admired the beauty and tried to make sense of the strange ideas the others were discussing.

"Oh, White means you're good and Red you're bad," said Algot authoritatively, with a toss of his head. "I'm sure when Far says someone's a Red he means they're a bad person."

"No, that's not right! It's got something to do with whether you speak Swedish or not," said Tyra. "In Vasa everyone at my Swedish school is White. That's what the head teacher says."

"That can't be true!" exclaimed Algot. "Far had people visiting here one day, and he told Mor they were good because although they spoke Finnish, they weren't Reds. They tried to speak Swedish, but they weren't any good. Fortunately, Mor can understand a bit of Finnish."

"Well, a new shop opened in Vasa, and the teachers told us not to go there because it was a dangerous Red shop and they only spoke Finnish," responded Tyra. "My teacher said the great composer Sibelius says that Swedish is the language of educated people and unless people use it our culture will become coarse, and we'll do nothing but squabble. He made it sound as though if everyone spoke Swedish we'd be good and we'd have no problems."

Algot shrugged. "Really? Well I haven't a clue what you're talking about! Have it your way, then!" he added, and bent down to pick more blueberries. Suddenly he straightened up. "You must be wrong, Tyra! Those kids down the road speak Swedish, and they're definitely Reds! Everyone says they are!"

"You know what?" said Hjalmar suddenly, rolling over on his grassy mound. "I don't think anyone knows what Red and White means. But one thing for sure, they're enemies!"

"Yep! That's the important bit. It means you can't be friends with anyone until you find out whether they're a Red or a White. I'm sure glad we're all Whites!" said Algot, adding "The trouble is trying to figure out what people really are."

"But it's crazy," persisted Hjalmar, bursting with all of his eight years' wisdom. "What has a Red person ever done to hurt me? Why should I be enemies with someone just because someone else doesn't like them? I mean, that farmer down the road with those boys is a real mean person, and I think he's my enemy, yet he says he's a White and he's supposed to be my friend. And those boys, who've never done anything to hurt any of us are supposed to be our enemies. Why don't we just mix ourselves up and turn pink!"

Algot and Tyra thought this was a huge joke, and laughed heartily. But Hjalmar's outburst made Tyra think, deeply. They were all silent for some time, but the more Tyra thought the more being pink sounded like a very good idea to her.

"What about the Nilsson family?" she asked, pensively.

"Oh, they're definitely White," said Algot, picking up his bucket and stooping to pick berries again. "No doubt about that!"

"That's good. But how long do people stay Red or White?" asked Tyra. "It seems a bit hard having enemies around all the time."

"Oh, definitely forever," said Algot. "I don't want to be friends with any of those Reds."

"But I thought you said you talked to those boys on the farm?" challenged Tyra. "Aren't you trying to be friends? Why are you trying to talk to them if you can't ever be friends?"

"Secret friends," said Algot, looking around to see if anyone was listening. "I'm not supposed to be friends with them. Mor and Far don't know I've talked to them so don't you tell on me!" Then he added defiantly, "And if you split on me Hjalmar I'll beat you up!"

Tyra laughed, a hollow laugh.

"If you look up in the trees you can see some interesting birds," observed Hjalmar from his sunny mound. "There are little black and white birds darting around catching mosquitoes, and a lovely red bird with brown wings that I think I heard Far call a crossbill."

"Really?" cried Tyra in excitement. "Show me! I've only seen greenish female crossbills." She began looking carefully in the direction Hjalmar was pointing.

"Why don't you both stop gazing at birds and start doing proper blueberry picking?" complained Algot petulantly. "I've almost finished two buckets, Tyra's done three, and Hjalmar you haven't even filled one yet!"

Reluctantly Hjalmar picked up his bucket and began working, while Tyra peered futilely into the branches for a red crossbill.

A few days later Anders arrived to bring his wife and daughter back to Vasa. Tyra, running to meet him, was concerned that he came with a borrowed horse, until she learned that Möja was close to foaling, and Anders thought the long journey too much for her. On the way home Tyra asked Anders what it meant to be Red or White. As the horse clopped along Anders used lots of strange words, like Bolshevik and communist, bourgeois and proletariat, but there was one word she did understand: Russian. She decided that being "Red" meant Russian, and being "White" meant speaking Swedish. But since there were so many other things about being a "Red" she did not understand, she would just be very careful who she talked to. And perhaps, she thought wistfully, people should stop worrying about being Red or White, and let Hjalmar have his pink dream.

Ten days after they arrived back in Vasa there was great excitement when Möja successfully foaled a beautiful, healthy filly. Möja was a rich chestnut red, honoring her name strawberry, but the filly was very pale.

"I know what we'll call her!" exclaimed Tyra, as she rubbed the nose of the little filly. "Let's call her Blek!"

"Blek?" said Anna, puzzled. "Why white?"

"Oh, Tyra and I have been having deep and meaningful political discussions about what makes people Red or White. It wouldn't hurt to call a horse after a political idea. I mean, she is pale, so no one should take offense. They might even laugh and get rid of the whole silly business!"

So Blek the filly was named, and more importantly, she rapidly became Tyra's special charge.

When Tyra and Anna went to Oxkangar the following year she was surprised to notice that Algot, and even Hjalmar, almost looked like men. They teased Tyra mercilessly about still being at school.

"Why, you're such an old woman!" they laughed. "We don't know anyone who's still at school when they're fourteen! You must be really dumb!"

Algot had a cheeky idea. "I know what! Are you staying at school because you're looking for a husband?"

Tyra took his jokes good naturedly, but after some days his banter became annoying. "You have it wrong," she said, disdainfully. "I'm at school because I want to be there. I enjoy learning."

"Want to be at school! You don't learn anything useful there! You must be crazy!" jeered Algot. "I'm going to leave school the minute I can. I've got one more year of *folkskola*, and then, hurray! I'm off!"

Tyra shrugged. They were harvesting a small field of flax that Karl had finally decided to plant. She loved her rough and cheeky cousin, but sometimes it was hard to explain anything to to him. Often he was just plain hard to accept. How could she defend her enjoyment of learning Swedish language and literature, the history of Sweden and Finland, basic German, and, of course, math and the geography and history of the rest of the world? The discovery that remarkable similarities existed between the German and Swedish languages fascinated her, although she preferred learning Swedish literature to German grammar! She wondered what other languages might be similar to Swedish, and if Finnish had any similarities.

Unfortunately, at Tyra's school, Finnish was not taught. This meant she could not read in the original the great Finnish epic *Kalevala*. However, the school library had a Swedish translation of some of the stories. She discovered Elias Lönnrot, who collected the folk tales that became the epic, was a doctor, and her favorite Swedish author Zacharias Topelius had written, "Everywhere it has been thought that the *Kalevala* is one of the most remarkable folklore products [that has] ever appeared and the Finnish nation is fortunate to possess such a work . . . It reflects the character of the Finnish people, and although much of it appears pagan and strange to our age, there is in it a profound wisdom, a simple beauty, and a moving love of the fatherland." Tyra learnt that Sibelius' mystical and rather mournful piece of music *The Swan of Tuonela* was based on one of the myths in the *Kalevala*. The hero of the story, Lemminkäinen, had to perform three apparently impossible deeds to win the hand of the daughter of the north. He must ski down the elk invented by the demon Hiisi, bridle the demon's gelding, and finally shoot the swan of Tuonela with one arrow shot. Most importantly, only a man free from all wickedness could perform these feats. Like many Finns, she understood spiritual implications in the story. But like this story, the whole *Kalevala* was incredibly serious, dark, and sad, portraying humor as inappropriate for Finnish men. Certainly many of the men she knew were solemn and unsmiling, and none very talkative. Although her teachers insisted on the importance and superiority of the Swedish language, she was aware some people implied that Finns were corrupted by the more light-hearted Swedish culture. Like the strange idea of people being Red or White, it was all very confusing.

Tyra, however, had the last laugh on Algot's disinterest in school, although she was too kind to remind him. In 1921 the busy and determined Finnish government passed a law making attendance at a "learning school" mandatory for all children. She thought it very funny that poor Algot now had to stay in school another four years, but his constant complaints about this terrible catastrophe were rather irritating.

Tyra listened patiently, and finally advised in exasperation, "Just stop grumbling! Think of it as a chance to make good friends and learn interesting things before you start work!"

"Interesting! Are you crazy! There's nothing interesting about school! And I've got plenty of friends, so I don't need any more. Anyway, Far says I can leave as soon as I look old enough."

"Really? You mean Morbror Karl doesn't want you in school? My Far's very happy for me to be there." Tyra paused, thoughtfully. "Far told me we should be proud of Finnish schools. Everyone in Finland can read, and that's not true of every country. Our leaders think reading's very important because we need to read the Bible, and that's why they make us go to school. Why, King Gustav Vasa, who gave my city its name, got the Bible translated into Swedish so that everyone could read it, way back when we belonged to Sweden hundreds of years ago. And Bishop Mikael Agricola, who studied with Martin Luther, translated the Bible into Finnish. That's why everyone in Finland can read. If you can't read you can't get confirmed in the church, and if you aren't confirmed they won't let you get married!"

"Married? Are you kidding? Who says I want that! Anyway, I can read enough to get confirmed, so why do I have to learn more?" Algot pouted. "It's only girls who get excited about getting married!"

"Don't be silly Algot!"

"Look Tyra, Far says I can help him on the farm. When I've done that for a year or two, I can join the army. Ah, then I can get a gun and go hunting for elk and bears up north. Hunting! Now that's what I *really* want to do. I'll go into Lapland and hunt reindeer, and maybe even a bear! That sounds like real fun to me!"

"Well, I never, ever, want to join the army. Soldiers do horrible things, and I don't like them!" Tyra turned angrily and walked off, her shoulders back, her head high. Algot stared after her, wondering what had become of his usually kind and co-operative cousin. He ran to coax her back and to his amazement, she was crying.

But that year the busy government made a decree even more startling than extending education by a few years, or banning alcohol. Anders brought the news when he came to collect Anna and Tyra from Oxkangar.

"You know," he said, wrinkling his nose cynically, "we're extremely lucky. Most Swedish-speaking people are being ordered to change their surnames, but we don't have to!"

"Come on! You must be kidding!" retorted Karl. "You get given surnames because of your father. You don't change them because you don't happen to like them, or someone tells you to change!"

"Well, they're saying in Vasa that anyone with a surname ending in 'son' has to change their name. I haven't found a newspaper stating it, but I met a couple of officials who confirmed it. You can choose your own name if you do it soon, otherwise the priest will assign you a name."

"Are you kidding? Look, that must be wrong! It's utterly ridiculous!" exclaimed Lisa. "That's simply the Swedish way. My great grandfather was called Erik, so my grandfather was Lars Erikson, and my father Axel Larsson. It makes perfect sense."

"But did you and your brothers use the name Larsson or Axelson?"

Lisa was thoughtful. "Now, that's an interesting point. You remember all that talk about making everything Finnish, and we were encouraged to make our names understandable for Finns? So our family decided to stick to Larsson."

"Well, our family name has been Rådman as far back as I know," declared Karl. Anna nodded vigorously in agreement. "We've never had a 'son' in it!"

"So Lisa," said Anders, very seriously, "you're lucky. You and your boys can stay Rådman as long as you like, but your brothers will have to figure something out."

"They can't be serious about this," said Anna, shaking her head. "I mean, why aren't they getting rid of all those Finnish names ending in 'nen'? Surely that's a bit confusing! I know what they're really doing! They're just destroying our Swedish heritage, taking away our identity!"

"Ah, maybe you're right. But those 'nens' are just what you said: Finnish. Yah, I think you're right, Anna. They're trying to make us Finnish," said Lisa. "It's not about name endings, but about who's Swedish and who's Finnish. I don't like this one bit."

When Lisa shared the name-change news with Sonja Nilsson, Sonja was very indignant. "Change my name!" she declared. "No one will make me do that! Why, that's the most precious gift Rolf gave me!"

But a few days later the law to change names was announced in church, where a register of births and deaths was kept. The Nilsson family had to lose their father's name, whether they liked it, or not. For Sonja it was a very painful situation, but her boys thought it was all rather silly and made fun of it. Eventually, however, they decided to honor the memory of their father, and call themselves Rolfholm, the house of Rolf. The name change was duly entered into the records of the village church, but no one remembered it, and they were called Nilsson for years to come!

Tyra, however, faced another problem when she returned to school. "Mor," she said as she dumped her schoolbag on the kitchen table and watched her mother stirring a pot on the stove, "several of my friends say I can't be a true Swedish Finn because I don't have a proper Swedish name. How did we get the unusual name of Lall?"

Anna stopped stirring the pan of onions and beetroot. "Are you ashamed of your name?"

"No, of course not. But I don't know anyone else with such a name. It doesn't sound Swedish, but neither does it sound Finnish."

The pan of vegetables was pulled to the side of the stove, and Anna sat down. "Has anyone ever commented on the color of your hair?" she asked.

Tyra frowned. "No, why should they? What's wrong with my hair? What's that got to do with our name?"

"Just wondering," said Anna. "So let me explain. You know my father was a blacksmith, don't you?"

"Of course, I remember Morfar. He was a kind old man."

"Yah, he was kind. Both my parents were kind. Anyway, my family has a very long tradition of the men being blacksmiths, hundreds of years of that type of work. Hundreds of years ago one of the kings of Sweden, the Gustav Vasa you've heard so much about, wanted to improve the production of iron in the country. Sweden has very good deposits of iron ore, you know. Anyway, he decided to get in some experts, because although Sweden had been producing iron for as long as the history of the country, at least a thousand years, he wanted to do it more efficiently. Anyway, the king encouraged people from Belgium, from the southern part called Wallonia, who were known for their fine iron products, to move to Sweden. They settled in the Dalarna area of Sweden. Dalarna means country of the valleys, or dales. Now, we think of mining as huge companies with massive machines digging large amounts of ore, but in those days it was families in small villages that did the work, with small furnaces in their backyards. So, you've guessed it, our family came to Sweden from Belgium and helped make the mines in Dalarna successful. I don't know exactly what year they came."

"But Dalarna in Sweden is a long way from here."

"I'm not sure what made my family move from Dalarna, but the most likely thing was shortage of food. Or just too many men good at working metals, and jobs were hard to get. Anyway, some of those people, originally from Wallonia, and now working in Dalarna, moved from the valleys and looked for work in other places. If you look at the map, it's not so far from Dalarna across the Gulf of Bothnia to the north of Finland. So it's not surprising my family came here. Because a blacksmith is working with hot metals all the time, his face becomes red, so I think that's how our family got the name of Rådman. It started as a nickname."

"Really? Just a nickname?"

"I think so. But your Far's family also came from Wallonia, and his name, Lall, is a real Walloon name."

"So, you're telling me it's a special name?"

"Yah, indeed it is!"

"That's wonderful. I like that story. I'll share it at school. But why did you ask me if anyone ever talked about my hair?"

Anna laughed. "Well, I'm sure you've noticed Swedish and Finnish people generally have fair, light-colored hair. But people from Belgium have dark hair. That's why you have dark hair!"

"Well, fancy that! I must say I *have* sometimes felt a little envious of the lovely blond plaits some of my classmates wear, but I never thought much about it."

"Never mind, daughter, you have lovely grey-blue eyes. The good news is our funny name means we don't have to worry about getting a new one!"

"That's good. Many of my classmates are very upset about it."

"Yah, Elin and Lukas Larson are very upset. They think it means they'll lose connection with Tobbe, and they're refusing to make any changes." At that moment Anna noticed her daughter's eyes get misty. "So you still miss him?"

"Yah, Mor. I'll never forget him. Please tell Fru Larson that Tobbe will keep their real name forever."

"Why, what a wonderful thought! I've been trying to encourage Elin to make the change, because if they don't they'll be given some horrible name they don't want. If I share your idea, it might help her feel better."

The Larsons, however, still procrastinated. The whole idea seemed to paralyze them. Not until the kind church warden reminded them that they had just one week to make their choice, or he would be forced to assign them a government-chosen name, was Lukas finally galvanized into action. He decided to make the exercise a game. He invited the Lall family over one evening, and organized a competition as to who could suggest the best name. Elin, who was always very tearful about the name change suddenly saw the funny side, and it became a hilarious Saturday evening. Lots of coffee, doughnuts, and apple cake were consumed.

What's in a Name?

"Now," said Lukas, his mouth full of good food, "the prize for the best name will be doing all the dishes afterwards!"

"So, with that sort of reward, does anyone want any coffee?" exclaimed Elin, smiling.

"We might as well have plenty of *fika* before we get our punishment! I vote for Larsfar!" offered Anna, grinning.

"Nah, it should be Elinfar," said Lukas, chuckling. "She's the boss in this house!"

"Try Vasaman," grinned Anders. "Or here's something truly original: *Träbit*."

"*Träbit*? Come on, now! Can't I just see the looks when I introduce myself as Fru Piece of Wood!" laughed Elin.

"I know!" piped up Erik. "This is a beauty, just what we need to be totally ridiculous. Let's be what they make in Far's factory. You can be Herr and Fru *Toapapper*!"

"Erik!" said his mother in horror. "Don't be naughty! That's taking fun too far! That's just too silly for words! You know very well your Far's company makes real paper, all sorts of good quality paper."

"Well, this whole thing is so silly, we just have to be silly back," pouted Erik, who was not repentant.

"Not with something you have to live with the rest of your life. Do you really want to be Herr *Toapapper* for life? Can you imagine any girl wanting to marry a Mr. Toiletpaper!"

"OK, so we have to be dignified do we?" sneered Jan. "So how about Generalissimo? Herr and Fru Generalissimo. That's surely serious enough."

That made everyone laugh, and they began playing with Mannerheim, Emil, Gustav, and Carl. "You could be Mannerlars, or Larsmanner," suggested Anders.

"The family originally came from Pedersöre. How do you think that would go?" asked Lukas, thoughtfully.

"Didn't I hear we aren't supposed to take the names of places?" remembered Anna.

"Then why can't we make our name Pederholm?" suggested Elin. "Surely that fits all requirements."

"Let me think about it," said Lukas. "All that toilet paper nonsense suddenly makes me realize this is a serious business. Just because I'm angry with those government twits in Helsingfors doesn't mean I need to give my family a silly name they'll be stuck with forever."

"Do you realize that it's not just our personal surnames we have to change," said Anna as she sipped her cup of coffee. "We have to start calling Helsingfors Helsinki, and Tammerfors is now Tampere."

"Yah," said Jan, "did you know our country isn't even Finland? Its Suomi, if I'm saying it right!"

"At this rate I won't know who I am, where I am, or where I'm going," spluttered Lukas. "We've only just got back our city of Vasa after years of being saddled with that Russian jerk's name. So what are we supposed to call it now?"

"Cheer up," said Anna. "They've only added another a to it to make it Finnish, so it's Vasa with two 'a's not much different."

"Well, aren't we lucky!" sniggered Lukas. "We might think Whites won that miserable war, but I think those Reds are taking over!"

A stunned silence followed this angry remark. Elin poured herself another cup of coffee. Erik and Jan made a grab for the same piece of apple cake, which fell to the floor, crumbled into pieces, and was retrieved with much scraping of chair legs and suppressed giggling. Anders cleared his throat loudly, and Lukas threw his pencil beside the empty sheet of paper he had provided for suggested names. "This is hopeless!" he exclaimed.

"Courage, friend," said Anders. "We'll come up with something tonight."

"Any more apple cake?" someone asked. Elin got up and carried over another cake from the sideboard.

"I've been thinking," said Tyra unexpectedly, and everyone turned towards her in surprise. This was the first time she had spoken all evening. "I've been thinking that you need to have a name you value. Something that's noble, and meaningful, and, well, special."

"Yah, yah, daughter," said Anders, a little irritably. "I think we all agree about that."

"Well, I've really enjoyed learning more about Swedish literature this year in school. It was Far who made me love Zacharias Topelius, but this year I've learned so much more about him."

She paused for breath. There was a great deal of foot scraping, and leg stretching, and throat clearing. No one was in the mood for a lecture on Swedish literature. They had a difficult and serious job to do, and her lack of attention was annoying.

"As I said," continued Tyra, after a moment's awkward silence, "I think Topelius had a really good name. Now, I think you all know that I was a very good friend of Tobbe." Elin covered her face with her hands at this. Tyra looked frightened and uncertain how to proceed. But continue she did. "Well, perhaps it's a silly idea. But I thought you could call yourselves Tobbelius, in memory of him. You know, Topelius originally had two p's in his name. You could drop one b if you like, like Topelius did, but either way, Tobbelius sounds very nice, don't you think?"

Elin's sobs broke the hush, and Lukas blew his nose and cleared his throat noisily. "It's a beautiful, perfect name," he said, reaching over to pat Tyra's hand. "A father usually names his sons, but why not have a son who gave his life for his country name his family? Thank you Tyra. Thank you very, very much. And Tyra, now *I* will do the dishes."

There was a gasp. Finnish men never, ever, did the dishes. Hurriedly, Elin wiped her eyes and raced to get the washing tub. It was unthinkable the mischief a man could do to dishes!

"Elin Tobelius. Now doesn't that sound good!" said Anna. While tears coursed down her face, Elin looked up from the dish pan, and smiled.

There was lots of laughter as the family bantered around its new name. Lukas, deprived of the excitement of washing dishes, insisted on grabbing a dish towel and drying the plates. But when they were all neatly stacked back in the dresser, a sudden impulse made Elin unpack everything, and put the kettle back on the stove.

"I've got plenty more *knäckerbröd* and *pepparkakor*, and it wouldn't take long to make some *plattar* and more coffee. The boys have two old *tablut* boards which we could all play. Perhaps it's fitting that tonight we should play a war game about Swedes and Russians!"

"I won't play, but I can act as advisor to others," laughed Anna.

"Let's have pairs of players and advisors!" suggested Lukas.

"Haven't played for years," said Anders, "but it was a fun game."

Anna insisted that no *plattar* was needed, and Elin could relax, but they all enjoyed nibbling on *knäckerbröd* and *pepparkakor*.

The evening that had begun awkwardly soon resounded with laughter. Sometimes Lukas and his boys won, sometimes Anders and the women. Nobody cared, not even the frequently cantankerous Erik and Jan.

They had just finished the third game when Anna looked up and asked, "Where's Tyra?"

There was a stunned silence. "I thought she was on your team," muttered Lukas.

"So did I," returned Anders, "but she isn't."

Anna jumped up and quickly found her warm hat and wrap. "She must have slipped home when we weren't looking," she said anxiously. "I must go!"

She found Tyra hunched beside the kitchen stove, still in her coat and hat. "You gave me a terrible fright!" scolded Anna.

"I'm sorry Mor," said Tyra softly. She looked up, calm and peaceful, but her red eyes betrayed that she had been weeping. "I didn't want to spoil the fun everyone was having. But, well—sometimes I just need to think."

Anna sat down and wrapped her arms around her daughter. When Anders got home soon after, Tyra was asleep on Anna's shoulder.

Chapter 6

Work

WITH HER SCHOOLING COMING to an end, Tyra realized she must think of possible employment. Unfortunately, neither Anna nor Anders thought she needed to work away from home, and showed no interest in discussing the matter with her. But she considered paid employment an essential part of being the new breed of emancipated Finnish woman.

In her last year of school she eagerly looked forward to attending *skriftskola* and achieving confirmation into the Lutheran Church. She was keen to learn what the church taught, but especially excited that confirmation would publicly proclaim she was now a woman. Without confirmation she would be a second rate citizen. In Vasa, *skriftskola* extended throughout the school year, and required a rigorous written knowledge of the teachings of the Lutheran Church, plus passing two stiff oral tests. Unfortunately, some alarming reports about the severity of the priest during the confirmation classes dampened her anticipation.

One reason she was eager to attend *skriftskola* was her hope that it would answer questions that had troubled her since the deaths of Rolf Nilsson and Tobbe. However, in the first class Tyra discovered there were more than fifty teenagers in her group, most of whom showed little interest in what was being taught, and there was much giggling, laughing, pushing, and shoving. Despite reports, Pastor Lindgren (previously Svenson) appeared remarkably tolerant of these teenage antics. She wondered how he had received his reputation for severity. He cracked jokes, uncharacteristic Finnish male behavior, and laughed at their adolescent clowning.

The class began with the history of the Lutheran church, which fascinated Tyra. After the terrible thunderstorm that claimed Rolf Nilsson's life, she empathized with Martin Luther. His experience with a fearful lightning storm transformed his life, changing him from an aspiring young lawyer to an Augustinian monk. Like Luther, she had struggled to know how to be good enough for God to allow her in to heaven. Luther's powerful teaching of the Christian doctrine of salvation through faith in Jesus Christ alone was most encouraging. As a teenager beginning to assert her individuality, images of Luther standing up to the mighty power of the Church of Rome were very exciting. Her friends teased her about her interest. But she was delighted when she took the oral test for this section and found she came top of the class.

However, the section on church teachings proved disastrous. The importance of hard work and self discipline were character traits her parents had already instilled in her. She had no problem with being obedient to her superiors, and was surprised to learn some people contested the law against blasphemy. That church, state, and school were intricately related, seemed natural. But as the class continued she became concerned about the dogmatic way the priest presented right and wrong, and his insistence that feelings had no part to play in Christian life. No one, he implied, had the right to question church teachings, not even to gain understanding.

Tyra made the fatal mistake of asking not one question, but two, in the doctrines class. The first was innocent curiosity, the sudden realization when the class studied the Ten Commandments that God's day of rest was declared to be the seventh day of the week, not the first.

She raised her hand. "Please Pastor Lindgren, why do we go to church on the first day instead of the seventh like it says in the commandment?"

The pastor's face turned deep red, and all giggling and jostling ceased abruptly. "That's a sinful Jewish attitude!" he shouted, and the whole class cowered. "Only a very wicked mind could possibly question the authority of the church to understand God's commands. See me after class!"

Fearfully, Tyra remained behind while her classmates fled from the room. "Wherever did you get that wicked idea?" demanded the pastor as she stood trembling before him.

"What wicked idea?" asked Tyra, wide-eyed. Was it really wicked just to ask about something she did not understand?

"That seventh day nonsense!"

"Pastor Lindgren, I just thought of it! Didn't Luther encourage us to keep the commandments and obey them? I thought we were meant to obey them just as they are. Aren't our practices and beliefs based on the teachings of the Bible?"

"Impudent girl! How dare you question me! Stay behind after class every week till you master this. For homework read the entire New Testament and note every mention of the first day, and how the old legalistic Jewish seventh day was changed to the glorious first day of the resurrection."

"Yah, Pastor."

"Luther had no love for Jews. Pigs he called them. For you to suggest that keeping the seventh day is what the Bible teaches is terrible heresy. This may keep you from confirmation this year."

"But Pastor . . . !" Tyra's eyes filled with tears.

"You may go," the man said roughly. Tyra, shaking from shame, from frustration, from the fear of hell, from the injustice of her situation, and especially from the shock of the changed behavior of the man she had always revered as her spiritual leader, walked dispiritedly away.

Anxious to redeem her wickedness, and to avoid the horrors of hell, Tyra read the New Testament, from the Gospel of Matthew to the Revelation of Saint John. The Gospels and book of Acts were easy, and she readily found references to the first day associated with the resurrection of Jesus Christ, and the time Paul preached till midnight and a sleepy boy fell out a window and almost died. But reading the complicated letters of Paul, and the strange images of the book of Revelation were challenging. Anna noticed her daughter's diligent Bible study, and asked what she was doing. With great embarrassment Tyra explained. To her surprise, Anna did not scold her, but admitted she had sometimes wondered exactly the same thing! She offered to help Tyra go through the difficult writings of Paul, and together see if they could find an answer. But neither of them found any text that mentioned a change of worship day. Anna advised Tyra to write out all texts that cited the first day, and say nothing about her private thoughts.

"Well, young lady, how many verses about the first day have you found?" asked Pastor Lindgren when she presented herself to him with her list of texts.

"Eight," she replied timidly, dreading further questioning, and hoping she had counted correctly.

"Good!" he replied. "Now, never forget them. Can you see how wrong and wicked you were to suggest that Jewish idea?" Tyra bowed her head, hoped it looked like a nod of agreement, and did not mention her confusion about what the eight verses actually taught. She was grateful he did not ask what she had learnt, and hoped he would state that her confirmation was now assured. But he did not. She could only hope. She certainly never planned to ask another question, but to her horror, she discovered she didn't have to ask a question to make a question. It happened soon after the Rådmans' next Christmas visit.

The visit proved that life was finally settling back to a normal pattern after the heartaches of war and terrible food shortages. The traditional foods and customs were enjoyed to the full. Tyra noticed that although it was only a few months since summer when they were together on the farm Algot and Hjalmar had grown even taller, and were now definitely young men. To celebrate their maturity, a highlight of the visit was having studio photographs taken with her cousins and friends. Despite much laughter and joking during the photography sessions, the final products made them all look extremely serious, almost morose!

Algot talked incessantly about his forthcoming work. Despite his declaration that he was needed on the family farm, he now cheerfully told them he had agreed to work for the local ferry operator. Because Oxkangar was an island, traffic to and from it needed to cross the narrow strip of quiet sea that separated it from the mainland.

"But won't you get bored, just going back and forth on that old barge all day?" asked Tyra teasingly. "Wouldn't there be more variety on the farm?"

"Look, on the ferry I only have to work a few hours a day. The rest of the time I can go fishing. Olav told me he makes as much money from fishing as he does from ferry work."

"Is Olav leaving the job?"

"No, at least not until he's taught me everything about ferrying, and of course about fishing."

"But," said Tyra thoughtfully, provocatively, "aren't you supposed to be back at school?"

"Now don't go on about that! I *am* supposed to be at school, but I've been lucky enough to grow and look like a man. Olav promised if he saw any school officials he'd warn me, and I'd have time to make myself lost. And anyway, Far says the nearest learning school is too far away for me to attend. I'd have to find somewhere to live, and Far says he can't afford to pay for me to do that."

"That's a pity," said Tyra, shaking her head. "I think you're making a big mistake."

"You're just a scared chicken. I told you I wasn't going to listen to some silly government and stay at school forever!"

"But what about *skriftskola*?"

"Just because you're going through all that doesn't mean I have to! I don't have to tell the priest I have a job, do I? And I assure you I'm not in any hurry to get married. And anyway, *skriftskola*'s at church, not school, so there!"

"I hope you can sort it," responded Tyra doubtfully. "I just don't understand why you don't want to learn."

"Now Fröken Uppity, I can learn as much on my ferry reading good books as you can parked on your rear end at school. By the time I'm twenty I'll know much more than you do!"

Tyra sighed. Algot didn't even want to understand.

The holidays passed swiftly, and all too soon it was time for the Rådmans to go back to Oxkanga, and Tyra returned to school and *skriftskola*. She was now wise enough to refrain from asking questions, but foolishly one day she spoke to the girl sitting beside her. Whispering and chatting occurred all the time during lessons, but Tyra forgot she was now a marked girl.

"I can understand that hell burns forever," she whispered, "but I can't understand why bad people just don't get burned up."

"No talking!" roared Pastor Lindgren. "Tyra, stand up! What were you saying?"

"I—I—was just talking about hell," she mumbled, as she slowly stood, shaking.

"So once again you're presuming to question the teachings of the Church? No doubt you were saying you wanted to visit hell?" sneered the pastor. "And just what were you saying to your friend that could contribute to our understanding of this important topic? Someone like you needs to know all they can about hell. If I remember rightly you and I had a discussion about this once before. I gave you very good explanations then. Didn't you bother to listen? Or are you still defying the authority of your Church and minister, like you've done on other issues?"

A hush fell on the restless teenagers. It seemed an hour before Tyra could make her paralyzed lips move. "I said . . . I mean . . . I wondered . . . I mean . . . I was thinking that I can understand that God can keep hell burning forever, but . . . I don't understand how wicked people aren't burned up."

The silence that now fell on the room felt like the ice on the wintry windows. Suddenly the pastor picked up his cane, strode two steps, and lashed Tyra's legs, twice. She staggered from the impact.

"Sit down!" he hissed between clenched teeth.

Fighting tears, she did. Why, she thought, as she sank to the floor, her legs throbbing painfully, had she been so foolish? What if the pastor reported her to her parents? How could she explain this second act of wicked doubting? Several of the class had been rapped across the knuckles by the pastor's ruler, and some boys had their ears pulled, but no one had been hit with his cane. He must be very, very angry.

When the written test for Lutheran beliefs arrived Tyra answered every question correctly, but was placed at the bottom of the class. She was so ashamed she dared not talk to her friends, but at least she knew confirmation was still possible. When the oral test for Lutheran practices was given she again answered every question correctly, but once more was declared bottom of the class. She knew several classmates merely mumbled their answers because they knew nothing, but Pastor Lindgren gave them full marks. Despite the pastor's anger, she was fairly certain she would achieve confirmation, and the pastor would not refuse to allow her to be confirmed with her friends.

But despite the troubles of *skriftskola*, Tyra's last year at school went well. All her teachers congratulated her on her performance, and the report she carried home at year-end was a glowing one. She was sad she had finished her studies, but optimistic about life. The confirmation ceremony would hopefully prove not only her membership in the Lutheran Church, but her entry into adult life.

The focus of most girls throughout *skriftskola* had been the dress to wear on the big day; for many boys, it was the party held afterwards. Anna made the requisite white dress, but Tyra had lost interest in wearing it. She just wanted to be be given a certificate and the fuss disappear. When, on Midsummer's Day, the entire *skriftskola* group lined up outside the church for a photo, her shame and embarrassment clearly showed. Her friends noticed she was not her normal self. The ceremony was solemn and impressive, the church packed with parents, grandparents and friends. But when Tyra took the solemn emblems of the Eucharist she found it hard to fuse the image of the magnificently attired, benevolently smiling pastor offering benign advice, with the cruel teacher who had caned her legs, and refused to answer her genuine questions. As they filed out of the church she hung her head, and struggled to mutter a few words of thanks when Pastor Lindgren passed out the traditional confirmation gift of a new Bible to each new member of the Lutheran Church. But the ordeal was over, she was publicly pronounced a woman. Nothing could change that! Suddenly she raised her head, and joyfully held out her hands to be shaken by her very proud parents.

Everyone was excited about the evening celebrations. Confirmation had been a beautiful day, and the evening was just as bright. In the park surrounding the church a band, of two violins, guitar, and accordion, played lively folk music, accompanied by spirited dancing of the newly confirmed adults. These dancers were the focus of attention, but many others joined the joyous occasion. Tyra enjoyed twirling around to the vivacious, traditional music, but was not impressed with some of her partners. They smelt strange, like Morbror Karl's *brännvin,* and behaved foolishly. Still, it was fun, and the humiliating memories of *skriftskola* were forgotten in the joyous realization that she was now a fully fledged woman. When the church clock struck eleven, the sun's rays, very low on the horizon, shone brightly on the happy youth.

"Coming to Hans' house?" asked a *skriftskola* classmate Tyra knew only a little.

"No, I promised Mor I'd be home by midnight."

"But Hans has some *lakka* and *sima*[1]. Come and join the fun!" her companion whispered.

"*Lakka* and *sima*? But that's against the law!"

"Alright, spoil sport Fröken High and Mighty, don't come! I thought everyone knew how easy it is to get alcohol from the backdoors of restaurants. Surely you know it's smuggled in from Estonia all the time! I thought after all those times you made the pastor angry you'd be someone who wouldn't be fussy about some stupid law! You must be the dumbest girl in Vasa! But if the police come we'll know who to blame! We'll make your life as miserable as we can, worse than that old priest did! So there!" The girl glared at Tyra, and ran off with a flounce of white dress and a toss of golden curls. She joined a group of guffawing teenagers. Tyra heard cries of "She's a Red!" and "Mor's little darling!" followed by gales of laughter. She felt terribly alone.

Just then her school friend Gunnel left the dancers and walked across the green lawn streaked with the long shadows of evening. In a moment of hush, when the musicians conferred what to play next, the unmistakable barking of a Ural owl was clearly heard in the distance.

---

1. Types of alcoholic beverage

"Did you hear that?" asked Tyra, shuddering slightly, and turning towards Gunnel. "Greta and her friends remind me of that owl. Predators, that's what they are!"

Gunnel put her arm around Tyra's waist. "They asked you to their party, didn't they?" Tyra nodded. "They asked me too. I heard that nasty Börje dare Greta to ask you. He was bragging that it would be extremely funny to make you drunk. They know you're a principled person, despite those problems with Pastor Lindgren. So, don't be upset. I'll walk home with you. I promised my parents I'd be home before the church clock struck midnight!"

In spite of everything, Tyra smiled. "That's exactly what I promised my parents!"

"By the way, Tyra, we were all horrified by the way Pastor treated you. He did the same to my brother three years ago. Pers was really interested and just asked simple questions he genuinely wanted answered. It seems the pastor can tolerate no end of foolish behavior, but woe betide anyone who questions his authority or the teaching of the Church!"

The Sunday following confirmation, Tyra was standing with her mother in warm sun outside church, waiting for friends, when her Swedish language teacher came to her.

"*Hej* Fru Lall! *Hej* Tyra!" he greeted. "Fru Lall, did Tyra talk to you about our recommendation that she attend the Åbo Akademi University in Åbo, or what they're now calling Turku?"

"Yah, Herr, she did, but my husband could not afford for us to send her there."

"Really? Tyra's been one of my best students. Her understanding of Swedish literature and language is excellent. With further training she would make a wonderful teacher."

"Thank you for your recommendation, but it would be impossible for us to help her to go to Åbo. Is there nowhere in Vasa she could train?"

"The Åbo Akademi is planning a campus here, but that hasn't yet happened. Please consider this, because I think Tyra would do well."

"Thank you, Herr. We'll think seriously about it," replied Anna, as the man walked off. She looked at her daughter, standing with downcast eyes. "Do you really want to be a teacher?" she asked.

"It would be nice," said Tyra, "but I don't know. Åbo is a long way away, and I don't feel ready to go to a strange city on my own, not even one with all the history that Åbo has. I do love Swedish literature, but I can read on my own. I always planned to help you and Far, not be a big expensive problem. So no, I don't want to go to that university."

"What would you like to do?"

"Get a job and help you and Far."

"But daughter, it's not natural for a young woman to have paid work! Your Far earns enough money to support us. Why don't you just help me at home and learn the things I can do, and we can talk more about this in the future."

"Yah, Mor."

A month later Anna and Tyra made the annual pilgrimage to Oxkangar, but with Algot away on his ferry most of the day, Tyra found it lonely. Hjalmar was a steady fourteen-year-old doing all the chores Karl needed. Tyra was happy to assist him, and in the evenings she read Swedish classics to Hjalmar, and to Algot if he came home early. Hjalmar showed a great deal more Finnish *sisu* than Algot was currently showing, but this disappointing realization made Tyra miss the Algot she loved even more. She looked forward eagerly to the times he came home, but now he smelt of cheap tobacco, and he only brought home one of the fish he was supposed to be catching in great quantities. Occasionally there were sharp words between him and Karl, notably when Algot asked for money. Either the ferry job did not pay well, or Algot was using more money than he earned. After a particularly noisy altercation with his father she tried to ask him about his earnings, but he angrily told her to mind her own business. Lisa overheard.

"Tyra, leave him alone," advised Lisa, after Algot stomped out. "We all find him difficult now. Must be just a stage he's going through, but I hope he grows out of it very soon!"

"He doesn't seem like the cousin I've had so much fun with for so long," lamented Tyra. "He's another person, and not a very nice one!"

"I know. Karl thinks he may be worried about army training. He could get out of going to school, but he won't escape the army."

"Perhaps you're right. But he doesn't go to the army till he's eighteen, isn't that right? And he always said he wanted to get a gun so he could go hunting."

"Yah, that's right about going into the army when he's eighteen. Anyway, bear with him, and say nothing to try to convince him of anything at the moment. Just keep him out of Karl's way. That's the most important thing you could do right now! Almost anything makes them flare up, and then we have another nasty scene."

"Certainly!"

When Anna and Tyra left Oxkangar Algot gave Tyra the same warm farewell he always did, as though nothing had changed. He was certainly her beloved cousin, but he had been absent for most of the visit.

Tyra's immediate employment plans were soon settled. She would assist her mother weaving linen sheets and colorfully patterned cotton floor mats, and her neighbor Elin Tobelius making rag carpets. Although imported cotton sheets were beginning to replace the traditional linen ones, Anna's sheets were still popular. Both the long, colorful, woven carpet runners that Anna made, and Elin's rag carpets, were essential Finnish home furnishings, and sold very well in the Vasa market. Although to a limited extent Tyra had assisted making these articles before, now she learned and mastered every detail of these classic Finnish furnishings. The plan was that the three women would make enough over winter so when the central market opened in summer Tyra would operate a stall selling what they had produced. Tyra was anxious about the marketing aspect of the plan, but more than willing to learn the skills of her mother and neighbor. Anders joked that he lived in a factory as the loom operated by one or other of his women rattled many hours a day. Tyra enjoyed the freedom of self employment. She and Gunnel had plenty of opportunity to explore the shops of Vasa, and go for long walks together in the nearby parks and waterfront.

The summer central market stall actually proved to be satisfyingly worthwhile. Elin's colorful rag carpets were extremely popular, and quickly sold out. Tyra was disappointed her mother's beautifully woven mats did not sell more quickly, until she realized they were priced more highly. However, well before the summer market ended, all of Anna's mats and sheets had sold.

The best part of the market was the chance to talk to other stall holders, and see what they sold. Tyra struggled to shout out her wares like other marketeers did, but she soon realized that if you had a quality product you did not need to make too much noise to sell it. One day on impulse she took some of her eggs and offered them to a produce stall holder, where she often bought vegetables for Anna. Not only was he delighted, but gave her half the sales, a tidy sum. She decided to get more hens and develop her own business. Anders muttered about his stable being taken over by poultry, but secretly was delighted by her initiative and pleased to make room for the flock of thirty hens his daughter acquired.

Soon after the first snows of the year had fallen, Tyra came to Anna with an unusual request. "Mor, Gunnel and I wondered if next Sunday we could attend the Orthodox church in the next block. It would be good if we got to know how our neighbors worshipped."

"But Tyra—we're Lutherans!" exclaimed Anna, utterly shocked.

"Yah, Mor. But they're Christians, like us, aren't they? We don't want to join the Orthodox church, but thought it would be good to know what happens there. And it's so close, just around the corner in the opposite direction from our church."

Anna sighed, nodding uncertainly. "All right. Let me talk to Far," she responded. "Our church is a White church, but the Orthodox church might be mainly for Reds."

Anna's comment about Reds made Tyra realize that going to the Orthodox church might be more dangerous than she had appreciated. But Tyra was young and adventuresome, and Gunnel even more so. When approached, although Anders expressed more political concern than Anna, he finally agreed the girls could go if he accompanied them. Anna then wanted to join them, and when Gunnel's parents knew of the plan they too were keen to accompany their daughter on this dangerous venture. However, it was finally decided that the smaller the group attending the less obvious their visit would be. It would be Anders, Tyra, and Gunnel.

"Well, how was it?" asked Anna anxiously when Anders and Tyra returned. Delicious smells of Sunday lunch permeated the house, and Anders settled himself at the table, ready to eat.

"Different," said Tyra.

"Lots of smoke," said Anders.

"Yah, there was lots of that. It's called incense, Far," smiled Tyra. "And there were lots of pictures on the walls, very fancy pictures of saints with gold halos."

"Did you recognize anyone?" asked Anna, a little nervously.

"Of the saints on the walls, or those attending?" grinned Anders. "Remember, I know half the town! But since you're worried, no one looked angry or aggressive, although a few were surprised to see us, I think. Several people spoke to us in a friendly way."

"Are you satisfied?" asked Anna as Tyra ladled potatoes on to a platter.

Tyra nodded slowly. "Yah, it was good to see. If the people attending the Orthodox Church are Reds, then they're nothing to get frightened about. But I decided it's better to go to our church where I understand what's happening."

Three happy, contented years later, Tyra and Gunnel were enjoying midsummer sun and the most recent confirmation festivities. While they relaxed on a seat in the church yard, two soldiers came and sat beside them. The girls quickly jumped up and were about to walk away from the unwanted intruders, when Tyra stared at one of them.

He roared with laughter. "I didn't think you recognized me!" he guffawed.

"Algot!" exclaimed Tyra with delight. "What are you doing here?"

"Yah, it's me. As you can see, I'm stuck in the army. I hate it! Oh, and this is my friend Axel."

Tyra turned from her beloved cousin and smiled politely at the young man. He was unremarkable except for his piercing blue eyes, a stocky, blond-haired, ruddy-faced youth, typical of many she knew.

"How long are you here for?" she asked, turning back to Algot.

"Don't know," he responded. "I'm stuck in this uniform for two years, but whether they'll leave us here in Vasa, or send us somewhere else, who knows. In the army we're just pawns, not men!"

"Can you come home for dinner?" invited Tyra.

Algot looked at his friend. "What do you think, Axel?"

"Nothing could be worse than army food," Axel said tactlessly.

"You better not say anything like that to my Mor!" exclaimed Tyra, shocked at the young man's candor. "But Algot, would you like to come? Mor and Far would love to see *you*."

"Of course," said Algot, without hesitation, and so they did.

After warm greetings for Algot, and polite introductions for Axel, Anna flustered around the kitchen finding food for two more mouths. She quickly added more potatoes to the bubbling pot, asked Tyra to prepare a bunch of new beetroot boiled with vinegar and sugar, and chopped and boiled a large cabbage. The roast pork would be ample she knew, and there was plenty of rye bread, milk, and coffee. It was good, hearty Finnish fare. She wished she had cinnamon rolls on hand, or time to make an apple cake, but the young men would just have to accept what she had. Anders was happy to chat while Anna and Tyra busied themselves with food. Finally, all was ready, and the family assembled around the table.

Tyra could not believe the rapidity with which her guests ate, and the amount of food they demolished shocked even Anders. Algot and Axel had no time to talk, they were so busy filling their mouths, and the Lall family was too surprised to make even limited Finnish mealtime conversation.

When nothing but bread and milk remained, Axel leaned back in his chair. "Ah, Fru Lall!" he exclaimed appreciatively. "I haven't had a meal like that for weeks! Thank you very much!"

"Aren't you glad I brought you here?" boasted Algot.

Tyra was annoyed. She thought Algot had come to see her family, and here he was claiming he only wanted their food!

Anna tried to break the awkward silence. "How are your family, Algot?" she asked politely.

"Mor's fine," said Algot. "Hjalmar's the good little boy looking after everything. And Far is as obnoxious as ever."

"I see," said Anders caustically, and silence descended again.

"And your family?" said Anna, turning to Axel.

"We live at Sorvich, a tiny village near Nykarleby," he answered. "Fru Lall, I really appreciate your meal. Army life is no fun. You don't realize how good it's been to spend this time with your family!"

"You're welcome! Algot, bring your friend next time you visit us," smiled Anna.

But army life is not intended for those who want to socialize. Algot was posted to different camps around the country, and Anna was rarely required to feed him or his friend. Once, to the surprise of everyone, Axel appeared alone at Vasa Central Lutheran church, and sat with Anna and Tyra. Anna dutifully invited him home for the midday meal. He accepted, ate heartily, said hardly a word the whole time he was with them, and left as soon as they finished eating.

"A bit rude that he should just come for food!" grumbled Anders.

"I think he's lonely, that's all," said Anna kindly. "Remember he told us Algot had gone to Oxkangar."

Shortly after Tyra's 23rd birthday, to her delight, she was offered a job, regular employment with a regular wage. The highly esteemed Herr Backman came to their home one Sunday afternoon to make her the offer. He was manager of the Lito-Björkell paper manufacturing company, and Anders did regular carting work for him, so he was no stranger. But his visit was a surprise. Anna welcomed him, and quickly made *fika*. She was amazed that such a busy man could find time to chat with them, and realized there was some purpose for his unexpected visit. She assured him Anders would be home soon.

"Very good!" said Herr Backman appreciatively as he munched his third piece of *knäckerbröd*, spread with cheese and lingonberry. He sipped his second cup of coffee thoughtfully.

Tyra brought fresh *applecaka* and placed it in front of their guest. "Please have some," she offered.

"Did you make the cake?" Herr Backman asked, eyeing the cake appreciatively. Tyra nodded. "Do you do much cooking at home?" he added.

Tyra sat down beside him. "I'm not as good as my mother, so she does most of the cooking. But I like to help as often as I can."

"And what do you do with the rest of your time?" he asked.

Anna stopped stirring pancake batter, and came to listen.

"I help my mother and neighbor make carpets. There's mother's loom in the corner," Tyra said, pointing. "Mor makes beautiful long carpets, and I'm learning from her. And our neighbor, Fru Tobelius, makes colorful rag mats. I sell all the carpets in the Vasa central market during summer." Herr Backman sipped his coffee thoughtfully. "Oh," added Tyra, "I also have chickens and sell their eggs, or at least a friend sells them for me."

"Sounds as though you're a busy young woman," Her Backman said thoughtfully. "Do you have any spare time?"

Tyra smiled shyly. "I like to be useful," she said.

"Our daughter is never idle," said Anna proudly. "She's a big help to my husband and me."

"I can see that," said Herr Backman. "Well, what I came to talk about was whether you could spare Tyra to help me."

There was a stunned silence.

Just then Anders returned. "*Hej*, Herr Backman!" he greeted heartily. "What brings you to my place? Got some work for me coming up?"

"I haven't got work for you, but I have for your daughter," laughed their guest. "I've just this moment asked if she would consider working for me."

"Really!"

Herr Backman explained that he hoped Tyra would work in the *papeteriavdelning* department of his company. He described this specialized work which involved packing elegant writing paper with matching envelopes into attractive wooden boxes. There was a large demand for quality paper products in both Europe and Russia, he proudly declared, and his company was in the vanguard for supplying this need. The work involved was not heavy, but it required someone who was meticulous, as the clientele for these products were mostly fastidious upper class European women. Poorly executed work would be deleterious for the company's reputation.

"Thank you for the honor of asking me," responded Tyra when he paused for breath, "but I would not want to desert my mother and neighbor."

Herr Backman tapped the table, and shifted impatiently in his chair. He was not used to being refused.

"You know, I think Elin and I could manage," said Anna unexpectedly, thoughtfully. "What sort of hours would Tyra have to work? Would they be fixed hours like the usual factory work, or would there be some flexibility?"

"As long as she could get the job done, she can work whatever hours she likes. I'm sure we could give her time off in summer to sell the carpets."

"That's a very generous offer. What do you think, Daughter?" asked Anders.

"Perhaps, under those conditions, I will try," said Tyra with a smile.

"Thank you very much," said Herr Backman as he reached for another piece of apple cake, and rested his hand on his well-rounded abdomen.

And thus Tyra joined the paid workforce of Finland. She was indeed a fully liberated woman.

Chapter 7

Karl

ANY APPREHENSIONS TYRA HAD about working for the Lito-Björkell paper company were quickly dispelled. Matilda, her work mate, a tiny woman with long blond plaits, unusually long even for a Finnish woman, had an even longer sense of humor. She was convinced it was her great fortune to work in Herr Backman's factory because the work was pleasant and her previous work mate had been there for years, leaving only because she married and moved to Helsingfors. Matilda could not understand anyone wanting to move to the "red" south of Finland, but concluded love was both strong and blind. Tyra enjoyed examining the intricate designs on the writing paper she packed into elegant boxes, both paper and boxes products of Herr Backman's factory. They reminded her of embroidery patterns she had learned to make at the *gymnasium*, and inspired her to do embroidery in the evenings while her mother rattled her loom. Matilda teased her about marriage when she brought her stitched cushions and pillowcases to work to embroider during breaks, but Tyra merely laughed good naturedly. Soon Matilda took embroidery lessons from Tyra, and they began cheerfully vying with each other as to who could produce the most delicate and intricate work. Tyra talked about her efforts making and selling mats for the Vasa market, and her family fun at Oxkangar. Matilda chatted about her large family of six brothers and one sister, and the mischief they got up to when they were children on a farm near Solv, where Anders had grown up.

    Vivacious Matilda encouraged Tyra to attend the dances regularly held to entertain soldiers from the nearby army training barracks. Tyra was reticent at first, but soon enthusiastically joined these gatherings.

Mostly these dances were held on Saturday nights, but sometimes during the week, and Tyra became such a dance enthusiast that she attended midweek dances as well. None of the young men interested her, but good-naturedly she agreed to comply with Anders' stipulation that she record the full names (and addresses!) of anyone she partnered. Although she knew she was over twenty-one, and a free woman, she respected her father's concern for her welfare.

Matilda had a distant cousin who was a member of the Finnish parliament, and joking about the frequent changes in government was a source of great mirth to her. Anders, however, did not find these government changes a cause for merriment, and was disgusted that as the decade of the twenties progressed, the Finnish parliament changed leadership more than once every year. "How can we possibly become a respected European nation when we can't even work out how to govern ourselves, and squabble like a bunch of silly school children!" he muttered angrily.

"Far, don't worry," Tyra responded, reflecting ideas imbibed from Matilda. "We're a new country just learning how to do things. We aren't doing anyone harm, and soon those people in government will figure out how to do it, and who's the best leader. Matilda tells me her cousin has changed parties twice, because he's still trying to work out which party is best!"

"He must be as stupid as all the rest, that's all I can say!" retorted Anders.

Sometimes the girls went into the main factory, but Tyra did not like the noise of the heavy machines. To her, these raucous beasts totally controlled their operators who had no time to stop and chat about life and the frequent changes in Finnish government. Older male machinists frowned at them, assuming they were wasting Herr Backman's time and money. Herr Backman, however, encouraged these visits so the girls could understand all aspects of his business, and meet other employees.

While Tyra enjoyed her work, Anna found adjusting to her daughter's absence difficult. Although Tyra was quiet, like her father, she was a cheerful presence. She encouraged Anna to share stories from her youth, to explain what it was like growing up in Russian Finland, and how different life had become. The times mother and daughter spent together were always pleasant, and Anna now realized how much she depended on her daughter.

The first day Tyra was at work Anna walked round looking for something she could not remember. Suddenly she laughed. Unconsciously, she was looking for Tyra! Later that morning when she finished weaving an intricate carpet runner in a design of blues and pinks, she felt a sudden sadness that she could not immediately get Tyra's approval. Nor could she ask for her advice about a new design, but had to await Tyra's return. She thought of running next door to Elin, but felt foolish in case Elin realized the true reason for the visit. Eagerly she peppered Tyra with questions about her job as they prepared the evening meal.

Herr Backman, as promised, agreed Tyra could work in the market over summer. He offered a generous six weeks' paid holiday, and when that expired, over the next month allowed her to work at her market stall in the mornings and do *papeteriavdelning* in the afternoons. He even generously agreed that Matilda join the carpet enterprise, and allowed both girls to do his work in the afternoons. Although he did not publicly admit this, there was less demand for *papeteriavdelning* during summer when affluent women were more interested in enjoying a holiday in the countryside than writing to friends. Matilda was delighted with the market, and her cheerful nature made her popular with other stall holders.

Apart from wanting to know exactly who his daughter was dancing with, Anders' contribution to Tyra's work was simple—he advised her which bank to use. Once a month he checked how her savings were growing, and talked to his daughter about the best use of her funds. He was delighted that not only did she save carefully, but showed signs of having good business acumen that he fondly attributed to inheriting from him.

Wars had taken a dreadful toll on the young men of Finland, very noticeable in church each week. The number of pretty young women in the pews far outstripped the number of young men. But despite this shortage of men, Anna and Anders did not want their daughter marrying unsuitably. Both had once secretly hoped Tyra would marry Tobbe, but his tragic death ended those dreams. They could see no sign that any of the young men she danced with interested her, and although she clearly loved dancing, she obviously preferred chatting with Matilda and Gunnel. Gunnel had learned to type, and found work in the office of another wood processing factory in Vasa. The three girls got together on Sunday afternoons, going for long walks around the harbor and parks, or enjoying *fika* in their homes. This proved an excellent way to develop baking skills. Occasionally Anders took them to Solv, where Matilda introduced Tyra and Gunnel to her family, and Anders showed them places he had enjoyed as a boy. Because her school holidays had always been spent in Oxkangar, Tyra knew little about her father's family. Both Anders' parents died before she was born, and she now enjoyed getting to know his only brother with the blacksmithing (now mostly car mechanics) business he had taken over from his father.

But in general, life was settling into a comfortable pattern, after all the years of war, semi-starvation, and uncertainty. Whilst the Finnish parliament might still squabble and change leadership every few months, and some things were not quite perfect (like young men being scarce in Vasa), Tyra looked forward to a happy life. She and her parents were content.

There was one unfortunate result of the family's busyness. They had no time to make the annual visit to the Rådmans, and for a few years the families did not see each other regularly, and when they did it was only for short visits. Anna and Lisa kept a faithful correspondence. Lisa's letters were full of joyful praise of Hjalmar and the hard work he was doing around the farm, despite continuing at school. She sometimes mentioned Sonja Rolfholm and the struggles she had because none of her boys was interested in farm work. They were adamant that their father's terrible experience destroyed any interest they had in taking over the farm.

Over the years Tyra had corresponded regularly with Algot, but his letters slowly dwindled to none. She was a little sad about this, but Anna was relieved. She had feared there may have been a romantic attachment between the cousins, and Algot's increasingly irresponsible behavior did not please either Anders or her.

Anna's loneliness without Tyra made her look forward eagerly to letters from Lisa. Although Tyra was happy, and caught up with her work and friendship with Matilda and Gunnel, Anna was determined to somehow engineer closer and more frequent contact between her family and her brother's. But one day in early autumn a shockingly brief letter arrived from Lisa, one that made Anna's heart stop.

Come at once. Karl is dead. Lisa.

Anna read and re-read the hastily scrawled note several times. It had to be true. The writing was unmistakably Lisa's. But—Karl, her brother, Karl—her only brother, *dead*? How could that possibly be true?

She must go to Oxkangar immediately, today. She had no idea where Anders was, but expected him home for the midday meal. If he would agree to make the journey, which he must surely do, that would still give them time to reach Oxkangar before dark. Tyra was at work just a few streets away. She could be contacted quickly and easily.

Hurriedly wrapping a thick shawl around her head and shoulders to combat the early autumn chill, she ran to the paper factory. Her mind was a turmoil of death-causing possibilities. As she ran panting into the main entrance she was embarrassed to meet Herr Backman. He greeted her warmly, noted her agitated manner, shortness of breath, and asked, "Why Fru Lall, what's the matter? How can I help you?"

Anna hesitated. She knew so little, what could she say? "There's been a tragedy. In my family. A dreadful tragedy. We need to go to Oxkangar. As soon as possible. That's where my family lives."

"Today?" he asked. "Immediately?" Anna nodded.

"And you've come to get Tyra?" Anna nodded again.

Herr Backman wasted no time with futile questions. "Let me come with you while you talk to Tyra," he offered. Clearly this woman was not telling him all she knew, which meant something really bad had happened.

Anna hesitated, but bowed her head in assent. She didn't know what else to do. Together, in silence broken only by Anna's heavy breathing from her unaccustomed hurrying, they climbed the stairs to the small, bright room where Tyra and Matilda worked.

"Why Mor!" exclaimed Tyra, looking up and instantly realizing her mother was in extreme distress. "Whatever brings you here? What's happened?"

"Something's happened to Morbror Karl. We must to go to Oxkangar, immediately. Come and help me pack so we can be ready when Far gets home."

"I'm giving permission for you to go," added Herr Backman. "You'll manage for a few days without Tyra, won't you, Matilda?"

Matilda nodded, a puzzled frown creasing her face.

"Thank you, Herr Backman," Tyra said quietly, putting her arm around her mother. Anna began to cry. Tyra turned to Matilda. "You *will* be fine, won't you?"

"Of course," said Matilda, her voice lacking its usual vivacity.

As mother and daughter walked the few blocks home, this time slowly so Anna could catch her breath, Anna told Tyra Lisa's message. Suddenly both of them realized its harsh brevity indicated something very bad had happened.

But they were level-headed women. Although distressed, by the time Anders arrived for his midday meal Anna and Tyra had everything ready for Oxkangar, including hastily purchased black fabric. Anders refused the meal they offered him, and sat, head in hands, thinking one minute of his cheeky, smart-aleck brother-in-law, and then mentally frantically rearranging his deliveries. Anna and Tyra placed rye bread and cheese in a basket, so Anders could eat along the way. As the church bells chimed two o'clock, the Lall family clopped out of Vasa. They arrived at the Rådman home as the last rays of sun crossed long dark shadows on the road.

Anders stabled the very tired Möja and Blek, muttering, "I shouldn't have pushed them so fast, it's against my principles," poured water into their trough, found oats for them to eat, and gently rubbed down their steaming, sweaty flanks. He valued his horses, and rarely pushed them beyond their strength. But occasionally, when dealing with something urgent, even his animals understood and responded. Both horses nuzzled him gently as he attended them.

Hjalmar met Anna and Tyra. "It's terrible for her," he said, picking up their luggage. Feeling like criminals they slunk into the kitchen, where Lisa sat at her table, a cup of cold coffee in front of her, weeping.

"I've lost both of them, my husband and my son!" she moaned desolately, looking up with deep red-rimmed eyes. "Sonja lost Rolf, but this is much worse!"

Hjalmar seemed afraid to speak, but finally said softly, "It happened about lunch time two days ago. The police came, and took Far away."

"Police!" exclaimed Anna. "Police! Why police?" Tyra added.

"Didn't Mor tell you?" Hjalmar replied, his face haggard and drawn.

Anna and Tyra shook their heads in bewilderment. After a deep breath and short silence Hjalmar added, "Well, you must know. Algot killed Far!"

Anna gave a heart-rending scream and sank to the floor.

At that moment Anders walked in from the barn. Lisa began sobbing uncontrollably, and Tyra dropped on to the nearest chair, the world growing very dim as it spun around her. Anders stood like a statue by the doorpost, unable to decide whether to support his prostrate wife or white-faced daughter. Hjalmar gently lifted his weeping aunt to a chair beside his sobbing mother, who threw her arms around Anna, and began to wail piteously.

"What—what happened?" Tyra found her voice, as her father sat beside her. "Please Hjalmar, we need to know."

"The problem is we don't know," said Hjalmar. "About noon Algot rushed in here white as a ghost and shouted, 'I didn't mean to do it! Honest to God, I didn't mean to do it! I know you think I'm a rotter. But he made me! It's his fault! He's in the barn.' We haven't seen him, I mean Algot, since."

"And Morbor?" prompted Tyra.

"We found him in the barn, just like Algot said, with a gun on the floor and a bullet hole in his head. There were three empty bottles of *brännvin* beside him. We called the police and told them what we knew. They took him away. The policeman told us Far can't be buried till they tell us we can, until they can work out what happened. Who knows when that will be!" The normally steady voice of Hjalmar was suddenly shrill with frustration and worry.

Tyra broke the sobbing silence. "Have you eaten today?" she asked Hjalmar.

"Yah, *knäckerbröd*," he answered, bitterly. "Dry *knäckerbröd*, that's all. Mor's too upset to cook, and I've got to look after the farm, no matter what's happened."

"You need more than dry *knäckerbröd* to cope with this. Shall I make *plattar*?" she asked. "That's simple and easy," she added.

Hjalmar looked startled, and turned uncertainly towards his weeping mother. "What do you think, Mor? Would you like something warm to eat?"

Lisa looked up, and wiped her eyes on the corner of her apron. "That would be lovely," she said. "Thank you. I couldn't bear doing cooking myself, but if you make it, I could eat it."

Tyra and Hjalmar hurried to the stove. The gentle clatter as Hjalmar helped find ingredients, and Tyra beat the batter for pancakes broke the emotional tension. Lisa stopped weeping, stretched her shoulders, and finally got up to find freshly made apple sauce in the pantry. Anders carried the remaining Lall luggage into the house. Anna set the table.

"Wow, you've made a difference already!" whispered Hjalmar to Tyra.

"I can't believe how dreadful it must have been for you these last two days. I don't know how you managed!"

"It's been terrible. Worse than a bad nightmare, like the ones I got about thunderstorms. You wonder if you'll wake up, find it all just a dream, and get back to normal life. I used to get bad dreams like that during the wars, when I was a kid. It still doesn't seem real."

Appetites that had vanished for two days were gently restored by Tyra's steaming platter of pancakes. Lisa's conscience for hostess duties was assuaged by her jar of apple sauce. The family silently replenished their lost energy and harmony.

Suddenly Anna gave an anguished, piercing cry. "Someone's watching us! It—it looked like Algot! I saw a face pressed against the window!"

"What's he come back to do to us now!" cried Hjalmar angrily, jumping up and moving protectively towards his mother.

Anders went to the door. "If you're out there, be a man and come in!" he commanded the night.

"Will you turn me in?" echoed the hollow voice of Algot in the darkness. "I know you went to the police, you brutes!"

"Come here, and I'll tell you!" demanded Anders sternly. Beyond his strong dark silhouette in the door, the hollow, ashen grey, unshaven face of Algot appeared.

"What do you want?" demanded Anders, as frightened by Algot as were the others, but standing staunchly with feet firmly planted wide part, and his hands on his hips.

"Food," said Algot. "Just food. I mean, what's wrong with you all? Isn't that obvious! Can't you see I'm starving! I hope you'll listen to me. But what a useless hope! None of you ever listened to me, but maybe just this once you will! I won't harm you, I promise, so stop staring as though I was a demon. I don't have a gun, can't you see that? But do you have one?"

"You talk nonsense," muttered Hjalmar. "It's you who wouldn't listen, not us! We have no guns."

"How can I trust you?" asked Anders, his voice shaking. "Do you *really* promise not to hurt anyone? On your own admission you killed your father!"

"Okay, I'll leave," Algot snarled, "but then you can have my death from starvation on the heads of all of you, you pack of hypocrites!"

Anders stood aside, his hands raised ready for defense. Algot tried to swagger in, but merely staggered, brushing awkwardly against Anders.

"Don't touch me," he said to his terrified mother. "And that means you too!" turning angrily to his white-faced brother. "I'll turn myself in when I'm ready. I'll have to do time for this, I know, I know, but I have to get myself ready first. I have to do some talking to myself, and maybe that God of yours Mor. Will you let me eat and talk?"

No one moved. No one spoke. Algot staggered to Anders' empty chair, and collapsed on it. He looked around at his family, at the remains of the meal, then grabbing the last four pancakes ate them ravenously, without even adding sauce. "Any more?" he said.

"Not until you talk," said Anders, bitterly, angrily.

"Alright," said Algot. "I'm starving. I guess I can talk for food."

In the deathly silence Tyra heard her own heart beating. She got up and brought the plate of dry *knäckerbröd* and a round of cheese to the table. Algot grabbed two slices of each and crunched them noisily. At first Tyra had experienced pity for Algot's plight, but now she felt revulsion. His selfish focus on his own needs, his oblivion to his family's enormous pain, repelled her.

"You all know I just got discharged from the army, right? Or perhaps none of you care enough about me to even know that!" Algot sighed, his mouth full of noisy crunching bread, which made understanding him difficult. He glanced at the wide-eyed white faces around him and sighed again, deeply. "Yah, I just got discharged from the army. The great day I was longing for! You can't believe how horrible army life was. Oh, how I hate the army! Do you hear! I hate it, every minute of the years of my life that I wasted there! Do this—do that—come here—go there! Pick up your brains and throw them in the sea! Don't think, don't feel! We were just robots doing what those beastly commanders in their fancy uniforms demanded. While their egos expanded like hot air balloons ours were trampled in the dirt beneath their lordly feet! But finally, finally I was free! At last! Discharged! Did you know when you leave the army they still try to hold you? They told us we were expected to join the civil guards, and be ready for action, as they call their mind-numbing activities. Now those civil guards publish a weekly paper called *Hakkapeliitta*. Do you know what that little Finnish tongue twister of a word means? It's so sweet, so kind! It means 'hack them down'! Oh boy! What a motto! That's what the army makes you do and think!

"Ah, but there was one thing we did learn in the army! It wasn't taught in the class rooms or those ghastly marches, or on shooting practice, but we all learned it very well. Where to get grog. Oh, my, oh my! We learned that skill really well, really, really well. It was the only thing that made life bearable. Drink yourself silly, and forget those beastly commanders. So, I got grog, good potent stuff, and I came home to celebrate."

"But you know . . ." began Lisa.

"Yah, yah, yah, I know, I know, it's illegal! So what Mor! When they train you to kill, what's legal and what's illegal? What does any of that mean? Now tell me that, my fine law abiding family! Tyra, you who was always so keen on what was right and what was wrong. Fröken Fancy Do-good tell me, why I should have to learn to kill, but not be allowed to kill my pain with drink?" Algot jumped up and paced wildly around the room, lunging at imaginary foes in a most alarming way. "Yah, it's legal to kill, to hack them down as they command, but illegal to have a bit of fun! What sort of country do we live in? Now tell me that, all of you!"

Suddenly he stopped pacing and lunging and sat down heavily. "Well, I came home. Home sweet home. You know all that stuff. Mor got tearful when she saw me. Little kid brother sidles up and says, 'How nice you're back home. Shall we go fishing?' So sickly sweet I ignored him. I mean, who wouldn't! I told Far I had some grog, and asked him to come out to the barn and celebrate my homecoming with me. I knew no one else would be interested in joining me. Far, he grinned and said yah, son, yah, what a good idea."

"Oh no!" wailed Lisa. "Karl hasn't used alcohol for 15 years!"

"Far was lily pure, you say? Well, I had no idea Far had such a problem with grog. He just gulped down that stuff like it was water! I'd had a few mouthfuls from my bottle, but he'd finished his, and a second, and wanted mine too, which I refused. He started calling me names when I didn't hand it over. All those nasty names he used when I was a kid, about how useless I was, about how bad I was about everything you can think of that's horrible, and lots of wicked words, that's what he said I was."

Lisa began weeping again. "He only did that when he was drunk," she whimpered.

"Oh, yah?" sneered Algot. "You never heard the way he talked to me out in the barn. He always had it in for me! He was mean, real mean, to me!"

"Why didn't you ask me to celebrate with you?" asked Hjalmar, suddenly. "Why did you just pick on Far to celebrate with you?"

"Herr Good-goody! Ask you to celebrate! You must be joking! All you could think of to celebrate was go fishing! I mean, what an imagination, or I should say, lack of it! I knew what you'd say before I even asked. You never did want to do anything fun with me! There's never been any fun in you! You're more likely to report me to the police than have fun with me!" Algot's lips curled as he hurled the sneering words at his brother.

"Algot!" exclaimed Lisa, angrily. "Be quiet! How dare you!"

But to everyone's surprise, Hjalmar reacted differently. "Oh brother!" he said, getting up and putting his hand on Algot's shoulder, "If only you knew how much I admired you. You were my hero. I felt so sad when you got home, walked straight past me, ignored my efforts to do something special, just the two of us, grunted 'Hello kid' then went off with Far to the barn. If only I'd been there!"

Algot looked as though he was going to break down, but he quickly recovered himself. "Well, you weren't there Herr Goody-goody, and what good could you have done anyway? Once Far started to drink there was no stopping him. Anyway, I took Far's name calling without fuss, but when he hit me because I didn't give him my bottle to drink, I hit back. I hit hard. He hit hard. We hurt each other bad. He fought so bad I picked up my gun to threaten him, to try to make him stop, but he really came at me then. I tried to shoot up to warn him to stop just as he made that fateful lunge and pulled the gun towards him. It went off straight into his head. And that is the honest truth, so help me God, if there is such a thing as God!"

Into the dreadful silence that followed, Anders spoke, his voice sharp with disgust. "You can't expect us to harbor you here. Do you want to go now, or shall I call the police?"

"Please, don't let him go!" wailed Lisa. "He's my son! We'll hide him in the barn!"

Algot stood up. "Don't you try threatening me!" he yelled, shaking his fist at Anders. "None of you, do you hear! I call the shots!" he growled. "If you won't give me more food, I'm leaving." He grabbed the remaining *knäckerbröd* and cheese and stuffed it all in his pockets, which bulged alarmingly.

"I won't turn you in," said Anders, "but I don't feed criminals."

"Anders, be gentle," pleaded Anna, wiping her eyes. "Please, be gentle!"

"I am," said Anders. "But I don't like people who have no self control. Even my horses know I am a patient person. But a man not in control of himself is not worthy to be called a Finn!"

"Who said I want to be a Finn!" exclaimed Algot, angrily. "I've had my country! I've had your God! All those nice things they teach in church, none of it makes any sense. Life is just a big black hole of hate and horror!"

Unexpectedly, Algot walked over, threw his arms around his mother, and began sobbing uncontrollably. "Mor, I love you. I'm so sorry, so very, very sorry, I did this! I never meant to hurt you. Truly, I never meant to hurt Far. I just wanted him to think of me as a real man, not a kid. Honest, that's the honest truth. I'll give myself up in a few days. Promise. Just give me time."

Suddenly he lifted his tear stained face and gazed at all of them. Then without warning he fled from the house. The family stared at each other in stunned silence.

"Well, at least we know what happened," said Anders flatly, sitting back on his chair, and reaching for *knäckerbröd* and cheese that were no longer there.

"I wish I didn't," said Hjalmar. "Algot's story just confuses me."

"I think we need some sleep," said Anna, glancing at the grandfather clock which began to strike midnight. "We've had a long journey, and you've had horrendous grief. Even if we can't sleep, we should rest."

"You're right," said Lisa, wearily. "I haven't slept since we found Karl. Well, at least I know it wasn't suicide. That's what really worried me."

"Suicide!" gasped Anna. "Oh, no! Did you think it was that? That would have been much worse, if possible."

Next morning dark-ringed eyes suggested little sleep had been enjoyed by anyone, but they all protested they felt better. Anna and Anders discussed the situation alone, then with Tyra, and at breakfast announced their plan. "Anna will remain with you Lisa until we know Algot's next move. Tyra and I will go back to work, and we'll come back as soon as you know something."

Lisa protested she would be fine, but Hjalmar rapidly agreed to the plan. Privately, he told Tyra he knew his mother needed to be distracted, but he had a great deal of work on the farm that needed his attention. They all agreed to wait up to one month before they went to the police again. The parting later that day was difficult, but tearless.

Ten days later a police officer notified the family that the murderer of Karl Rådman had been found. His son Algot had given himself up. They would release Karl's body for burial.

Now shame overwhelmed the family. How could such a decent, respectable, law-abiding family publicly acknowledge they had nurtured a murderer? To Matilda's kind enquiries Tyra said her uncle had died suddenly, but refused all further discussion. It was impossible to talk about the unthinkable. How could she talk, to anyone? Was Algot right? Was life really just a big black hole of hate and horror? With Rolf Nilsson's senseless death, the horrors of war, Tobbe's death, all that red and white nonsense, people losing their names, and now this most dreadful crime, what good could there ever be in life? Was it merely an extension of the hell she had feared so much? Worse, where was God, if there was a god, in all this mess? But that thought frightened her most of all.

Anna Lall on her wedding day, 1900.

Johan Rådman, Anna Lall's father.

Anders Lall, husband of Anna, and Tyra's father.

Confirmation Class, Tyra 3rd from L, front row.

Collage of Tyra, her cousins and friends. Algot is on the L of top L photo.

A/B LITO-BJÖRKELL O/Y
(f.d. Julius Björkells Litogr.Tryckeri A.B.)
STENTRYCKERI, BOKTRYCKERI &
PAPPERSFÖRÄDLING

Telegr-adress:
LITOBJÖRKELL, VASA.
Telefon:
566.

Wasa,

På begäran få vi härmed intyga, att T y r a   L a l l
varit i tjänst å vår papeteriavdelning från den 1 september 1929
intill denna dag. Under denna tid har hon till vår fulla belåten-
het utfört åt henne överlämnade arbeten samvetsgrant och ordentligt
varför vi, då hon nu på egen begäran lämnar vår tjänst kunna på det
bästa rekommendera henne.

Wasa, den 15 april 1931.

O/Y LITO-BJÖRKELL A/B

A. Backman

Tyra's work reference.

Tyra aged about 20.

Tyra.

Tyra.

Karl Rådman.

Finnish Funeral Hearse.

Axel Östring in army uniform.

Elna Marie Hendriksson Östring,
1905–1932.

Östring family, L-R, Edit, Mor Anna, Johan, Anni Astrid, and Erik.

Östring family, back L Axel. R Elna.
Front L Mor Anna, and R Father Emil Hendricksson Östring.

Östring family home, Sorvich.

Part Two

Blood, Sweat, and Tears

Chapter 8

The Funeral

Tyra pinched herself to make sure she was awake and not in the midst of a gruesome nightmare. For more than two hours she had stared sightlessly at the dark, hulking shape of her father as he drove the familiar cart, listening to the mesmerizing, rhythmic, clop of horse's hooves. What, she wondered, was her usually quiet and now utterly silent father thinking? How did he feel about being the uncle of a murderer? For her, she was not merely cousin to this murderer, but a best friend of this wicked assassin. Despite the widening philosophical gulf between herself and Algot, she had remained very fond of him. She felt utterly betrayed by his behavior.

She and Anders had returned to Vasa, as planned, a few days after the frightening encounter with Algot. Now, with a providential light fall of snow to brighten the dark, desolate, leafless autumn countryside, they were returning for the even more desolate funeral of Karl. The trip, like everything in the last few weeks, was utterly unreal, a robotic, puppet-like existence where mind and body were suspended, disconnected, animated merely by the strings of necessity.

Anders had taken pains to take special care of his daughter for the trip, making sure she was warm and comfortable, and she was grateful. She wriggled fingers and toes, stretched arms and legs under the warm quilts packed around her. But the silence as they clopped along was crushing, a heavy burden highlighting the meaninglessness of life. She did not want to talk, but she was afraid of the silence that forced her to think. The death of Rolf Nilsson was senseless; the death of Tobbe was senseless; but surely this was the most senseless death of all. For a man to kill his own father—how could sense ever be made of that? And that man, that dreadful killer, was her own beloved cousin, the person with whom she had spent so many happy hours of childhood, the cousin she thought her special friend. Since the passionate night encounter with Algot her father had maintained a stony, stoical silence, deepening her heartache. She went to work. He went to work. She made food for them both. But they never talked except about the most basic necessities. Even her mother's frequent letters were about food preparation, Hjalmar's farm activities, and other trivia, and not about *the* issue. Friends and family were important to her, but it appeared they caused her deepest pain. It was not merely the sadness of it, but the weight of shame and the meaninglessness of life that overwhelmed her.

Suddenly Anders turned. "Are you comfortable, child? Are you warm enough?" he asked gently. Coming unexpectedly in the midst of her gloomy thoughts his use of the diminutive "child" brought tears to Tyra's eyes.

"Yah, thank you Far," she answered gratefully. "What about you? Are your hands warm?"

"Yah, they're good hands in good gloves. It's not that cold, and there's no wind. Come, sit a little closer, and we can chat."

His request surprised her, but gratefully Tyra inched close to her father, pulling the coverlets with her. She wanted to talk about the troublesome things of life, but she too resorted to trivia. "Do you get tired of holding those reins?"

Anders gave a quiet chuckle. "I've been holding reins since I was a boy!" he said. "I love working with a good horse. Once you know each other you hardly need to touch the reins. It's a great feeling. Come and try for yourself. There's plenty of room beside me, and the road along here is very smooth."

When she was settled, Anders passed the reins to Tyra. Immediately Blek slowed her pace. "See," said Anders, "how quickly she responds. She's testing you. She's getting tired, and would like a rest, so she's seeing if you will let her. She trusts you."

"Should we let her have a rest, Far? We've come a long way."

"Not in this weather. She needs to keep going, not so fast that we'll exhaust her, but to keep her warm and safe. It would've been good to have Möja with her, but Möja's getting too old for this long journey now. Unless for emergencies, like that awful trip a few weeks ago, I only use her for short trips around Vasa. I'm glad Lukas is willing to feed and keep an eye on her. Now, tighten up the reins a little, and see if Blek speeds up." To

Tyra's delight the mare immediately began to walk a little faster. "Good girl!" praised Anders. "You have a feel for horses. I should let you do this more often."

"I'd love that, Far. Do you remember when Tobbe and I used to clean Möja's stall? We both enjoyed doing that. Does Mor like to drive horses? I don't remember her driving."

"Interesting you ask. She knows how to drive the cart, but she doesn't enjoy doing it. Her hands are made for weaving and cooking, not for holding reins, or looking after horses."

"You know Far, I've been feeling so sad, but guiding this horse makes me feel better. I'm supposed to be in charge of her, but it feels as though she's showing me where to go, as though she's leading me. It feels great! My job has always been feeding the horses, but this is fun, really fun! Far, you said Möja's getting old. You're not thinking of getting another horse, are you?"

"Yah, I am, but I won't get rid of Möja. She's been such a faithful companion for me over so many years. We've walked many a long mile together. I just have to figure out how to feed and keep three horses."

"Oh, that's good to hear, Far. I know some people who—well—don't care about their animals and they—well—get rid of them."

"I'd ask a horse doctor to painlessly 'get rid of' Möja as you call it if she becomes ill and in pain. She's part of our family, and we need to care for her."

Anders leaned back, and took a deep breath. "Child," he said, patting Tyra's hand gently, "this business about Algot and Karl is about as bad and sad as it can get. I've never seen your Mor so distraught. I don't know what words I can say to make it better, and I'm not that good with words at the best of times, but I do know it's very hard on you as well as her. I know how much you loved Algot. And Karl of course was Anna's only brother. She had no sisters. Please know that I care and try to understand how hard it's been for you both."

"Yah, Far. Thank you." The gentle clopping of Blek's hooves soothed the silence. So her father *had* been thinking about the dreadful tragedy. "Far, I just struggle with the whole idea of death and hell." Tyra blurted out her deepest pain. "All that awful war stuff, and people hating each other."

After a pause, Anders responded. "You know what? So do I! What those preachers say doesn't make sense. I don't read the Bible like your Mor does. Frankly, I don't have time, and when I do I fall asleep! But this business of an everlasting hell of torment organized by a God who's supposed to be love itself must be nonsense. I figure either hell is nonsense, or God is."

"Oh Far! Don't you believe in God?" cried Tyra, apprehensively. With shock, she realized that she herself, during the dismal earlier silent hours of the trip, had wondered exactly the same thing—if there really was a God.

Anders reached over and again patted her hand gently. "Don't worry, child. I'm ready to toss out hell, but not God. I don't want a second hand preacher's religion. I like to think for myself. I think God will destroy wickedness, but I don't think he's going to keep hell going forever."

Her father's declaration was both comforting and bewildering. After her experience in *skriftskola* the idea of thinking for herself made Tyra anxious. "I wonder if I'll ever see Algot again. I couldn't even say goodbye before he was out into the night! It was so dark, and he was so alone. That's what really bothered me, his being so alone in the dark. But then, is it wrong for me to think about him, to care about him, a wicked murderer?"

"Of course you can think about him! He's a person, no matter what he's done. You'll see him again. He'll have time in prison for his deed, probably five to ten years. But then he can get on with life. And child, we've all done stupid things. That's one thing I can agree with those preachers about—there's no such thing as a perfect person. We all need God to forgive us. Just some mistakes are a bit worse than others, and hurt a lot of other people. Well, that's what I think, but who knows what God thinks!"

Tyra gasped. "Ten years! He'll be an old man by then!" she exclaimed.

Anders chuckled, despite the gravity of the topic. "Older, but I hope wiser. And thirty is not too old to start decent living. He's been a headstrong young colt up to now, but despite all his rough talk that awful night, I sensed a real change in him. No doubt he's been doing some very tough thinking wherever he's been hiding these past few weeks. But it's very hard on his mother. And we all worry what work he'll do when he gets out of prison. People are not kind about employing ex-prisoners, and he clearly doesn't want to work on the family farm."

"I think Hjalmar will help Aunt Lisa," suggested Tyra. It was easier to talk about him, than Algot's seriously uncertain future.

"You're right. Hjalmar is very different from his brother. I think he'll quickly learn to manage the farm. What's more, he'll be able to get out of army training to help his mother."

"Oh Far! I never thought of that. But of course, he was about to go into the army."

"He was. Well, this might be one good thing that comes out of this miserable business. Algot was right about the army teaching men to kill. But he was not right to buck against authority. Learning good discipline never hurt anyone. But sadly, the army also taught Algot to use alcohol, and it's my opinion that stuff was the real murderer of Karl. It just shows you, even when there are laws against it, if people want grog they get it! It's wicked stuff!"

"That's what I think!" exclaimed Tyra. "I'm so glad you don't get drunk, Far. Yet many of my friends think vodka makes a man a real Finn! I don't understand why a man has to behave stupidly to prove he's a man. Can you explain that?"

"I can't," replied Anders, angrily. "I used to occasionally have a small drink with friends to be sociable. It was easier to do that than have them mock me, I'm ashamed to say. But when I saw what Karl did to your mother after that barn burnt down and his neighbor died, I vowed I'd never drink again, and I haven't. Some day you'll marry, child. Please take this advice from your Far. Make sure he's a real man, who who doesn't poison his brain with drink."

Tyra gave a short, hollow laugh. "I'm not going to get married, Far. There aren't any decent boys around. Like Tobbe, they all got killed in that awful Red and White war. But one thing for sure, if prince charming ever does come along, and he drinks he won't have any chance with me!"

"I remember when I met your Mor," said Anders, softly, nostalgically, after a pause, as he stretched himself to get more comfortable. "Wow, was she beautiful! Incredibly beautiful. And kind. I never thought she'd even look sideways at a mere cart driver like me. At church she was always surrounded by a ring of admiring men. But she ignored them all. The fact that she was up there in Oxkangar and I was hard at work in Nikolaistad did complicate things. I met her when your Morfar ordered new roofing for his barn. No one else wanted to make the long trip to Oxkangar, but I was young and adventurous and willing to go. It was amazing how often after that I managed to find reasons to make the trip. I almost begged people to give me orders to go there. After a while my friends twigged there was a girl I was interested in, but how could I tell them I was interested in her but she hadn't even seen me! I spent lots of time talking to Karl about farm things I knew nothing about and had no interest in, even though I grew up on a farm, just to get to know Anna.

Karl wasn't my sort of man, but I tried to make friends with him, even though he thought I was a joke. I guess he knew it was Anna and not him that I was interested in! Then one day I heard Anna tell her mother she wanted new shoes. When no one was looking I found her wooden pattens by the door and measured them, then bought her a pair of black leather shoes, really expensive ones. I told the shopkeeper they were for my sister, and we discussed amazing things like fashion and style that I knew nothing about. Then I took those shoes to Oxkangar. But how was I to give them to her? Finally, I just gave her the box and said 'You might like these' and ran off to talk to Karl. Even in those days he liked to drink, and I didn't, and he made fun of me and joked about what he called my 'girlie' ways. I was leaving the farm later that day without even saying goodbye to Anna, when suddenly she was at the gate to meet me. I tell you, I pulled hard on the reins! 'These are beautiful shoes, Anders,' she said. 'I don't know how you knew I needed some. Is it true what Karl says, that you don't drink?' I was so surprised, and embarrassed, that I couldn't say a word. All Finnish men are supposed to drink, and I thought she was laughing at me, like Karl did. 'Please be honest,' she said. 'Well, no, I don't drink, not like most men. I like to use my brain,' I somehow said. I felt so foolish. She just stood there looking at me, real strange like. And then she suddenly exclaimed, 'I'd really like to see more of you!' I blurted out 'Thank God!' And we married two months later."

Tyra leaned over and laid her head on her father's broad shoulder. "My mother was a lucky woman!" she said softly.

"Not sure about that," said Anders with a quiet chuckle, "but I certainly was a lucky man." And he gave a deep contented sigh.

With a surge of understanding, Tyra recognized she had found what gave meaning to her father's life. The love between her parents was deep and tender. But... how could that ever be for her? Where could she find love like theirs?

They continued in silence, a silence no longer oppressive. The snow lightened their path, and a slender moon rose over the bare tree tops. Stars began to twinkle. Their journey had such a sad purpose, but Tyra realized with amazement she had learned more about her father on this trip than she ever had before. It was a huge, unexpected benefit. Suddenly, in the distance a wolf howled, and a cloud passed over the moon. She shivered.

"Don't worry, child," said Anders, retaking the reins. "Wolves only attack the sick and weak. And we're nearly there. Just over that small rise

The Funeral 133

is the ferry. I wonder who's running it now. Algot was in the army for a couple of years. I can't remember who was there when we made the trip a few weeks back! I guess you'd say I had other things on my mind!"

Usually they had to wait for the ferry, as it ran on demand, not schedule. But tonight it was tied to the wharf on their side, ready and waiting for them. Anders recognized Olav the ferry man, and greeted him politely.

"Back for that dreadful funeral?" Olav said flatly. "Lisa asked me to wait. Said you were coming. Dreadful business. Terribly sad for the family. But that second boy's a good lad. He'll look after his mother."

"Very sad," responded Anders curtly as the ferry clanked into action. "Thank you for waiting, Olav." They made the short crossing in silence.

Anders paid Olav, giving him a generous tip. "Thanks for your help," he said. Olav protested about the extra money, but soon accepted. Few people argued with Anders' quiet dignity.

"It's so hard talking to anyone about it," said Tyra as they clopped the last two kilometers. "Impossible, really."

"No need to talk, and believe it or not, people will soon forget. Just be polite, because they mean to be kind, at least most of them do. Olav liked Algot because he gave him the ferry job. It's hard for him to talk, too. So many people have been hurt by this miserable tragedy."

"Heartache seems to spread much faster and further than happiness," observed Tyra, with a deep sigh.

"True, but look, there's the house!"

"Far, it's been so good talking to you. I don't think we've ever had such a good time together!" Anders turned and gave his daughter a smile straight from his heart. There was no time for anything more, as Hjalmar was running to meet them. He insisted on taking charge of Blek, and ushered them towards the house

For a few seconds the warmth of the farmhouse kitchen overpowered both travelers, but soon thick creamy potato soup, fresh rye bread, and cinnamon rolls that Anna had prepared were warming cold bodies back to normal. Lisa busied herself making coffee.

Hjalmar returned from attending to Blek, and Tyra was struck by his mature manhood. He sat beside her. "I have good news," he said.

"We can do with that!"

"Yah. But this is *really* good news, at least I think so. I've been given deferred army training. Apparently any time in the next ten years I could be called to do it if what they called 'my circumstances change', but meanwhile I can help Mor. They didn't say, but I suspect," and he lowered his voice, "the change in circumstances would be if Mor remarried."

"That *really* is good news. I mean, the no army training part," Tyra agreed.

"Yah, I'm really pleased. It was awful to see what the army did to Algot. Perhaps it would not do the same to me, but his reactions really disturbed me. It was strange, he was so keen to learn to use a gun, but I knew he was afraid to go into the army. Then after he was drafted every time he came home he was more angry, more wild, more unhappy. He never talked about what happened to him in the army, but if we asked him anything he would stomp off angrily. He became a chain smoker, and I could smell alcohol on him most of the time. Honest, I tried to be friendly, but he treated me so bad I just had to keep out of his way. I told Mor I thought the army was getting to him and she agreed. So I was pleased to tell her I didn't have to do training. I don't think I'd let it get to me like it did Algot, but it sure doesn't seem a fun place to be!"

"It must be a huge relief to you both that you don't have to do training right now."

"Yah, Mor stopped crying when I told her. And the good thing is winter's coming, when there's least to do around the farm. I'll have time to work out how to manage before things get busy. I've been going through Far's books, trying to work out what crops are most profitable. I know money isn't the only aspect of farming, but I need to know because I can't do everything well to start with. So my plan is I'll focus on the most lucrative to begin with, and then try other things."

Tyra looked at her 17-year-old cousin with respect. "Hjalmar, you've been doing so much thinking! You amaze me! Did you know Olav the ferryman was talking about what a good job you do?"

"Really? That's nice of him. He knew Algot well. They had a few arguments, but Olav was very patient with him. But I just think of Mor, and that makes me want to do my best."

Anna got up to place a fresh log on the fire. "I need to tell you something. Tomorrow they want black horses," she said apologetically to Anders.

He nodded. "That's good. Blek needs a rest."

"Of course," said Anna, "How foolish I am! I've been worrying that you would be distressed by having to use other horses."

"But anyway, do they want me to drive?" Anders asked, surprised. "Won't they have their own driver?"

"I'm so stupid!" cried Anna, with a wan smile. "I'm just so used to you being the driver I never thought the undertaker would have that organized. I've been doing the cooking so Lisa could make the arrangements. She's been so silent I didn't dare ask anything."

"The undertaker will have everything under control, so relax my dear woman."

A knock at the door startled them, until they heard Sonja's voice. Lisa and Hjalmar bumped each other in their race to open it for her. Hjalmar won. Sonja's arms were loaded with four large loaves of bread, while a bag bursting with two roast chickens dangled from one elbow.

"Brought something for tomorrow," she said.

"Sonja!" exclaimed Lisa. "You're too kind!"

"You never know who comes to a funeral," continued Sonja, stepping inside and dropping her gifts on the table. "I remember how much you helped when Rolf died. I also remember how much food people ate. Oh, my! Could they eat! I was so worried I'd run out, so here are things to help you relax. I've a batch of cinnamon rolls I'll bring in the morning."

Lisa threw her arms around her neighbor.

"That's good of you," said Anna. "I've made platters of *griser* with strawberry jam, they just have to be rolled in sugar. Some cinnamon buns will be wonderful!"

After Sonja left, Anna motioned Tyra to view the pantry. "I've done nothing but cook since you left," she declared, gesturing at plates of food on the shelves. "We could feed all Vasa!"

"Mor, this will be a big relief to Lisa tomorrow."

No one slept well, and all were up early next morning. Tyra was used to the sight of her parents and Lisa in dark clothes, but felt very conspicuous in the somber black dress and coat Anna had carefully prepared for her. She liked to wear bright, cheerful colors, especially red. When Hjalmar walked past and said, "You look good today, Cousin. Your dress matches your hair," she was embarrassed, although she knew he meant it kindly.

The undertaker with hearse arrived promptly at 8:30, just as the sun was weakly sending rays over the horizon. They could have used Blek after all, Tyra thought, as she saw the black horse pulling the white coffin heavily draped with black cloth. Blek would match the coffin. But after her father's comments about Blek needing rest, she was surprised to see Anders with his cart and Blek in harness, coming from the barn.

"It's much too cold for the family to walk. Don't want anyone slipping on ice today, do we?" he announced. Seeing her surprise, he added, "I'll take you to the church, bring Blek back to rest, then walk back to the church."

Lisa and Anna were grateful for the ride. It kept them from needing to speak to neighbors on their way to the service. "So many of them!" Lisa mumbled with embarrassment mingled with shame and anger. "Just gossips, all of them!"

"Maybe they care," said Anna. Lisa merely snorted.

The church was very familiar, but for the first time Tyra suddenly noticed the ugly set of stocks beside the entrance, brutal tools designed for malefactors. With horror she remembered there was a set of these same cruel instruments inside her own church porch. What sort of people were placed in that brutal device? she wondered. Wasn't church supposed to help sinners? Would anyone think of putting poor Algot there? Did there have to be a hell on earth as well as one after a person died? And where was Algot now? Was he thinking of them? He must be, she decided. Did he want to be with his family to say a last goodbye to his father, or was he glad to escape the ruthless comments of the people he had lived among all his life?

The hymns chosen were painfully gloomy. Someone was determined to ensure the occasion was as sad as it could possibly be. Later Tyra discovered the minister had made the choices. He told Lisa it was the most depressing funeral he had ever conducted, and decided the hymns should reflect this. The sermon had frequent disheartening references to the fate of those who committed great crimes, and tactless descriptions of the horrors of hell. If the family felt in need of spiritual comfort, which they surely did, they received none from the priest's words. The only time Tyra's emotional tension lifted was when the congregation sang the *Vårt Land*. She had vowed never to sing it again, but the familiar words transported her beyond her present misery. But even as she sang, she knew patriotism could never satisfy her longing for meaning in life.

The more she thought of Finland the more she wondered if the country was the source of her pain. Rolf Nilsson died because of her country's weather. Tobbe died because of her country's war. And her uncle Karl died, and her beloved cousin was banished, because of her country's perceived need of a large, well trained army. Love for her country was certainly not the answer to her deepest longings.

The Funeral

After the funeral, the graveside service was indecorously rushed, but no one complained because the cold was intense. The minister's formal invitation for people to return to the farmhouse for refreshments was unnecessary. The amen of the last prayer was barely uttered when the entire congregation hastily set off on foot for the Rådman farm. Tyra was grateful of her father's foresight in providing the cart for the family; it gave them space and privacy, although she knew she must face the comments of people while they ate. She wondered how her father managed to get the cart so promptly, then realized he had not been present at the graveside service.

Lisa set herself as mistress of the coffee pot, restricting her distress to platitudinous small talk that avoided painful discussion. In her agitation she spilt more coffee than she poured, but no one was too concerned. Hjalmar made himself responsible for keeping the fire burning much more brightly than needed, and gathered wood so frequently that he rarely faced the gossips. Anna's chosen responsibility was food, which left her little chance to speak to anyone. Anders decided the minister and undertaker (especially their horses) needed his undivided attention, and everyone else could fend for themselves.

Thus with horror Tyra found herself the target of the beady-eyed old ladies whose need to know the details of the death was insatiable. Her defense was simple. "I live in Vasa," she repeated over, and over again. "I was not here when Morbror Karl died." When they persisted she said, "You will have to ask someone else," and they, of course, were much too busy with other concerns to talk to the old scandalmongers.

Just when Tyra thought she could cope with the barrage of questions no longer, a young man in army uniform walked towards her. How completely inappropriate! she thought with fierce, irrational anger. Why should a soldier come to this funeral! Abandoning her hostess duties, she turned quickly and walked determinedly towards the hall, intending to take refuge in the bedroom upstairs. Unfortunately, the young man was persistent.

"Tyra!" he called. "Don't you remember me?"

"No!" returned Tyra disdainfully, "I don't!"

"Wait a moment, please," he pleaded, his voice urgent. "I want to tell you Algot and I were good friends and I'm so sorry."

The pain in his voice sounded genuine, so she stopped. "So you say," she said with icy politeness, turning to face him. Suddenly the memory of good times with Algot rushed over her. "Why, you're Axel, aren't you?"

"Yah. I'm sorry to come in uniform, but I've just been discharged. I had nothing else decent to wear."

"Oh. Oh, I see." Tyra could not bring herself to say his costume was acceptable.

There was an awkward silence, then Axel said, "It's very crowded here. You look tired. Is there somewhere we could talk?"

Tyra was about to say an adamant no. There were bedrooms, most inappropriate for a young man she hardly knew. And the barn? The big animals made it warm enough, but it was hardly suitable to be out there alone with this virtual stranger. Axel must have read her thoughts, because he said awkwardly, "I've left my horse in the barn. Hjalmar said it was alright."

"Your horse?" returned Tyra. "How far did you come?"

"I rode from Sorvist, near Nykarleby, early this morning."

"But . . . ! But that's almost forty kilometers away! You must have left very early!"

"I did, but Algot was a special friend."

"That's amazing. You must be the only person here because of Algot, and not his father."

"Possibly."

"Have you seen Algot since . . . since he did it?"

"Yah, I have. But can we go somewhere to talk?"

"The barn's the only place. Do you mind? I mean, it was where . . ."

"Not at all. I'm a farmer, you know, when I'm out of these clothes!"

Tyra led the way, feeling awkward and conspicuous. The sun, low on the horizon, was now shining brightly, and the clouds of the morning had drifted away. The barn was warm, heat from the cows doing a good job. Axel pulled out a bale of hay, and motioned Tyra to sit, while he got another for himself. Nearby, Blek whinnied for Tyra's attention.

"That your horse?" asked Axel.

Tyra smiled, a small, sad smile. "I don't usually talk to people in barns," she said awkwardly. "The only person I know who used barns for things other than farm purposes was Morbror Karl, and his purpose wasn't good. I remember when I was a very small girl, about my eighth birthday I think, we came here like we always did in summer, and there was a terrible thunderstorm, with lots of lightning. The farmer next door, Rolf Nilsson, was killed when his barn was struck by lightning and caught fire. Morbror Karl was very upset, and came out to this barn where he brewed *brännvin* and drank too much of it. When my mother and aunt tried to help him he hit my mother hard, very hard. I'll never forget her bruising. She thought I didn't notice how bad it was, but I did, I certainly did."

Axel was silent. He seemed oblivious of the horror story Tyra had just told him, and she was suddenly mortified she had shared such a painful family secret with this virtual stranger.

"Your neighbor's wife is Sonja, right," said Axel, deep in thought.

"Yah, but how do you know?"

"Well, she has a brother who was good friends with my family. His son Erik was good friends with my older brother, Johan." Axel stopped. Suddenly he looked down at his trousers, and said angrily. "Yah, I hate this uniform I'm wearing! Did Algot ever tell you what it was like in the army? All the time I was there I couldn't get my brother out of my mind!"

Tyra waited. When Axel remained silent she prompted, "Your brother?"

"Killed. Killed just before the battle of Tammerfors. He was on a train, and someone put a bomb under it. The beasts! He was only seventeen!"

"Why, I remember that!" exclaimed Tyra, surprised. "I was with Sonja when she got the news about him. She was very upset."

"Really?" said Axel, gently now.

"Yah, I got my mother to comfort her."

"Well, that's a surprise. We were so caught up in our misery we never thought other people might be sad about what happened."

"Axel, I'm sorry I was not friendly a while ago. It was silly really. I just felt I couldn't cope with another person asking stupid questions about Morbror Karl. And then you were wearing that uniform, and I hate everything about war, and I felt angry with you for coming and reminding me of Algot instead of my uncle. You know, Algot and I were good friends. Today everyone is talking about my uncle, but I keep remembering Algot, wondering where he is. I never thought that you too might have lost people in those awful wars. I was good friends with our next door neighbor, and he was killed in that Tammerfors battle too. We don't even know how he was killed. Tobbe and I grew up together. He was six years older than me. Very quiet he was, but very good to me. I miss him. But it must be much worse to lose a brother."

"Finland is such a small country every family must have lost a family member or close friend in that fighting. A civil war is the worst kind of war. And we perpetuate it by all this horrible army training! All this hatred! Did you ever talk to Algot about the army?"

"We never talked, but we noticed he was more and more unhappy. He became a heavy smoker, and we often smelt alcohol on him. We never said anything, because it's illegal, but we found out, after Morbror Karl died, that everyone in the army used it. I think alcohol was the real murderer of my uncle!"

"I agree! I must say Algot was worse than most of us. I sometimes drank some *öl*[1] to join in with the others, but it never seemed right, and I was ashamed. But Algot used vodka, and used it often and as much as he could get. I tried talking to him once, but we came to blows and I never tried again."

"What, you mean he hit you?"

"He was drunk, and I was a fool for trying to talk to him then. Don't be upset with him. No one is normal when they're drunk!"

"Yah, I saw that with Morbror Karl. But it's a disgrace people use that stuff even when they know it's illegal!"

"Being illegal is not the issue! Did you know there have been more arrests for drunkenness since they brought in that prohibition law? There are so many hurting people in our country, so many families and friends torn by the wars and fighting, all that Red and White stuff, and yes, all the language disputes! Alcohol is our traditional way of dealing with pain."

"Shame on us!" retorted Tyra. "We're mad, making more pain to kill pain!" She jumped up defiantly.

"Anyway," responded Axel, after an awkward pause, "what I wanted to say to you was I don't think Algot is such a bad person. I hope that won't shock you. Did you know he came to us after he did it? I hid him in our barn for two days and he did a lot of talking, when I dared go to him. He told me he would never, ever drink any form of alcohol again, that he knew what it had made him do. He was so ashamed of what he had done, although at first I thought he was just plain angry with everyone. He also talked about how miserable he'd been in the army. He talked about his father, lots. Did you know Algot thought his father didn't value him? Algot's not the farming type. He knew his younger brother was much better on the farm, but every time he tried to talk to his father about doing something else his father just sneered at him, even when he got that job on the ferry. He claimed his father often told him he would never be

---

1. Beer

The Funeral

good at anything. Of course, I don't know if that's true, but he certainly believed it. He was very interested in selling things, and good with carpentry stuff in the army. We often got him to fix things for us. He was envious of your father who took his father's produce and sold it in Vasa. He often said he wished Anders would offer him a job. He even said he wished he could learn weaving from your mother! Yah, he talked about you. Yah, he talked about you a lot." Axel suddenly stood and walked rapidly around the barn, as though there were things he wanted to say, but didn't dare. "Yah, he talked about you often. He admired you. He isn't such a bad person. Just a really mixed up man. I'm sure he'll do the right thing when he gets out of prison."

Tyra returned to her hay bale, and sat down. "Thanks," she said, softly.

"Oh, by the way, I nearly forgot! How crazy can I be! Forgetting the reason I wanted to talk to you! Algot gave me a letter to give you." Axel stopped pacing, then sat down hurriedly, pulled a crumpled piece of paper from his pocket, and handed it to Tyra. She stared at him, and for a few moments could not speak. Axel stood up, awkwardly holding out the paper.

"Did . . . did he know you would . . . would come to the funeral?" she stammered when she controlled herself.

"He asked me to come, and I promised," Axel replied, looking down. Tyra took the note and read it, wiping stray tears from her eyes.

> "Tyra, I hope you can understand. I am so dreadfully sorry, dreadfully, dreadfully sorry. I wanted so much to please Far. I never hated him, but I thought he hated me. Give my love to mor. I am going to think about that god of yours when they lock me up. I hope I'll be a better person when I come out. Algot."

Tyra folded the note carefully, handed it back to Axel, and wiped her eyes. Suddenly she was very aware of Axel's eyes intently focused on her. They were very blue, and very piercing. "We should go in," she said, blushing self-consciously, mortified that Axel would notice her embarrassment. She dropped her gaze from Axel's face, as a confused jumble of ideas rushed through her mind.

"I shouldn't be out here. I feel foolish talking with you. I'll go in to the house on my own, and you follow later. Please talk as though you've been looking after your horse."

"Of course," said Axel, pocketing the letter, and suddenly grinning mischievously, his bright eyes twinkling. "We can do the rest of our talking in the house. But I didn't think you'd want me giving you that letter in front of those old busy bodies!"

"Why not?" exclaimed Tyra defiantly, as she jumped up and almost ran from the barn.

Chapter 9

Axel

TYRA LEFT THE BARN in undignified haste. Such a strange idea had taken possession of her that she dared not stay a moment longer. Axel's behavior was—well, not what she expected. Could it be, perhaps, was it possible, maybe, that he had come to the funeral not just because he had promised Algot he would? After all, he could have posted her the note from Algot. Eighty kilometers on horseback just to give her a letter? The more she thought, the more crazy this idea seemed, unless, maybe, he had another reason for coming. And that reason, she had the strangest feeling, which she hardly dared admit to herself, was that he wanted to see her. Everything he had said and done was perfectly correct. She had no reason to be embarrassed in the slightest, not really. But—she could not get rid of the astounding thought that his presence at the funeral was not for her uncle, not for Algot, but for her. She walked around the barn twice to try to rid herself of the preposterous idea, but that just brought memories of his appearance at the church in Vasa, awkward and alone. On that occasion she had angrily believed he was just hungry, that he came merely for food. Perhaps he was—? Suddenly the thought that someone might see her walking aimlessly around the barn sent her running quickly to the house.

Crossing the farmyard in the cold but sparkling air restored her poise. She assured herself that her foolish thoughts were unfounded, and had a course of action planned by the time she reached the farmhouse door. This plan could prolong her discomfort, but it might also clarify things, and clear her mind from preposterous ideas. She went straight to her mother.

"Mor, you'll never guess who's here! Remember Algot's friend Axel? He visited us once or twice in Vasa. This morning he rode all the way from Nykarleby to come to the funeral. Right now he's in the barn attending his horse, but it wouldn't be good for him to ride back tonight. It's already dark. Do you think Aunt Lisa would let him sleep here?"

"Axel? Oh, yah, I remember him. The army friend, wasn't he? I remember when he came to our home alone and hardly said a word! What a surprise that was!" Anna nodded thoughtfully. "I'll talk to Lisa, but perhaps you should introduce them."

"He'll come inside soon, after he's finished attending to his horse," replied Tyra, as Anna hurried off with yet another empty platter. It was amazing how much grieving people could eat, they both thought.

Tyra was puzzled to realize, as she waited for Axel to appear, that talking with him had lifted the burden of gloom that had pressed so heavily on her over the past few weeks. The meaninglessness that had enveloped her since Karl's death, that made her question life itself, was drifting away like morning fog. Axel had put a great deal of effort into coming to the funeral, simply because he promised his friend he would. That meant he appreciated Algot, in spite of the dreadful thing Algot had done. Maybe there were other reasons, those reasons she hardly dared articulate, but the sudden realization that a good person could appreciate an apparently bad one, brought a whole new dimension to her thinking. People were not just bad Red or good White, law abiding citizens or wicked criminals. Her father's insistence that Algot could start life again when he was released from prison now seemed a real possibility. She had no idea how to thank Axel, but she could at least thank God for sending him to her.

When Axel came in, after what seemed a long time for the waiting Tyra, she quickly asked him to meet Lisa.

"Actually, we've met before," he said, shrugging, "but she probably won't remember."

Tyra nodded, thinking it would be natural for Algot to bring his friends home. "Well, still talk to her," she insisted.

"If you like," said Axel, shrugging again.

"I'd like you to meet one of Algot's friends," said Tyra, uncomfortably aware of Axel's undesirable army uniform, but still ushering him to her aunt who sat mournfully alone beside the coffee pot. Lisa blanched at the word "Algot" but quickly regained her composure.

"Yah, I remember you!" she said, looking up with a slight frown and gazing steadily at Axel. "But I can't remember your name."

"This is Axel," began Tyra, and he finished, "Östring. I visited you about a year ago."

"Ah, yah. Now I remember," responded Lisa. "Actually, it was more than a year ago, because Algot took you fishing. Right? So it must have been the previous summer."

Axel laughed. "He did indeed. Remember the first day when we caught nothing? We were out all day in the sun, and came home burnt and sore, with nothing to show for it! Algot was very grumpy about that. But the next day really made up for it! We could hardly get the boat to shore we had so many fish!"

The strain lines across Lisa's face relaxed, and she gave Axel a wan smile. "We ate fish for weeks after that! We had so much smoked fish Algot suggested I take some to the market. Algot loved doing that."

Axel nodded. "See what I told you," he said, turning to Tyra triumphantly. "Algot enjoyed selling things."

"Really?" said Lisa, her eyes wide. "We never thought of that. Karl always said he just wasn't much use around the farm. He'd get very frustrated with him, I'm afraid. They had some dreadful arguments."

There was an awkward pause, and Axel began to walk away. Tyra took a deep breath. "Aunt," she said, "Axel rode here from Nykarleby very early this morning. Would you mind if he slept here tonight because it would be a bit much for his horse to go back tonight."

"From Nykarleby!" exclaimed Lisa. Axel stopped, and turned back towards her. "Of course you must stay! It'll be no trouble at all."

"Thank you," said Tyra and Axel together.

With conspicuous lack of sensitivity, the heartbroken guests began leaving as the food showed signs of running out. Lisa and Anna were exhausted, relieved to see them go.

Tyra noticed the weariness of her mother and aunt and offered, "What would you like me to cook tonight? I don't know about you, but I haven't eaten since breakfast, and I'm hungry."

"We've plenty of berry jam," said Anna. "Do you want *plattar* or porridge with it? We have enough eggs for pancakes."

"Tyra makes awesome *plattar*," said Hjalmar, overhearing, so pancakes it was.

Around the table, as the pile of pancakes diminished regularly and Anna and Tyra were kept busy replenishing it, Axel told funny stories from army life, including some about Algot. Hearing "the murderer" spoken of so normally helped the family relax. Yes, he was undoubtedly a criminal, but he was also a person.

"He volunteered for kitchen duty," Axel began. "Most of us hated it. You know the saying, 'women work inside and men work outside'. But Algot turned cafeteria duty into a sought-after job. Soon everyone was offering to be a kitchen hand. He'd quietly fill his pockets with small amounts of special food. Things like cheese, which was rationed to a slice a meal (well, that's what we claimed!) That's how I tasted tomatoes. They were making one of those enormous pots of nameless, tasteless army food, and some of these things called tomatoes were thrown in. Algot tasted a piece and liked it, and brought one out for me to try. I asked around how to grow them."

"Sounds like stealing to me," said Lisa, sourly.

"No, anyone on kitchen duty could eat what they liked. The army knew most of the men hated that job. But Algot not only shared extra food with us, he was a good mimic. He'd have us doubled in laughter when he parodied the officers and their eating habits. Trust me, we all loved him."

"I'm glad," said Tyra.

Axel began laughing. "I remember one of the funniest things he did! Algot volunteered for extracurricular activities, anything to get out of army routine. The captain or whoever would say 'We need . . . ' and up would go Algot's hand. Well, once, when he wasn't listening, he put up his hand to clean the officers' latrines. He got huge guffaws about that from the rest of us. But the last laugh was on us. Algot took his time about this detested duty, all day in fact, and while we slogged away at cross country marches, exhausting ourselves, he cleaned those latrines to perfection. He was a fussy person, always did things very carefully and neatly. Somehow he even found some lavender stuff and sprinkled it liberally around those stinking latrines. The unit commander was so pleased with his efforts that he gave him a huge carton of cigarettes, as well as, you'll never believe, a bunch of cornflowers! Algot used those cigarettes to get the rest of us doing his chores for weeks afterwards! But here's the funniest bit! The commander gave Algot his cigarettes after he'd inspected the latrines. What he didn't know was Algot had emptied the yuck onto ground behind the officers' barracks. There were flower beds there, so it was easy to sneak the yuck into them. I tell you, those flowers really grew! Of course the officers had no idea what had happened, but honestly, on a warm day that area stunk! Those officers wouldn't have dared open their windows at night!"

"Sounds like Algot," said Hjalmar, chuckling. "He liked doing pranks around the farm too, but Far wasn't very pleased about that. I think they were just too alike!"

"I must tell you," added Axel, laughing so hard he had trouble finishing his story, "the army even got a plumber in to try to work out where the stench was coming from, but no one discovered the reason!"

After breakfast next morning, as the sun was rising, Lisa suggested Hjalmar give Axel and Tyra a tour of the farm. After the cold of the funeral morning, the weather remained good, and the light fall of snow had almost melted away. But to Lisa's surprise Hjalmar quickly returned.

"Back so soon?" she said. "You aren't a very good host!"

"I'm not needed," smiled Hjalmar, rolling his eyes knowingly. "Tyra knows this place as well as I do."

"But . . ."

"Have you ever felt superfluous? Those two can see only themselves!"

"Oh!" gasped Anna. "Really? I never thought of that!"

Tyra took two hours to show Axel the farm, at least twice as long as Anna expected. When she and Axel returned, to Anna's amusement, they were earnestly discussing crop rotation, and Axel's planned experiments with tomatoes. Tyra had never eaten a tomato, so Axel extolled its flavor and nutrient value. "I'm sure Far would be interested," she said as they entered the kitchen.

"In what?" enquired Anders, raising his eyebrows.

"Oh, Axel was telling me about a new kind of fruit he's planning to grow, tomatoes. They're very nutritious, and taste good too."

"Aren't they something that grows around the Mediterranean?" asked Anders, skeptically.

"Yah," agreed Axel. "But I've discovered if you grow them under glass they'll ripen in Finland in summer."

"The boy's innovative, at least," thought Anders. "Good luck with your efforts," he said aloud, doubtfully.

Lisa observed her niece closely. The normally quiet Tyra had a new glow about her. "Axel," she said, "are you in a hurry to get home, or could you stay another night? I think you're good for the morale of all of us."

"I can stay tonight," said Axel, very quickly, glancing at Tyra. "I'll just have to work a bit harder when I get home." He laughed cheerfully.

Anna and Anders exchanged looks.

While the family ate their midday meal of thick slices of rye bread, fat rounds of cheese, some potato pancakes that Anna had quickly prepared served with apple and lingonberry sauce, jugs of fresh milk, a few left overs from the funeral feast, plus the inevitable coffee, Hjalmar began reminiscing about Lall family summer visits.

"We kids loved going egg hunting," he said to Axel. "I wasn't much use. I liked roosters. They were pretty, and I loved chasing them. But Tyra was good with hens, and amazing at finding nests. Far gave her some chicks. Tyra, what did you do with them?"

"Looked after them and let them lay eggs!" smiled Tyra. "And let them have more chicks. Remember, Morbror gave me a rooster? I had quite a flock. At first Far sold the eggs for me, but when I began to sell Mor's rugs in the Vasa central market, I got a friend to sell my eggs."

"Our hens always stopped laying in winter. They were too much trouble to bother with," commented Axel.

"Oh, many people think that, but they don't treat their hens right," said Tyra. "They keep them cooped up. But to get hens to lay well they need plenty of space, and lots of greens to eat. Even in winter I made sure my hens had space, and I'd look for weeds for them. I didn't have enough eggs to sell in winter, but we had plenty for our family. That's why I learned to make *plattar*!"

"She sometimes even brought her hens into the house to give them space!" groaned Anna.

"But that's impressive. It makes sense," said Axel, nodding his head admiringly. "I should try that."

"Axel," said Anders, standing and stretching, "if you've finished eating, would you like to help me with the horses?"

"Sure," said Axel, jumping up. "I'll check that my horse is in good shape for the trip home. My mother wouldn't be happy if she wasn't, because she helped me buy her. I'll leave early tomorrow, so best I look now."

Hjalmar ran after them, leaving the women with the dishes. "As always, men work outside and women work inside," grumbled Anna, gently.

"Ah, well, washing up for just our family is a dream compared with what we did yesterday," declared Lisa, her hands deep in suds in the wooden tub. "I'm so glad you were here. I don't know how I would have coped without you!"

"How can people be so hungry when they're supposed to be grieving!" grumbled Anna. "I dreaded foolish questions, but hardly anyone spoke a word to me!"

"Me either," said Lisa gloomily. "They'd shove their empty cups at me then go off and talk to their friends."

Tyra listened, but quietly gazed out the window towards the barn. Anna and Lisa watched her and smiled. "Let me cook tonight," announced Lisa, to Anna's surprise. "We've plenty of potatoes and chicken left over from yesterday, and I have big crocks of pickled beetroot in my larder. That should keep the men happy. Oh, and we still have some of Sonja's cinnamon buns, so dessert's sorted."

The men were talking animatedly when they re-entered the kitchen. The women sat silently knitting, Lisa wrapped in a sad reverie, staring into space, her work often falling into her lap unattended.

"Good smells in here," declared Axel.

"This young fellow knows a thing or two about farming," declared Anders, nodding at Axel.

Axel laughed. "Anders gave me a horse lesson. I sure didn't know much about them before! Mor Anna will be impressed!" He paused, then grinned, "Not that she knows much about horses herself!"

Lisa rose and bustled in the kitchen, Anna quietly assisted her, and the men sat beside Tyra.

"Tell us about your family," urged Anders. "You're here at this dreadful time, and know our troubles, so we should know a bit about you."

Axel took a deep breath. "Not much to tell," he said. "There's not much left of my family."

Tyra looked up.

"Tragedy?" said Hjalmar.

"Nothing like yours," responded Axel. "Just sadness." After an uncomfortable silence, he continued. "You know about Johan, my oldest brother, the one your neighbor Sonja knew. He was killed in that senseless train bombing during the so-called war of independence. I was only eight or nine when he died. Actually, I'm the second youngest child of my mother, but the next son in the family when that tragedy happened. There were five of us originally. My mother died when I was very young, about two I think. My younger sister Edit was just a tiny baby." He broke off.

"That would be tough," said Tyra, breaking an awkward pause.

"I can't remember my mother," resumed Axel. "She died of what we call the coughing disease. It must've been hard for her to cope with five children when she was sick, but we didn't understand. My father, Emil Hendriksson, had a farm in Sorvist, near Nykarleby. But why tell you that? You know that's where I live.

"My father couldn't cope with the farm and five children, well, actually only four when my Mor died, so he remarried soon after. My new mother, Anna, was kind to us, but she wasn't my mother. Everyone commented how neat and tidy and capable my mother, the late Johanna Backman, was. But with Mor Anna, our house was always—well—a mess. Of course, I was just a boy, so I didn't notice things like that, but my sister Elna did.

"My second oldest brother Albert died before I was born. There was something wrong with him, I don't know what, but Far told me he never talked, and he died before I was born, or perhaps when I was just a baby. Far told me he was seven years old when he died. When I was only about seven, two of my younger sisters died. That was in 1916. I'll never forget that year. It was terribly sad. My little sister Edit died, she was about six, and then Mor Anna's little girl Anni died two days later. They both died of the coughing disease. My older sister Elna, she's wonderful. She's like my mother, beautiful and kind. When she's at home our house is lovely. She cooks good food too.

"My new mother had three babies. Anni Astrid who died was the eldest. Erik's the second oldest, he's four years younger than me. He's at home now, he and Johan. (Yah, another Johan. My father wanted to remember my brother, and Emil Johan number two was born about the time my oldest brother died, so Far said he was to be called Johan, not Emil. I call him John.) Erik's fifteen now, coming on sixteen. You remember when the law came in that everyone had to go to learning school?"

Tyra looked up, and Lisa said, "That's when things went wrong with Algot!"

"Well, when that law came Mor Anna was keen all her children go to school. Our village was so small it didn't even have a *folkskola*. Anyway, Mor Anna talked Far into letting Elna go to Nykarleby, where there was both a *folkskola* and a learning school, with Erik and Johan Two. Elna's just beautiful. She's so kind and capable. But it must have been hard for her caring for her little brothers. She's still young herself. Elna says she's well, but I often hear her coughing.

"I never knew whether Far was just sad so many of his children and first wife died, or whether he too got the coughing disease, but anyway, he got sick himself. He died four years ago. So there you are. My family is my older sister Elna, stepmother Mor Anna, and two half-brothers, Erik who's sixteen, Johan who's eleven, both still at school, and myself. Now everyone lives at home, and a neighbor takes the boys into Nykarleby for school.

"When Far died Mor Anna sold off most of the farm so she could survive, but that's made a problem for me. I hope she's careful with the money. We still have the old family home, but it's more like a barn than a home. It's very big! Takes a lot to make it warm, and perhaps that's why so many of my family died from the coughing disease. I wanted Mor Anna to apply for me to get out of the army so I could support the family but she chose to sell the land. It's worked for her, but it means now I don't have a farm.

"Yah, selling the farm was good for her, but terrible for us boys, because now we have no inheritance. But I've saved all my army allowances, and I'm looking around, and there's a little village not far from home, Brännon we call it, that has a house for sale with some land and I think I can get it. When I get back home I'm seeing the owner. If I can buy it, I'll start farming on my own, then maybe I'll have work for Erik and John when they leave school. That's my plan anyway." He sighed, and leaned back.

"Thanks for telling us," said Anders. "When you're in grief it's easy to forget other families have their troubles too. By the way, wouldn't government land reforms help you buy land?"

"Yah, probably, but there are lots of people wanting land now, so many! The big landowners know they have to sell, but they can be very tricky."

"How far is Sorvist from Oxkangar?" asked Hjalmar, a thoughtful look on his face. "Maybe I could visit you sometime."

"About 40 kilometers. Not exactly the trip a busy farmer, which you're going to be, could make too often. But you'd be welcome if you came. Any time."

"You could write," suggested Tyra helpfully, "if you want to keep in touch." Both men laughed.

"Writing's not my thing!" admitted Hjalmar.

Axel suddenly looked at Tyra. "I'm not much at writing, but if you wanted to write to me, I'd try."

Tyra blushed crimson. "If you write, I would answer," she said primly.

"Tyra has a fulltime job," said Anders, frowning. "I doubt she's got time for writing letters."

"You'd be surprised what women can manage if they really want to," observed Anna as she joined the group, her eyes twinkling. "But I came to tell you supper is ready."

Next morning, Axel was ready to leave by 7am. The weather was clear, but cold. A half moon lightened the landscape. Hjalmar and Tyra were up to see him go, but the older family members apparently needed more sleep. Tyra made sure Axel had plenty of rye bread and cheese to munch on the road, and Hjalmar offered a canteen of fresh milk. Axel mounted his horse without even offering to shake hands, but Tyra cheerfully waved him goodbye at the gate.

"How was it?" asked Matilda gently when Tyra retuned to work three days later. "Are your family well? Are they coping?"

"Yah, they're coping. My cousin will manage the farm fine. But you know, it's incredible how much food people eat at a funeral. I had no idea grief made them so hungry!"

"Free food!" declared Matilda, shrugging. "Some people turn up to every funeral!"

"Really?" exclaimed Tyra.

Matilda looked at her, and noted a far away look in her eyes. She was no longer withdrawn as she had been for the weeks leading to the funeral. "Tyra," she asked, "how old is your cousin? The one that's taken over the farm?"

"Hjalmar? Oh, just a boy. Seventeen. Just finished school. He's got out of army training so he can manage the farm for my aunt. We're very pleased about that."

"I see," said Matilda.

Matilda had attributed Tyra's recent refusal to attend any dances to grief at the loss of her uncle, but her continued rejection of dance invitations, despite a generally cheerful manner, made Matilda very suspicious that this cousin was something more than just a 17-year-old boy.

Two weeks later a letter, post marked Nykarleby, was waiting for Tyra when she arrived from work. Anna handed it to her with a grin. Tyra quickly pushed the letter in her pocket, and began to help prepare the evening meal as usual, determined to show no excitement. Anna whispered the news to Anders when he arrived home, but both refrained from comment. After they had eaten, and dishes washed and stacked in the dresser, Tyra escaped to the bedroom to open her letter. But what she saw utterly astounded her. With difficulty she read, but did not understand:

> *Tira I got hom. Hav sik cow. Mor is glad hors I road good. Erik helps do things. He fel don ice on skul steps but not hert. Spok to man at Brännon He wonts mor munny. I talk to him nice. Try to get him help me. He not lissen. He is landlord man. Not very nice.*

I talk tuff. I think I win him down. Mor Anna sad I not by my farm yet. Johan at skul. Hop yoo rite. Plese rite. Axel.

Tyra stared at the letter. How could she make sense of it? Suddenly, reading it aloud as though it were spoken, she began to understand. Clearly Axel could not spell, and his writing was primitive. This was embarrassing. Was he—normal?

Later that evening she spoke to her father, hoping he might help her understand. "Far, did you ever write to Mor? She lived in Oxkangar, and you lived in Solv, so did you write?"

Anna, working her loom on the other side of the room, threw her head back and laughed. "Daughter, in those days we all learned to read. That was the law and without reading we couldn't get confirmed, as you know. But no one was concerned about writing. As long as you could sign your name, no one worried about anything else. I could hardly read your father's letters his spelling was so bad! He only wrote one letter that I remember. Anyway, we got married quickly after I agreed to get to know Far. He gave me some beautiful shoes and I realized he was keen on me. I already liked him a lot, so we quickly decided."

This revelation amazed Tyra. "Far told me about the shoes when we were driving to the funeral. But Far, you read so well! I just love to hear you read. It's one of the things I loved when I was a child. I can't believe you can't write!"

Anders gazed thoughtfully at his daughter. "Most of my customers pay me on the spot, in cash or goods. I rarely write bills. If I need to do that, I get your Mor to help, or she checks what I've written. We started work young when I was a boy. My father was a blacksmith, like your mother's father, and like him he tried to do a bit of farming too. My Far was good to me. When I was thirteen he gave me a horse and let me start working on my own as a carter, but I still had to help him every spare minute I had. As soon as I could read, enough to satisfy the priest, I left school. I've taught myself to write since, enough to get by. Your mother helped and encouraged me."

"Why did you have to satisfy the priest?"

"Well, remember, the only reason to learn to read was to get confirmation. It didn't matter what the teachers said, I just had to prove to the priest I could read."

"But now, doesn't everyone have to go to learning school as well as the *folkskola*? That was only back in your time."

Anders laughed. "That's what you might think, young lady, but it isn't as simple as that. I mean, I'm not that old! For many country kids getting to school is still very difficult. There's often no learning school in their town, or even *folkskola,* and to go to school they have to find somewhere in a big town to live. That costs the family, and many families don't have enough spare money. These parents aren't bad, they simply can't do what the law says they must."

"That's not good!"

"Maybe, but it's a fact of life. Take that young Axel, for example. He told me when we were looking at the horses that he couldn't go to learning school. In fact, with all the health problems in his family, he didn't even finish *folkskola*. You remember he was only eight when his older brother died? Axel was the next boy in the family, and so he was forced to leave school when he was nine. That means he had only three years of schooling."

"Only three years? Really? He told you that?" There was relief in Tyra's voice.

"He did. Didn't you know?"

"No. But well, it might, well, explain some things."

"Like the fact that he can't write?"

Tyra blushed. "But he must be able to read well because I'm sure he said he'd been confirmed."

Anders chuckled. "He told you that, did he? Well, don't forget you were privileged, child. Not many youngsters, especially girls, get as good an education as you did. And for most farm boys they can't even see the sense of learning. Remember Algot, and the fuss he made about staying at school, foolish lad! But Axel got no choice."

"Thanks for explaining Far," said Tyra.

"And by the way, what exactly did that young fellow write to you?" asked Anders.

"Nothing much Far. He wrote about trying to buy a house and land in a village called Brännon. Remember he talked about that to us? He seems keen to start farming on his own, and being able to offer work to his brothers."

"And why do you think he's telling you all that?" asked Anders, raising his eyebrows and grinning.

"I don't know. Just something to write about."

"Oh, yah, right!" said Anders, and looked knowingly at Anna, who pursed her lips and nodded.

Axel

Tyra decided to take time before replying to Axel. Despite the flutters in her heart, she needed to think carefully what writing to him might mean, and what was suitable for her to write if he was just lonely. She wanted to be friendly, but not too friendly. After a week of careful thinking she wrote:

> Hello Axel. I hope you are well, and the sick cow is better. Keep trying to buy the land in Brännon. I am glad your brother is at school. Did you go to school for long? I think school is important. I was very lucky. My parents helped me and I stayed at school till I was eighteen. I really liked learning Swedish literature. I enjoy reading. Tyra.

She read and re-read her composition. Finally, she crossed out "I think school is important." And then, after carrying the letter around in her pocket for another week, and feeling very self-conscious, she mailed it.

Two weeks later she received another letter, this one written in different handwriting:

> Tyra, thank you for your letter. It is good you like reading. My brother Erik also likes reading very much. He is good at school. He says he would like to talk to you about Swedish literature, and hopes he can meet you some day. I don't know much about that literature stuff. I got Erik to help me write this letter. I hope it is better than my first one, and you can understand it better. I did not have much time at school. When my brother was killed my father needed me to help him on the farm. I was nine years old. Erik says he will help me learn to write, but I don't think I have time for that. I have done more talking to that man in Brännon and he finally says he will to sell to me. I will give him the money I saved from my army pay, and then work for him for one year. He wanted me to work two years, but I won that discussion. I think he might know I did not have much time at school, and he thinks he can cheat me easily. Axel.

Tyra did not have to think long about a response to this letter.

> Axel, I don't mind if you can't spell very well. I think it is better for you to write to me yourself, and don't get Erik's help. Erik will be busy at school. Please write in your own way. Tyra.

She was about to seal the envelope when she suddenly took the letter out, unfolded it rapidly, and added:

> *I am very glad I could spend so much time at school. But book learning is not as important as who we are inside. Do you read? I love to read, and to learn new things. You can read and learn new things yourself. I would like to hear more about the farm in Brännon. Tyra.*

With quick strides she walked to the post box, and pushed the letter in the slot before she could change her mind.

Tyra waited, and waited, for a reply. Christmas, New Year came and went, and nothing was heard from Nykarleby, or Brännon, or Sorvist. Matilda noticed her work mate was more quiet, but questions about the cousin in Oxkangar just made Tyra smile, with assurances that he and his mother were coping well. Privately, Tyra was anxiously reorganizing her feelings, deeply embarrassed that she had made a serious mistake about Axel's attitude to her. After all, they had really only met once under very strange circumstances, and the one thing she had never thought to ask him was if he had any friends. Anna and Anders wisely refrained from comment. Then late in February a short note arrived.

> *Tyra, sory I hav not ritten. I hav bene bisy at Brännon. The howse and barn neded lots of werk. I am cumming to Vasa nex month to get things for the howse. Can I see you. Axel.*

He was answered by return mail, rather more hastily than wisely, Tyra thought, as soon as she posted it, along with an invitation to stay in Rådhusgatan while he visited Vasa. Tyra wished he had given some dates, but she understood his visit would be dependent on weather, and probably not occur before April. Anders made deliveries contingent on weather conditions, so this was not new to her. But on the second of March, when snow was still thick on the ground, Axel surprised everyone by arriving in Nykarleby by bus, wrapped in a thick sheep skin jacket, and carrying a very small satchel. Tyra was at work when he knocked on the Lall door, and Anna greeted him cautiously. Standing awkwardly on the door step, clutching his tiny satchel, he said he had come to town to order supplies for the building and repair of his house in Brännon.

"Doesn't Nykarleby have a building supply store?" asked Anna thoughtlessly.

"Yah, and so does Jakobstad. But I've looked there."

"How long are you here for?" probed Anna.

"Two nights. Does Tyra work near here?" Axel jigged from one foot to the other, impatiently.

Anna nodded to his question and wrote out the address of the Lito-Björkell company, along with directions to get there. Axel took the proffered paper, thrust his satchel at Anna unceremoniously, said, "Can I leave this here?" and abruptly strode off without saying goodbye.

When Axel walked into the *papeteriavdelning* department in company with Herr Backman, Matilda, though hard at work, was sharing funny stories about the antics of her younger siblings.

"There she is," smiled Herr Backman, pointing to the laughing Tyra. "I'll leave you to chat together."

Matilda stopped mid sentence, her mouth open. Tyra's face turned rich red, but her eyes sparkled with delight. "Axel! I didn't expect you!" she exclaimed.

"Tyra," said Herr Backman, turning at the door. "If you want to take tomorrow off work, you may. Axel explained he's here for only one day."

"Axel," said Matilda, her eyes open wide, "have you ever been to Oxkangar, and do you know Tyra's cousin?" Axel nodded, and stood awkwardly fingering his hat while Matilda doubled up with laughter.

"Thank you, Herr Backman," stammered Tyra.

Strange, but Axel never went near a building supply shop during his brief trip to Vasa, but he did walk around Vasa with Tyra (despite the snow and bitter cold!) discussing the best type of stove to install in a kitchen (she could only think of the one Anna had in Rädhusgatan), how big a good pantry should be (she estimated the size of Anna's), how much barn space Anders thought was necessary to house a horse (Axel had to wait for Anders to come home to have that question answered), and other building design features. His letters might have been brief, but he had no difficulty describing in great detail all he had done to restore his new house, and clearly was eager to obtain Tyra's approval. He also had good news.

"The house is sound, and the barn's in reasonable condition. But the property has only two hectares of land. It's been used to grow potatoes mainly. But I want to grow more crops. Two hectares is not enough to make a living from. I found some neighboring land, which looks pretty wild and unused, and discovered it's owned by the church. I visited the priest. He didn't seem too businesslike, but I offered to lease the land. He had to talk to the church warden and who knows who else in the hierarchy, but eventually they offered to lease me the land for 50 years! Well, actually that's what I asked for, although they hemmed and hawed about that and said it had to have bishop approval for so long. They finally told me the verdict last week, and I've signed a bit of paper. I pointed out it did not actually say I had use of the land for 50 years, but the priest said it was unlikely anyone else would want it, and as long as I use it properly I can have it. Now that gives me another ten hectares to work with, which will make a big difference. If I get the tomato growing to work, and have grain crops and potatoes, a cow and a few pigs or sheep, and chickens in the barn, I think it would work well. Does it sound like a good plan to you?"

"Why, yah," replied Tyra blushing, surprised he should want her opinion.

"Good," smiled Axel. "I was hoping you'd like the idea. And what do you think, Anders?"

"Me?" said Anders, hurriedly. "You don't have that much land to work with, but it could be enough. If Tyra's happy about the arrangement, I should be."

"I've just got to work off full payment over the next year, and then the place is mine. The chap I bought it from is tricky. I signed all the documents, but when I wanted to talk about starting work for him he said, 'Oh, we'll work that out later.' Then he came to me and said 'There's nothing for you to do over winter, so we'll start the work part of the contract in April and go till October, and then you can do the same next year.' I protested vigorously and said I had plans of my own, and a year was a year, not two six months. Finally, he agreed, I hope. I'll do logging work for him this month, and the same next winter, and hopefully by next March I'll be free. That's if he doesn't try something tricky again. I don't trust him, and I've now got the contract properly written up by a lawyer. But the lawyer says the working bit is unusual, and since he didn't put anything in writing he may be free to make his own arrangements with that. When I work for him I slog, and then with doing my own work at night, I'm exhausted. I'm too tired to think of writing," he grinned sheepishly. "But next time I come I'll bring some photos of my family."

"So you're coming back, are you?" grinned Anders. "Are you invited?"

"Husband!" exclaimed Anna.

Axel returned to Nykarleby on the early morning bus. He promised Tyra he would visit again "soon", and write more often. As he climbed aboard the ancient, rattling vehicle, he took both Tyra's hands and shook them for much longer than needed. Then, pressing an envelope into her palms, he said, "Elna said I could give you this. She made it for you."

Once the bus had left, Tyra opened the envelope. Inside was a beautifully embroidered handkerchief.

Chapter 10

Nykarleby

Tyra fingered the delicately embroidered handkerchief in her pocket. Of course it was not for use, but it was very comforting to feel it there. It confirmed Axel's serious intentions about his friendship with her, and that he had talked to his family and apparently gained their approval, or at least his sister's. Axel's arrival in her life just when she urgently needed support after the terrible loss of both her uncle and Algot conferred a significant spiritual quality to the friendship, and she strongly believed he had been sent by God. It indicated she must think, seriously. Clearly, Axel was hard working and steady. He was willing to try new things, and to learn as much as he could. She had not noticed whether he had any special interest in religious issues, but that was normal for most of the men she knew. She wished she could have talked to Algot to learn more about his friend, but of course that was impossible. She decided there was no point in discussing Axel with her parents or Matilda, as they did not know him any better than she did, and she must make up her own mind.

But after Axel's next visit Anders gave her a strong helping hand. "Tyra," he said, "we need to do some serious talking."

"Yah, Far."

"I've noticed you don't go to the dances any more."

"Yah, Far."

"So, we need to talk about Axel."

"Yah, Far."

"That young fellow has serious plans about you."

"Yah, Far."

"Don't say 'Yah Far' again! It's annoying! I want you to listen!"

"Yah, Far. I mean, I'm listening, Far."

"Good. Now, your Mor and I have done everything we can to help you have a pleasant life."

"And I appreciate that, Far."

"Good. You also have a very pleasant job with Herr Backman."

"Yah, Far, I mean, I do, Far!"

Anders shook his head. "This talk is meant to be serious, but you're making it funny! Your face is composed, but those soft grey eyes of yours tell me you're laughing! The point I want to make Tyra, is do you understand what being a small farmer's wife is like? There's no doubt Axel is hard working, and willing to try new things to make a living. He's a decent lad, although he *is* pretty young. Mor and I like him. But do you realize what you'll have to do on his farm? You won't be having pleasant days chatting with Matilda while you sit on a comfortable stool and pack pretty boxes of fancy paper. You'll have no time for dancing. You'll be out in all weathers, summer and winter, helping with animals and who knows what else. I doubt you'll ever have time to do weaving like your Mor does, or that embroidery you like. None of us has seen this Brännon or his house there. He showed us a photo of his family home and described it as very big, but what size is the Brännon house? Is it just a hut? What about water and lighting? Has he got a stove installed yet? He didn't last time I talked to him, and I don't know how he was doing his cooking and keeping warm. He's been pretty vague about what sort of a toilet he has. I think you could be in for some very rude surprises and..."

"Far, I *have* thought about all that. Honest. True, Axel has asked me to marry him, but he's waiting to get his affairs sorted so he can offer me a good home, as he puts it. As to his being young, I'm pretty sure I worked out that when you and Mor married you weren't even twenty, either of you, and Axel is well past that! To be really honest, the only thing I don't like about him is he smokes, but then you have a puff on your pipe in the evenings, and I don't know any man who doesn't smoke! I don't know why men want to smell bad, but they all seem to want to do it." Tyra paused, and smiled. "Far, you know his full name and his address, just like I promised you for all the boys I danced with! I promised you I wouldn't marry someone who drinks, and Axel doesn't except for the very occasional beer, and he insisted he would not drink even that if I was unhappy about it. I've never seen him drink at all. I've been proud to work for Herr Backman, because the wood and paper industries are very important to our country. But I also know that famers are essential, and

I'll be proud to help Axel. I'm healthy and strong. I hope God will let me have children, and you will let me take some books, or buy me some, so I can read if I ever do get time. Far, don't worry about me. The only thing I have worried about is I'll be a long way from you. I don't like that. Of course there's the bus, and I'll visit as often as I can, but as you pointed out, I'll have plenty to do helping Axel."

"Well, you do seem to have thought about everything. We just wanted to make sure. Life is tough enough without living in dream land!"

"Thanks, Far, for caring," replied Tyra, smiling broadly, those soft grey eyes twinkling.

"I always said you had a large dose of good Finnish *sisu* in your character! It will stand you in good stead on Axel's little farm. Axel is a plucky boy. And although he *is* young, he's been carrying the load of man in his family since childhood, and is very mature for his years."

"Thank you, Far."

The summer wedding, on the 2nd of July, 1931, was a simple and quiet affair, as was the custom and necessity of the times. Axel was 22 and Tyra a month off 25. Pastor Lindgren married them in the late morning, with Anders and Anna, Gunnel and Matilda, and Herr Backman in attendance, and, to Tyra's surprised delight, the whole Tobelius family was there too. Pastor Lindgren was full of affable bonhomie, apparently totally amnesic of his verbal and cane attacks on Tyra, but his presence made her nervous. Axel protested a little about going to a studio on the way home, but once there he was co-operative with the photographer. Anna provided a wonderful luncheon feast, even better, Tyra thought, than the usual Christmas fare, although she was excited and ate little. She discovered Elin Tobelius had done much of the cooking to help Anna. Such a good neighbor was a treasure. She was glad her mother would continue to have this good woman beside her, and hoped she would find good neighbors in Brännon. During the meal Axel whispered, "If you can cook like your mother, I'm a lucky man!" Tyra smiled. She was doing a lot of smiling these days.

Tyra's luggage was packed and the guests helped carry it to the nearby bus station. One piece exuded much cheeping: Hjalmar's wedding gift was a basket of chicks. The bus driver noted Axel's stiff new suit and Tyra's spotless white dress, and quickly realized they were newlyweds. In a rush of kindliness he ushered them to the front seats, and fussed over them and their luggage in a most embarrassing way. However, Tyra supervised the chicken basket. She was placing it in the luggage carrier above her head when the driver offered the passenger seat beside him, and she gratefully accepted as it was much easier to keep watch over the chicks that way. In summer heat the trip was long, an uncomfortable journey on rough, dusty, gravel roads, but when in love, time flies, and the driver did his best to make the trip as pleasant as possible for them, including making an extra, unscheduled, dinner stop at a restaurant he recommended they try.

Erik, with horse and cart, was at the Nykarleby bus station when they arrived as the sun was setting in a long blaze of golden pink. After quick introductions he and Axel hoisted the suitcase, boxes, and chicken basket into the cart, while Tyra clambered aboard. After dreaming for weeks of the moment she would arrive at her own new home, she was so tired she almost fell asleep to the familiar clopping of horse hooves. But when Axel cried, "Here we are! Here's Brännon!" she was wide awake. Her first thought was "What a nice little village!" and as they turned into the track that led to Axel's house, "Why, it's not a hut! It's a nice little *rådhus*!" The house was freshly painted in traditional red, with window frames and sills a bright, clean white. Her heart swelled with pride. Suddenly she thought, "I'll spend the rest of my life here!" Two pots of cheerful scarlet geraniums framed the door. Axel gestured towards them and said, "From Elna."

Erik had a large saucepan of traditional pea soup (not Tyra's favorite!) quietly bubbling on the stove, and ample rye bread available, but Tyra was so tired she struggled to muster the politeness to eat even a few spoonfuls. But she did notice the brand new wood-fired stove installed in the back wall of the kitchen. Clearly she would be able to cook! While the brothers talked long in the waning light of the slowly setting sun, she quietly slipped into the bedroom and was fast asleep when Axel came to check on her. Hurriedly, he removed his uncomfortable wedding finery, and slipped into bed beside her.

Tyra woke to bustling sounds in the kitchen, and the smell of rolled oats porridge. She had to shake herself to remember where she was, and was staring at the blotched, unpainted lining of the bedroom walls when Axel came in.

"Sorry I didn't have time to paint those before we got married," he said apologetically, gesturing at the grubby walls. "But I do have porridge and coffee ready if you're interested. Elna sent some apple sauce and rye bread, and I have some fresh cream from the cow."

"What time did you get up?" asked Tyra, embarrassed. She looked at a clock hanging lopsided on the wall and saw it was ten past six.

"Oh, not long ago. Elna will be over soon with Erik in the cart. She so wants to meet you."

Tyra wanted to spend time alone with Axel exploring her new home, but she asked, "Whose cart it is?"

"Mine, but I share it with the family."

Tyra nodded. "Really? Anyway, I'd like to get dressed before breakfast," she added awkwardly. "Will I have time? And where's the toilet?"

"Toilet's in the barn," said Axel. "Use the chamber pot, it's under the bed. I'll put the kettle on."

Tyra was dressed and spooning rolled oats porridge into her mouth, when a gentle knock announced Elna. "No," Elna said to Axel's gestured offer, "I've already eaten." Tyra wondered what time country people normally got up. Hastily she stood to politely shake Elna's hand.

"I hope you don't mind my coming so early," Elna smiled, "But I did want to make you feel welcome. Axel promised you'll come over for lunch and dinner today, since this is your first day here and you should rest. But I wanted to make sure you are happy about the plan."

"I would love to see you and the others," said Tyra, only a little untruthfully. "How far away are you?"

"By road, or by path? By road it's about three kilometers, but I always cut across the fields, except in winter, and its less than two that way."

"Oh, dear, I've just remembered my chickens!" cried Tyra jumping up. "I must check them."

"Don't worry," assured Elna. "Axel told me about them, and I've already fed them. They're contented. Come and see them when you've finished eating, and have a look at the rest of the farm while you do."

"Yah, I'd like that."

"Elna will do a good job looking after you. I need to fix some things on the farm. See you later!" Axel gave Tyra a friendly pat, and she tried to hide her disappointment at his disappearance.

Tyra finished her porridge and Elna led the way to the barn, fifty meters across a small meadow dotted cheerfully with daisies and cornflowers. "The barn is convenient, even in winter," said Elna, proudly. "The path is easily cleared. Axel usually does it, but I've done it for him when he's busy. It's easy."

They entered the barn. "Axel hasn't got around to building the toilet properly yet," said Elna bluntly. "That Oskar who owned the land worked him so hard. It's a wonder he managed to paint the house, but he was determined to do that for you." Secretly Tyra thought she would have preferred a toilet to a house paint, but she was sure everything would come in time. In an area hastily penned off with hay bales were Tyra's half-fledged chickens looking very content with lots of oats and barley at their feet. A bony red cow left off feeding when they entered, and gazed with soft brown eyes. Tyra rubbed her neck.

"That's Kossa," said Elna, her voice full of approval for Tyra's interest. "She's not young, but she gives plenty of good milk. She usually has the run of the garden, but Axel kept her down here so the flowers could grow for you. He's been too busy to attend to her yet, so let's take her out now. The horse isn't here, Erik's taken it."

"Shouldn't we give the cow a more appealing name? I wouldn't be too happy if people called me girl, or woman," laughed Tyra. "I think Vallmo[1] would be a nice name for her. What do you think?"

"Ask Axel," said Elna, puzzled. "We don't bother too much with animal names."

"Oh, it helps make them part of the family," said Tyra. Curiously, she explored the barn, full of cow, dung, and hay smells. "Axel said he was growing potatoes," she said suddenly, "but I don't see any."

"Oh, that's his plan for the new piece of land he's renting from the church. He hasn't had a chance to clear it yet, but if he lets Kossa, I mean Vallmo, and the horse in there for a few days it'll be cleared quickly."

"Some sheep would help," said Tyra with a faraway look in her eyes. "We could spin and weave their wool. People say they're foolish animals, but I like them, and I always thought having a few would be fun."

"What a good idea!" exclaimed Elna. "You know, we thought you were a city girl and wouldn't know anything about farming."

Tyra sat on a hay bale and looked at her new sister-in-law. She was beautiful, and obviously very kind. But her flushed cheeks and thin body made Tyra wonder about her health.

"My father always had horses," she responded. "You probably know he's a carter, and has wonderful Belgian draught horses that he's very proud of. Sometimes he's let me take the reins when I'm out with him, and he's very pleased with my driving. And I spent all my summers on my uncle's farm at Oxkangar. We didn't just play; we had to help with the work. And I listened to the adults, because what my morbror did always interested me."

1. Meaning poppy

"Axel will be very pleased about that."

"Oh, he knows. He was friends with my cousin from that farm."

Elna nodded. "That's right, Axel mentioned something about that. Anyway, Erik will help Axel with the farm chores today, so he can finish early and join us for lunch at the house, I mean our family house. It will be good for us to spend time on our own before they arrive."

Tyra, again, would have preferred to spend time alone with Axel, but she understood her new family was trying to be kind and make her feel welcome, that Axel was working hard for her, and decided there would be plenty of time to spend with him later.

The sun was shining brightly when the young women set off across the fields. "I like this route because it's shorter, and also safer," announced Elna.

"Safer?" questioned Tyra, alarmed.

"You know about that Lapua Movement, don't you?" asked Elna.

"You mean those people who smashed the communist press in Vasa last summer, and thousands of them marched to Helsingfors?"

"That's it!" nodded Elna.

"Yah, it was terrible. My Far happened to be nearby and saw a couple of men beating up Eino Nieminen who they claimed was a Red army officer. I'm certainly not a Communist, but I don't think we should treat anyone like that! I wish our country would accept each other instead of all this endless fighting and blaming that we do!"

"I agree!" declared Elna. "And remember they kidnapped good ex-President Kaarlo Ståhlberg last October, and took him and his wife to Joensuu, near Russia. I don't think they were really going to take them across the Russian border like they did other poor people they didn't like, but it was very bad behavior. You know, the Lapua people might call some people Red communists, but the Russians call those same people White and treat them very badly. No one around here liked what happened, so there hasn't been much local support for Lapua anti-communist activities, but you never know. Rumors have it there are still a few activists around here. Their leader is a farmer, so that gets him local support. Just be careful, I say, who you talk to in the town. Anyone in this village is safe. Axel knows everyone here and says none of them are into political activity."

"I thought living in the country would be quiet and peaceful," said Tyra, with a sigh.

"It is, normally," assured Elna, "and I shouldn't be talking about this on your first day here, such a special day. Axel talked so much about you, and he's worked day and night to have the house ready for you. It's such a pity he didn't get time to paint the inside, but that awful man kept insisting he work for him. But you'll be pleased to know he has signed off all the papers, and the house is fully Axel's, well, yours too!" she laughed.

"I've never done any painting," said Tyra, "but I'd be willing to try."

"Oh, I don't think you need worry about that. Erik is a good lad and he'll help Axel. Once they have the farm under control I'm sure they'll get on with painting the inside of the house."

The fields were full of ripening rye and oats, mingled with cornflowers, daisies, a few remaining spring poppies, and some pink twin flowers. Several times Tyra noticed Elna was short of breath, but she did not like to comment. However, when they came to a style over a fence Tyra asked to rest, though she felt fine.

"Oh, yah, I could do with a rest," said Elna, breathless and gratefully sitting on the lower step of the style while Tyra leaned on a fence post.

"Nykarleby is on a river, isn't it?" asked Tyra. "I confess I was too tired to notice much last night."

"Yah, and that river is the Lapua! You can see why I warned you to be careful about talking! We're at the mouth of the river, a little port. We used to be famous for exporting tar to Sweden. It's a nice town, at least I think so. You know something funny? That tar came from Finland, but once it got to Sweden they called it Stockholm tar, and it was exported to the rest of the world as that! I believe the English were very keen to buy it for their navy, until they got steel ships and didn't need it anymore."

Despite growing up in the port city of Vasa Tyra was not very interested in shipping. She nodded politely.

"Ah, there's our house," said Elna, standing and pointing to a large barn-like building visible across the fields. They resumed walking, and as they neared the house Tyra saw it had not been painted for a long, long time, and there were no pots of geraniums by its door.

"Elna," she said, "I haven't said thank you for those beautiful geraniums Axel said you gave us. I really appreciate them."

"So you noticed them!" Elna smiled, and her eyes twinkled joyfully. "I love flowers, but Mor Anna says they're just work and isn't interested in them."

"What a pity!" exclaimed Tyra.

The sound of their footsteps brought Mor Anna and young John to the door. Both with great formality offered their hands to shake Tyra's, before inviting her inside. Tyra was shocked at the shabbiness of the furniture and the chill inside the house despite the warmth of the summer's day. Elna bustled away to make food, John got up to help her, and Tyra was left to make polite conversation with her new step-mother-in-law. It was hard work. Elna was interested in everything and conversation flowed so freely as they walked that Tyra felt she had known her all her life. But Mor Anna appeared tired and worn, struggling to make herself interested in her daughter-in-law. Conversation was such an effort Tyra wondered if she had somehow done something to offend. Since Axel was the first in the family to marry, Tyra wondered if Mor Anna resented her presence, or was merely uncertain how to relate to a new family member.

With great relief Tyra heard a horse and cart heralding the arrival of Axel and Erik. Axel had a red-faced, newly-shaved look, and was wearing a bright plaid shirt that was rather startling. With confident ease he sat beside his new wife, and began talking with his step mother. Tyra envied his natural flow of conversation with a woman who, until he had arrived, had shown no interest in the world around her.

Elna's meal was huge, revealing preparations that must have taken days. By the time Tyra got to the final course, bowls of luscious strawberries and whipped cream, she could barely eat a spoonful, but somehow finished her serving. Just when she found herself dreading the thought of spending the afternoon trying to make conversation with Mor Anna, Axel suggested they go for a walk, and the rest of the family join them. Still no chance to be alone! groaned Tyra inwardly.

"Let's take Tyra into town and show her everything," suggested Erik, and John quickly agreed. "We could take the cart and chat together," he added.

Mor Anna declined the invitation, but the youthful members of the family were keen. Jokingly, Tyra offered to drive the horse. One look at the mare told her it was an old and very placid animal, nothing like the powerful Belgian horses her father used. She was confident it would be easy to control, and cause her no trouble.

"Are you sure? Can you?" asked Axel in doubtful surprise.

"I'm not a carter's daughter for nothing!" Tyra laughed. "You know the powerful horses my father uses, and I can manage them. Let me try!" With obvious uncertainty Axel handed the reins to Tyra and off they set. The old horse behaved beautifully, and Tyra felt Axel relax.

"She drives better than you!" observed John tactlessly. "You and that horse fight, but now she knows who's boss!"

Tyra looked at her new husband and saw his embarrassment. "She knows I like her, that's all," she said, quickly. "I've been looking after horses all my life. I can tell she's not young, and she will do a good job if I'm patient with her. What's her name?"

"Name?" said Axel, puzzled. "She's just the horse!"

"If you want a horse to respond well you have to name her. That's how they know you're their friend," said Tyra firmly. "Can I name her?"

"Anything you like!" said the surprised Axel, shrugging. "It makes no difference to me."

"Wow! She's bossing you already!" said John admiringly.

"We'll both name her," Tyra added hastily.

"Good," said Axel briskly. "Now Erik can take over the driving so I can show you the sights and you don't need to concentrate on the road."

Erik was only too happy to oblige. Proudly Axel pointed out St Birgitta church, painted a lovely golden yellow, and still standing after two hundred years of pious use. He showed great interest in the small power station being built on the banks of the river, and proudly announced that electric lighting would come to Brännon in the very near future. "It will make winter so much easier!" he assured Tyra. He carefully indicated where he liked to buy groceries, and the school he hoped their children would attend, which made Tyra blush.

"Why don't we hitch the horse and take a walk," suggested Erik. "Along the river it's nice."

"You know, this is a very pretty town," Tyra said admiringly. "I never expected anything half so nice."

Axel looked at her sharply. "You're very brave to come somewhere you didn't expect to be nice!" he observed.

Tyra enjoyed walking along the placid Lapua River, but again noticed Elna tired easily and had trouble keeping up with her brothers. "I'm a bit tired after the trip," she said, "let's go back. We can come another day."

"Let's!" said Elna, gratefully.

They returned to the barn-home of the Östring family. Mor Anna smiled faintly when they entered, but made no attempt to assist Elna to prepare the evening meal, which Tyra quickly offered to do, and the young women chatted while they worked. Elna had already made an apple cake, and they prepared a soup of potatoes, leeks, carrots, salmon and dill.

"I've made a *leipäjuusto*[2] for you, too," said Elna proudly. "We can have that with our coffee."

"Really!" exclaimed Tyra, impressed. "I've never made that cheese, only bought it. But I really like it. Actually, I like all cheese!"

"Oh, making it's easy, I'll show you how sometime," offered Elna.

Tyra looked around and, seeing Axel and his mother in conversation took a deep breath. "Elna," she whispered, "is Mor Anna happy about me? She didn't seem to want to talk."

"Of course she's happy," responded Elna, quickly and quietly. "It's just her manner. I was about six when my mother died, and Axel just a toddler. Far remarried very soon afterwards. Mor Anna was kind. But she's had a lot of sadness, and since my father died she's been very withdrawn. She won't even come to church, which she always did every week, no matter the weather, even though the priest came and tried to talk her into going. She was interested in embroidery, but now she just sits."

"Embroidery. Hmm, that gives me an idea. Thank you for that. I like embroidery myself."

"Come upstairs to the bedroom," whispered Elna, "I'll show you something."

In the bedroom, which seemed more like a dormitory to Tyra, Elna rummaged in the drawer of a battered old dresser, and pulled out two photos. She handed one to Tyra, a picture of a mother with four children.

"That's Mor Anna with her children just months before my little sister Edit Johanna and her own daughter Anni Astrid died. Edit is standing by herself at Mor Anna's right hand. Notice how short she is compared with Erik, even though she was quite a bit older! Poor little thing, she must have been sick even then and we didn't realize it. Look how pretty little Anni Astrid was! The boy on the far left is Erik, and the baby is little Emil Johan. By the way, Johanna was my mother's name. She was Johanna Backman. And Emil Johan the baby was called Emil before my older brother Johan died in the war. After his death, it seemed to comfort Far to still have a son called Johan. But you can't please everyone, and Axel doesn't like that because he says Johan was his brother. So we call him John."

Tyra examined the photograph, noting the girls in identical dresses, the smartly clad boys. "Where are you and Axel?" she asked suddenly, looking hard at her new sister.

---

2. Also known as "squeaky cheese", similar to haloumi cheese.

"We didn't want to be in that photo, I'm ashamed to say. Edit was just a baby when Far married Mor Anna, and they got on well right from the beginning, but I was still grieving my mother. I wasn't too friendly to Mor Anna for a long time. Axel was a troublesome toddler, and although I could handle him, Mor Anna found him a trial. She did her best to be kind to both of us, but Axel was never very close to her."

"Yah, I suspected that. He talks a good deal about you, but not much about his step-mother."

"When Edit Johanna and Anni Astrid died just two days apart it was terrible for all of us, but especially for Mor Anna. It was March, 1916, the fifteenth and the seventeenth. It was awful. So one day, a couple of years later, after my brother Johan died in the war, I realized why Mor Anna might be sad all the time, so I asked Far if Axel and I could have a photo with both of them to remind her that she still had other children." Elna passed another photo to Tyra. "Axel was not enthusiastic and I had to talk hard to get him to agree, but finally we got that picture taken at the local studio. Notice how straight Mor Anna is sitting in the first photo, and how she seems drooped and shrunken in this second one. I don't think she ever got over my sisters' deaths, and somehow she felt responsible that Far lost two of his sons. When Far died she just collapsed into herself."

Tyra examined the photo carefully, and Elna suddenly observed, "When I see myself with Axel in this photo, I realize both Edit and I are pretty short. I think our mother must have been a short woman, too."

Idly, Tyra turned the photo over. "Hmm, I notice your father was Emil Hendriksson."

"Yah, didn't you know that?"

"No, I didn't, or don't remember, if I did. So that means you had to get your name changed like so many people in Finland?"

"Yah, of course. But I kept the Hendriksson as my middle name. So did Axel. What was your name before?"

"We didn't have to change. Our name has always been Lall. It comes from Wallonia, the southern part of Belgium. My family come from blacksmiths brought to Sweden by King Gustav Vasa. How did you choose the name Östring?"

Elna laughed. "Devilment, I think! Far was very angry those Finns in Helsingfors could even think to take his name from him. At first he adamantly refused to change, but finally realized he had no choice. Of course you know Finland was called Eastern Sweden, so that's how he came up with Östring, meaning from the east. So, we declare we're eastern Swedes! No one in Helsingfors could complain about that name, because there's no 'son' anywhere in it! You can be a rebel without doing anything nasty to other people!"

"A family of rebels, eh?" laughed Tyra.

"Yah, I'm afraid so. Not bad rebels, just not orthodox! We like to think for ourselves. But that name, Östring, did cause a few problems. Many people just didn't think it was a serious one, and for years still called my far Hendriksson. He was perfectly happy about that! I think when my mother died Far was so distressed and busy he didn't get around to putting a marker on her grave. Years later, when the church warden reminded him and he went to the ironmonger, the man thought Östring was a joke, and wrote her maiden name!"

"A wasted grave marker, eh?" smiled Tyra. "You know, I like to think for myself too, but it got me into trouble when I was in *skriftskola*. Thanks for sharing Elna. Knowing all that will help me a lot."

"Sorry you had trouble in *skriftskola*. I survived by saying nothing, but Axel was yelled at a few times for asking questions. But we better get on with the meal, or we might have some more rebels around here!"

As Tyra and Axel drove home later in the golden evening, she announced, "I've thought of a name for our horse."

"A what?" said Axel absently, busy thinking about how he could fit in painting the house, making the toilet, clearing his new land and planting it, and . . .

"A name for the horse. Löfte. Don't you think it's a good one? It means promise."

"It's a mighty fancy name for an old horse, but you can call her that. I'll just call her häst."

Tyra giggled. "Axel! That's not even the right name! She's a *kvinnlig* häst, a girl horse!"

"Oh, well, if calling her Löfte makes you happy, I'm willing. There's no doubt about you, you've got a quick brain!"

"Thank you. And Axel, can we go to town tomorrow and buy some paint?"

"What! Buy paint? Of course not!" he responded roughly. "I've got many more urgent things to do."

"But I can go with Elna, not you. All I need is the cart. Don't you understand, I'm here to help you. You don't have to do everything all by yourself any more! I probably won't do as good a job as you, but I'm sure I can paint inside our house while you do other things. Remember, women work inside, and men work outside!"

Axel dropped the reins and Löfte came to a bewildered standstill. For a few awkward minutes he sat staring into the far distance, golden from the waning sun, then suddenly he threw his arms around his new bride and gave her a tight hug. She rested her head on his shoulder and murmured, "We're in it together now, don't ever forget!"

"Löfte," he said as they sat entwined, "it's a good name, a wonderful name for our horse, it really is. Even if we get a new one, we'll still call her that, you know, Löfte I and Löfte II, like the kings of Sweden. And look, you don't need to paint the bedroom, I'll find time to do it. But you can get the paint tomorrow, with the cart, if you like."

Next morning, when Elna and Erik arrived, this time well after breakfast, Axel announced that Tyra would take the horse, that is, Löfte, and cart into Nykarleby, with Elna, to buy paint, while he and Erik walked to the new land and began clearing it.

"He must really trust you," said Elna admiringly as they trotted along. "Do you know everything about horses?"

"Of course not!" protested Tyra. "Although both my grandfathers were blacksmiths I have no idea how shoe a horse. But my father, who's a carter as you know, said I was good with horses, and he encouraged me to drive."

The hardware store attendant was surprised when two young women arrived wanting paint for their house. After he offered the traditional bright red and yellow they assured him they wanted something gentle, a pastel color suitable for inside a house.

"What if I mix white with this nice yellow, and see how you like that?" he offered. When he saw their uncertainty he suggested he add yellow drop by drop into a white paint tin, till it was the shade that appealed to them. This option pleased Elna and Tyra much better. "But be careful," he warned. "Paint gets darker when it dries. I'll make it a bit lighter than you want."

"Sounds good," said Tyra briskly, "and give us all the advice you like." The man swelled with pride, and began sharing many practical tips.

"By the way, who's doing this job?" he asked.

"I am," declared Tyra quickly.

"You? Really?" he stopped and scratched his head. He was not used to young women painting houses. "Look, I'm going to give you an extra brush, because I have the feeling you girls can do this job together. And by the way, Fru Östring, make sure you use that young Axel's old clothes when you try this paint job of yours! Painting's a messy business, unless you're experienced!" Tyra blushed to be called Fru for the first time, and did not dare pretend she was an experienced painter. "And here's all the sandpaper you need," he added, thrusting a wad into the pink Tyra's hands. Seeing Tyra's blank expression, he showed her how to use the sandpaper. Tyra was rapidly losing her confidence about her house decorating project.

"How did he know who I was?" she asked incredulously when they were safely outside.

"Well, he knows who I am, and where do you think Axel got the paint for the outside of the house? I bet Axel told him he was getting married, along with careful descriptions of you! Axel's very proud of you!" Elna laughed, and Tyra blushed.

"Let's have something quick to eat, then start painting," said Tyra when Löfte was back in the barn, and they were in the kitchen.

"But Mor Anna is expecting us for lunch," protested Elna, in obvious consternation.

"Oh," said Tyra, thrusting down her frustration. "I must let her know that tomorrow I'll be busy," she added firmly.

As they began the walk across the fields she suddenly realized where Axel had been "doing his cooking" and that she would need to use considerable tact to get her new family to understand that she and Axel would not be permanently dependent on them for food. Then she remembered Elna's disappointment. She thought of the big old house, cold and dreary, with Mor Anna sitting stolidly, remote from life, on her chair. "Elna," she asked, in the middle of her sister's knowledgeable discourse on local birds, which she was enjoying, "Do you have any friends here? Sorvist looks very small."

"Oh, I have several good friends in Nykarleby," said Elna. "Would you like to meet them?"

"I'd love to!"

The three women ate alone, without conversation, and the men had not arrived when Elna and Tyra left Mor Anna and set out for Brännon. Tyra explained carefully that she had duties at Brännon that needed her immediate attention, and excused herself from returning for the evening meal, or for any meals the next day, although she had quietly invited Elna to join her whenever it was convenient for her to do so. By now Tyra had worked out ways of allowing Elna to rest as they walked, and when they reached Brännon she insisted Elna stay in the kitchen preparing food while she rubbed down the walls with sandpaper as the hardware storeman had shown her. The huge quantities of dust that sandpapering produced made her quickly cover the bed with a sheet. Barely half a wall was completed before she felt exhausted, but doggedly she continued. After a while she learned to "see" what needed rubbing, and saved herself much energy. When Axel had not returned by supper time she suggested she take Elna home in the cart, but Elna refused, insisting she was happy to wait. Tyra was disappointed when Axel finally returned, said "I thought we were eating at home", quickly ate the potatoes and chicken Elna had prepared, and hurried to do more work in the barn. Tyra walked Elna home, returned alone, and was sound asleep when Axel came in.

"What are you and Elna doing today?" asked Axel next morning before he left with Erik and John. "I need the horse today. We plan to plough the new fields and hopefully get them planted out."

"Oh, we'll stay here today," Tyra replied noncommittally. "I've got some jobs I want to do." The moment he left she changed into the old dress Elna had given her and began painting. It was fun, although it took a while to develop a technique that didn't drip paint all over her hands and the sheets of newspaper spread on the floor. By the time Elna arrived midmorning she had painted one wall and almost finished another.

"It smells terrible!" cried Elna when she walked in, "Open all the windows and the door!"

Tyra surveyed her handiwork, and expressed disappointment that it looked rather blotchy. "Don't you remember Hans told you it would take at least two coats of paint?" said Elna, encouragingly. Tyra had not remembered what the shopkeeper had said, but she kept hard at her work, and by lunch the bedroom had its the first coat of paint.

"Have a little rest," Elna advised, after lunch, and Tyra was shocked that when she lay on the bed she fell fast asleep. But she was even more shocked when Axel arrived home late in the afternoon, said with a disapproving wrinkle of his nose, "What's the bad smell? What on earth have you been cooking?" and never noticed anything!

"We've been cleaning," giggled Elna, conspiratorially. "Special girl cleaning. Now have your supper, and take me home in your cart because I'm tired." By the time Axel got back Tyra was once again sound asleep.

Next day Tyra applied the second coat of paint, Elna came to keep her company and cook. This time, when Axel arrived home and complained about the bad smell, the girls could no longer contain their mirth. Irritated, he walked into the bedroom and stopped short.

"You've done it!" he exclaimed. "You've painted the bedroom!"

"You're not angry?" asked Tyra, timidly.

"Angry! Of course not! I'm just amazed. It's great!" He stood in the doorway admiring his wife's handiwork, then said, "How about helping plough the field tomorrow?"

"Women work inside, and men work outside," quipped Elna, and he roared laughing.

"I'm taking two days' to recover, and then you're going to introduce me to your neighbors here in Brännon," said Tyra. "They must be wondering who this strange woman in your house is! Put them out of their misery! After that I'll paint the kitchen."

Axel looked stunned, then said, "Yah, in two days we should finish the field, and yes, you should get to know your neighbors." But he need not have worried, because the next day neighbors began arriving with loaves of rye bread, platters of apple cake, crocks of preserves, jam-filled *griser*, and baskets of strawberries. Elna, it turned out, knew them all, and they were waiting for her signal to know when it was convenient to meet the new bride. Tyra admitted that socializing was as hard work, maybe more, as painting a bedroom, and certainly her decorating activity was a major talking point in the village. Paint smells, she discovered, carry quite a distance!

Tyra soon learned the best place to get to know her neighbors was the village well, about 50 meters from her kitchen. Axel had carried buckets of water to the house every morning, but she discovered by filling them in the evening, he would leave the job to her. All her neighbors were pleasant people, but one woman, though at first quieter than the others, eventually proved a good friend and most helpful. Little did Tyra realize the dramatic influence Takla Höglund and her husband Karl would have on her life. Karl was a butcher, and most notably, was the distinguished owner of one of the few trucks in the district.

With the help of Erik and John Axel cleared, ploughed, and planted in potatoes the rented church land in record time. "It's a bit late in the year," he admitted when he triumphantly announced their achievement, "but as long as we don't get early snow I expect to harvest a good crop." He then declared he had work in the barn, and every day Tyra heard him hammering there. For some reason he didn't want her around while he worked, so she fed the chickens before he began his hammering, then after their evening meal, and during the day left him to his work.

Flush with the success of her bedroom painting efforts, Tyra commenced painting the kitchen. It proved much more time consuming and fiddly than the bedroom as she had to work round stove, windows, and benches, but eventually she achieved her goal, and rejoiced in more thanks from Axel. With both of them working hard, they were now ready for bed at the same time, and joyfully became fully man and wife.

Tyra developed a routine with Elna and Mor Anna. It was clear that although Elna said she had good friends, she very much enjoyed the company of her new sister, and was eager to spend as much time as possible with her. She would arrive at Brännon late morning, have lunch with Tyra, and Axel too if he had finished his work. Often she was happy to prepare food for them all to eat, while Tyra completed some project. After lunch both women walked to Sorvist, or occasionally Tyra drove the cart if Axel did not need it, and they had *fika* with Mor Anna. Tyra's hunch that embroidery might become a link with her mother-in-law proved true. Although Mor Anna now rarely did embroidery herself, she took an interest in Tyra's handiwork, and enjoyed discussing it with her.

One early autumn evening Axel arrived for his meal a little early. "The potatoes have good heads of flowers," he announced, "I should be able to harvest them soon."

Since he had said the same thing for the last few evenings, Tyra was at a loss to say something intelligent about his precious tubers. She smiled encouragingly.

"Would you like to see something in the barn?" he asked with surprising eagerness.

"Of course," Tyra replied, curious, ready to go. She thought she knew what he would show her. She had been hinting that she needed a proper place to house her hens.

"I did all the work except the seats," he announced as they walked. "The carpenter did a good job with them," he added.

Tyra was mystified, hens not exactly needing seats, but the last twenty paces were soon traversed. Then, instead of going to the big barn door and showing her a pen for hens, Axel led her to a small side door, and swung it open with a flourish. "Well, what do you think?" he asked with pride.

Tyra was speechless. She didn't know whether to laugh or drool thanks. There in front of her, in a small room carefully boxed off from the rest of the barn, was a toilet, with not one, but three toilet holes. Two, in a well-polished bench beside each other, were obviously adult sized, and beneath them, with its own polished bench, was a child-sized one!

"They're . . . they're . . ." she stammered, desperately trying to suppress giggles.

"In winter, it's good to go out together. And when we get a child, well, he should be with us," said Axel earnestly.

"They're lovely!" she exclaimed, and could contain herself no longer. Her merry laughter echoed through the barn.

"Nice and sensible," Axel was saying, while she doubled up with mirth. "They drain down to the animal manure channels and together will grow good potatoes!"

By now Tyra was exploding with laughter. "I'm not sure I'll be able to eat any of those potatoes," she said between chortles and wiping her eyes.

"Why not?" asked a dumbfounded Axel, staring at his wife in amazement. "I thought you'd be delighted with my toilets!"

"I am!" laughed Tyra, giving her husband a hug. "I just didn't expect the fertilizer part of the plan! You men are so different from women!"

Chapter 11

News

THE WEATHER WAS KIND to Axel's potatoes, and after reflection, Tyra decided fertilizer was fertilizer. She ate his potatoes and enjoyed them; they were good, very good. Sacks of them piled high on the cart quickly sold in Nykarleby, and another two cartloads went to Jakobstad, a town twice the size of Nykarleby about sixteen kilometers to the north. They still had plenty for their own use.

Winter. Dark, cold, lonely winter, inevitably came. With the arrival of snow and the long darkness, Tyra began to understand her father's concerns about being a small farmer's wife. The promised electric lighting had not yet arrived in Brännon. All through summer and autumn Tyra watched the progress of workmen setting power poles along the road from Nykarleby. But to her disappointment they did not make it to the village before winter blackness took over, and the village was left to its unlit fate. Vasa had been lit electrically for years, and with the riverside generator now completed Nykarleby had good winter lighting. But the darkness in the village was challenging. Axel's triple toilet was suddenly gratefully appreciated. So was his supply of efficient lanterns. Despite the darkness and the cold, he and the men in Brännon banded together and took the horse and sleigh out to do forestry work. Tyra and the village women were left to cope on their own during the long, dark days.

And those days alone were long, very long. It was not safe to visit Elna, plodding through heavy drifts of snow, so they looked forward to Sundays when Axel drove the sleigh. Tyra came to depend on her neighbor Takla Höglund, and they spent considerable time together. Takla helped Tyra understand many things that had puzzled and frustrated her. For example, when Tyra complained about the vendor of the land Axel bought, and his demand that Axel not only pay money, but work for a year to pay for the property, Takla laughed, and explained: "Axel was lucky! Karl still has to work for this house! Yah, we own it, but not quite. Most of the land around here was owned by the Church, but Karl was able to buy this block. However, the deed states that the priest can demand Karl work for him for ten days every year! And there's no time limit to that demand!"

"You aren't serious, surely?" exclaimed an incredulous Tyra.

"I am. Karl never knows when the priest will ask him to work, and he can be very demanding. Karl stopped going to church to avoid the man, but we can't stop him visiting us. Karl is one of the few people around here with a truck, as you know, and usually the priest asks him to move something heavy. But it hasn't made for a good relationship between them, I can tell you! I struggle to get Karl to church even on the mandatory Christmas and Easter! Karl's trying to run a business, and it's hard, let's say sometimes impossible, when someone demands you work for them whenever they feel like it. The priest's calls always seem to come when Karl is busiest!"

"That's incredible! I thought Axel was hard done by, but now I realize he was lucky!"

Finland's wonderful new Yleisradio (General Broadcaster), begun in 1926, proved a great comfort to many people during the winter dark and cold. Tyra and Axel spent many hours in the "evenings" listening to it, although what exactly was evening when there was daylight for only one hour a day was a conundrum. So despite Takla's company, and the Yleisradio, Tyra's days alone meant her mother's letters acquired new importance, and she looked forward to them eagerly.

She learned with delight that her parents would visit at Christmas. She had suggested to Axel that they go to Vasa for Christmas, but Axel was committed to his forestry activities, and she didn't press the idea. Although Tyra was a competent cook, she worried how she could prepare all the traditional Christmas foods, but her concern was wasted. When they climbed off the bus Anna and Anders staggered under the load of enough food to offer Christmas fare to feed the whole of Brännon!

"This thing stinks!" declared Anders, clambering down the bus steps, hands filled with food parcels, as he thumped the vehicle's paneling with his elbow. "They say horse poo smells, but nothing can be as bad as diesel fumes! The driver insisted it was too cold to open windows, so I didn't even have a fresh breeze on my face!"

"You could have gone to sleep!" laughed the driver, good naturedly.

"Had to keep an eye on your driving!" quipped Anders, and the driver, raising his eyebrows, grinned. Both men of the road, they had known each other for years.

"I miss my horse," the driver conceded, leaning against the warm hood of his engine, "but in winter this machine is definitely the way to go. You get used to the smell. And my hands never freeze gripping this wheel!"

By the time Axel drove Anders and Anna to Brännon in the lantern-lit, bell-tinkling sleigh, behind slowly plodding Löfte, Anders was complaining of the cold, and everyone was laughing at him.

What a wonderful week they had! Anna and Anders made appreciative noises about all Axel had done around his property, especially the warm stoves installed in kitchen and bedroom, and he and Anders went off in the sleigh to view the empty potato patch in the dark! Tyra's dozen chickens, now fully grown, were laying enough eggs for regular meals of *plattar*, enjoyed with strawberry jam, apple sauce, or the cloudberry jam Anna brought with her. It was truly festive when the whole village got together to sing carols, accompanied by someone's strident mouth organ and a scratchy old violin they thought was wonderful. Axel brought the Östring family over to join the village, and Anna was impressed with Elna's cooking, especially her *leipäjuusto* cheese which she urged Tyra to learn to make. Even Mor Anna became animated and chatted with Anna Lall. The day after Christmas they had a welcome surprise when Hjalmar arrived on skis, and he too needed to be shown everything. But Hjalmar, committed to his mother, left the following day, and all too soon Anna and Anders returned to Vasa. Tyra once more must cope with the dark and cold, too often alone.

Then, just as the days were beginning to lighten, on the 27th of February, 1932, the Yleisradio evening news brought Elna's warnings about the Lapua movement into sudden and unwanted focus. A peaceful meeting, the announcer reported, of the Mäntsälä Social Democrats was violently interrupted by armed Lapua extremists, and a national coup attempted.

"Well, at least it's far down south," commented Tyra. "That attack on the printing press in Vasa was much too close to my home for comfort. Far said the attackers were ferocious. He was very relieved to get away unnoticed."

"What's wrong with them!" fumed Axel. "Why do they want another government? We had thirteen changes in the twenties! No proper country behaves like this!"

"Matilda and I used take bets on how long each government would last," laughed Tyra. "She had a cousin in the diet, so we got news very quickly. Herr Backman thought it was entertainment and not meant to be taken seriously!"

"Well, those Lapua people are serious about this! They're disgraceful! More like kids scrapping than serious government! Surely we should settle down to law and order by now, and be a civilized country!"

"We're a brand new nation with a wonderful chance to do things right, and all we're doing is making fools of ourselves fighting each other!" lamented Tyra. "How can we be so stupid! We've been independent for about fifteen years now, surely we could learn to do something right!"

Over the next few days the country listened anxiously for news of the rebellion. Highly respected President Pehr Evind Svinhufvud made an impassioned broadcast urging militia involved in the coup to return home, and promised only the rebel leaders would be punished. The President was known for his important role in setting up the new parliamentary system in 1906, and being the first Speaker for it. He had delighted Ostrobothnians (of which Lapua and Nykarleby were part) by refusing to Finnicize his noble Swedish name. He was the first head of state for newly independent Finland in 1917, and was recognized as a conservative Swedish Finn, sympathetic to some of the aims of the leaders of the Lapua Movement. To the relief of the country, his speech proved successful, the rebellious men dispersed, and the leaders, including General Wallenius who was a famed Jaeger trooper, were arrested a few days later, and, as promised, sent to prison.

"Well now, General Wallenius might meet up with Algot!" quipped Axel with a grin. "Sounds like prison is becoming quiet a sociable and fashionable hotel!"

The comment shocked and did not amuse Tyra, but did help her recognize that maybe prison was not such a bad place after all, not the ultimate disgrace she had always thought it to be. Not if a respected army general could be sent there.

A few weeks later, with spring brightening the landscape, and after a week of no snow, Tyra decided to visit to Elna, whom she had not seen since Christmas. She waited until late morning when the sun was well over the horizon, and enjoyed the brisk walk across fields still patchy with snow. When no one answered her knock she called out and walked in. Elna, wrapped in quilts, was lying on a couch, and Mor Anna, as usual, was sitting motionless nearby.

"I'm not feeling so good today," Elna apologized, making an attempt to sit which made her cough violently. "We've all been a bit sick here," she spluttered between coughs. When her cough settled, she half rose to set the kettle on the stove, but fell back amidst the quilts with another fit of coughing. Momentarily free from the puffy quilts, Tyra was shocked to see how thin and wasted she was.

"We've all been sick," repeated Mor Anna, "but we're fine now, except Elna who isn't getting better as quickly as the boys."

"Elna, don't worry," Tyra said, shaking her head. "I know where everything is, and I'll get something to drink." She hurried to the stove and began bustling with kettles, glad to hide her face. There was no doubt, although the rest of the family had been sick, beloved Elna had the dreaded coughing disease, and, unthinkably, was dying. How could they have not realized sooner? Why had she, Tyra, not spoken to Axel about her concerns? Why, the first day she met Elna she was worried about her, but somehow everyone just accepted Elna's delicate health. Why had she not expressed her fears more forcefully? How could life be so cruel that they should lose Elna, Elna of all people, Elna the heart of the family? The Östring family had already lost a mother, probably their father, and two children, to the coughing disease, as well as two sons in tragic, premature death. Why did they have to lose beloved Elna?

Somehow she made polite talk. Mor Anna sat stolid and remote as usual, but whenever Elna tried to talk coughing wracked her body. Tyra handed around cups of coffee that no one drank, offered *knäckerbröd* and cheese because it was all she could find in the kitchen, and hurried home through the now darkening shadows to make nourishing chicken soup and sustaining rye bread to take to her sister next day.

"Axel," she blurted out as soon as he arrived home, exhausted after a hard day behind his plough, "can you drive me over to your family tomorrow?"

"Don't be ridiculous!" Axel began, and then saw Tyra's face in the lamplight. She had clearly been crying, and he had never seen her look so upset. "What's wrong?"

When Tyra shared her concern, her absolute certainty that Elna was dying, it was Axel's turn to sit down quickly and try to take in the enormity of the impending tragedy. Elna! Surely not his beloved Elna!

By the time they returned to the family next day, with loads of food and large bundles of carefully dried firewood (Axel was right, the house was cold and in urgent need of better heating), both had composed themselves and could talk vapidly about the weather, the possibility of snow, and even the Lapua crisis. As planned, they left early and, while the short daylight lasted, went straight to the doctor in Nykarleby, but it was a futile attempt. The doctor, although he came immediately, had nothing to offer except advice to keep Elna comfortable, and prescribe a cough mixture that made her sleepy. Outside the house, in the gathering dusk, he talked to Axel, and confirmed Tyra's fears that Elna was dying.

Tyra visited regularly, but Axel shrank from seeing his beloved sister in such a decline. He would take Tyra to the door, call out a gruff but supposedly cheerful "hello," check the supply of firewood, and race to his allegedly essential work, leaving Tyra to get home across the fields as best she could.

After one visit, Elna beckoned for Tyra to come close. "You're all being so kind to me," she said, smiling, "but I do understand the truth. Don't worry. I believe in God, and know he will save me. I'm not afraid to die. I know I'll meet you in heaven." Tyra grasped her sister's hands, but could not speak.

Elna lived long enough to see the lilacs bloom, and her favorite grape hyacinths fill a vase on the kitchen table. She joyfully noted the spring return of fieldfares, watched a great tit build its nest in an apple tree, and daily asked to be taken outside so she could hear the songs of the birds she loved so much. She was a cheerful presence to the end of her life.

One day Tyra arrived at the house and was shocked to see Mor Anna bustling in the kitchen. Wordlessly Tyra placed the food she had brought on the bench, and looked uncertainly at her mother-in-law.

"I didn't realize how sick she is," Mor Anna said softly, apologetically. "We'd all been sick. I got better quickly, so did the boys. Yesterday when the doctor came and told me the truth I was shocked. I'm struggling to believe it. I've relied so much on Elna. But I will take care of her. I can do it, and I will."

And she did.

Tyra did not expect Mor Anna's efforts to last, but she should have had more faith. When Elna died on a lovely spring day in mid May, Mor Anna took care of arrangements, and continued to care admirably for her two sons still at home. The terrible lethargy that had enveloped her since her husband's death was thrown off, and she had a new purpose for living. Previously Elna had done almost everything around the home, but now Mor Anna began cooking and cleaning, and even planted flowers in the garden. Tyra found it very hard to visit her without Elna being there, but she tried to go at least weekly. Sometimes she took Takla with her, and that certainly made things easier, until she finally realized that whatever terrible lethargy had burdened Mor Anna, it had truly gone. Elna's death blunted the anger Tyra felt when she learned the government had repealed the prohibition laws. Facing the terrible injustice of Elna's death, the injustice of alcohol was just another part of the mess of life.

Those most troubled by Elna's death were Axel, and fifteen-year-old John. Axel was the sole survivor of his once happy family. His four siblings and both parents were dead. He buried himself in work; fortunately the farm was demanding all his spring energies. Tyra received grunts over her carefully prepared evening meals, then he disappeared into the barn for more work. Erik, the poetic philosopher, coped reasonably well with his sister's death. He had finished his last year at school, and, although looking for more permanent work, before being called into army training, was happy to help Axel. John seemed to have taken over his mother's lethargy, and nothing, whether pleading, bribing, or scolding, made any improvement in his behavior. Sometimes he came with Erik and did a reasonable day's work, then when he was most needed, he moped around the house refusing even to get water for his mother. Axel was frequently very impatient with him.

Tyra was making nettle soup one day when Axel walked in early for his evening meal. A flourishing patch of nettles grew beside the barn, and Takla had shown her how to pick them without getting stung and turn them into good soup with milk, flour, and butter. He flopped into a chair, and silently watched his wife working.

"I'm glad I've got you," he blurted out unexpectedly. "Elna meant so much to me. She was more than a sister; she was really my mother. I don't remember my own mother at all. It was always Elna. She was so kind and patient, cooked so well, kept the house running smoothly. I was so happy when I saw you were good friends. I never thought I'd lose her, never. But I have you. And you were her friend, and that makes me feel good."

Tyra stopped stirring her pot, and gazed at her husband.

"I'm glad I have you, too. I didn't know Elna like you did, but I'm really sad she died. She seemed so calm, and faced her death so bravely. She was sure she would meet me in heaven. But I struggle with death and dying. Well, not so much dying as what comes next, you know, hell and all that. When I was young, in *skriftskola*, I tried to talk to Pastor Lindgren about it, but he just got angry with me."

"Those priests!" exploded Axel. "They don't know anything!"

"Oh, they try, I'm sure," said Tyra softly. "They just don't seem to understand what it feels like having someone you think is really special go to hell, and then burn forever. He seemed to think it was a mortal sin to ask questions, but how else could I learn?"

Axel looked at Tyra sharply. "So you've worried about that too, like I have? Elna was so good she'll have to be in heaven and talk to the good Lord and get us all there too! But sometimes in church they make it sound as though everyone has to do time in hell, and I wonder what sort of a god would ask my wonderful sister to do that!"

"I trust that God will do what's right."

"I don't know. I guess I'm not as trusting as you are! When I get to one of those places I'll have some pretty tough questions to ask that old man in the sky!" Axel stared into space. "That priest, the one I went to about our land, I don't think he was interested in anything about me except the lease money I agreed to pay. He never said anything nice when I told him I was getting married. I guess it's commonplace for him, but surely he'd know it was special for me! Yah, all those land reforms the government made must be hitting them a bit. I think the church owned half Finland! Ah, well, I guess it was much easier to take land off the rich gentry than the church, but I don't trust those priests. It won't be long before the government turns its greedy eyes on church land and confiscates that too, mark my words, and then I might be in trouble. When I was in confirmation class we didn't dare ask anything, just like you. It was yah sir, nay sir, just as you say sir, to the priest!"

Tyra smiled, although she wasn't sure it was right to talk about God the way Axel did. But she admitted she had some tough questions of her own. "Yah, I had the same problem," she admitted. "The priest even caned me because I asked a question."

"What! You mean than grinning hypocrite that married us?" Tyra nodded. "Just as well I didn't know that then! Anyway, I came in to tell you I've done it. Got everything planted out, potatoes, barley and rye."

"That's wonderful," said Tyra, looking with admiration at her husband. "You've been working hard."

"And I've been thinking. We need something to give us a steady income through the year, rather than just relying on crops once a year. What do you think about getting another cow, and more hens? We're selling eggs locally and that's good. But what if we got more hens, and I took eggs to Jakobstad regularly, and maybe some chicken meat too. And if we made cheese from our milk, we could add that."

"Good ideas! I'm happy to help with whatever you think would sell. The last thing Elna did for me was tell me how to make *leipäjuusto* cheese, or what she sometimes called *juustoleipä*. I haven't felt like trying to make it yet, but I'll see if I can make it good enough to sell. But eggs, now I do know about them. I'll get Hjalmar to send more chicks, and start breeding my own. I'll tell him rooster chicks are as good as hen chicks because we can sell them. I don't know where to buy another cow, but you can deal with that, I'm sure."

"Ah, you're a good woman," grinned Axel. "As good as Elna." And that, Tyra knew, was the highest praise he could give. Then he smiled. "I forgot to tell you the cow is already in calf, and I hope it will be a heifer! I took Vallmo to old Hans' bull just before winter."

"So that's why she's getting fat!" laughed Tyra. "I should have guessed."

And though a heifer the new calf proved to be, Tyra's efforts to make *leipäjuusto* cheese did not satisfy her. It was never as good as Elna's. She served it to her husband who praised it, but rarely made enough to sell. However, Hjalmar sent two large baskets of chicks, and they flourished. Tyra was in the poultry business with her husband. Her dozen hens soon became one hundred, and after a few months they had a steady flock of about three hundred. They cluckingly fulfilled Axel's dreams of a good steady income.

Then late autumn an unusual letter arrived from Anna. After news about Elin and the Tobelius family, and an exciting message from Matilda about the perfect man she had recently met, Tyra read:

> *After we got back from our visit to you at Christmas I signed up for some Bible study classes. I've been missing you, and thought it would help me meet people. The class is pretty small, only about ten of us, but the two young men conducting it are very pleasant and patient. They are happy to answer any question, and they make it all so simple and logical. I was a bit sad when Pastor Lindgren spoke against them in church as Judaizers, whatever that is, but decided they were such nice young men and I enjoyed their classes so much I would ignore him. I asked them lots of questions about death and dying, and they never got angry with me. I thought you would be very interested to know that they have proved clearly from the Bible that we don't go to heaven or*

> hell when we die. Isn't that great news? We just rest quietly in the earth, like a sleep. When Jesus comes back he'll resurrect, that is, wake us up, and take all those who love him to heaven, and those who don't will be destroyed because they would not be happy in heaven anyway. But they won't burn forever, just long enough to be obliterated. They explained that when the Bible says 'forever' it means as long as something lasts. The Bible says the smoke from the destruction of Sodom went up forever, but we all know Sodom is not burning now. Isn't that good news! I'm going to ask those young men for books that I can send you, because you would find it very interesting, and answer all those questions that I know have been troubling you for a long time.

Tyra reread the passage twice to make sure she had the sense right, then sat back on her kitchen chair in bewilderment. Was it possible that her youthful doubts about how something could burn forever, and the injustice of the whole punishment system of hell, were actually not so stupid after all? Did the Bible really not teach an everlasting hell? She looked forward eagerly to the arrival of the books.

But instead of any books, in early summer another letter came from Anna, with more surprising news.

> Well, what those young men have shown me from the Bible is all so sensible, I decided to join their Christian group. In the classes they showed us how we should be baptized like John the Baptist baptized Jesus (remember when the dove of the Holy Spirit fell on Jesus?), and so I got baptized properly (right down in the water, completely) and now I also go to church on Saturday, which these men have shown is the seventh day of the Ten Commandments. Remember how Pastor Lindgren made you do all that reading about the first day? Those texts all clearly showed that Jesus rose on the first day, but there is no mention of changing the commandment, I'm sure you remember. Ever since the pastor made us do that I've had doubts because there was certainly no mention of a change to Sunday in any of them. The young men explained lots of church history, and it seems the change came from Greek ideas and a Roman emperor's decree hundreds of years after Jesus. Anyway, Pastor Lindgren is not at all happy with me. We had a long, and I am afraid to say rather heated talk. I told him I was just doing what Luther told us to do, making the Bible the base for my beliefs. He did not like that! Finally, he agreed that if I continued to pay my church tax and go to his church at Christmas and Easter he would not report me to the authorities. That scared me

a bit, because I didn't know I was a rebel, which is what he called me. But he couldn't answer any of the questions I asked him like those young men did. Sorry I haven't sent the books yet, but don't worry, they'll come soon.

Tyra was shocked. Her mother was the last person she could even begin to think of as a rebel, but here she was not only learning strange new ideas, but doing them as well! Everyone, Tyra thought, got baptized, nicely sprinkled with holy water, when they were born, or soon after. What on earth was her mother talking about going right down in the water like Jesus? She got out her Bible and read the passages about John the Baptist, and was shocked to discover her mother was right. Jesus did go right into the water, and there was no mention of any sprinkling. The ideas about death and hell and dying were comforting, but Tyra was worried. From experience she knew it was not a good idea to go against the priest. However, being summer she was much too busy to waste time and concern about these things. If her mother's books ever did arrive, maybe she could look at them during the long darkness of winter. Things might be easier this year, because the men with their power poles had finally reached the village, and were busy stringing wires to every house. Having electric light in the house would make everything, but especially reading, easy. She wanted to talk to Axel about these new ideas, but he worked such long hours, and fell asleep as soon as he sat down in the evenings, sometimes almost while he was eating, that there was little time to talk seriously about anything with him. Sometimes she had to wake him to eat!

Thursdays and Fridays became very busy for Tyra. All week she collected eggs and carefully placed them in baskets in a cool place she prepared under a tree, and engaged Erik to make an egg house for her. Then on Thursdays she packed them in straw, meticulously checking for any that were no good. Finally, very early on Fridays, she helped Axel load the cart that he and Löfte took to Jakobstad. It was hard work every day keeping her flock of hens together while letting them roam freely, but she knew this was important if they were to remain healthy and lay well. She was proud of her contribution to the family wellbeing.

Axel was not yet growing the tomatoes he was keen to develop because he was so busy developing his other enterprises. No one else in the area had grown tomatoes, which meant he had no one to advise or help him get started. However, he did know that building the glasshouse was the first step. Since glass was expensive he asked around for old windows discarded by builders. His trips to Jakobstad proved useful for this, and he slowly accumulated a pile of old glass of various shapes and sizes. He became quite paranoid that one of the animals or a careless person would smash his precious pile, and ruin his plans. At first he insisted the glass be kept in the house, but Tyra contended she was in grave danger of tripping over the higgledy piggledy pile, and smashing it herself. The bedroom, she insisted, was not the place to stack building materials!

"Really?" he exclaimed, shocked at her careless indifference to the project. "This hothouse is very important, don't you understand!"

"No doubt," said Tyra firmly. "But you can get Erik to fence off the place you plan to put your glasshouse, and keep the glass and other building material there until you're ready to build it. He did a good job building the fence and house for my eggs, and I'm sure he'd do the same for you."

"Did he really? So he was the one who made that?"

"You don't think I did it myself, do you!" she laughed.

Tyra won, and had her bedroom back again. Erik was happy to help. He planned to begin a joinery apprenticeship, but was conscripted into the army before he could begin. On home leave he was both willing and able to make anything. He did such a good job Axel decided he would hire him to help build the glasshouse when the main farm work was done, and the long winter set in. Axel's big concern now became the placement of his proposed hothouse. Many times Tyra saw him walking around carefully inspecting variousplaces, and looking anxiously at the sky.

"I want the sunniest place for the glasshouse," he finally revealed. "Your Far was right, tomatoes are a Mediterranean fruit. I have to catch all the sun I can."

It was early autumn and Tyra was busy packing eggs when the postman arrived with another welcome letter from Anna. Tyra did not think her mother could have any more significant news to report after her Bible study revelations, but she was wrong. She firmly tried to fix the number "59 eggs" in her head, carefully closed the gate to the egg box, and sat on a large rock in the garden where she read:

> *You'll be pleased to know Matilda is getting married. She came around to tell me the good news. Wasn't that nice of her? Her fiancé is a young man who also works for Herr Backman. They'll get married next summer, and she hopes you can come for the wedding. And now I must tell you Pastor Lindgren visited me again. I confess I was more than a bit worried when he knocked on the door. But don't worry, he was not nasty, not a bit. In fact, he came to make an apology! Really, truly. I invited him in, although*

I wasn't too sure if it was a good idea. After lots of hemming and hawing he asked me if I had stopped coming to his church because of what he had done to you. I asked what he meant, and then he shocked me. He said he had caned you because you asked impudent questions in skriftskola! I couldn't believe it! I told him you were such a good child, and I was sure he had misunderstood you. I told him you had never mentioned that he had done any such thing, which seemed to surprise him. But then I remembered how he had been the one to make us find all those first day verses, so I told him that's when I began to wonder about the church's teachings. I reminded him I was taught that Lutheran church teachings were based solely on the Bible, but the changed day of one of the commandments had no mention anywhere in the Bible. He seemed sad about what I said, so then I told him how sad you were about people dying, and that you really wanted to know about death. I told him how you had lost several very important friends and that's why you wanted to find out what really happened when a person died. He apologized again for hitting you, and admitted he dreaded the skriftskola classes and found them exhausting because most of the students had no interest. Every year he had to teach this group of restless and bored students, and he had come to detest the job. And then, you will never believe this, but I promise I am telling the absolute truth! He said he too often wondered about hell, and when people asked him about it he was so uncomfortable he was liable to get really angry because he had no answer. Can you believe that! I felt so sorry for him. So I promised him I would go to his church a little more often, just to show people I was not angry with him. (After all, I can go to our fellowship on Saturday and his church on Sunday without causing trouble to any one.) He seemed very happy about that, and then he especially asked me, in fact begged me, to write to you and ask for your forgiveness for caning you.

Tyra took a deep, deep breath, and looked up at a passing cloud. She shivered slightly, and realized the evening was getting cool. Egg counts vanished from her mind. Not in her wildest thoughts had she ever expected a message like this from dreaded Pastor Lindgren. She would have to tell Axel about it, but carefully, certainly not when he was tired. So, Pastor Lindgren was human after all, a man with the same worries she had. Why had he been so afraid to admit his concerns? She knew he had a wife, but there were no children, at least none she knew about. What tragedies had he experienced, that he too was worried about death and hell? He was wrong to beat her, but a beautiful peace stole over her. She would read those books her mother promised to send very carefully, when, if ever, they came. And yes, she would send a message by her mother to Pastor Lindgren, and tell him she had forgiven him, or at least she was working on that.

As the sharp rock beneath her cut into her buttocks, the long grass tickled her legs, and the evening breeze chilled her body, she wondered how much suffering was the result of people being hurt and damaged by others. Take Algot, for example. If only his father had been able to see that his son was hurting, and hear his pain, listen to him, and help him. What about that dreadful Tammerfors war? Why did "Whites" fight "Reds"? She had to admit, even now, as an adult, she still had only a very hazy idea of who Whites and Reds really were. She knew that many people had suffered under Russian rule, and that "Reds" in the minds of those people represented a continuation of Russian power. But both "Reds" and "Whites" were people, Finnish people, just like her. Her parents were passionately against Russian rule, although she doubted they would ever join any fighting. When would this endless, senseless cycle of pain and retaliation ever end? And now she had discovered that Pastor Lindgren, the man she had revered as a child and been terrified by as a teenager, was struggling with his own hurts and serious doubts. Why did he have to pretend he had all the answers when he didn't? Couldn't he study the Bible for himself, and come to his own careful conclusions, or was he afraid he would lose his job if he taught anything different from the official teachings of the Lutheran church? She had always been proud of her church, knowing it had stood up to the might of the Roman Catholic Church, and declared its teachings were based on "sola scriptura." Oh, it was all so confusing, she thought, as she stood up and rubbed her tender bottom. Someday it might all sort out, but, she thought, only God could do that.

Anna's promised books finally arrived, but they were accompanied by a young man[1]. In late autumn, when work on the farm was easing, this smiling young man knocked on her door and introduced himself as the person who had baptized her mother. He was going to run some Bible study classes in Nykarleby, he said, and invited her, and anyone else she would like to include, to attend. Tyra asked Axel to come with her, and even shared the amazing story of Pastor Lindgren's apology, but he

---

1. Whilst the name of this man remains unknown, the leader of the Adventist church in Finland at this time was Pastor Adolf Blomstedt, father of renowned orchestra conductor Herbert Blomstedt. See *A Great Song*, by Ursula Weigert.

was not interested. He suggested she attend the classes and let him know what she thought of them, but he was much too busy to be bothered with such things. To her surprise, however, Erik, recently returned from army training, when told of the Bible classes offered to drive her into Nykarleby each week, and attend with her.

She hardly knew Erik, partly because he had been away in the army. He was a quiet young man, and Elna often hinted he was quite a scholar. "He writes poetry" her sister-in-law told her proudly, but Tyra had never seen any of his efforts. What she did know was he crafted beautiful woodwork and occasionally presented her with a wooden tray, or carved bowl. He did not attend church very often, certainly no more than his older brother, so Tyra had not suspected he had any interest in spiritual things. But he eagerly soaked up the lessons from the Bible studies, and when the young teacher asked who would like to be be baptized by this strange new way of getting right in the water, Erik was the first to raise his hand. Tyra hesitated, not sure how Axel would respond, and unwilling to displease him. She asked for time to think about it, and the teacher was happy to accept that. He admitted that for health reasons he would not actually baptize anyone in winter, but would return to perform the ceremony in summer. Meanwhile, he encouraged his students to study the Bible carefully for themselves, so they could be fully convinced about what they believed. When he returned they could make their decisions. "They" were two elderly couples, two widows, one with two teenage children, and of course herself and Erik. Erik came over one or two evenings a week, despite the winter darkness, and under the new electric light, studied the Bible with her. Axel invariably fell asleep, but, to her relief, expressed no disapproval of their activity. Sometimes Takla came and listened to the discussions, but she never said much. Erik, however, was deeply in earnest, and put more pressure on her to make a decision to be baptized than the young pastor had.

Before summer fully arrived, Tyra had wonderful, and very distracting, good news of her own, news that totally preoccupied her. At long, long last, she was pregnant. With great difficulty she waited until she was absolutely sure before telling a slightly incredulous Axel, and writing to her jubilant mother. Anna feared her daughter suffered from the same problems she had becoming pregnant, but Tyra achieved pregnancy after only three years of marriage. Anna's letters now said little about Bible study, but were parcels containing new articles of essential baby attire. Tyra wondered if her mother planned to outfit an orphanage of children! But secretly she was extremely grateful of her mother's help, as she struggled with diminished energy to keep up her share of the farm's essential work.

By the time she was visibly with child the troubling morning nausea had subsided and she was in excellent health. Her gratitude to God was overflowing, and she earnestly wanted to show him how thankful she was. One Saturday she asked Erik if he would like to go with her to Nykarleby and meet with the other Bible class students for a "Sabbath" meeting. Although neither of them had ever done this, he quickly agreed. She had no idea what to expect, and felt very conspicuous and apprehensive as she and Erik walked into the tiny room where the group met. Despite trusting Anna's spiritual judgment, she was still anxious that this new group was somehow a weird cult, the sort of wicked convention Pastor Lindgren had occasionally warned his congregation about. But, just as she and Erik sat down, the group started singing a familiar hymn, one very popular in Lutheran churches, whose tune she had always loved, and with words that now suddenly removed all her doubts that this group of Sabbath keepers was anything other than a deeply committed assembly of Christians. The words flowed over her with calming reassurance, especially for her forth coming labor and delivery and the solemn responsibility of motherhood. For the rest of her life this hymn served as a strong personal guide. All the terrible fears of death, and dying, the horrors of hell, and the ever-present daily worries of ordinary farm life vanished like a snowflake on her hot stove as she heard, as though for the first time, the words of the beautiful hymn. Karolina (Lina) Sandell-Berg, the author of the hymn, was a well-known nineteenth century Swedish hymn writer, and the tune was a beautiful Swedish folk melody. How, Tyra wondered, had she missed the significance of the hymn's words? Now they served as her guide for the future, and the choices she needed to make.

> Day by day, and with each passing moment,
> Strength I find, to meet my trials here
> Trusting in my Father's wise bestowment,
> I've no cause for worry or for fear.
> He Whose heart is kind beyond all measure
> Gives unto each day what He deems best—
> Lovingly, its part of pain and pleasure,
> Mingling toil with peace and rest.

Every day, the Lord Himself is near me
With a special mercy for each hour;
All my cares He fain would bear, and cheer me,
He Whose Name is Counselor and Pow'r.
The protection of His child and treasure
Is a charge that on Himself He laid;
"As thy days, thy strength shall be in measure,"
This the pledge to me He made.

Help me then in every tribulation
So to trust Thy promises, O Lord,
That I lose not faith's sweet consolation
Offered me within Thy holy Word.
Help me, Lord, when toil and trouble meeting,
E'er to take, as from a father's hand,
One by one, the days, the moments fleeting,
Till I reach the promised land.

When the young Bible teacher returned in mid summer and asked if she was ready and willing for baptism, she immediately agreed. It was not a decision she made lightly, but once made she was fully committed. Erik was delighted that she would join him and the rest of the small Bible study group. Axel agreed to attend the ceremony, although he maintained an apparently disinterested silence afterwards except for one incredulous, "Why would you want to go swimming in your clothes with all those people!"

But Tyra, as she solemnly submitted to being lowered into, then raised from the water, felt a deep sense of peace. She still considered herself a loyal Lutheran, one following the footsteps of the great Protestant reformer. She was not rebelling, but simply continuing to make the Bible the basis of her faith and conduct. The recognition that the horrors of hell that had tormented her for so long was simply a momentary destruction of all that was evil, at the end of the world, in preparation for the new, recreated earth that Jesus Christ had promised, was a source of great reassurance.

Having made her choice for the future, Tyra faced motherhood with the calm assurance that God would help her meet the challenges. Her commitment to God, she was certain, would ensure she had no more problems. Life from now on would be plain sailing. She wished Axel was more interested in the Bible truths that had become so important to her and Erik, but she was confident he would make a very dependable father, and he had already proved to be a good provider.

Christmas later that year with her parents was fun, but large and awkward with imminent delivery, she was unable to enjoy the festivities as much as usual. Predictably, Axel and his work mates were out doing winter wood chopping in the forest, stacking their neat piles of sawn timber into tidy cubes called *motti*, when the strong pains of labor came upon Tyra. She was thankful her mother had decided, despite her mild protests, to stay on in Brännon after Christmas to help her daughter with her imminent delivery. Anna actually had little experience with childbirth, and when Tyra's pains began, she panicked and struggled through deep and slippery snow to ask Takla to get Karl, in his truck, to call the midwife.

Takla came to sit with Tyra, and assess the situation. She had often assisted the busy midwife, and well knew she would make a fuss if called too soon. "It's always slow, especially for the first," she encouraged the anxious Anna, and sweating Tyra. "I'm sure Axel will be back before you go into real labor."

As another agonizing spasm engulfed her, Tyra wondered what "real labor" was supposed to be like. Takla began collecting towels, while the buckets and basins of water Anna had carefully prepared were heated on the stove. With great relief Tyra heard the approach of the returning men, although Axel was not the first to arrive.

"Get the midwife!" Anna begged the bemused Karl. "The baby will arrive any minute!"

When the midwife came everything was a professional bustle and hive of activity. Axel was pressed into hauling more water from the well than he believed could possibly be needed, but obediently he trudged back and forth to keep the midwife happy. He decided midwives were the bossiest women he had ever met, and was not surprised that this one had never married!

Finally, with a last agonizing cry, in the deep winter darkness of the 19th of January, 1935, the day after Axel's 26th birthday, Tyra gave birth to a bonny baby boy, whom they promptly named Nils Axel. Of course he was the most beautiful baby ever to arrive on earth. But as Tyra held him to her breast she was especially grateful he was born in the long winter darkness, when work on the farm was at its least demanding and she had ample time to enjoy him. Even Axel's forestry took second place, for a week or two, as he found excuses to loiter around his home and admire his son with bemused amazement.

"You know," he told his lumber-jacking friends who came to admire the new addition to the human race, "I have a special appreciation for my cow and what she went through to get her heifer!"

Chapter 12

Another War, Again, and Again

Tyra dandled Nils on her knee, and felt a contentment she had not believed possible. Her aching questions about hell and death had been answered, and she had surprised herself by her courage in making a stand for biblical truth as she saw it. The gift of a son, and both she and Axel were sure Nils was just that, confirmed her sense of purpose and destiny, that God was definitely blessing her. Life was purposeful, meaningful. God would work out everything just fine. The miseries of the past were over, and she could look forward to the future with confidence.

The excitement of Finland's amazing triple win in the 5000-meter race in the 1936 Berlin Olympics gripped the proud country, and confirmed her overall optimism. Such a small country, such a new country, and yet three of their men had beaten the best in the world! Finland was ranked world fifth in these Olympics, with seven gold medals and six each of silver and bronze, equal to the huge country of France, and slightly ahead of their Nordic neighbor Sweden which had double the population. Listening to their radio each evening Tyra and Axel fully shared the national pride and excitement. But behind all the pomp and glory were niggling concerns. The United States, Britain, France, the Netherlands, Czechoslovakia and, significantly, Sweden, had initially called for a boycott of these games because of growing concerns about the policies of Germany's new Chancellor, Adolf Hitler. However, with her now firm belief that God was in control, those issues did not greatly concern or seriously trouble Tyra.

"We've had enough discrimination in this country to know what that feels like," observed Axel, after another news report on Germany.

"But that Hitler guy sounds lethal. I don't like it." he shook his head in consternation.

"It's supposed to be a Christian country, Lutheran like us, but they seem to have forgotten that Jesus Christ was a Jew," replied Tyra, clearly surprised at the realization.

"Well, well, well! So he was!" exclaimed Axel.

But farm activities dominated their thinking. Axel was much more interested in his new glasshouse than sporting events or Germany. The sunniest place on the property, he finally discovered, was right beside their own house. He postponed wood cutting that winter, and while the weather was still fair a friend helped him pour a solid concrete floor with low concrete walls, and troughs to fill with soil where the tomatoes would grow. Then, after a day's lumbering with his friends, he used his "evenings" to fit the various collected window frames into place, and eventually the glass house rivalled their home in size. Once the sun shone properly in May it heated beautifully, but Axel decided to augment the vagaries of weather and installed an old wood stove to fire up if temperatures dropped too low. He built a large tank beside the house to hold water from their roof so the precious plants could be watered in the long, hot summer. Packets of tomato seeds were bought at significant cost, and while it was still cold and dark Axel planted them in trays inside their snugly warm house, trays around which Tyra had to negotiate her housework. With great excitement they watched the tomatoes grow, tall and luscious, producing wonderful plump red fruit. Axel now had to persuade people to buy his unfamiliar delicacy. He and Tyra discovered tomato with cheese on rye bread was delicious, so she suggested he take samples when he sold eggs in the markets. Soon demand for his crop was greater than he could supply, and with delight he resorted to raising his price.

Nils grew at a rapid pace, another delight to them both. Privately his mother was a little sad there was no sign of a sibling, but he was such an agreeable child she quickly cheered. Mor Anna took a great interest in him, and often walked over to visit, which made life easier for Tyra.

"We need some pigs," announced Axel the spring after Nils turned two. "The eggs and chickens are doing well, tomatoes I'm sure will be good, cows are providing plenty of milk, and crops are good. Some pigs would top it all. They sell well, and just eat rubbish."

"No!" said Tyra firmly, watching Nils making a castle from small cubes of wood. "Not pigs. I've learned from the Bible pigs are dirty animals, not fit to eat."

"Are you crazy?" expostulated Axel, jumping up. "We aren't Jews! Every Finn eats pork! Anyway, we don't have to eat it!" Axel was willing to indulge his wife's ideas, including not smoking around her because she said it was unhealthy, but this was taking it too far. He could not understand the idea, which she claimed was from the Bible, that a person should look after their body because it was a gift from God. Her insistence that smoking was unhealthy went against the advice of all his friends, and even doctors. But, for love of her, he did not smoke when she was near him. However, to refrain from doing something that would clearly benefit them financially was utterly crazy. It was time to assert his masculine leadership!

"Tyra, I try to help you, but you are being ridiculous. I don't make a fuss about your crazy Saturday ideas, but you can't have your way in everything. Pigs are easy money, and we need that. Just be reasonable woman."

"I am," said Tyra firmly. "But I do most of the animal care, and you know that. I refuse to care for pigs. Please, for my sake, no pigs. Remember, they aren't the only animals we could farm. What about sheep? We talked about them when we were first married. They wouldn't be expensive because we have plenty of grass."

"They'd be much more work! Who's going to shear them? Don't tell me you plan to do that!"

Tyra permitted herself a faint smile. "I'm sure you'd enjoy slicing wool off sheep. But if you don't want to, I'll find someone willing to earn a little money, like Erik. I don't mind work. When I was a child Morbro Karl grew flax."

"Not suitable here, and anyway, what's that got to do with sheep?" butted in Axel. "You do annoy me sometimes with your irrelevancies!"

Tyra sighed, but was not beaten. "Well, my mother is an expert weaver. I don't think she spins, I never saw her do that, but she has many friends who do. Now if we had a few sheep we could sell the wool for spinning, and as I said, Mor has spinning connections. When the animals get old we'll sell them for meat."

Axel scratched his chin. "You sure are persistent! You have an answer for everything! Well, I'll think about it. But if I decide on pigs, you better not make a fuss!"

Two weeks later Axel arrived home from his weekly trip to Jakobstad with a cart carrying six bleating lambs. "Orphans," he grinned sheepishly, "and very cheap. They'll have to be hand fed till they're older, but the cows are producing plenty of milk, and feeding them might be easier than trying to sell milk when everyone else is doing the same thing." He paused, and began unloading his bleating purchases.

"Oh, Axel, thank you for listening!" said Tyra, resting her hand on his shoulder. "I'll look after them very carefully. I can ask God to bless these animals, but I couldn't do that with pigs!"

Axel made a snorting sound, but he patted her hand gently. "And by the way, I've found someone who'll teach me the basics of sheep shearing. He says there's nothing to it!"

Tyra smiled triumphantly, and settled into lamb feeding routine. Nils was a willing helper. Takla told her not to bottle feed lambs too long, or they became boss sheep, so the weaning process began as soon as possible. Tyra was kept very busy that spring and summer, very glad Mor Anna visited regularly and she did not have to make the weekly trek to the old house herself. Two of the lambs proved to be rams, but they provided excellent wool, and one of them good meat. The other Axel used for breeding purposes. Life was good.

One day Erik spoke to Tyra. "I'm worried about John. He's finished school and is due to go into the army. Perhaps he's just worried about that, but he doesn't seem well to me. Come over when you have time and talk with him."

"No problem," responded Tyra, who, despite all her chores, visited next day. When she arrived Mor Anna began bustling in the kitchen. Tyra felt slightly guilty for not warning her of the visit, but there was no hint of displeasure in Mor Anna's demeanor. John was sitting in a chair reading the paper.

"Are you glad you've finished school?" asked Tyra, seating herself beside him.

"Yah."

"What are you doing this summer?"

"Nothing." John continued staring at his paper.

Tyra changed tactics. "John, why don't you take Nils for a walk around your garden?"

This time John looked up. "I'm too tired," he said, and his face flushed. "Leave me alone!"

"Well, come with me," said Tyra gently, persistently, and as John reluctantly stood up she immediately regretted forcing him. He was so thin! As thin as . . . Oh, no! It didn't bear thinking about. "Let's go and sit in the sun," she said, taking Nils by the hand and ushering him outside. John followed slowly.

"You're to go into the army soon, aren't you?" she probed kindly.

"Can't," said John flatly. "They won't have me. The army doctor says I have the coughing disease and they don't want me."

Tyra took a deep breath. Erik was right, John was sick, very sick, with the same dreaded malady that took Elna's life.

"Have you told your mother?"

"No."

"Or Erik?"

"No."

Tyra took another deep breath. "John, you need to see the doctor. There are new treatments now."

John gazed at her steadily. "I know you care!" he blurted out. "I know you're trying to be kind. But it's no use. The army doctor took a picture of my lungs. He called it an X-ray. And he didn't call it the coughing disease, but a fancy long word I wrote down, tuberculosis. There were lots of them looking at me, and they all said I was too far gone and there was nothing they could do for me. Well, I'll tell you the truth, they did tell me to come home and go to the doctor here, but they admitted I was bad and I know that in our family there's no hope with the coughing disease."

"Oh, John! When did they tell you that?"

"About two months ago. Now don't you go telling Mor!"

"But John, she should know. It's not kind otherwise."

But Mor Anna did know, by intuition, and shared John's fatalistic attitude. Her only action had been to give John his own room in the hope he would not spread the infection to Erik. Axel was extremely quiet for several days after Tyra shared the tragic news, and as usual buried himself in work. Erik spent much time in the Nykarleby library borrowing books for his brother. Tyra visited as often as she could, but rarely took Nils with her, grateful of Takla's kindly support. Takla had no children, and was glad to "borrow" Nils for the few hours Tyra could bear to part with him. In the autumn of 1938 Emil Johan Östring became the fifth, and probably sixth, victim in his family to die of tuberculosis. He was just twenty years old. Mor Anna was stoical, Erik heartbroken, and Axel defiantly silent. Tyra busied herself with Nils, her animals, her tiny church fellowship, and her Bible. This time death did not terrify her, except, which she hardly dared allow herself to think about, the possibility of Nils catching the dreaded disease. She had taken time, lots of time, to talk to John, and was convinced he had committed his life to God. But it was still very hard.

After John's death Axel persuaded Erik to buy a cottage that became available in Brännon. The dilapidated old Sorvich house was put up for sale, but there were no buyers. However, the proximity of the new cottage to Tyra and Axel, her grandson Nils, and its much more practical size, convinced Mor Anna that the move to Brännon was wise, and she soon joined Erik. She arranged for neighbors to rent the old house as a barn. Axel and Erik were delighted to have Tyra nearby to help support their mother.

Early one morning, a few weeks after Mor Anna's move, Tyra was busy feeding her flock of hens that had spread widely over the field around their home. Nils loved joining this activity, regarding it as his special fun, and like his uncle-cousin Hjalmar could not resist chasing some of the more skittish birds.

"Come back here!" Tyra called loudly as he ran towards the road. Nils laughed and kept on running.

"You're just the same as ever! Still looking after hens!" called a cheerful voice from the gate.

Tyra looked up sharply. The voice sounded familiar, but she did not recognize the man under a wide-brimmed hat, a man who suddenly leaned down and picked up her precious son! Alarmed, she moved rapidly across to the intruder, who was talking to Nils in a much too friendly way.

"You don't recognize me, do you?" the man laughed, pulling off his hat and hooking it on a fence post.

Tyra stood there, indignant, puzzled, and unsure. Then suddenly she knew. "Algot!" she exclaimed joyously. "Algot! When did you get here? Is it really ten years since I saw you?" She thrust out her hand to shake his, but despite his armful of boy he enveloped her in a bear hug.

For a few moments neither could speak. Tyra regained her poise first, and remembered her manners. "Give me time to get these birds fed, then stay and have something to eat and drink with us. Axel isn't far away, though I'm not sure where he is right now."

"Yah, it's me," responded Algot, blowing his nose with his one free hand. "I'm free, very free. People like me don't have much work to do. I've got all the time in the world," he added with a sigh. "While you look after the chickens I'll get to know this young fellow, whose name I don't know, and he can help me find his Far."

"That's Nils, our son," introduced Tyra belatedly.

The hens did not notice their dramatic reduction in care that morning as they were shooed off to peck weeds around the barnyard. Nils, with an unerring compass for his father, skilfully led Algot to the glasshouse where Axel was ladling water on tomatoes. Nils loved this task, which dismayed Tyra, because of the mess he made of his clothes. With Algot now hatless Axel recognized him immediately.

"Well there, there, there!" he grinned. "So you're out? Did you meet General Wallenius?"

Algot thought this a huge joke and roared with laughter, but admitted he had not had the pleasure of the celebrated man's company. "But you know," Algot said, pulling Nils away from a bunch of plump red tomatoes, "although prison was tough it wasn't all bad. I learned a trade there, carpentry. I hated the farm, and felt stuck and didn't know what else to do. Hjalmar's doing great there, and with a trade I enjoy I can get on with my life, that is, if people will give me a chance."

Axel nodded sympathetically. "Have you been looking for work?"

Algot shook his head. "Not yet. I—I just need to get used to being a person again. It's a whole new world in there, compared with real life. You can't think for yourself, just have to fit in with the regulations. But you know, prison helped me kick my habits. Both of them. No more alcohol for me, never, ever. I know it's deadly for me and I must never touch it, never. And no more smoking either. That was my idea, because I noticed smoking made me want to drink."

Tyra arrived, and hearing the last comment said, "Algot, you smell so good now! Keep it up." Axel shot her a frown. Smoking was manly, and that was the end of that, he thought, whatever Tyra may think. It was alright for Algot to make his choice not to smoke, but woe betide him if he was on some campaign to stop others!

The men, with Nils hoisted to Algot's shoulders, went off to inspect the potatoes and grain. Tyra began preparing food. She was glad she had a good supply of rye bread. There were two apple trees beside the barn when they moved into Brännon, but the first couple of years their crops were small and wizened. Axel dug deeply around the trees, applied liberal amounts of farm manure, and now they were laden with choice fruit. An apple cake was quickly made, along with a nourishing pot of potato and leek soup. She knew Algot would not mind if she did not serve traditional Thursday pea soup. And, being Thursday, before market day, she had a plentiful supply of eggs which were quickly turned into cheese omelets.

"It's amazing what this man of yours has done with his farm," enthused Algot when they returned. "Those tomatoes taste great, no wonder they sell so well. He was always very inventive in the army, always full of good ideas, I remember. Even I could get excited about farming the way he has so much going on!"

Tyra offered to make a bed in the kitchen, and Algot quickly accepted her invitation. Axel pressed him to join the market expedition next day, and Algot was keen. Over the next few days he willingly did woodworking repairs needed around the house and barn. Time flew, and a week rushed past before Algot finally, reluctantly, said he should return to Oxkangar to work for his brother, now happily married.

"But I'll be back!" he assured them, as he cheerfully waved good bye and walked into Nykarleby to take the bus to Oxkangar.

But the good life did not last. On the first of September, 1939, Germany invaded Poland and war engulfed the world, again. Fearfully Axel and Tyra listened to the radio to learn what would happen next.

"I don't like it," said Axel. "Something's going to happen. Germany and Russia aren't friends. Yeah, something's going to happen, and we're right in the middle."

But night after night Finnish radio gave bland news and played pleasant music.

"I don't like it," said Axel, again. "Something's going on and they're not telling us. I'm going to get a shortwave radio and see if we can get news from Sweden."

But news from Sweden was not much different. Finally, someone in the village discovered there was a Swedish language channel from the British Broadcasting service. And Axel was right, something was going on, although the full details of this were only revealed years later, after the war. Russia had pressured the Baltic countries to allow it to have military bases on their territory, and they had agreed. But Finland's situation was worse. Russia had pressured Finland not only for military bases, which demand Finland rejected, but, incredibly, demanded Finland give up sovereignty of its choicest territory in Karelia so that Russia could have what they claimed was a better defense of Leningrad should Germany decide to invade. Fiercely patriotic Finland resisted this preposterous demand.

"Oh no!" exclaimed Axel listening to the radio on November 30, 1939. "Russia claims Finns have bombed some village called Mainila."

"No!" cried Tyra.

"Oh, no! Oh, no!" Axel suddenly cried. "It's much worse than that! Russia bombed Helsingfors today!" The color drained from Axel's sunburned face. Tyra put the squirming Nils off her knee, and sat staring into space. They both knew what a war with Russia meant.

Another War, Again, and Again

Five days later Axel received call up papers. Like it or not, he was part of the Finnish Territorials. He was ordered to outfit himself (skis would be an advantage the summons declared) and report to headquarters in Jakobstad within 24 hours. It was incredibly cold, incredibly dark. Axel and Tyra stared at each other, Nils playing cheerfully on the floor, the stove cruelly radiating home warmth, and tried to take in their situation.

"You have no choice, you must go," said Tyra.

"Yah."

"I got your best boots repaired last week."

"Yah."

"The crops are all harvested, the tomatoes finished. Then . . ."

"Tyra, do you understand? Do you have any idea of what war at this time of the year is going to be like? How long this will go on for?"

"Yah, I understand. It will be dreadful. Dreadful!" She got up, her legs like lead, and began packing. It was the best she could do. His warmest clothes, that was all she could think of. He was a farmer, and a winter woodsman who had good winter clothes. How strange, how very strange, she thought, that the army supplied no clothing, no equipment, nothing, but who was she to question? The reason actually was simple—the Finnish government was woefully unprepared for war. Axel's head reeled trying to think of all he should tell Tyra to enable her manage while he was away. But his mind would not, could not, focus.

Tyra drove Axel and Erik, with Nils, to Jakobstad (because of his mother, Erik was exempt from military duty, at present, but he still had to register). Tyra had never driven in snow and dark before, but it was the least she could do. Axel made sure she had plenty of lanterns to make the return journey safely. The cold was intense, the dark deep; it was no joyride. But Löfte, though old and not powerful, plodded faithfully. They got to Jakobstad safely, and she returned to Brännon without mishap.

Only then did she allow herself to put her head on the table, and weep. Would she ever see her husband again? Where was God, and his promises, now? She tried to pray, but anxiety took over.

Nils stood beside her, puzzled. "When's Far coming back?" he asked, bewildered. "Will he be back tomorrow?"

After a few minutes she pulled herself together. First, there was Nils. In a few weeks he would be five years old. She must put everything she had into caring for him, no, more than caring for him, preserving him. For this she could pray earnestly. There was plenty of rye and barley in the barn. They had several bags of wheat flour. Her apple and berry jams were stacked in her larder. The hens laid enough to keep them in protein. Yes, they had food and could cope. Karl Höglund was still in the village because he had not been called up, yet. Yes, Karl would help, and advise her when spring came and she needed to do something with the fields. Could she manage the plough? Perhaps faithful Löfte would somehow help her do it.

A sudden knock at the door made Tyra freeze. Terrified, she opened it, and almost hugged Karl. "Just want you to know I'm here to help," he said, and was gone.

At first Tyra thought she would not need Karl's assistance, but she soon realized it was essential she have someone to help sell her eggs. Karl proved the ideal person, and was happy to sell her eggs along with his meat.

Sadly, Tyra realized Anna and Anders would not, could not, come for Christmas now. Helsingfors was bombed viciously. Vasa, the port, was another target for Russian bombing raids. How were her parents coping? She did not know. She could only try to pray. When fear overwhelmed her, she remembered:

> Day by day, and with each passing moment,
> Strength I find, to meet my trials here;
> Trusting in my Father's wise bestowment,
> I've no cause for worry or for fear.
> He Whose heart is kind beyond all measure
> Gives unto each day what He deems best—
> Lovingly, its part of pain and pleasure,
> Mingling toil with peace and rest.

Listening to the news at night, whether from Finland or the BBC, was torture, and she abandoned the habit. She focused on keeping herself and Nils healthy and strong, and looked after the animals on whom they were so dependent. But she could not escape news. Everyone talked about it. That winter was extremely harsh. Shoveling snow to keep the path to the toilets clear, hauling wood for the stoves, and water from the well were major daily undertakings. In the past, Axel had done most of the winter animal care, but now it was all entirely up to her. She was so tired she often spoke sharply to Nils, and then felt miserable because she loved him dearly. He was missing his father, and was often unruly and difficult to manage. Especially hard were the blackouts. Reading was one thing that always helped restore her mentally, but with the farm now totally dependent on her, she had no time for reading during the day, and at night with only the glow from the wood stoves because of the blackouts, reading was almost impossible. But Nils was not bothered by the blackouts, and chatted happily beside the flickering stove light. They told each other stories, stories from the Bible, stories they invented, stories from Finland's past. She thought Nils was her responsibility, but he was her lifesaver.

When the first letter from Axel arrived by "field post", Tyra's joy was unbounded. With a wry inner smile she noted that athough his writing was very untidy, his spelling had improved considerably since their courting days. She had not realized it, but she had quietly raised his level of education. She read edited versions of these precious letters to Nils, who struggled to understand why Far had gone away so suddenly, and left them to live all by themselves in the cold and snow.

Late Christmas Eve, when the old crooked clock on the bedroom wall said 9:10pm, there was a knock at the door. Tyra froze.

"Aloh," came a muffled cry, lost in the wind. "Open! Quick! Freezing!"

"Who's there?" Her voice a whisper of fear.

"Who's there?" she called again in her deepest voice, trying to sound strong and perhaps a little masculine. Normally she loved knocks, heralds of visitors and company and enjoyable times. Now they were dangerous, threatening.

The knock came again, more insistent, more demanding.

Wind howled around the roof, and she heard no reply.

Dazed and shaking, Tyra opened the door a crack. There to her amazement was Algot, bundled up in heavy sheepskins, removing his skis at the foot of the stairs. He shook snow from his hood, shoulders and gloves, stamped his boots energetically, picked up his skis, jumped up the stairs, and rushed inside.

"Mor sent this," he announced, removing a small package from inside his jacket, and placing it on the table.

Tyra, still recovering from her fright, just stood there. What did Algot want of her?

"Go on! Open it!" he urged.

Cautiously Tyra opened the package. It contained *pepparkakor* and, unbelievably, *gubbröra*. She gave a small cry of delight.

"Now, don't do the girl thing and cry!" he commanded, which of course, she did, from pure relief.

"How long are you here?" asked Tyra, as she dabbed her eyes.

"As long as you like! Mor said I should keep you company over Christmas, and do any jobs that need doing. So, you're the boss, madam! I'm at your command!"

Hearing Algot's voice, Nils came running from his toys beside the wood stove in the bedroom, and jumped at his "uncle".

"*God jul!*" he cried. "Mor said we weren't having Christmas this year because Far is away, but now we can!" He saw the special Christmas foods on the table, and went wild with delight. "We really can have Christmas, after all!"

"We can indeed, young fellow!" Algot dug deep in his pocket, and pulled out a strange-shaped parcel. "And just to prove it, here's your present, although I think I made it for your Mor, so be good and share it."

Nils unwrapped his gift, a beautiful spinning top. "Oh!" cried Tyra, and walked out of the room. She returned a few minutes later, blowing her nose, just in time to watch the top spin perfectly across the floor.

"I promise I won't cut off its point or tie dirty string on it!" laughed Algot.

"Oh Algot, we did have good times, didn't we!" smiled Tyra, wiping her eyes. "How could either of us have ever imagined what life would do to us!"

Algot stayed two weeks, doing much to help Tyra. But she noticed, now that she spent time with him, that he jumped at loud noises, and sometimes reacted aggressively if Nils got too boisterous. He was kind and attentive, but not relaxed.

"Was . . . ah . . . um . . . prison tough on you?" she asked one evening, after Algot had spoken sharply to Nils.

Algot sighed, and his shoulders relaxed. "I'm sorry I get so jumpy at times. But, to answer your question, I benefitted from it," he said slowly, as he put Nils off his knee. "But no one there was kind. It wasn't as bad as the army, believe it or not, but another version of do this, do that. At first I rebelled and got struck many times. But I did learn, eventually. They taught me a trade, and that's useful, and I'll be forever grateful for that. I can do odd carpentering jobs around Oxkangar, but I don't have steady work, and nothing is settled, not yet."

Tyra nodded. "Just want you to know I'm very grateful of your help. Nils is a normal little boy. Sometimes I get impatient with him too. But he's a good kid. Don't be afraid to tell him to stop doing something if you don't like it. You'll find he listens very well."

"Thanks. I wasn't sure if you'd be happy if I disciplined him. I want to help you, trust me. There are still so many people who whisper about me. I like to move around, keep out of the gossip lines, and well, keep people guessing. Mor has Hjalmar and his family for Christmas, and they were very happy to share me with you. You see, I'm a pariah, so they can't socialize with me around. They benefit if I get out of sight, and hopefully you will too!"

"It's been tough, your situation," said Tyra.

Algot nodded. "Terrible," he said. "For everyone. I shudder at what I did. But I'm a better person now. Far was very tough on me. Perhaps that's why I don't want to discipline Nils. I'm not sure why he took it out on me, and not Hjalmar. Maybe we were too much alike. I don't think he was happy farming, but he felt trapped into following the family business. He should have skipped the farm and done blacksmithing. Anyway, I now know he was unhappy, unhappy about something I didn't and still don't understand. So I no longer feel the bitterness I once felt towards him. I just hope Mor can forgive me. She treats me well, but I'm not sure she trusts me, yet. There was a good chaplain in the prison. He helped me come to terms with myself and God. But I sure paid a price for my stupidity!"

"We've all been stupid. You aren't the only one."

"Tyra, when I was a kid you were an inspiration to me, you were special. Not romantic special, so don't worry," he quickly added, as he saw a blush creep over her face. "I wanted to ask you so many things, but it never seemed the right time. Things about God and good living, those sorts of things. And you know, Axel was a really good friend to me in the army. He kept me sane, kept me doing the right thing. He's the best man I know, and I was so glad when I heard he was going to marry you. Tyra, I pray for him and you. That's why I came here to do a little bit to help."

"You're a big help," Tyra smiled. "Much bigger than you realize! Erik does his best to help me, but he has his mother to attend to, and his work, so there is still a lot for me to do. Sometimes I feel I just can't keep going." But, she admitted to herself, God had an interesting sense of humor. There she was, praying earnestly that her husband would be preserved from the nameless, faceless, murdering Russian hordes, and who should God send to help her but a murderer!

Two weeks later, she was on her own again, with the dark and the cold. Axel wrote regularly, and she eagerly looked forward to the "field post" stamped letters. Radio reports, however, were discouraging in the extreme, claimimg Russia had three times as many soldiers as the Finns, thirty times more aircraft, and one hundred times more tanks. The odds were impossible. How could the tiny Finnish army possibly win against such a horde? The Russians, with all their planes, constantly dropped bombs in unexpected places, although railways seemed their favorite targets. It was reported that no permanent damage was done, because the resourceful Finns quickly repaired any damage, but how could she know? How did the Russians decide what to bomb? Would Nykarleby be next, and could they aim properly? She looked after her son and tiny farm, and prayed, prayed fervently like she had never done before. News from both Sweden radio and the BBC indicated their terrible war was currently the only major site of European hostilities. Neighboring Sweden and Norway sent volunteers, which helped Finnish morale. And yet, and yet, it all seemed so impossible, and the winter was so extremely cold and dark and long.

When spring crept in her troubles increased. Desite beginning each day at 4:30am, she never seemd to cope with all the field and animal work. Every week she sent Axel, through the army field post, a packet of food, and often clothing. Ominously, he never gave any indication about where he was located.

War made everything strange. One day she heard that General Wallenius, the rebel leader Algot was supposed to meet in prison, was back as a leader, in command of armed forces in Lapland! Either the army was desperate, or Wallenius was not so bad after all. And there were the much praised Lotta Svärd, women volunteers helping the army. She had no interest in joining such a group, but it was strange they got so much praise, while there was no recognition for women who kept their farms running without their men. Well, she didn't need recognition: love for Nils and Axel was enough.

Then suddenly, in early March, it was all over. Finland, the government declared, had won!

Well, sort of.

Moscow signed something called a peace treaty, but, unbelievably, the losers claimed not only Finland's second largest city, Viipuri (Vyborg), but considerable industrial territory in Karelia, resulting in, most devastatingly from Tyra's perspective, more than 400,000 Finns having to be evacuated permanently from their homes. The Finnish population was only about four million, so this was a huge issue for a large sector of the community. But Finland was still Finland, independent from the belligerent Russians. That was something.

But where was Axel? Was no news indeed good news?

Then one day a ragged man with a bushy beard, wearing tattered clothes, and smelling very badly, opened the kitchen door and walked in. "Got anything to eat?" he said, grinning. Axel was home.

Nils went wild with joy. Tyra gave a cry of delight, and then, hugely embarrassed, fell on his shoulder and wept.

"I could make *plattar*," she finally said, straightening up and brushing away her unwanted tears, "or do you want something else?"

Axel laughed. "Anything, just anything, will do! Oh how wonderful! I'm home!"

Never had Tyra enjoyed making pancakes more than she did that day.

"Tell me about it," she asked, while he ate.

"Someday," he said, "but not now." He ate ravenously, *plattar*, cheese, *knäckerbröd* and anything she could find to set in front of him. Then he went into the bedroom and without changing his filthy, smelly clothes or even taking a bath, slept for twelve hours straight. He smelt so badly Tyra made a bed for herself on the floor in the kitchen. Next day he got up at daybreak, took out the plough, and ploughed one of the fields. Only then did he take a long, long sauna in the little shed behind the barn, shave, and ask if there were any clean and decent clothes he could change into. He was back on his farm, and that was his focus. Over the next few months he slowly told her small snippets of what life was like during the war, but if Tyra ever questioned him, he immediately clammed shut. It was easier to get on with the farm jobs than talk about the horrors of war.

Erik, he quickly told her, was successful in registering as an army medic and not a combatant soldier, but after an injury he was sent back home.

"Strange, he never mentioned he'd been injured!" exclaimed Tyra.

"He wouldn't," said Axel. "Somehow we all thought getting injured was a disgrace. And it was worse for him. They treated him rough at first, I mean really rough, because of his noncombatancy, but he stuck to his choice, and they finally gave in. But I don't know how he did it, dealing with all those ghastly wounds, all those dead and dying people, and nothing to defend himself with. I agree with him about not fighting, but I think he had a much more dangerous job than the rest of us. No wonder he was injured. Not for me, that medic job he had. I'm glad he got out of it. Glad for Mor Anna's sake, too."

Tyra could only nod, and keep packing eggs for market, feeding hens and sheep, milking the cows, ever mindful to remember the demands of a five-year-old boy.

"The only clothing they gave us," he told her one evening as he pulled off his muddy boots, "was some white coats to wear over everything else, so we'd be camouflaged in the snow. But that didn't do much for the cold. That cold, oh boy, you can't begin to know how bad it was! But at least we had tents, more than those poor Russian boys had. That huge and mighty Russian army didn't even supply them with tents! Living out in the freezing cold they were, and every fire they lit just begged us to shoot at!" He shook his head in disgust.

They were packing eggs for market one day when Axel inadvertently dropped one. The bright yellow yolk spread vividly across the bare earth. "Huh, that was a dumb thing to do!" he said, looking at the mess. "You know, I was good at throwing Molotov cocktails," he added suddenly, looking ruefully at the broken egg. "I hated doing it, but it was the only weapon I had, most of the time. We called their airplanes Molotov breadbaskets," Axel laughed, bitterly, "because they promised food but dropped bombs. So we laughed about the generous cocktails we threw back at them! Those cocktails wrecked their tanks very nicely, I must say. We messed up scores of tanks that way. Oh, my! Did they have tanks! There was no end to those brutish machines! Great long lines of them, rolling over everything! We put big boulders in their path to stop them, but they just rolled up and over them! After a while we learned to make better blockades. I was a *pioneeri*, or engineer. At least I didn't do much with a gun. If we captured one of their tanks we immediately put it to use. We wrapped tanks (the ones we captured) in white cloth to camouflage them, but the Russians didn't bother with anything like that. My, they had good horses, too. Wasted, those poor beasts were. Such a terrible shame. Ah, but our reindeer did us proud. Good beasts, they were, very faithful, very reliable."

He brought in wood for the stove one morning, dropped it in the woodbin on the porch, and stood looking at it. Suddenly he picked up a pair of straight sticks lying on the top of the pile. "They gave us skis to use," he said, looking at the sticks, "those of us who hadn't brought our own. Hadn't used skis for ten years, but it didn't take more than a few minutes to relearn. Sure helped us to sneak up on the enemy!"

One evening a radio broadcast extolled the victory of Suomussalmi, and Axel suddenly turned to Tyra. "That's where I was. We did a good job it seems, but it was terrible. I still get nightmares! Those Reds drove long lines of tanks and men along Raate Road towards Suomussalmi, but it was insane. Absolutely insane! Just forest on either side of the road which tanks couldn't drive through, and a rough, narrow, one-way track. We could easily pick them off with our *motti* tactic. Oh, there were mountains of Russian bodies, piles and piles of them, the poor beggars. Must have been thousands and thousands of them. Just boys they were."

Tyra realized she would never fully know what her husband had been through, but now she had some idea of where he had been. For some reason this gave her peace, the simple geography of his location. She heard that in the battle of Raate Road Finns used the tactic of *motti*, meaning they divided the long Russian army convoys into pieces, encircled those enemy parts, then destroyed them. She found this sadly amusing as Axel made *motti*, tidy piles of neatly stacked timber, when he did lumber-jacking in winter. Soldiers had wicked humor!

On a mild May afternoon Tyra was playing with Nils in the small field surrounding their home. A large rock stood in the middle, a wonderful plaything for Nils. He scrambled up the rock, leapt high in the air, and landed onto the soft grass surrounding it. Suddenly she heard the ominous tramp of boots. Three men were coming towards her. One wore a ragged uniform, the others were mere boys hanging back in obvious fear.

"Herr Östring!" shouted the uniformed man officiously. "Herr Axel Östring! Where is he?"

Tyra faced him. "I'm Fru Östring," she said as calmly as she could. "What do you want?"

"Where's your husband?" repeated the man gruffly. "It's about these prisoners."

Tyra cringed at the word "prisoners" but allowed her face to show nothing. No wonder those boys are frightened, she thought. "I'll find him for you," she responded, wondering greatly.

She had no idea where Axel was, and feared he was on the church land some distance away. Fortunately, he was in the barn reorganizing his hay. He came out brushing wisps of dry grass from his clothes. "Yah?" he said, scowling at the uniformed man suspiciously.

"Herr Östring?"

"You heard! Yah," replied Axel testily.

"You fought the battle of Suomussalmi?"

"Yah! What's that got to do with you?"

"These Russian prisoners are to help you. They can sleep in your barn. Shouldn't have any problems, but let me know if they are troublesome. Sign here."

Axel felt he was signing for a farm commodity, but he wrote his scrawling signature on the proffered paper. Herr Uniform stuffed it in his knapsack, turned and stamped off. Tyra and Axel were unexpectedly the proud supervisors (or was it owners?) of two Russian prisoners of war!

The Russian lads clearly had only the clothes they were wearing. With much pointing and chest tapping Tyra and Axel established their guests were Mikail and Vladimir,[1] and got them to understand they were to call their hosts Tyra and Axel. Tyra was not comfortable about the sudden arrangement, but apparently they had no choice. She did not like putting "guests" in the barn, but again she feared there was no option. But she could feed them, which she did generously. Nils, however, thought the newcomers were primarily for him to play with, and instantly did more to break the tense situation than all adult attempts at smiling. Axel later admitted that on a trip to Jakobstad he had signed a document indicating his interest in Russian prisoners of war as laborers. He thought it a slightly insane idea, and doubted it would happen. Well, sometimes insane things do happen!

Axel was so used to coping alone that at first he had trouble knowing what to do with his sudden role as "employer". But soon Mikail and Vladimir were doing many things he had planned for months, but never found time to do. As the summer moved on Axel's Russian increased, and the young laborers' desire to learn Swedish was insatiable. Tyra proved a willing and able Swedish language teacher. "No want home!" they insisted several times. Their obvious appreciation of Tyra's cooking was flattering. Vladmir especially liked to help her look after the hens and animals, and he and Löfte developed a close relationship. Both were kind to Nils. "Horse rides," hide 'n' seek, chasing, and other games need no language, and the three quickly became friends.

When winter cold arrived Tyra decided the barn was no longer a suitable bedroom for their "staff," as they now thought of the Russian lads, and she had lost her fear of Herr Uniform. She persuaded Axel to allow the young men to sleep in the kitchen. She was rewarded for her kindness by many little acts of helpfulness. Sometimes, as they ate around her spotlessly scrubbed pine table she could hardly believe that the terrified cold loneliness of the previous winter had ever been a reality. How could the "enemy" her husband had fought against under such terrible circumstances prove to be so much fun, so useful and helpful? In those

---

1. Pseudonyms.

long, drear, and dismal months, terrified by life, she had thought all Russians were ghastly ogres. But these young men were not only useful farm laborers, but friends to be enjoyed, to have fun with. The whole war situation was completely overthrown, a ridiculous travesty of life. Instead of belligerent politicians discussing national frontiers, all they needed was to get people to work and play together, to learn to understand each other, and all would be well. Tyra was aware the terrible war still raged throughout Europe, and of the irrational demands Hitler's minions were still making. But in the quiet, obscure, tiny village of Brännon in faraway northern Finland, international peace reigned supreme.

Late the following May, Mikail and Vladimir were out with Axel when Herr Uniform returned, again demanding Herr Östring. He was unhappy when he was forced to wait while Tyra walked to the fields to call her husband. Axel arrived hot and bothered, and in no mood to parley with officialdom.

"They're doing fine!" he shouted before the man could say a word. "I've no complaint and happy to continue to employ them."

"You don't employ prisoners! Russian prisoners of war are being relocated!" Herr Uniform snarled. "Get them to Jakbstad by tomorrow lunch, or you'll suffer!"

"What's wrong?" demanded Axel.

"New government orders," was all he was told. "Now you heard!"

"What if I don't?" asked Axel defiantly.

"Then you go with them! None of your sass, my man." Axel reluctantly did as he was told. Not only were Mikail and Vladimir in tears as they climbed on to the cart, but Tyra and Nils were very distressed. Axel covered his misery with a gruff exterior, but felt like an executioner as he flicked the reins and Löfte plodded off to Jakobstad, taking the luckless Russians to their uncertain future.

And then, on the 25th of June, 1941, Finland, at the instigation of, and in collaboration with Germany, declared war against Russia. They called it the Continuation War, supposedly a continuation of the Russian-instigated Winter War. Axel received his mobilization papers, again, with orders to report to Jakobstad within 48 hours.

"What are you going to do?" asked Tyra. "Shall I pack clothes for summer or winter?"

"Never!" snarled Axel. He pushed his mobilization papers into the kitchen stove, and stood there watching them curl, blacken, and burn, then marched out to attend to his farm.

Chapter 13

Fugitive

FEAR GRIPPED TYRA. Axel's behavior was utterly irrational, and she no idea what to do about it. Every time she tried to talk to him he quickly stumped out to the tomato house, and left her talking to herself.

Axel had received his second summons for military duty, which, like the first, he angrily shoved in the kitchen stove and watched burn to ashes. Autumn was a busy time for any farmer, and without help from the Russian prisoners, and with most of his friends called up and gone to the army, he worked from Finnish dawn until Finnish night. Years later his son insisted it was friendship with the Russian prisoners of war that had spurred Axel's strong anti-war sentiments. Certainly Nils remembered those young men with great affection.

Tyra, however, believed it was listening to reports of what was happening in Germany that incited his strong disapproval and hostility, and she sympathized with his determined opposition. This renewed conflict was not a life and death survival against Russia like the Winter War had been, but instigated merely by German interests, despite the Finnish government's attempt to give it a connecting name. True, Germany had been helpful in the Winter War. But the aims of the German government were clearly wrong. BBC news revealed its world dominance intentions, and dreadful anti-Jew policies. Yes, she understood Axel's opposition because she herself was opposed, but she was deeply troubled. She suggested he apply for noncombatant medical personnel status, like Erik had done before in the Winter War, but Axel brushed the idea aside.

"No one would listen to me," he said angrily. "Erik had your church backing, but I don't. And I couldn't do that type of work. I'm a farmer, not a half-baked pretend doctor!"

"Well, they've allowed Erik to stay home to care for his mother," Tyra retorted, "so why don't . . . !" But Axel gave an angry snort, and stalked off.

Tyra dared to hope the government had forgotten her husband, but in mid September his "final" summons came. Axel must enlist, or face court martial and prison. He was not told to report, but ordered to be ready in two days, when military officials would collect him. He had no choice. But this ultimatum only seemed to galvanize his determination. Without considering the impact his choice would have on himself and his family, he made other plans.

"No, I won't be a stooge for that Germany! Never!" he declared defiantly. "I gave everything I had to fight for my fatherland in that fiendish Winter War, but I'm not, I repeat, not ever, do you hear, never fighting for Germany! You know those nice lads we had here helping us? How can I fight people like them? You think I've done no listening to you, but I know God always gives us a choice. He never forces. I like that. That's the right way to govern. I'm willing to help my country, to defend it, but never to fight for some evil power like that one in Germany!"

Tyra had no answer. "What are you going to do?" she asked, fearfully.

"Hide."

"Hide! Are you crazy!"

"It's the only option they leave me."

"But where?"

"If I don't tell you, you can truly say you don't know where I am. Get me warm clothes, like you did when I went to war, and let me have all the *knäckerbröd* and cheese I can carry."

"But—but Axel! It's not right! And it's winter!"

"Of course I know it's winter! Don't worry, I'll be back. Just help me, like I said."

Tyra searched her apprehensive heart. She had always supported Axel, but should she help him defy the government? Everything in her rebelled against the thought. But when she remembered Germany's policy against Jews her mind was made up. God could never condone such an evil government, and it would not be wrong to oppose it. She did not agree with his idea of hiding, but she understood his purpose. She collected his warmest clothes, new and in good condition because his old ones were reduced to tatters in the Winter War, wrapped two big rye loaves, *knäckerbröd*, and a large round of cheese in cotton shopping bags, and prayed fervently. "I'll leave more in the sauna house so you can collect it if you can," she offered, fearfully.

It was very dark, very cold, and snowing lightly when Axel walked out the door, leaving Tyra in an agony of ignorance. Sleep vanished, and she found she couldn't even find words to pray. She just closed her eyes and wrung her hands.

Two military officials stomped up her steps early next day and demanded Axel appear. Truthfully she said she had no idea where he was. They demanded they search the property while she stood faint with fear and lack of sleep. Within minutes they turned her immaculate home into disheveled chaos. Finally they clomped angrily around the barn, making the animals bleat and bellow with fright, threw bales of hay around indiscriminately, and shouted furiously at her when they returned having failed to discover anything.

"Where is he? He must report!" one screamed.

"Prison!" hissed the other. "And you too, for helping him!"

She stood silent, a small woman with a small boy clinging to her skirt, both terrified.

Nils was old enough to understand these men were very angry, and they were angry with his father. She could tell Nils his Far had gone "somewhere", but he was smart enough to realize his father was somewhere he was not supposed to be. After more angry shouts and curses, including a shove that made her stagger against the door, the men left, promising to return.

She was getting into bed late one night a week later when she heard a slight scuffle in the kitchen. She froze. Was it just the wind?

Again the sound came, a human sound of heavy breathing. Paralyzed by fear, she controlled herself with difficulty, and cautiously opened the bedroom door. It was dark, very dark. Suddenly she realized she could no longer see the glow of the fire in the stove. A man was huddled over it, begging for its warmth.

The figure had not heard her. Was it a Russian prisoner returned? The figure flipped back its hood. Was it . . . ?

"Axel!" she whispered urgently.

"Yah, it's me. I had to get warm," he said between teeth chattering violently. "I'll go before morning."

"No!" said Tyra. "Stay! We must talk."

"Did they come?"

"Yah, they came. Angry, very angry, searched everywhere. Made a mess in the house, upset the animals, they did."

Stove warmth slowly eased his shivering. Axel came close to Tyra, whispering. He'd hid in the forest, but the cold was too severe for him to survive hiding alone. He had to change plans.

He clung to her, wordlessly begging for her support. Tyra heard her heart, both hearts, beating wildly. What would he ask of her? For a long time they clung to each other, then finally Axel spoke.

Would she, please, please, would she help him hide in the barn? The big animals would keep him warm. She could bring food when she fed them. It was not a wonderful idea, not the best idea, but it was worth a try because it was the best he could think of as he huddled, freezing, alone, in the forest. And right now, could she put Nils in his summer bed so they could be together?

Tyra snuggled closer to her icy husband and tried desperately to think clearly. His hiding in the barn terrified her, but she had nothing better to suggest. Of course, he could not survive hiding on his own in the forest, and she was enormously relieved he had returned to her alive. She was willing to do anything to help him.

"I'll try," she whispered, as they fell asleep, together.

Axel was gone when she woke, but she knew where he was. Nils stirred, and asked why he was cold in his summer bed instead of warm with his mother, the first of many painful interrogations she struggled to deal with. Impatiently she sent him to look for kindling sticks, though she knew she had plenty.

She made a large pot of rolled oats porridge, and while Nils ate his she sneaked a bowl inside the bucket of hen food, which she carried down to the barn. She placed the steaming bowl on a high bale of hay, and when she retuned later that morning the bowl was empty. She berated herself that she had forgotten to bring the bucket so she could take the bowl back to the house without being observed. But she never made that mistake again.

Every day was a nightmare of subterfuge, concealment, and exhaustion from trying to cope with the farm work. Simple comments from neighbors and friends could startle and feed her growing paranoia that sometime, somehow, she would say or do something that would expose her husband. The easiest way was to avoid all social contact, but that was also impossible without attracting undue attention. A few kindly comments made her realize most people assumed her increasing reserve and silence was due to anxiety about Axel at war. She encouraged this. She would rather look a fool than risk her husband's safety.

Through the achingly cold winter of 1941–1942 Axel hid in his barn, and Tyra kept him alive with her food. He slept in soft hay, covered with quilts that one by one she furtively carried down. Amongst the hay, with the big animals, it was surprisingly warm. She was grateful. Occasionally a piece of clothing would lie beside the food bowl. Shoved deep into the bucket she now always carried, covered with hay and eggs, washed furtively, and dried under her bed, she returned the garment inconspicuously beside the food bowl. They never spoke, but on rare occasions embraced. Who knew who might be listening, unseen in the gloom of winter? Most mornings the manure trough was cleaned, animal food mysteriously appeared in the mangers. Axel was doing his best to help.

On December 6, 1941, the BBC reported Britain had declared war on Finland for its collaboration with Germany. Although devastating news for the country, it reassured Tyra to realize she and Axel had international vindication.

In January Nils turned seven, ready to start school. How could she deal with the questions he might ask, his teachers might ask, his friends might ask? Should she keep him back from school? But that would mean more trouble with authorities! Perhaps school would distract him, leave her with more time to cope with the farm alone. She had to decide on her own. When the time came, reluctantly she enrolled Nils, taking turns with other women to deliver their children to school.

When it was her turn to take the children to school, she sometimes went shopping, but food in Nykarleby was in devastatingly short supply. At first puzzled, she realized farmers were called into the army before they could harvest properly, then the army requisitioned most available food. She herself had received notice that she must supply her quota of eggs and wool to the army. Newspaper photos showed groups of women trying to harvest after all the men were called up. She dared not tell anyone she had a good supply of potatoes, rye, oats, and barley in her barn (food Axel had not sold before he went into hiding), although the village knew of her hens, and regularly requested eggs. She insisted people come to the house, and carefully avoided taking anyone near the barn.

Algot visited again at Christmas, dispensing food and gifts as before. Tyra was delighted to see him, but distressed he might notice and comment on her strange "chicken" food. Fortunately he never did, and helped her by playing with Nils. Nils liked to go to his friend Ben Öhling, who lived on the edge of the village, but Tyra's heartaches made her a hermit, and she ignored his pleas. In summer, he was free to walk to Ben's place on his own. Now Algot could accompany him to visit his friends.

Algot asked about her parents in Vasa, surprised by how little she knew. "They've had a terrible battering from bombs there," he said, "and food shortages are particularly bad in the cities, we've heard." Tyra nodded sadly. With shock, she realized that her own troubles had drowned all other ideas, and she had barely given her parents' plight a thought.

Wrapped in guilt from the crime of forgetting her parents, she was surprised when suddenly Algot looked at her and exclaimed, "You've still got your gold wedding band! Why weren't you tempted to swap it for one of those iron things the government offered?"

Dragged from her incriminating reverie, Tyra shook her head. "Axel gave me this. For his sake, I can't support this war. I can't understand why any government would make such a demand of its women."

"They say they've raised a lot of money getting women to give up their wedding bands, but how they'll get the gold out of the country to buy the aircraft they want beats me. What do you mean you can't support this war?"

Tyra looked at the floor, and then said softly. "Simply, because we're collaborating with Germany, and that is not a good country right now." Algot nodded thoughtfully.

Diffidently Tyra added, "My faith is in God, not governments. And my marriage promise was to Axel and to God, not the government."

"I see what you mean," said Algot pensively.

Later, Algot was proved right about getting money out of Finland. The women's noble sacrifice of their wedding rings proved useless, and the gold simply lay in a bank vault. Algot left promising Tyra to return in spring to help with ploughing. "I'm no good at it," he laughed, "but I can do better than you! The plants won't mind if the furrows aren't straight!" Tyra made sure he had a bag of well-packed eggs to take to his mother and Hjalmar's wife.

A few days later, when Tyra thought she could keep going no longer, a letter arrived from Anna. Again, Algot was right. The situation was dire in Vasa. So dire that they had decided risk the journey and come and live with her. "Your Far is no farmer," Anna wrote, "but he'll do what he can to help. There's no food here, just long queues with nothing to buy. With you we'd at least have something to eat, and we can help you grow it. The bombing of Vasa is now so bad it's more than either of us can tolerate. It makes your father's work impossible."

Anders and Anna arrived, on a bitterly cold mid January day, in the familiar cart pulled by the faithful Blek, both protesting vigorously they had only driven from Oxkangar that day. Sadly, beloved and dependable Möja had developed breathing problems, and Anders reluctantly decided to end her days. Anna brought every article of warm clothing they possessed, all her woolen blankets and quilts, her loom and knitting, some favorite cooking pots, pellets to use as mattresses, and, surprisingly, pieces of embroidery Tyra had done as a child.

Tyra's delight at seeing Blek mitigated her sadness at the news about Möja. As she ushered Blek into the barn she could not help but notice the difference between the mighty, powerful Belgian draught horse and the aging hack Löfte. But fine breeding was not her priority, and she was grateful for the faithful services of gentle Löfte. She talked loudly, foolish nonsense about her parents, to the horses, hoping Axel would understand, and then she left a cryptic note in Axel's next bowl of porridge to try to explain.

Tyra agonized, but finally decided her safest course was to tell her parents who was living in the barn, fervently praying they would support her and Axel. Although Anders favored the so-called Continuation War on the grounds of national security, they did agree to support their daughter. Anna quietly shared with Tyra her total support, and admitted she too thought supporting the German government's policies was wrong.

"Want me to take anything to Jakobstad market?" offered Anders, eager to be of use to his daughter.

"No Far, it's too dangerous. We get bombed here too! What I need is help in the fields. Erik helps a little, but I need more help."

Anders, however, took it upon himself to "sell" Tyra's eggs locally. It was a barter system he operated, eggs in exchange for a pot of jam, a piece of fish, an old dress to be cut up for Anna to weave, and on one very special occasion a small packet of wheat flour. When he noticed the heavy, ragged fleeces of the remaining five sheep, he went looking for Axel's shears. A few trial snips convinced him he could never manipulate them, but on his trips into Nykarleby he asked around and found an old man who could shear. Tyra did much shouting to explain to the old shearer where to do his work, and successfully directed him to a "safe" place well away from Axel.

Anders also located a woman who spun, and the rough sweaters Anna and Tyra knitted from the old spinner's imperfect thread, surplus to their own needs and the government's demands, were eagerly "bought" by women who found nothing in the shops. Anders got precious wheat flour that way, and insisted Tyra make *plattar* one night (a few of which she secreted to the barn). And Anders' triumph was unlimited when he found a ram to service the ewes, certain he would double the flock by spring.

But as spring sunshine cheered the countryside, it became harder for Tyra to conceal what she was doing. One morning on her way to the barn she met Takla, and the smell of warm porridge emanating from her chicken feed bucket was overpowering.

"Got some nice warm mash for your hens?" smiled the hopefully unsuspecting Takla. "Good to see you, Tyra. You've been in hiding all winter! I see your parents have come. That's good. Now you won't be scared say hello! But don't forget to ask for help with that man of yours away! Oh, I've missed your lad. Send him over any time you like."

Tyra wondered what else her neighbors had "seen" but she thanked Takla for her kindness, confirmed the arrival of her parents, agreed to send Nils when he came from school, muttered about being very busy without Axel, and hurried off as soon as she politely dared to feed her hens and man.

Then, early in April, in the grey of not-yet-day, before even hard working farmers were out of bed, without warning, two military police arrived, again. "Search warrant!" one shouted as they hammered on the door.

"Search warrant! Open up! Open up!" The hammering was powerful, insistent.

Tyra's heart almost stopped beating. In the leaden light of predawn she could see nothing, but understood everything. Her father, sleeping in the kitchen, climbed out of bed and slowly opened the door.

"Who are *you*?" an officer yelled, staring hard at night-clad Anders. But Anders' white hair and weather-battered face clearly declared he was well past military age. The police made no challenge to his muttered "her father", but with an insolent "move aside!" they pushed him away and marched into the house.

The search was systematic, as disruptive as before, and badly frightened the sleeping Nils, whom they unceremoniously tipped out of bed.

For a few agonizing moments Tyra dared hope they would leave the barn alone, but no, they soon headed there. She could only pray fervently that the police yells had alerted Axel, and he had escaped. She listened anxiously for the sounds of a confrontation in the barn, but there was an ominous silence.

Half an hour later the heavy tramp of boots announced their return, and roughly held between them was a bedraggled, dirty, long-haired, bearded Axel. They frog-marched him triumphantly to the door, roughly shoved him at her, and from their accusing yells Tyra expected that she also would be arrested. Anders and Anna cowered by the stove, protectively trying to cover Nils.

"You!" they shouted, shoving accusing fingers at Tyra. "You . . . !"

But Nils took one look at his father and sprang at him joyfully. "Far! Far!" he cried, his voice full of delight. "You've come back! I've missed you so much!"

Axel made an attempt to hug his boy, but his guards prevented him. Nils was undeterred, and threw his arms around his father's legs.

The police looked uncertain. The boy had clearly not seen his father for a long time. Perhaps the man had just returned to his barn.

"Scoundrel!" cried one officer thrusting his fist into Axel's chest. "Cowardly villain!"

"Deserter!" shrieked the other, and spat on Tyra's clean floor. "You'll go to jail!"

Axel had no chance to say goodbye, no chance to hug or say anything to his family. Tyra could not bear to look at him, and simply stood helplessly, paralyzed by fear. Roughly pulling him from the distraught Nils, the officers marched Axel down the road, down to who knew where, for who knew how long.

Suddenly, at the corner of the road, Axel fell flat on the road, and ducking the blows of his captors, turned his head and shouted, "Pray for me, Tyra. Pray for me!" The officers prodded him to his feet, and he was soon lost to sight, but his final words reached her, "Do your best!"

Tyra tried to answer, but her throat contracted, and her whispered words were carried on the four winds, spreading slowly across the face of the mutilated earth. But heaven heard. In the coming months and years, never did Tyra pray so hard.

Tyra desperately hoped none of the villagers saw the disgraceful spectacle, but the noise had been so great she knew it was a futile dream. She turned from the door, and set about comforting the distraught Nils and shaking Anna. Suddenly she could do it no longer. She collapsed in a weeping heap on a chair, only slowly realizing her father was beside her, murmuring words of comfort. "Oh, God!" she cried, "I can't take any more of this! But thank you Far!"

The crushing sense of failure paralyzed her for a couple of hours. What could she, should she, have done to prevent Axel's capture? But the murmuring words of her father slowly penetrated her thoughts. She had concealed her husband for almost seven months, her father reminded her as he gently patted her hand. She had done her best, her very best. Had someone betrayed them? Had the police merely come as a routine? They would never, ever, know. But now she must do everything she could so that her son, her mother, her father, would survive. That meant she had to survive, too. Because someday Axel might come home.

She stood up, and began preparing porridge for them all.

When Algot, unsuspecting, arrived a few days later to do the ploughing, he noticed the pall of gloom that hung over the family. He set to work making long wiggling furrows in the fields, for which Tyra gave heartfelt thanks. Anders and Erik went with him, and together they planted out rye, barley, and potatoes. They hunted for tomato seed, but could find none.

Nils had a grand time while "uncle" Algot was visiting, and he continued a useful distraction for his grandparents. With pride they read and re-read his first school report, nodded sagely, making repeated remarks about how his good work was so much like his mother's.

"Well, my girl," said Anders after Algot left, "I'm glad Axel's not here to see what we've done to his fields. Our furrows are awful. But we should have food, although I don't know what the rest of the country is going to eat."

"We'll share what we have with people around here," suggested Tyra, anxiously wondering what Axel was eating. "Be kind about the exchanges you take from those starving people!" she added, and Anders nodded, in full agreement.

Then great joy erupted in the family. A letter arrived by "field post"! Axel was safe. Yes, he had spent a few horrible weeks in prison, but was now serving in the army reserve in the Helsingfors area, apparently as some type of guard. Although he was rather vague about what he was doing, Tyra believed he had work in a prisoner of war camp. Axel wrote regularly, all through the war, sharing simple daily activities. However, with the unrelenting farm duties, as well as caring for Nils, her aging parents, and household chores, Tyra struggled to find time and energy to write her return letters. She managed to write only about one to every four that Axel sent. Far more important than letters were the regular dispatches of food and clothing she sent him. The Finnish government was no more prepared for the Continuation War than they had been for the Winter War, and the provisions they offered the men serving it were woefully inadequate.

One cold, crisp, starry evening, as Tyra trudged wearily back from the barn, overwhelemed by exhaustion from relentless farm work, she was startled to hear a bird call. Only one call, so short she could not identify it, but it brought hope. She gazed up at the stars, and suddenly realized that God was looking after Axel. He could have been at some war zone where horrible casualites were daily occurring, but instead he was in Helsingfors. True there were bomb raids there, and people sometimes were killed, but it appeared to her the safest place for him to be. Perhaps some sympathetic official had respected his protest about the war, and whilst forcing him to serve his country, had organized for him to be excused from active military duty. For the first time in months she bowed her head and prayed, a prayer of pure gratitude.

Soon after the joy of hearing from Axel came more official demands from the government. Not even Axel's relative safety could stop her grumbling about this! Despite all she sent Axel, and he could share with others, she must provide a set quota of eggs and wool to the military authorities, and worse, the number of animals and hens she owned would be inspected to ensure she was doing her utmost for her country. Without compunction, the normally law-abiding Tyra hid twenty-five hens in the sauna house, while the remaining half of her already seriously depleted flock roamed free. She had struggled to meet her government quotas, and if they were increased she was sure they would starve. But the inspectors must have been too busy, for they never arrived, much to the relief of some sauna-cooped hens.

Throughout the war Tyra struggled to cope financially. Many of her letters described how she had taken yet another loan from the bank, or paid off a loan. Often the loan was to pay for the rent of the church land she and Axel farmed, a rent that never dropped despite the poverty of the war-torn country. Rarely did she buy things for herself, but frequently she carried home warm clothing to send Axel, who served in a military that provide neither sufficient good food nor suitable clothing for its forces. Gratefully, she often turned to Erik to stand guarantee for these loans. Every week she sent a packet of food to Axel, usually something she had baked, and a kilogram of her own homemade butter, most of which he sold for good profit. She urged him to be as frugal as possible, asked him to stop attending the cinema because of bombing raids, and begged that he stop smoking so he could save money. She proved herself an astute businesswoman, while Axel spent most of 1942 leaning on a post, bored witless, dreaming of what he would do when he returned to his farm.

One afternoon Anders returned with furrowed brows from his daily farm inspection. The grains and potatoes were growing, but were not as tall and healthy as in the past. Did Axel do something he and Erik had not, he wondered.

"Did you apply manure before you ploughed and planted?" asked Tyra, busily weeding a small patch of precious beetroot.

Anders clapped his hands. "That's it!" he exclaimed. "We never thought of it. Greenhorn farmers we are, it never occurred to us. Well, you and your mother better do some heavy duty, serious praying so those crops grow! I might be able to sneak some manure in later, but not while the stalks are so small."

Tyra smiled, wanly. She often wondered if her desperate prayers were heard, but apparently her father thought they were worthwhile. Perhaps God wasn't so much meant to hear her prayers, as to encourage a change in her attitude. But she felt permanently exhausted and angrily wondered what God was doing. Like her father, she too was ignorant of many things Axel did on the farm. She could only hope the unskilled efforts of her father would eventually produce a good crop, and, amazingly, they did. The potatoes were small, but good, the barley was a bumper crop, and the rye worthwhile. They had food, even some they could share for small barters. Tyra was grateful of the small additions to her larder that Anders achieved, and the small amounts of money he sometimes acquired, although there was nothing to buy with it.

One afternoon, with a feeling of absolute desperation, wondering how she could possibly add another task to her already overloaded days, she headed into the nearby forest to pick blueberries for essential winter nutrition. But the dappled sunlight on the fresh green bushes, the soft symphony of birdsong, and the cool whispered breeze on her fevered face calmed her spirit, and a sense of gratitude filled her heart. With a small inner smile, she recognized this gratitude was a gift from God.

Early in September, Tyra received another welcome "field post" letter from Axel. He had often mentioned he was trying to get leave to visit home, but at last he had been successful. He was allowed to visit them for three days! He arrived by bus, extremely thin, and exhausted after the long journey, too tired to even inspect his pastures. He ate voraciously everything Tyra placed in front of him, and spent most of his time watching her with sad, hungry eyes as she cooked. He returned to Helsingfors loaded with 30 eggs, three loaves of bread, and a thick, warm jacket for which Tyra had taken yet another bank loan to purchase. He made her promise she would come and visit him before winter set in, and then walked to the bus in Nykarleby for the long journey back to Helshingfors. Tyra was left sad and utterly drained. The thought of undertaking the long trip to the capital city horrified her, but she had promised, and she would keep that promise.

Nils' return to school in September added to Tyra's deep anxiety. Russia was bombing much more frequently, apparently indiscriminately across the country, even occasionally Nykarleby, reports declared.

"Mor!" announced Nils one afternoon as winter cold closed in again, "Our school rattled. An airplane dropped a bomb by the river."

"Was it a big rattling?" asked Anders, turning away from the radio.

"Yah, fairly," answered Nils uncertainly. He had no idea what was a big rattle or a small one, except that the rattle he had experienced was scary.

"I think it's the electricity generator they're trying to knock out," said Anders. "That's what they always targeted in Vasa. The Nykarleby generator is close to the school."

Frequently Nils reported "rattling" windows, and then one day came home very excited. "It landed right in the school yard!" he exclaimed. "We all saw it! A real bomb and it screamed and went whoooom! Dirt flew in the air and there was a huge bang. We had to get under our desks, and when nothing more happened the teachers made us go down to the basement and stay there for the rest of the day."

But either the Russians ran out of bombs or lost interest in Nykarleby, for there was no more bombing for the rest of that winter.

It was early March, and snow was still thick on the ground, when Tyra finally made the trip south to Helsingfors. Nils wanted to accompany her, but after much thought she decided to leave him at home with her parents. She would only be away for a week, and was sure they could manage. The Russians targeted railways relentlessly, and although the resourceful Finns repaired damges quickly, it was still a potentially dangerous way to travel. So she chose to go by bus, but was miserable with bus sickness throughout the whole long trip. She was glad stay in Helsingfors with a friend from Nykarleby, Anna Kyllonen, who introduced her to chicory coffee that somewhat helped settle her heaving stomach. Although grateful to be with Axel (to whom she presented 50 eggs!), she hated the big city atmosphere, its blackouts, sirens, and restless crowds. The journey was exhausting, the time with Axel far too short, and worse, all the time they were together, the thought, not only of their parting, but of the nauseous trip home, weighed heavily on her heart.

As they farewelled at the bus stop Axel removed his gloves, and Tyra was horrified to notice that he no longer wore a wedding ring!

"Your ring!" she exclaimed. "Where is it!"

Axel hung his head, a little shamed. "We get so little food, I pawned it so I could buy some cheese. We get watery pea soup day after day after day, and I suddenly just couldn't face any more of it!"

"But what will people think if you come home without a band!" remonstrated the horrified, and hurt, Tyra.

"Don't worry, I'll get money to redeem it. Your butter sells very well, you know!"

Tyra sighed and wondered how she could somehow manage to increase his butter supply.

Axel was able to visit Nykarleby twice that year, but Tyra came to dread these occasions because she found she spent the time sadly anticipating when he would leave. It was better to dream of his possible visits! When he knew how she struggled with travel sickness, Axel never again asked her to visit him. But he continued to write faithfully, about twice a week.

She returned home from her trip to find Anders had injured his hand while trying to plough, and it had become infected. He was clearly too unwell do do any field work for some time. Her mother was also unwell with a heavy dose of bronchitis, and sat shivering by the kitchen stove most of the day. Nils, understandably, had not been happy while she was away, and had been very disobedient for his grandparents, refusing to help collect eggs and firewood. Combined with the sorrow of leaving Axel, the long exhausting journey, and then the misery she found when she arrived home, Tyra wondered how much longer she could keep the farm and family going.

In fact, she was so tired she almost dreaded Algot's now customary Christmas visit in 1943. But it proved good to talk to him about Axel, and share what he was doing in Helsingfors, something she did not feel comfortable doing with most other people except her parents.

"Good old Axel!" he exclaimed. "He's a real man, a true Finn! I'm proud of him for standing up for what he believes, although guarding prisoners doesn't sound much fun. Axel was always such an active person, so full of energy. I can't imagine him standing around doing nothing much all day! I'll do all I can to help you. I feel so bad that he with a family was made to go to war, but they won't let me, who's just as trained as he was!"

For the first time Tyra wondered what Lisa thought of Algot's trips to Nykarleby, but could only presume she approved. This year Algot's food gift was strawberry jam, and a small boat he'd made for Nils "to float on the river in summer". Tyra's supply of wheat flour was almost gone, but she was very grateful of Lisa's jam to serve with barley porridge. Memories of childhood wartime barley meals were not happy, but now she was glad of anything to eat. Grass still grew, and with its hay the cows still provided milk, although, because milk prices had fallen so low, Anders was suggesting they sacrifice one cow to eat. This Tyra resisted vigorously. Ironically, the sheep Axel had not wanted proved to be the most lucrative part of their small business. Nettles still made soup, and she learned from Takla how to make an imitation coffee from dried nettle leaves. At first she considered it rather unpalatable, but at least it was something they could pretend was *fika*. After a while she grew to like her make-believe coffee, and noticed she was not so anxious when she stopped using regular coffee. She shared this observation with her mother, who agreed she too felt calmer without coffee. They both decided to permanently give up using coffee. However, she did urge Axel to try to find some chicory seeds to bring on his next visit, as she had learned from her friend Anna Kyllonen that they made an even better coffee substitute.

Algot, however, was concerned that they had no sugar for their "coffee". "Leave it to me," he said mysteriously when he left. "I have a plan to get some sugar."

"But I've tried every shop in Nykarleby!" protested Tyra, with a wan smile.

"Mor told me the same thing about Oxkangar. But you know, there are advantages in being an unwanted human like me. I can do things those good boys fighting in that gruesome war can't do!" He grinned at Tyra, and slid off into the darkness on his skis.

In late January 1944 Tyra was horrified to get a "field post" from Axel, this time telling her that he has been transferred from Helsingfors to "Aanislinna". At first she had no idea where this was, until Anders, whose ear was always glued to the radio, discovered it was the current war-inspired name for Petroskoi, the capital of Karelia on the shores of Lake Onega. Tyra's heart dropped like pure lead in her chest when she heard that. Karelia! Not only was it where bitter fighting occurred, but it was incredibly cold! Axel described how he was doing carpentry work supposed to help rebuild the area, and shared that often they were billeted to deserted cottages, where there was no electricity or heating. The conditions he lived in were appalling. But, from scraps of wood saved from his "work", he made Tyra a sewing box. Incredibly, he was able to send this treasure to her, with 300 Finnish marks carefully concealed inside. It became a very precious family keepsake.

Six weeks after he had left, when snow still covered the ground but the spring of 1944 was just beginning to push back the blackness of winter, Algot once more knocked on Tyra's door. "Hjalmar told me it's too early to plough," he said apologetically, "but I have to give you this." He handed her a package.

Tyra looked at the label, and cried out in disgust, "German! What do you mean by giving me this stuff?"

Algot chuckled. "Ah, that so-called German package came from Sweden. Never mind it might have been made once upon a time in Germany! Just taste it. It's not poison. See, I'll show you." He opened the packet, lightly touched his finger on the powder, and licked it.

Tyra looked at the white powder, and stared at it uncertainly. Gingerly she touched a tiny portion and licked her finger. "Why, it's sweet!" she exclaimed. "What is it?"

"Saccharine," said Algot. "As I said, I got it from Sweden. Now you can have sweet *fika* whenever you like!"

"But . . . but how did you get it? Where did you *really* get it from?"

Algot chuckled mischievously. "From Sweden, just like I told you."

"Come on," said Anders, "Tell us. People here don't go shopping in Sweden!"

"Well, the Kvarken of the Gulf of Bothnia freezes over in winter, as you know. I was an Oxkangar ferryman, so I well knew about it. You can ski from the north of Oxkangar right across the Kvarken all the way to Sweden on good solid ice. It's only fifty kilometers, and there are islands along the way to take rests. So, on a cold, clear day, I did just that. Umeå on the other side is a big town, lots of people milling around. No one asked me awkward questions, they assumed I was a Swede just like them. I found a money changer who accepted my story about visiting Finland a few years before, and swapped my *marks* for good *kronor*. Actually, the way that exchanger looked at me I think he knew I was a war refugee from Finland, but he was decent, didn't comment about my accent, and made no fuss. I bought wheat flour for Mor, and lots of this saccharine stuff, all I could carry. Let me tell you, it sells really well! I've been doing a roaring trade! Apparently the Germans made it for years, but no one was interested and it's been sitting on shop shelves gathering dust until this war began and we can't get British sugar. I admit I like sugar better, but this stuff will do me in the meantime. I thought you'd like some."

Tyra shook her head in amazement. It seemed like eating blood money knowing how much effort had gone into buying this strange new "sugar", but her gratitude was deep. Axel might not like collaboration with Germany, she certainly hated the war Germany had instigated, but she was sure he would approve of Algot's German-Swedish saccharine.

"Algot," she said, impulsively, diffidently, "I was terribly upset when you . . . when you . . . ah, you know what I mean to your father."

"Go on," he prompted, grinning broadly. "Don't be shy, just say it! I'm willing to admit to anyone I'm a murderer, that's a fact. But I'm definitely a reformed one!"

"Yah, I can see that. You're a changed man. But I want you to know how much I appreciate what you've done for us."

"That's OK," Algot grinned, and somewhat awkwardly gave his cousin a pat on the arm. "I always thought you were a bit special. I just hope my efforts to sweeten your *fika* redeem my spoiling your top once upon a time!"

Anders laughed heartily at that, Anna frowned in puzzlement, and Tyra blew her nose.

"You know, Algot, you've been a life-saver for us," Tyra continued after a sniff or two. Anna and Anders nodded assent. Then to everyone's surprise, Tyra began to sing, very softly at first, more strongly as she gained courage.

> Day by day, and with each passing moment,
> Strength I find, to meet my trials here;
> Trusting in my Father's wise bestowment,
> I've no cause for worry or for fear.
> He Whose heart is kind beyond all measure
> Gives unto each day what He deems best—
> Lovingly, its part of pain and pleasure,
> Mingling toil with peace and rest.

As Tyra began the second verse, Anna joined in, her voice slightly tremulous.

At the third stanza both Anders and Algot were humming in a rich baritone harmony worthy of any Finnish male choir.

There was a long, utterly serene silence.

"Tyra," said Algot, so softly it was almost a whisper, "I hope you believe that Axel will return. That's what I pray for you. I'm no holy man, but I think Axel will be back."

"I try to believe that, but its very hard," admitted Tyra. "You know Algot, the Bible says all things will work together for good to those who love God." Tyra stopped. She was no preacher. "Algot, that's what I was trying to say before. We all thought your situation was a terrible disaster, but look what a help you've been to all of us through this awful war; your family too. I can't imagine where we'd be if it wasn't for you. It's so strange, all those poor men out there being ordered to kill each other, and they won't let a murderer join the army!"

"So I'm some use after all?" grinned Algot, but there was a catch in his voice.

Anna blew her nose vigorously. Anders got up and walked around the room.

"Algot, look how you've helped me! Look how my parents came just when I needed them most. They thought they were helping themselves, but really, they were helping me. And look how healthy Nils is. The school doctor thought he was too thin and wants me to give him more milk, but you can see how healthy he is. I heard the other day about all those orphans from Karelia being sent to Sweden, so young, and all by themselves by train, so far away. Tens of thousands of them, can you believe, sent by their own parents. Perhaps if I lived in Karelia I'd be worried too, but I can't imagine parting with Nils. The idea breaks my heart. So, you see, I have much to thank God for. I admit there have been plenty of times over the past few years that I have said lots of angry words to God. Now don't be shocked! I try to trust God to look after Axel, but sometimes God has to listen to some very bad grumbles from me. I confess I'm not sure how much longer I can cope with the farm. By the way, Axel is in Karelia now."

"Oh, No! Really!" exclaimed Algot. "That's not a good place to be?"

"No."

Another long silence. Tyra wiped her eyes, and Algot blew his nose.

"They must be desperate, those children's parents, I mean," said Anna sadly.

"I don't understand them," responded Tyra. "Perhaps because I always wanted another child Nils is so precious. Nothing would induce me to send him away, nothing. Yah, those parents must be desperate to send their children away, with no idea where they are going."

"I think you're right, they were mostly from Karelia," said Anders matter-of-factly. "Those families have lost everything. They have nowhere to live. They either had to leave everything, or become Russians. Most, it seems, chose to leave everything. That's why Axel can stay in those deserted cottages. The people just walked out and left everything. Those parents couldn't help their children, though I confess I don't know why parents didn't choose to go with them. Maybe Sweden would only accept children, who knows! Their situation was the result of that winter war we were supposed to win. That's why we're fighting this war, to get back their homes."

There was a tense, awkward silence. Tyra was sure she heard Algot mutter, "Propaganda! Pure German propaganda!"

"Axel mentioned in one of his letters that he had been near the Russian border, and seen school children round a fire in their playground. I realize now he was in Karelia. Those poor children!"

"Well, what can I do to help you, if it's too soon for ploughing?" asked Algot, generously trying to breaking the tension.

"If it's too early to plough," said Anders, clearing his throat, and anxious to capture his nephew's strength, "how about helping me spread manure on the fields? We forgot to do that last year! It won't hurt if it's on top of the snow!"

Algot threw back his head and roared with laughter. "I bring you something sweet, and for my trouble you get me shoveling animal poo!"

"Pay back for letting me empty the stink pond!" laughed Tyra. "You always had trouble with smelly things," she remembered, smiling.

Algot grinned. "You remember that?" he asked. "It was the retting pond, remember? Oh boy, did that stink! Somehow you never minded it, I don't know how. Well, since you're such a good uncle, and cousin, I'll help." And he stayed to help with ploughing also.

Axel's next letter filled Tyra with deep concern. He had been in hospital, sent all the way from Aanislinna to Helsingfors. He was vague about what sickness ailed him, but very clear that he hoped to stay in hospital for as long as possible. Not only did he get two jugs of milk a day in hospital, but he had access to newspapers and books which gave him much joy. Although unfortunately he was soon discharged from hospital, he was back there a few weeks later. He had been billeted in a house crawling with budbugs, lice and other vermin, and over-zealous attempts to fumigate them out had made many of the men sick, Axel one of them.

By summer 1944 Finland was in a grim situation. A large army was sent in by Germany to try to halt the renewed Russian assault on the Karelian peninsula. BBC news was full of the story. All gains the Finnish army had made earlier in the so-called Continuation War were overthrown. Night after night Anders sat glued to the radio clucking his tongue in frustration and disappointment. Tyra, desperately worried about Axel's whereabouts, busied herself mending worn clothes and had no time to join him beside the crackling set. Axel's letters gave Tyra little comfort. He was back stationed in Karelia, the reason very unclear. She could not help a surge of intense jealousy when in one letter he described how he had been ordered to help a woman with her haymaking because her husband was at war. Why was he kept helping other women with their work instead of being sent home to help her with their own farm? Once again deep anger at the Finnish government for involving them in the war roiled inside her. She longed for the end of hostilities, but was burdened with increasing pessimism.

Then suddenly, early in September, 1944, Finnish radio, usually bland and noncommittal, announced that an "understanding" between the Soviet Union and Finland had been reached. Hostilities would cease. Late October came the news that the conscripted army was being discharged. The war, it seemed, was over. But there was not a word about constripted territorials, except the dire news than many Russian prisoners of war, maybe half of them, had perished from disease and starvation. Had Axel been with these hapless men?

"I'll believe war has ended when I see it!" growled Anders. "I don't trust Russia!"

When the BBC reported the same news, Anders reluctantly conceded that maybe the war was over, but eventually, sadly, he was proved correct. But much more tragically, while out working in the barn one late November evening, Anders developed sudden severe chest pain. He staggered to the house, and collapsed into his chair beside the kitchen table. He was unconscious when the doctor, hastily summoned by Karl, arrived. Indeed, as he feared, Anders did not live to see the end of the war.

Both Tyra and Anna were utterly devastated. They had braced themselves for the possible loss of Axel, but neither had even remotely considered that Anders would not survive the war. Neighbours and friends rallied around them. Lisa and Hyalmar came from Oxknagar. Tyra lived in a dark nightmare of misery.

"I'll have to talk to the priest not to mention hell," said Anna firmly, to Lisa's obvious surprise, but Tyra's relief. "Anders and I talked about hell several times, and I know he understood the truth about it." The pastor was more than willing to confine his remarks to generalizations that did not include a homily on the horrors of hell, and he was kindness itself to the grieving family. His unpretentious funeral address simply emphasized the saving power of Jesus Christ.

"I wish your Far had come to understand all my beliefs," said Anna, tearfully, to her daughter.

"Me too, Mor, but I'm sure he believed in God, so we can leave God to work things out. I'm glad of the new understanding of the Bible I have, but it's really knowing Jesus that counts. I'm sure Far loved him."

Anna nodded sadly. "I think you're right," she said.

Privately, Tyra was very pleased when Hyalmar asked if he could buy Blek. In all the misery of losing Anders, and not knowing where Axel was, it was a small comfort. Anna, however, insisted on giving the faithful carthorse to him, and smiled cheerfully as they drove away from the barn. But later Tyra found her weeping bitterly by the kitchen stove.

"I'll be all right," said Anna weakly as she wiped away her tears. "It's the best thing that could happen to Blek, but that horse was a very good friend."

"I know," said Tyra, and wiped her own eyes.

Although she tried hard, for weeks Tyra, numb with grief, was a mere robot performing as best she could. The continuing uncertainty about Axel made things worse. His letters now arrived both infrequently and erratically, merely hinting that he was no longer in Helsingfors. Tyra had no idea where he really was.

But for permanent peace, it was not Russia, but Germany, that proved untrustworthy. Because Germany did not withdraw its troops from Finnish soil by the date of the agreed terms of the armistice, about two weeks later Finland embarked on the third of its wars, the Lapland War against German troops on its territory. Angry German soldiers, feeling betrayed by Finland's change of loyalty, pursued a scorched earth policy and devastated much of northern Finland. They destroyed virtually all roads, railways, telecommunication lines, and about half the homes and other buildings in the northern Bay of Bothnia and Lapland areas.

But when the Germans were finally expelled on the 27th of April, 1945, the war, for Finland, was finally, finally, over.

But there was little for the country to rejoice about. Finland had lost significant territory, even more than after the Winter War. The Karelians were permanently expelled from their homeland. The majority of all Finns were starving, and the loss of human life had been appalling.

And for Tyra, the only thing that mattered to her was the one thing she did not know: when Axel would return home. After the loss of her father, she was too despondent to dare to even think about Axel's return.

Chapter 14

The Unthinkable

Tyra's thoughts tormented her. The Finnish army was officially disbanded, the war was over, yet not a word from or about Axel. How could she have ever thought that understanding a few theological questions would ensure a happy life! Since she had found answers she had been tested beyond her wildest nightmares, and there was no end in sight to the torture. She could not confide her heartaches to her mother, the one person who was normally strong and comforting. Anna still had a hacking cough, still grieved the loss of her husband, and was also deeply troubled by the lack of news about Axel.

Nils had celebrated his tenth birthday on January 19, 1945, while the Lapland War raged. Birthdays were not big celebrations in Finnish culture, but Tyra made an effort for her son's special day. He, her mother, herself, had survived. Better, Nils was healthy, a tall, and gangling boy. He consistently received outstanding school reports, and his teachers spoke of him in glowing terms. Yes, he was a gift from God. For weeks she carefully protected a precious bag of wheat flour, and a crock of apple sauce. To mark his birthday they had the best *plattar* she could make.

On May 8, 1945, barely two weeks after the last German soldiers left Finland on April 27, jubilation erupted throughout Europe. The entire European war was finally, finally over! Even the disparaged and usually bland Finnish radio broadcast triumphal music and programs. The BBC went wild with delight. Hitler was dead! Europe could begin the painful task of rebuilding its devastated nations.

Tyra and Anna were pleased—no more fighting, no more bombing, and, hopefully, soon a lot more food. But where was Axel? His last letter had spoken vaguely of "patrol" duty, with no explanation of what or where this was. Nils began asking awkward questions. If the war had ended, why didn't Far come back? Had he died like his Morfar had? Had he been killed like so many other soldiers had, and if so, why didn't they tell him?

Erik and Algot planted the fields in meandering furrows. Tyra learned something from their ploughing attempts. Whilst Blek, the special Belgian, was a powerful and incredibly good draught horse, she was much less effective than nondescript Löfte when pulling a plough. No doubt this was due to her lack experience, but it proved that one should not judge by externals, not even a horse!

A few days after VE Day Tyra was, as usual while it was barely light, in the barn feeding her hens, sadly remembering the times she had placed food on the high bale for Axel, and all the dreams she had for their life together, when she turned and saw a ghost! Standing in front of her was an apparition, thin, wasted, hair disshevelled, clad in absurdly ragged and ill-fitting clothes. She gasped, and sat quickly on a hay bale.

"Tyra! Oh, Tyra!" the apparition cried, then very un-Finnish, very un-ghostlike, the apparition sat beside her, enfolded her in its bony arms, and hugged her tight. Hugged her as though it would never let her go. The deep, jerky breathing of the apparition was the closest to sobbing Tyra had ever seen her husband.

"Where have you been? What have you been doing?" Tyra finally asked as Axel briefly released her.

Axel continued his strange, irregular gasps, while he frequently turned to hug her. Slowly, very slowly, the sobbing gasps subsided to normal, regular, breathing.

"You've just come?"

"I got here late last night. You had people with you. I—I didn't want anyone else. I decided to wait till I could see you alone. One more night wouldn't matter."

"How did you get here?" Tyra said, still trying to convince herself it was not a dream.

"Getting out of Karelia was a nightmare, and I daren't tell you about it. The army is quick to pull you in, but slow to push you out! They gave me what was supposed to be the bus fare home, but I was so hungry I spent half of it on food. So I only got half way. I don't know where they got these clothes I'm wearing, but they didn't encourage people to share rides with me. Since about Vasa I've walked."

"Oh, Axel! That's 80 kilometers! I've missed you so much. Didn't you remember, it's only Mor with me now." Tyra began to weep softly.

"Yah, I remembered that this morning, but I still wanted just you. Is Nils OK? How is your Mor coping?"

"Nils is good, really good. He's growing so fast. You won't recognize him. Mor is still very despondent. We both have been. Oh, it's been so long! How many years?"

"Too long," said Axel. "Much too long! Let's go inside."

The sight of Tyra walking from the barn with a man, especially a ghostlike man, caught the attention of Anna. Suddenly, she knew! "Nils," she called softly, "come and look."

Nils wandered to the window, and gazed with puzzled disinterest at the cheerful spring morning. Suddenly he too knew!

"Far!" he cried, and with a long whoop of delight, he flung himself out the door and down the path. Then he stopped dead, kicked dry leaves and rocks, and feeling a turmoil of emotion, hopped on one foot waiting for his parents.

"Did you shoot lots of Russians?" he asked hopefully. "Or Germans?"

"My, you've grown!" said Axel, patting him on the shoulder, a shoulder not far from his own. "You're almost as tall as Mor now!"

"Mor made me eat lots of eggs, one every day. She said that would make me grow, but she didn't eat any herself! Eating eggs is better than drinking milk," he added.

Tyra smiled. "The school doctor told me to make him drink two deciliters of milk a day," she said, "but Nils hated it. And since we had plenty of eggs, I thought they would do the job. I must confess it would have been good if he had drunk the milk, because I had lots of customers for the eggs, but few for milk."

Axel grinned, and gazed joyfully at his son, hardly believing he was so tall.

Anna could contain herself no longer, and ran from the cottage. Her cries of joy brought Takla and Karl running. Soon others in the village, including Erik and Mor Anna, joined them. There was much back slapping and hand shaking. All the time Tyra tried to convince herself it was real, that it was not a dream, and the strange apparition beside her really was her husband.

"Well, let's see what needs to be done in the fields," said Axel when all the laughter and chatter began to settle, "while Tyra makes me some food." Tyra smiled her broadest smile. That comment, that simple hungry, work-focused comment, could only come from her Axel, her own Axel, safely returned to her. God was indeed very good. And one thing he surely needed, in urgent abundance, was food!

"I'll make food while you wash and get into decent clothes," she insisted, "and then you can go to your fields!" Axel pulled a face, gave her a cheerful pat, and complied without protest.

"Do I have to go to school today?" piped up Nils, hopefully, when Axel was towelling himself and about to change into the clean clothes always kept for his visits. While no one was looking, Tyra gathered up Axel's cast off rags, and hid them in her wood bin, ready to be burned.

"Of course!" said his grandmother.

"Nah," said his father. "Come with me."

Axel could not wait for food before he checked his farm, and while Tyra made porridge Axel and Erik set off to admire the wobbling furrows Algot and Erik had so faithfully made. Axel laughed cheerfully at the meandering lines of fresh green grain, but privately was astonished his family had done so much to keep his farm going. Or was it from Tyra's prayers that he and his farm had survived? he wondered. He pretended he had not already seen the animals in the barn when Erik took him there, and was loud in his praise of their healthy condition. He noticed the flock of hens was significantly reduced, and Tyra admitted that recently, to get needed essentials, they were forced to sell eggs and cull hens faster than they could replace them.

"And my tomatoes!" Axel remembered. "How did you get on with those?"

"Didn't," said Erik, flatly. "We couldn't find any seeds."

Axel chuckled. "Come and I'll show you!" He led them into the bedroom, and in a fold in the mattress was a packet of precious tomato seeds. "I usually plant the seeds earlier, but let's see what we can do with them in the glass house. I hope they're still fertile, after all these years." He shook his head in bewilderment, and sighed deeply. "Yah, too many years!"

The glasshouse was a tangle of weeds, but Axel was delighted. It gave him something to do, and proved his return was needed. After a bowl of Tyra's now-ready barley porridge, he was out pulling weeds. The fowls made contented short work of their festive mound of greens, and the sheep and cows contributed manure to the success of tomato growing.

Meanwhile, Tyra agonized what to feed her man for lunch. He was so thin, so gaunt, he needed as much nourishment as she could provide. She decided she could not offer him more of their staple boiled barley, not even with the egg Nils usually got, not on such a special day. Risking his possible displeasure, she decided to sacrifice a hen, use half of their remaining potatoes, and begged a crock of preserved beetroot from Takla, who insisted she also accept a cup of precious wheat flour, enough to make one pancake for each of them. Tyra opened her last crock of apple sauce to garnish the pancakes. They wouldn't eat like this till new crops came in, but she had to make something special for such a day.

While the Finnish government tried to sort out major political confusion, and top leaders in the country were sent to prison for "war crimes", Axel gratefully worked on his farm. When Algot went to priosn because of his misdeed the family felt enormous, overwhelming shame. When General Wallenius went to jail because of his Lapua involvement, only to be extracted speedily to help with the Winter War, prison suddenly seemed like a game. When he, Axel, spent a few weeks there because of his conscientious objection to the war, he had been mortified. The shame was so deep he would never speak to anyone about it, not even Erik, although, of course, Tyra knew. But now, the very people, like President Risto Ryti, who had ordered him, Axel Östring, to prison for opposing war collaboration with Germany, were being sent to prison themselves because they had shamefully supported Germany and its policies! What a weird world!

Tyra, however, was very happy. Not only had God answered her earnest prayers and brought Axel safely home, but her mother's health rapidly improved after Axel returned, and she was keen to do all she could to help with the farm duties, making Tyra's work load easier, much easier, than it had been since she had married, fourteen years before. There wasn't much to buy in the shops, but wheat flour from Russia trickled in slowly, allowing the occasional meal of *plattar,* and even an apple cake sometimes. Strawberries arrived in the market, blueberries ripened in the forest, complementing *plattar* and the ubiquitous barley. Potatoes were coming on, and Axel allowed an occasional plant to be dug, and some of his precious tomatoes were picked for home use. Axel rapidly gained weight, Tyra's hollow cheeks filled out, and her arms and legs felt a strength they had not experienced for years. Nils soon rivalled his mother, then father, in height.

"The market isn't the same," Axel remarked to Tyra one evening, when he returned from his weekly trip to Jakobstad. "Lots of the old faces have gone."

"In the fighting?" she asked.

"Yah, sadly, but many are just leaving the country. The economy isn't good, and they're worried those communists in government have so much power. After fighting Russia for years it's hard to watch politicians falling over themselves trying to make friends with the Soviet Union!"

"So where are people going?"

"Everywhere I think, but Sweden is a favorite destination."

"That makes sense, but won't the Swedes stop that?"

"Maybe, but I think they feel guilty that they got away virtually without any harm in the war, while we suffered so much. And they need workers, I hear, especially in that huge iron ore mine up there in Lapland."

"You mean the one the Germans tried to get control of? The one not too far from the Norwegian border?"

"Yah, that's it. Kiruna. Biggest in the world, I hear. Doesn't sound like too much fun working in a mine in arctic conditions, but they say the pay is very good. The chap with the stall next to me in Jakobstad has gone there, and today another man was talking about doing the same. He thinks a few years of work there will make his fortune, and then he can go anywhere he feels like."

"You're not thinking of doing that?" asked Tyra, anxiously.

"Me? I'm a farmer, not a miner. I can't imagine anything worse than working in a mine. As long as I have land, I'll stay here!"

Tyra breathed a sigh of relief.

That winter was so different, so very different. The dark was still dark, and the cold still cold, the snow still icy and slippery. But they had hope, they had each other. Life was good. But at the height of this blissfulness Tyra was dismayed to find herself feeling decidedly unwell as spring slowly burst on the snow drenched countryside. At first she thought it was because she was eating too much rich food, food that for years she had been unable to obtain. She decided to go back to her war-time diet of mainly barley, but that made no difference. Then one day she realized her sickness was always worse in the morning, and what's more she had not had a menstrual period for more than two months. Could it be, could it possibly be, that she was to have another child?

It was hard to contain her joy, but she decided to wait until she was absolutely sure. After all, in only a few months she would be forty. By the end of May she was sure—tiny movements were pummeling her abdomen which was definitely starting to swell.

"Axel," she said one night as they lay in bed, "put your hand here. Can you feel it?"

"You're getting a bit fat!" he said, carelessly, thoughtlessly.

"Oh Axel, you men are so slow! I'm going to have a baby!"

"A what!" cried Axel, sitting up, all attention now. "You mean after all these years? Are you sure?" Tyra nodded happily.

"Well, well, well! Oh, boy! What a surprise! So that's why I survived that horror!" Axel grinned triumphantly.

Winter darkness was beginning to close in, and a heavy fall of snow lay in deep drifts, when on the morning of 31st of October, 1946, Tyra went into labor. Axel was away with his final autumn cartload of goods for the Jakobstad market, so once again Anna trudged through deep snow to beg Karl Höglund to fetch the midwife. Again it was all hustle and bustle, and officious efficiency, until amazingly, Axel stamped in the door, shaking snow from his heavy coat and boots, just in time to hear his second son give his first cry.

"A healthy baby boy!" declared the midwife. His parents gazed at him in wonder, their miracle child.

It took no discussion for both to agree that Anders form part of his name.

"I'd like Sven," declared Axel. "So Swedish and manly!"

"True," smiled Tyra weakly, as she propped herself on the bed. "And I'd like Roland. It's regal. This child is special! I just can't believe God has finally, after all these years, given me another child. I had long ago given up even thinking about it! But it's wonderful!"

Thus the brand new boy became Sven Anders Roland Östring, the pride and joy of his parents, his big brother now almost twelve years old, and his doting grandmothers, not to mention his uncles Erik, Algot and Hjalmar who were quickly informed of the wonderful news. But somehow, because mothers have a way with such things, he was always known as Roland, unless some government official got in the way.

"Next week we'll have a minister at church," announced Tyra carefully to Axel in early March, when the baby was four months old. "Roland will be dedicated, and I hope you'll come."

"What?" said Axel absentmindedly. "You mean some sort of christening?"

"Sort of, but not exactly. No, he's too young to choose God, but this is a promise we make to be good parents for our children, and teach them about God."

"That's a bit different. Never heard of anything like that before. Are you sure he shouldn't be christened properly? The local minister didn't seem too friendly when we went to church at Christmas, but I guess he would co-operate."

"No, I don't think christening is necessary. When he's older he can choose to be baptized. But do come with me this Saturday."

"Please, do," added Anna.

Axel shaved carefully, dressed in his uncomfortable best suit, knotted a tie around his neck, slicked his hair with water, and proudly carried his second son into the meeting hall of Tyra's church fellowship of a dozen people. The tiny congregation made a great fuss of both father and son, and to his surprise, Axel enjoyed himself. The young minister read the Bible story of the dedication of Jesus, offered wise advice to the beaming parents who were almost old enough to be his parents, and prayed earnestly for the health and welfare of the whole Östring family.

"Nice people, those friends of yours," said Axel as Löfte trotted them home in the cart.

Baby Roland became the embodiment of family hope. He made Nils, as he entered his teens, feel strong and manly. Axel decided he had endured all the privation of war and prison for the purpose of fathering this new son. Tyra and Anna clucked and fussed over the baby's needs, convinced he was a special gift from heaven, compensation for all the sorrows of the war. The villagers, Takla in particular, marveled that he brought so much joy to so many. Algot declared that he gave extra excuses for him to continue his regular visits, that is, until one day he shyly announced he was planning to move to Sweden.

"Haven't you got enough work round here?" asked Axel bluntly. "I'm sure I could find you more if you like."

"Thanks, but I still have a past. I've met this lovely girl in Vasa, Gunnel's her name. She knows my story, but is still prepared to marry me."

"Ah, now I get it!" grunted Axel. "So she's the cause! Are you off to that mine where they pay people a fortune?"

"No. It was my idea to go to Sweden. I didn't want Gunnel bothered by gossips all our lives. I've found a permanent job with a building company in Eskilstuna, west of Stockholm, and after we're married, we'll head there. She's a typist, so there'll be no trouble for her getting work, if she wants it."

"So, this is good bye?" said Tyra sadly, wistfully watching Algot dandle Roland on his knee.

"Not quite. Gunnel has agreed to come and visit my family and you before we leave. I've thought a great deal about this. For years I never thought anyone would marry me." He stopped, and grinned at Tyra. "Remember how you took me to task about not studying or getting confirmed and not being able to get married? Well, believe it or not, I listened. I was a bit late, but I got confirmed in prison. *Skriftskola* was a lot kinder there, from what I heard, than what you went through. The priest helped me understand that God would forgive me, and that I could live a better life. But anyway, I can legally get married!"

"Algot, I'm sad for us, but very pleased for you," said Tyra, pensively.

"Gunnel's a bit younger than me, quite a bit. Fourteen years in fact. All the women my age are already married, at least anyone worth marrying! Gunnel's family had a tough time during the war, but it's made her game for anything, even marrying me!"

Algot was true to his word, and a few weeks later brought his new bride, shy and blushing, to meet them and say goodbye. Everyone liked her, but the parting was strained. It was utterly foolish, but hard not to blame her for depriving them of their Algot.

"Love her, Algot," Tyra said gently. "She's a lovely young woman. We'll miss you. I can never thank you enough for all the help you gave me in the war. I don't know what I would have done without you."

"Tyra, your faith in me has given me the strength to start a new life in Sweden. I don't want to go, but this is the best plan I can think of, to make life decent for Gunnel."

"Well, all the best, my friend," said Axel, clapping Algot's shoulder, as he helped them down from the cart at the Nykarleby bus station. "I think you must've known I was going to ask you to help me reroof the barn!"

"Hey, Far, I can help you do that!" piped up Nils enthusiastically.

Axel looked at his son. Algot nodded approvingly. "Let him, Axel," he said. "He'll do a good job. And Nils," he added, pounding the lad's back, "you write and tell me what sort of a job your Far makes of the new roof!"

"Sure!" declared Nils. "When can we start, Far?"

"I'll need to think about that," said Axel, surprised at the proposed change in personnel.

After Gunnel and Algot left, Nils began excitedly talking with his father about what needed to be done to reroof a barn. His enthusiasm finally dispelled Axel's doubts, and that summer father and son, after farm chores were done, worked tirelessly on the project every evening. Eventually a fine photo of the renewed barn was sent to Algot in Swedish Eskilstuna, and Nils was a proud boy when Algot wrote a very complimentary reply. "I'll get you a builder's apprenticeship in Sweden," the letter ended.

"That could be fun," said Nils, "but when can we start making the room for me in the attic?"

"Son, I have no time to help you," declared Axel, "but you can work on that yourself."

"All by myself?" asked Nils, wonderingly. "Are you sure?" Axel nodded.

"Don't make a mess!" said Tyra. "I don't want wood shavings all over our beds!"

"Don't fall down the manhole!" added Anna, while she watched Roland play with his blocks on the floor.

Nils grinned broadly, and immediately got a ladder to climb into the attic and inspect what needed to be done to bring his dream project to fruition. While Axel rotated his crops and trotted Löfte II (Löfte I having been retired to quietly nibbling grass) to Jakobstad with his produce, Nils worked on his attic project, and transformed the cluttered space into a tidy room for himself. Occasionally during summer Axel got Nils to help him with the Jakobstad trips. The lad uncomplainingly helped pluck the culled hens, and sorted dozens of eggs, but when they got to the market he would cringe behind the cart.

"Far, I just can't do it! I feel so ashamed shouting out all that garbled stuff about our superior eggs! So many other people sell chickens and eggs, it's just a heap of noise and nonsense!"

"Son, that's why we need to call out! We used to be the only ones selling chicken and eggs in this district. It was your mother's brilliant addition to our farm products. But now many people try to do the same thing. So many have small plots of land, like us, and they're all trying to do the best they can with what they've got. Letting people know we're the original Östring egg producers helps them know they're buying a quality product. Surely son, you're proud of our eggs? Marketing must be done, or we'll be out of business. At least we're still the only ones selling tomatoes!"

"Far, you can do this, but I can't!"

Axel was angry, but grudgingly admitted the truth that competition for selling eggs had increased significantly. The government's land redistribution policy was helping people, but it was also breaking up the old, traditional, large grain estates, and the many small holders like himself were all vying for a share of the same market. Sometimes he thought of discarding the egg business, but knew Tyra loved her hens, and they did bring steady ready cash, as long as he put in the effort to sell them. He couldn't bear to tell her that her special contribution to their income was not living up to their expectations. He congratulated himself that he had bought a piece of forest when he got home from the war; Tyra had been surprisingly reluctant about that venture, but now she enjoyed the yearly visits to check their property, and to collect their own blueberries without all the neighborhood teenagers competing for their share. The forest gave them no income at present, but it was a source of blueberries, essential firewood, and was something to fall back on in years to come, something for his boys. Green gold, Finns had always called their forest.

So despite hard work, Tyra and Axel were content. Their boys were growing strongly. Tyra and Anna had their church fellowship, and friends in the village. They had a stable income, and Axel was confident he could adapt to new products if the hens did finally prove to be unprofitable. He began reading agricultural magazines to see what else he could experiment with and grow. He smiled somewhat ruefully when he realized the sheep were proving a very good venture, and wondered if he could experiment with breeds of sheep to produce better quality wool for specialty markets. Maybe even a few goats to produce mohair, yes, he'd think about that. He shared the idea with Tyra, and she was enthusiastic. Perhaps he could intentionally grow more blueberries in his forest, and sell those. Yes, there were plenty of things he could do with his land.

On a fine late summer day in 1949 Tyra was watching Roland play in the small yard in front of the house. Like Nils, he enjoyed leaping off the large rock in the middle of the home field and landing in the soft grass that surrounded it. It was a favorite occupation, and although she did not always have time to be out with him, today, for once, all her chores were done.

"Fru Östring?" a voice broke her tranquility.

She looked up. It was, it was—?

"Urho Järvinen," the man said, noting with irritation her hesitation. "I'm the local Lutheran minister."

"Oh, hello Pastor Järvinen," said Tyra, slightly embarrassed to have not immediately recognized such a prominent member of the community.

"Is your husband home?"

"No, not yet, but Axel should be back any moment. I'll put the kettle on, if you would like to step inside and wait for him."

"I don't need anything to drink," the man said curtly, "but it would be better waiting inside than out in this heat."

Tyra wanted to say she was enjoying the sunshine, but she led the way to the door just as a cloud passed over the sun, and the darkness inside the house momentarily blinded her. She pulled out a chair and motioned her guest to sit. She noticed he seemed very ill at ease.

"That's your boy?" the man asked, pointing awkwardly at Roland who was tugging at his mother's skirts, wanting to return to his favorite game on the rock.

"Yah, that's Roland," said Tyra proudly. "He's so special to us, because we didn't think we could have another child."

"Children come easily enough in my experience," said the man coldly, awkwardly. "So you have another son?"

"Yah, Nils is fourteen, almost fifteen. He's down the road visiting his friend Ben."

"Ah, yes, the Öhling family. Very pious people."

Tyra was not sure how to respond, especially as her guest maintained his stiff and frigid manner. Did he want to ask why she did not attend church regularly? She knew perfectly well the pious Öhling family attended church for Easter and Christmas, but no more frequently than she and Axel did. He must have something else to discuss with Axel.

Fortunately, she soon heard the crunch of Axel's boots on the path, and hastened to meet him. "Pastor Järvinen has come to visit us," she called as clearly and blandly as possible. Axel scowled, but had composed himself by the time he entered the kitchen.

"Evening, pastor," he said, brusquely. "Very dark in here after the bright sunshine outside."

This time the pastor scowled, then cleared his throat. "How long have you farmed here, Herr Östring," he began.

Axel was startled. "I've been here almost twenty years," he replied. "Everyone knows that!"

"You never applied for a land grant?"

"Well, the only other land available when I came here (apart from what I bought with this house) was church land, so I applied to the church, to the priest who was before you. We signed an agreement, a proper legal agreement for me to have its use. Of course, I freehold own this house and the land around it."

"The government is very serious about reallocating land, you must realize."

"Of course, and I'm glad. But I didn't want to be greedy, so I didn't apply for more land. I've bought forest, and I would like more land if any became available. We don't have much money, but my wife is very frugal, a very good manager, and we cope well. I could easily buy more now if any became available, but I know of none."

"I see," said the minister, and there was a long, awkward silence before he continued, "Well, I have come to let you know that the government has reallocated all church land."

"Really!" exclaimed Axel, standing up.

"Sit down my man," commanded the priest. To his own immense surprise, Axel obeyed.

"That agreement you signed with my er . . . um . . . predecessor was never legal. Maybe a nice gentleman's agreement, but . . . well, how long did you think you had use of the land?"

"Fifty years. The priest and the warden were both there, and they both agreed. They signed it in front of me, just like I did."

"Was anything put in writing?"

"Of course, I've just told you! I signed it and saw those churchmen sign it. And I've paid my rents faithfully, too. There must be a record of that! It was a real struggle for my wife to keep up rental payment during the war, but she never failed to pay. Just a minute, and I'll show you."

"There is no need to show me anything! Simply, there's no record of any such agreement in the official church records. Certainly nothing that was sent to Helsinki, and that's where the decision comes from."

There was a stunned silence. A long, long, stunned silence.

"There must be!" exclaimed Axel finally, leaning forward and clutching the edge of his seat. "The old pastor now lives in Jakobstad, as you know. I could visit him. I could easily ask him. Of course he would remember, even if you don't. He must have misplaced the paper I signed!"

"He's far too old to be taken seriously, and anyway, what he has to say is of absolutely no relevance. It's completely out of our hands, I mean the church's, and our jurisdiction. The land has been reallocated by officials in Helsinki."

The darkness in the room was palpable.

Axel finally found his voice. "Why didn't someone offer it to me? You must know I've been farming that land for twenty years. Everyone knows it! I didn't just squat on the land like a gypsy, or some Red refugee!" As the priest opened his mouth to speak, Axel cut in: "After all, you've come here to tell me I've lost it. Why couldn't you walk out here and tell me what to do so that I wouldn't lose it? How can you, a priest, stand there before God and tell me you've taken away my land, just like that? We'll starve! It's my livelihood for my family! Just tell me that!"

"Since there was no record of your right to the land, none in Helsinki at least, it was a government decision that it should be allocated to a refugee from Karelia."

"Karelia! A Red refugee, just like I said!" exclaimed Axel bitterly.

"I don't think someone like you, someone without patriotic fervor or honor, has the right to make political judgments like that!" hissed the priest. "Don't think your history is unknown! We all know what you did, or rather, didn't do! If you had been a proper war veteran, or a loyal member of the Church, it might have been different. The Church has only received a fraction of the market price for the land the government is reallocating. We have not profited from this situation. It's government orders, and the Church as a loyal supporter of the Finnish government must comply."

"But I am a veteran!" exclaimed the astonished Axel.

"Not a proper one, my man, and you know that! While others risked their lives, you had an easy job there in Helsinki. A very easy one."

As the pain of his war experiences flooded Axel's mind, he lost the will to fight. He drooped in his chair, suddenly aware of the mess his shuffling boots were making of his wife's clean kitchen floor. Only the presence of the apparently callous minister prevented Tyra from reaching over and touching her husband.

"Pastor," she said, her voice trembling with pain, "how long do we have before we must get off the land?"

"Oh, the Church and state are compassionate," replied the minister with a condescending nod. He got up up and pulled his well-made jacket around him, as if to exclude imaginary contamination from the peasant farmer and his no doubt uneducated wife. "You will be allowed to harvest the crops currently growing, which I have observed are potatoes and barley. The new ownership will take effect from January."

Axel stood up and angrily opened the door. "Leave! Get out! You can walk around my fields and spy on my crops, but you haven't the decency to offer me the chance to redeem the land. I wonder what your God would have to say about that sort of behavior! No wonder I don't waste my time going to your church too often!"

"Axel," pled Tyra softly, "don't talk like that."

"What would either of you know about religious matters?" exclaimed the priest angrily. "Wicked sinners who never attend church!"

"A great deal more than you, and certainly my wife much better than you!"

Suddenly, unexpectedly, Tyra stood, white-faced and trembling, and walked to the door, blocking the priest's exit. She turned to face him. As always, she was gentle and soft-spoken, but there was the glint of tempered steel in her grey eyes as she declared with a passion Axel had never seen before, "Pastor, I demand an apology, or at least your acknowledgement that we are not wicked sinners who deserve this terrible punishment that you have just delivered. I am a very loyal Christian, a true follower of the noble Martin Luther. He made the Bible the base of his belief and Christian practice, and I do exactly the same. As for the Lutheran Church, my husband and I pay our taxes faithfully, and we attend church at all the required times. We are in your church as often as virtually everyone else in this village. We have faithfully paid our rents to you, always on time. My decision to fellowship with a small group of Christians who study the Bible regularly and worship on the seventh-day of the commandment according to the Bible is mine alone, and my husband should not be held accountable for it. My husband has not had any disagreement with the Lutheran Church, and you do him a great wrong to suppose he does, or ever has done. Yes, he did seriously disagree with the decision of our country's government to collaborate with the Hitler-led German government, and he was punished for that. But, he was proved right, and you must acknowledge that. Eventually the government itself recognized that it had done wrong, and you know very well that many of our war time leaders are being punished as war criminals because of that collaboration. You know I am telling the truth, and God in heaven also knows it's the truth!"

It was an unusually long speech for the normally taciturn Tyra. To her own and the pastor's surprise, she remained standing by the door, gazing at him with flashing eyes. It was the pastor who finally dropped his gaze from her stricken and trembling face.

"Well, if you must know, I am sorry for you," he said awkwardly. "I really am sorry for you."

Pastor Järvinen suddenly regained his poise, pulled his jacket more tightly around himself, brushed past Axel, and looked as though he would push Tyra aside to get out the door. But Axel, throwing his arm around his wife, drew her protectively towards himself. The priest, with downcast eyes, rushed by and stumbled down the stairs, semi-blinded by the sudden bright sunshine outside, without saying goodbye, without looking back.

He almost collided with Anna returning from her daily visit to Mor Anna. As she entered she was shocked to see Tyra weeping, and Axel sitting awkwardly, protectively, close beside her.

"Who was that? Whatever's wrong?" she asked, alarmed.

"Everything," said Axel.

"Almost!" said Tyra.

While Axel buried his head in his hands, his elbows propped on the table, Tyra dried her eyes, and indignantly explained what had happened to her incredulous mother.

"But . . . that's unbelievable! Surely you can talk to someone? He can't just walk in here and tell you to get off land the whole town knows you've been renting for twenty years! How will you manage?" asked Anna. She paused, then announced proudly, "Remember, I have money from my house in Vasa. You could always use that! We could all go to Vasa!"

"That's a generous offer, Mor. You are very kind, but please, that house, and money from it, is for your needs." Tyra looked up, and tossed her head defiantly. "Mor, I have confidence that Axel will work something out. He has built our farm from nothing. We're not poverty stricken. We can make other plans. And I will do whatever it takes to help him!"

She had to sound confident, to somehow convince herself, and encourage Axel. What the future held she had no idea. God had brought Axel home from the war—but for this? To take away his land? The anger that swelled up in her heart was almost overwhelming. She had committed herself to God and was sure if she did all the right things God would do the right things for her. But it didn't work like that. War, prison, years of long separation, and now this! Losing his land was an unthinkable catastrophe for any farmer. How would he, how would they, ever survive? Was this the way God treated his loyal followers? She wanted to talk to God, to pummel him with questions, to, well, yell at him for allowing such a dreadful, unthinkable thing to happen.

She looked up, and wiped her eyes. The sight of Axel's ashen, stricken face, suddenly galvanized her. She had relied on him, leaned on him, but now he really needed her. She thought she had helped him during the war, but this would be a much bigger, much harder challenge. She knew she needed more than her own strength to do what would be necessary. The worst thing was she had no idea what was going to be required of her. But, she was willing to give God another chance.

Suddenly, strangely, she began humming softly to herself, singing to give herself the courage she so desperately needed. Axel looked up and frowned. He was in no mood for music, anyone's music, any type of music, and especially not churchy music. Tyra's confidence was very low, but she sang to remind herself that somehow things had worked out in the past.

"Don't be ridiculous, woman!" Axel exclaimed. "This is no time for silly ditties!"

Anna got up and left the room.

Tyra ignored her husband, took a deep breath, and, skipping the second verse of the hymn, hurried to the last.

> Help me then in every tribulation
> So to trust Thy promises, O Lord,
> That I lose not faith's sweet consolation
> Offered me within Thy holy Word.
> Help me, Lord, when toil and trouble meeting,
> E'er to take, as from a father's hand,
> One by one, the days, the moments fleeting,
> Till I reach the promised land.

Axel opened and shut his mouth, and Tyra expected an angry outburst. Then he looked up, and his eyes were strangely softened. Gratefully he had recognized what she was singing, and suddenly he smiled. "You're quite a woman! You really are! I don't know where your promised land is, but I sure will need your help finding mine!" he exclaimed gruffly.

Tyra and Axel, Wedding Day, July 2, 1931.

Tyra and Axel's house, on right, in Brännon.

Tyra with farm horse and unidentified rider.

Nils aged about two.

Namn: Anna Lall

har blivit döpt

den 20 augusti

och upptagen som medlem i

Sjundedags adventist samfundets

församling i Vasa

den 17 sept. 1932

J. Henson

Predikant

Dyra syster förbliv du vid det som du har lärt och som du har fått visshet om. Du vet ju, av vilka du har lärt det." 2 Tim. 3:14. "Kämpa trons goda kamp, sök att vinna det eviga livet, vartill du har blivit kallad, du som och inför många vittnen har avlagt den goda bekännelsen." 1 Tim. 6:12.

Minnesord.

1 Joh. 2:1.

Anna Lall's baptismal certificate.

Finnish soldiers.

Tyra and Nils with family cow.

Tyra and Nils with family pet.

Erik Östring.

Kiruna Mine and Town, circa 1955.

Östring's house, (note snow) Kiruna.

Tuullovaara Mine.

Roland in Kiruna.

Nils and Erik in Kiruna, 1953.

Nils and Roland in Kiruna.

Nils (facing camera) in mine.

With Finnish friends in Kiruna. Back Row, Nils second L, Axel far R. Front row, Tyra has Roland, wearing dog-shirt, sitting on her knee.

Family group, Kiruna, L to R, Nils, Tyra, Axel, Roland.

Axel, circa 1955,
when the family left for Australia.

Nils with Family's first car.

Med sorg tillkännagives att
vår kära mor och mormor

Anna Greta Lall

(f. Rådman)

insomnade fridfullt 30. 12. 1955
i Oxgangar i sitt 74 levnads-
år. I ljust och tacksamt min-
ne bevarad av oss släkt och
vänner samt adventförsamlin-
gen i Nykarleby.

**Tyra och Axel Östring
Nils och Roland.**

På de sällas gyllne strand
där i evighetens land
helgon vandra hand i hand.
Möt mig där!
Hän från jordens kval jag flyr
dit, där stormen mer ej gnyr
men en evig morgon gryr.
Möt mig där.

Som vänlig inbjudan med-
delas alla som önskar följa
den avlidna till den sista vi-
lan, att jordfästningen äger
rum på Oxgangar begrav-
ningsplats söndagen den 8 ja-
nuari kl 13. Samling i Sofia
Lerstrands gård kl 10 samt
efter gravläggningen.

Death Notice of Anna Lall, December 30, 1955.

Axel and Tyra at Roland's wedding, 1972.
The young man to Tyra's L was the best man, Dr Keith Powers.

Grave of Tyra and Axel, Mullumbimby, NSW, Australia.

Part Three
Love

Chapter 15

Kiruna

An untouched apple cake lay on the table between Tyra and Takla, beside two cups of cold chicory coffee. Two suitcases and three small boxes were stacked by the door of the kitchen, now otherwise strangely empty. The women reminisced about the many experiences they had shared over the past twenty years. There was much to talk about.

"It must be hard leaving your Mor and boy behind," said Takla, sighing.

Tyra swallowed, took a deep breath, and nodded. "We've thought hard about it. But it's best for Nils to complete school here. He's doing well, and we don't want to cause him trouble."

The conversation drifted to general topics, to laughter about humorous events that had occurred. Takla stretched her legs. "I'll write regularly," she said. "I won't forget you."

"Thank you," said Tyra. "I was a young bride when I arrived here, full of hope. You've been good to me. I'll never forget you. You and Elna. It was so sad to lose her so soon after I came here. You were so much help in those early days. Yes, so much help. It's just as well we don't know the future! We've had some tough times, haven't we?"

Takla nodded. "We have. Every one has. But we've had each other, we've been good friends." She paused, cleared her throat again, then took a very deep breath. "Tyra, I don't know how to say this, but I want you to know that Karl and I know what happened to you and Axel during the war."

Tyra looked up, a rush of fear, surprise, and embarrassment flooding her face. "It was lonely," she said. "Very."

"It must have been, but it was more than that, and you know it. I want you to know that I know. We were relieved when your parents came, and that cousin of yours dropped in. What a fine young man! How lucky you were to have him! I wanted to talk to you then, but you were so stoical. But oh! The morning I saw those men drag Axel away, it broke my heart. At first, we thought he was foolish to resist the call up, but later we understood he was right. It was our leaders who were wrong. We admired you both."

"Really?"

"And Tyra, we know why you're leaving now."

The relief that had momentarily flooded Tyra's face was quickly replaced with more fear, surprise, and embarrassment. "What—what do you mean?" Tyra stammered.

"Well, Axel told Karl there is no money in eggs, that he needed ready cash, and that's why you're going to Kiruna." Takla paused, and studied her friend carefully. "But Tyra, you don't need to be brave all the time. We Finns are just too stoical for our own good, and you must be the worst! The minister visited you, didn't he?" Another pause, Tyra sat with eyes downcast. "When Axel told Karl about the eggs, he let slip that he didn't have enough land to continue farming. Now Karl gets around, and he's also been, most unwillingly, at the beck and call of those priests, ten days every year ever since we've lived here. Well, about the time the priest visited you, he also called on Karl and told him he wouldn't be needed for church duties anymore because church land was reallocated by the government to refugees, but the documents for our ownership of the land had been recognized by the officials in Helsingfors. Karl was delighted with the news, but casually asked what would happen to people who were leasing church land. Pastor Järvinen suddenly got angry, and at first refused to talk. Finally, he admitted there might be people who would have to get off their land. Of course we immediately thought of you. Tyra, Axel didn't deserve to lose the use of his land. That minister is a very unhappy man, merely taking orders, afraid of officialdom. It doesn't sound as though anyone put up a fight, just took orders. Karl thinks it won't hurt them much, because they still get tithes and the church tax, but I'm not so sure. You only go to church on the required days, like Karl and I do. There are always lots of people there then, but trust me, on other Sundays there's hardly anyone at church, probably less than at the little fellowship you attend. Pastor Järvinen must have hated coming to visit you."

"Really?"

"Anyway, that's all I have to say. Karl is grateful Axel has given him the use of your barn and the land around the house. We'll look after things for you, especially your Mor and Nils, till you get back from that mine in Sweden. Promise."

"You know, I don't want to go," said Tyra, suddenly, impulsively, leaning towards her friend, and shaking her head miserably. "I really don't! I've made so many suggestions, come up with so many other plans for Axel. I've begged, I've pleaded, I've even refused to go! But Axel is deaf to everything I say. So, I'm going to Kiruna to support Axel, and trust God we're doing the right thing. I know Axel will hate working in a mine, but he's convinced this is the best option he has. Coming here 80 kilometers from Vasa when I was a young and adventurous bride seemed a huge journey, but this Sweden expedition is almost a thousand kilometers. I have no idea what it will be like. My mother wanted us to go to Vasa, and use her house. She suggested Axel try carting like my father. But Axel is a man of the land, and he's certain that Kiruna is the best way to get money quickly so he can buy more land. He's hopeful that once he earns enough in the mines—and they do pay well—we'll come back, buy a piece of land, and get on with the farming he loves so much. Nils is excited about being 'man of the house' for my mother. He has two more years of school, before he starts a career. His teachers are very pleased with his work, and strongly suggest he consider teaching. Even now, they get him to help teach some of the younger students. Nils is excited about the teaching idea, and he could do some of the necessary training right here, which would be good. One positive thing, after what has happened to him Axel has agreed for Nils to try other work besides farming. Mor has you and the church fellowship for friendly support, so I'm sure she'll be fine."

"I couldn't do it!" declared Takla, shaking her head. "I just couldn't! How can you give up your home, your friends, your family, everything, just to support Axel's crazy idea! Why should you give up your life just for him? Men are impossible!"

"Takla, as I said, I don't want to go. But I've prayed about it. I believe if I do this, somehow something good will come of it. Losing his land so unexpectedly has been terrible for Axel. His faith in God is weak, or at least it is now. He was very depressed for a while, and I was really worried. I decided supporting him with this Kiruna adventure was the best thing I could do."

Takla shook her head again and frowned, whether in disapproval or disbelief was not clear. "I guess Roland's too small to know what's going on?" she asked.

"He is. Mor has taken him to the barn to say goodbye to the animals, and to give me a bit of packing peace! He's a good kid, but packing with him around is a nightmare! He wants to pull everything out, and play with it! I came in yesterday and found him using my underwear as a hat! Right now Axel and Nils have gone to what was the church land. I've no idea why they want to torture themselves, but perhaps it's to say goodbye."

Takla nodded. After an awkward pause she added, "Our drinks are cold, and my cake untouched. I'm sorry Tyra. This visit was not meant to be so gloomy! But, we've had a good talk, and we're real friends, not just chat mates. Karl and I not only wish you all the very best for this big adventure, but we'll be praying for you too, trust me. But please, have a piece of my cake, and the rest you can share with your family later."

"Thank you Takla, thank you very, very much," said Tyra, as she slid a piece of cake to her plate, and watched it lying there.

"Mor!" cried Roland, bursting in the door with all the confident exuberance of a three-year-old. "Mormor says she's going to look after all the animals, especially Löfte I, while we go on our trip. She says Karl's going to look after Löfte II. And you know what? She says we're going on a train! Oh, Mor, I've always wanted to do that! A train! A real train! Won't that be fun!"

Tyra smiled wanly, as her mother followed Roland into the kitchen. Roland grew quiet when he saw Takla, but stood eyeing the apple cake. "Yes, you can have some," Tyra smiled. "Get a plate from the cupboard, and I'll give you a piece. Takla made it for us, wasn't that nice?" Roland grinned broadly.

"I've been trying to make it sound fun for him," declared Anna, helping herself to a piece of cake, and munching thoughtfully.

"Mormor says Nils will have his attic room and she'll have our bedroom all to herself!" said Roland between mouthfuls of apple cake. "Won't that be good for her? She can sleep in as long as she likes!"

"Tyra, try not to work too hard today," said Takla as she rose to go. "You have a long journey ahead of you. Karl will be here to take you to the station in the morning."

"He knows it's not the regular station?" asked Tyra, a tinge of apprehension in her voice.

"Yah, yah. Five thirty the train leaves, so he'll be here at four thirty. That should give you plenty of time." Suddenly she bent and unexpectedly gave Tyra a kiss on the cheek.

Karl kept his word, and was at the door with his truck well before time. Quickly the vehicle was loaded and his passengers climbed in. Anna was tearful, but did her best to encourage her daughter. Nils grinned proudly as he waved good bye. Takla pressed Tyra's hands warmly, but neither could speak. Axel had a face like stone as he bid his brother and step-mother farewell.

It was a beautiful May morning. Lilacs bloomed in hedgerows. Tyra noticed fieldfares chattering beneath the trees, and as they passed a small lake a heron rose majestically from the sedges. She wanted to comment on the beauty around her, but her heart was too full. Axel had his eyes closed most of the journey, apparently deaf to Karl's attempts at small talk.

The train was waiting, belching billows of black smoke. Roland, who had dozed most of the truck ride, became excited. "It's so big!" he exclaimed. "Can it really pull us all the way to Sweden? Look at all that black smoke!"

Tyra brought pencils and paper to entertain Roland on the long journey, but eating and gazing out the window, between dozes, kept him happy. The worst part of the journey, for all of them, were the frequent train changes, when their luggage had to be pulled down, pulled out, pulled from under, counted, then carried to another train, which was often waiting many meters across an unfamiliar station. There it all had to be re-stowed. Station personnel sometimes helped, but it was still stressful. Fortunately, the weather, though cloudy, was kind, and they did not have to battle rain. By the time they reached the international border with Sweden, it was bright and sunny. Axel was surprised how easy it was to cross into Sweden. Obtaining Finnish passports had been a laborious process. But a quick glance, a quick stamp, and they were out of Finnish Tornio and into Swedish Haparanda on the opposite side of the delta of the mighty Torne River. With a couple more passport stamps they were in Sweden.

Axel insisted his most important task at the border was exchanging Finnish *marks* for Swedish *kronor*. While Axel sorted his money, a chore that lasted a long time, Tyra celebrated their arrival in Sweden by pulling out the remains of Takla's apple cake. They ate hungrily, Axel between *kronor* counts. Earlier they had nibbled on *knäckerbröd* and cheese, but it was good to eat something special. Another train change at Luleå allowed Tyra to persuade Axel to use his new *kronor* and buy food from the station cafeteria, cinnamon rolls and *griser*. From Luleå they entered the longest, and final, leg of their journey, the four hour ride to Kiruna. Axel was delighted to note this train had a diesel engine, and they would no longer need to keep the windows tightly shut to keep out the acrid smoke that stung their eyes and stained their faces. The entire journey lasted more than fifteen hours, but, except for Roland, excitement kept them wide awake.

Once safely on the final Kiruna-bound train, with his money carefully sorted, Axel relaxed. "Quite an adventure this! Had plenty of time to think about life! I've been meaning to tell you this funny story for a long time," he began as they chugged out of Luleå station, "but I was always too tired when I got home from market. Whenever I went to Jakobstad there was always an official roaming around checking on us. They wanted to know how much land we had and how much tax we owed. I was amused how vague some farmers were about what they farmed. One officer came up with the idea that he would count the animals people farmed, and then apply some fancy calculation he had. I was honest about how many hens we had, and he didn't bother me. (I didn't waste time telling him that I farmed other things beside hens!) He had no idea what tomatoes were, and didn't bother me about them.

"Anyway, one poor chap, Stefan, was a refugee from down south just starting out as a small farmer, and this official really harassed him, persecuted him, I'd call it. According to his complicated calculations Stefan needed twice as much land as he claimed, and had three times as many hens as he claimed, and therefore owed a lot of tax. This argument went on for weeks, while we all stood around waiting for the explosion. We joked with Stefan, but it wasn't funny, and we knew it.

"Then one day I arrived at market and Stefan, for once, was looking pleased with himself. That should have warned us. 'Anyone want to come with me?' he asked. We wanted to know what he was up to, but he was all mysterious. Finally, my stall mate agreed to look after things for me, and I went with Stefan. Honestly, I was just curious, wondering what he was up to.

"Stefan grabbed a couple of baskets of live hens, and to my surprise we headed for the municipal council building. When we got there he demanded to see the head tax bureaucrat. Those hens made an awful lot of noise in their baskets and made everyone stop and look at us! Of course this tax person was not available. Various people asked what the problem was, and Stefan said he had to pay too much tax and wanted his situation revised. No one was willing to listen to him, but they sure turned to look at the hens. There was no way they could avoid hearing them! Then some officious woman up on the third floor (we were sent all over the building) ordered him to leave. At that point he suddenly opened his baskets of hens and yelled he'd had enough of everybody, that his hens weren't half as valuable as those useless officials claimed they were, so the useless blankety blank officials could have them, special blankety blank gift! They weren't good layers anyway, he yelled, as the birds fluttered and squawked out of their cages.

"Oh, my, what pandemonium he caused! You should have seen the mess! There were hens and feathers fluttering everywhere, flying up to desks and perching on official papers. I even saw one hen sitting on a tax officer's head!"

Tyra began laughing. Memories of her own efforts to hide hens to reduce tax filled her mind. "How many hens did you say he had?" she asked. Axel now was laughing so heartily he had to had to wait till he caught his breath.

"Probably only a dozen, but it seemed much more," he chortled. "Those hens had been cooped up for hours, and they'd been messing themselves, and wanting to mess, which they now did all over that fancy municipal building. Stefan stormed out of the building with a hen or two fluttering after him, and left an uproar inside! It must have taken them days to clean up!"

"Did the 'ficious lady laugh at the hens?" asked Roland, boggled-eyed

Tyra shook with laughter, and some of the surrounding passengers, doubtless eaves-droppingly bored by the long journey, began laughing too. Tyra finally controlled her mirth. "Did he give up farming poultry, or did they leave him alone?"

"Both. By then he'd discovered what many of us knew already, that there were too many poultry farmers. Soon afterwards he started selling potatoes and beans and I didn't see any more eggs or chickens in his stall."

After a few more chuckles, Axel was quiet for a while, then added, "I kept them guessing, because most of the small farmers concentrated on only one or two products. I always sold our excess grains to the grain merchant in Nykarleby, so the Jakobstad officials were not aware of that, though I didn't make it a secret. I don't think they could associate hens, tomatoes, potatoes, grains, and certainly not sheep! Those officials have no farming knowledge."

"I sympathize with both Stefan and those officials," announced Tyra. And then she had the astonished Axel doubled with mirth as she told how long it had taken to clean the sauna after her own tax evasion efforts.

"Does anyone farm around Kiruna?" asked Tyra suddenly, stretching her cramped legs.

Axel began laughing again, but soon became serious. "Actually, I was stupid enough to ask that too! The growing season there is about three weeks. Can't think of anything that would grow that fast! But, I heard they grow awfully big mosquitoes, if you're interested in them!"

At that moment Roland wanted to use the toilet, and Axel volunteered to escort him. Both found balancing on the swaying train challenging. Tyra sat watching the flat countryside flash by, thinking about huge mosquitoes with nothing to eat but humans. Light snow covered much of the land, with clumps of pine forest, black and stark against the snow. Occasionally tiny hamlets of three of four brightly painted cottages, no doubt foresters' cabins, nestled beside the trees. She wondered what time it was, and in a spasm of intense emotion, longed for the old clock on the bedroom wall, the one that never would hang straight.

"Will anyone meet us when we get there?" she asked, anxiously, when Axel returned with Roland.

"Yah, the mine manager said he'd be there himself, or arrange for someone else. He seems to have a special sympathy for Swedish Finns, as called me."

"Hmm, that's kind. Funny, I don't think of myself as a Swedish Finn, but that's what we are, I suppose. I wonder what Swedish children learn in their history about Finland?" mused Tyra. "Do they know we were once one country? I was really surprised when Nils told me he learned Finland is not part of Scandinavia, but a Nordic country, whatever that means. Not sure what they were fussing about, but somehow the connection between Finland and Sweden seems lost. Nils didn't even know about the name changes of Finland."

Axel nodded. "I wasn't at school long enough to learn much, but you were, weren't you?" He gazed out the window. "Oh, by the way, I won't be working in the main mine, but in a smaller one near a town called Tuulovaara. It's about five kilometers from Kiruna. I got advised by the men at Jakobstad market, ones with family already up there, that the manager for this mine was a decent chap, and treated Finns well. From my contact with the manager it seems they were right."

"Will we live near that mine, or in the town?" asked Tyra.

"The mine provides accommodation, but I don't know where it is. Let's wait and see."

As the train rumbled north into the Artic Circle passengers began to take more interest in their surroundings. "I want to be the first to see it!" declared a young man, sitting opposite.

"See what?" said his older companion sleepily.

"You know, the iron mountain! The Kiirunavaara."

"Oh, it'll be on the right," the older man said, yawning. "Obvious it is. You'll see a bit of a lake below the mine hill, as the train comes in."

"Good, I'll get a good view," returned the young man. He looked at Roland. "Hey, you've been a good kid. I'll call you over when I see the mine."

"Will it be soon?" asked Roland eagerly. "Is it a very big hole?"

"Don't know about a big hole, but I hope it will be soon! And where do you come from, young fella?"

Roland looked at his mother to answer this strange question. She spoke quietly to him, and he answered confidently, "Oh, we're from Nykarleby, in Finland."

"Yah, thought you sounded different. That's a long way away! Got a sort of lilt in your voice, although I must say your Swedish is very good. You must've been practicing to speak so well! But I wouldn't have picked you as Finns, not the way your husband was telling that funny story. Finns are usually so serious! What time did you start this journey?"

Roland again looked uncertainly at Tyra. She smiled, and answered the young man herself. "Many people in Finland speak Swedish. Finland used to be part of Sweden, you know. And we Finns aren't serious, not all the time! But to answer your question, we began our trip at 3:30 this morning, Finnish time."

"You're kidding? Finland once part of Sweden, eh? Fancy that! Didn't know that! But, oh my, you must be keen to go to the mine to get up so early, or your husband is. My uncle here has worked in the mine a couple of years, and he thought it would be good for me to set myself up. The pay's pretty good, you know. Oh, by the way, we're from Umeå."

"Umeå? That's only about 50 kilometers across the Kvarken from where we lived. Oh look," cried Tyra, pointing out the window, "see, a pair of swans on that frozen river!" Axel nodded, tired and not in the mood to get excited about birds. The young Swede grunted. He too had no interest in mating birds. But he nudged his seat mate and pointed out the window. The older man nodded. "Yah, that's it!" he said.

"Come here young fella!" the young Umean called Roland. "You can see the mine over there!"

Roland ran over expectantly, but frowned, "It's just a big hill, and it looks very dirty!" He puckered his nose. "It's all black! And like a staircase. Don't they have trees?" Other passengers erupted in mirth.

"Have a look out the other side of the train. There might be trees there," suggested the Umean. But Roland remained unimpressed by tiny bushes, black branches with no leaves, around the houses of the city they were rapidly entering.

"Don't they have forests for blueberries?" he asked with concern. But the train was coming to a halt, and people were more interested in grabbing their luggage and reaching their destination than answering a small boy's anxious questions about his favorite food.

Axel scanned the platform for a mine manager, but had no need to worry. True to his word, the man was there, waiting with a small truck. Introductions were made, luggage loaded, they climbed in. "I don't meet everyone," he explained to Tyra, "but I do try to meet families. Men workers come and go, but if we have families, they stay much longer." Tyra gave an exhausted smile.

He drove them a few kilometers to a block of apartments, painted the classic deep red like their own home, and helped carry their luggage to the second floor. He unlocked the door with a flourish.

"Welcome to Tuullovaara! The mine's down the road, easy walking distance Axel. Won't stay now, you'll be tired," he added thoughtfully. "Beds should be made. Axel, let me know when you have your own bedding, and I'll arrange for the mine stuff to be collected. There's milk, bread, two types, coffee, and cheese in the cooler in the kitchen. Keep that cooler shut, or everything will freeze overnight! Bus leaves for the main town every half hour morning to evening. Take the next couple of days off to show your wife around, Axel, then report for orientation on Thursday. Sleep well," he added, ruffling Roland's hair as he left.

"It's very comfortable," said Tyra, walking around the apartment and admiring two bedrooms, a kitchen, a bathroom, and a living area. "And look at this! It has a flush toilet! But I'm exhausted. Let's sleep."

Roland was fascinated by the new toilet, and for a few days his need to use it was extremely frequent. "I just pull the chain, and it makes a waterfall!" he announced with gleeful admiration.

Next morning Tyra woke to an insistent a small voice. "Mor, there are big buckets on wires outside. Why?" Axel got up to see what Roland was talking about, and explained the buckets carried ore from the mine where he would work.

"You need iron to make things like nails, and wheels, and axe heads," Axel explained. "But let's explore the town," he added, moving from the window and returning to Tyra, who grunted and rolled over sleepily. "Remember, he said I have two days to show you around, and then its work!"

"Work? What's new!" grumbled Tyra. "See what you can find for you and Roland to eat, and then you can explore. I'm simply too tired." Exhausted from her trip, she was soon fast asleep again.

Axel shrugged, looked at the sleeping Tyra, and fed Roland. Then buttoning his son warmly in yesterday's travel-strained clothes, he took him to explore Tuullovaara despite the bitingly cold wind. "There's the school you'll attend," Axel pointed out, as they trudged along. "Right close to our house, now isn't that good! Can't see a market, but we'll find that."

When they returned Tyra was still asleep, but she woke when Roland ran in and began excitedly telling her of all he had seen. She soon revived enough to venture out and explore, the icy wind still cutting straight through their layers of clothes. Waiting for the bus was miserable, although inside the vehicle was warm and cozy.

"This town looks prosperous," commented Axel. "Very prosperous. There's money here, that's for sure. Lots of it, I'd say."

"Oh! Look up there!" pointed Roland, catching the sentiments of his father. "There's a building with gold people on it! People here really are rich!"

Tyra and Axel laughed. "That's a church!" they said. "Those gold people are saints. But it does look rich, doesn't it?"

"People here are rich," insisted Roland. "Are saints people with lots of money?"

"Your religious education of your son needs a lot of improvement!" teased Axel, nudging his wife.

The bus pulled into the terminal, and the driver indicated where they would find shops. With hats pulled down and scarves wound tight they walked up the cobbled street. A few people sat on benches in a sheltered corner, sunning themselves, dirty snow piled high on the cobbled road beside them.

They found the shops were all tucked inside sturdy buildings, ensuring comfort no matter what the weather conditions. Despite the sun and a clear blue sky, the bitter wind made indoor shopping most welcome. Tyra was agog with what was available in these shops, and eager to explore as many as possible. Roland, however, quickly tired of looking at plates, bedding, warm clothes, and other necessary supplies that so excited his mother. Not even a ball hastily purchased was successful in prolonging his shopping enthusiasm. Finally, his pleas to look at the golden people on the church were heeded, and the family walked across the cobbled streets to the imposing red church. Roland was excited to find, in small corners without snow, that real green grass grew in the park beside the church, the only grass in the town.

"Look! It has a special church for children!" announced Roland, pointing to the church's elegant bell tower as they crunched up the path. The church door was open, and they were glad to escape inside from the relentless wind.

"Oh!" sighed Roland, as they stepped across the threshold. "Oh, it's so pretty!" The high windows, electric chandeliers, beautiful altar painting, and striking red carpet against the dark wood of pews and walls was indeed very attractive.

"Better than anything I saw in Finland," muttered Axel. "There sure is money in this town." He found a brochure in the church porch, and proudly informed Tyra the church was dedicated in 1912, and the striking altar painting was the work of a real Swedish prince, turned artist, Prince Eugen of Närke.

"This place is special," Tyra agreed. "That organ must sound magnificent. I wonder if there's a Sabbath-keeping fellowship here?" she added wistfully.

Final task for the day's outing was visiting a food shop. Tyra cooked farm produce, and used fruit from her trees, from the forest, and from the hedgerows around her home. But there was none of that in Kiruna, and she was fascinated by the variety of food available in the shops. Axel wanted barley and oats and rye bread and cheese. Tyra added apples and oranges, and a strange long yellow fruit she had heard of, but never eaten.

"What do you want those banana things for?" grumbled Axel, whose patience with a market was long, but with shops very short. "They're probably poisonous! What's wrong with good apples? I'm not made of money for you to go trying out oddities!"

"You brought me here, and I'll try everything that's available," Tyra insisted, her eyes flashing mischievously. "I promise if you can grow anything here, I'll cook it and eat it!" They bought four bananas, and headed home.

"Can I hold the golden fruit?" pled Roland when they settled on the bus. Tyra laughed and gave him the banana bag to carry, which he did most carefully. That evening they ate two of the "golden fruit," divided with meticulous care between the three of them.

"Delicious!" said Axel, as he chewed his piece of banana thoughtfully. "I must find out more about them."

"What! Are you going to grow them inside our apartment?" exclaimed Tyra, laughing. "They come from the tropics, not the arctic circle! You can put tomatoes in a glass house, but these things grow on trees!"

"Do you think Nils knows about them?" asked Roland, savoring the last bite of his portion. "Make sure you tell him, won't you Mor?"

Next day Axel vigorously resisted more shopping, and reviewed his clothing ready for the mine. Tyra did her housework, astonished that by ten in the morning she had completed her day's chores. There were no hens, no sheep, no cows, no horses to care for. The water flowed from a tap, and did not need to be hauled from a well. Had she come to Kiruna merely to have a holiday? The idea of spending her days doing nothing was not appealing.

Just before lunch there was a knock at the door, and a woman held out a large fish pie. "Welcome to Kiruna! Enjoy this!" she said. "Fish is really good here. You'll be wanting to do fishing yourselves on the lakes and rivers when you get days off. My husband will show you." She placed her pie on the table, and quickly left.

"Friendly people" said Axel. He sniffed the pie. "Smells like salmon. Perhaps I should find out about fishing instead of bananas."

"Fishing, now that's a much better idea! Did you notice her accent? She's from Finland," said Tyra.

But after enjoying fish pie for lunch, even Axel was restless from the unaccustomed inactivity and confinement indoors, and grudgingly agreed to take the bus to explore more of the city. To Tyra's delight, by walking in a different direction, they discovered a large, well-stocked library. Perhaps leisure time could be used to advantage after all! She signed up for membership, and borrowed two books. Turning to leave, she was delighted to find Axel behind her, ready to get his own library card!

"This is great," she said as she cradled the books. "I never had time to read in Finland, but now I'll finally have the chance!"

Axel left early next morning to attend orientation. Tyra washed the fish pie plate, and went looking for her neighbor. She could see only one other door on the second floor, but her tentative knock quickly brought yesterday's donor. "I'm Mira," the woman smiled, "come on in!"

Tyra was right, Mira came from Finland, and better still, there was another "Swedish Finnish" family with the Tuulovaara mine. Mira had endless advice for coping with arctic Kiruna, and was keen for the three families to meet. Tyra talked about Nils left behind in Nykarleby with his grandmother, and how she looked forward to his visiting them. Tyra was amazed how quickly and enjoyably the morning flew by, and agreed to meet her new friend regularly for *fika*. The next time they met a woman called Greta joined them, along with her daughter and son. The children had fun together, and Roland, willing to cooperate with any game, became their mascot.

Axel arrived home from his orientation smothered with dirt. He insisted he had done nothing except listen to advice, so Tyra wondered what he would look like when he finally started mining. Perhaps washing clothes would be her arctic occupation.

Two evenings later Axel arrived from work chatting, and ushered in the mine manager. "We've come to see you," Axel grinned.

"Yah, Fru Östring, I have," said the manager. "We're very happy with your husband, and he's going to be an asset to us. But I have a personal request. I need someone to do housework. My wife works in the mine office and we agree she needs some home help, no more than two hours a day. You can suit yourself about times. I noticed your boy is a quiet kid, so you'd be welcome to bring him with you. Will you help us?"

"Thank you for thinking of me," replied Tyra. "Would you mind if I talk with Axel about this?"

"Not a bit. Just let me know soon. We pay good wages here. Our average wage is about the same as downtown Stockholm business area. So working would be worth your while." The manager stood to leave.

"How are you liking it?" Tyra asked Axel when the manager left. "And how come you're so clean tonight?"

"I'm not liking it," said Axel, "but as he said, they pay well. If I can last a few years, and we save carefully, we'll get enough to buy land. And as for cleanliness, when we finish a shift in the mine we have to take a thing called a shower, and change out of the mine gear the company supplies. So the clothes we bought I'll only have to use for getting to and from work."

"Well, that's a relief. I wondered how I could cope with keeping you clean!"

"It's dreadfully dirty work, I tell you. A horrible job! Sometimes I feel I can't breathe, buried there inside the middle of the earth, with nothing to look out on! I'm a farmer, used to wide open spaces, with the sky on my head, and the wind in my face. Mining is not me. Most of the time there's barely room to stand, just a tunnel. It's dangerous too, although they try hard to make us safety conscious, and to learn to avoid problems. That's what those two days of orientation were all about."

Tyra quickly made up her mind about the manager's work offer. If she had paid employment Axel would not have to work so long in the mine, and she would not have to stay so long in this strange city. The life of a city housewife, she discovered, was boring, really boring, very different from the satisfying long hours and hard work of a small farmer's wife. Armfuls of books from the library could help her escape, but they did not make life meaningful. With two hours of work a day, her life would still be very easy compared to life in Nykarleby.

"Axel," she announced, "I've decided to take that job the manager offered."

"Good. Give it a try," he acquiesced. "Oh, by the way," he added, pulling something from his pocket, "the mine secretary showed me where they leave the mail. These letters should make you happy." He passed her a fat envelope postmarked Nykarleby, Finland.

"Perhaps I should wait till I've given you something to eat," said Tyra, taking the package with sparkling eyes.

But Axel shocked her. "Eating can wait," he said, grinning broadly. "Go ahead and read me what they say."

Chapter 16

Exploring

"Listen to this! What wonderful news!" exclaimed Tyra, a few weeks later, as she read another letter from Anna. Axel looked up. Tyra had often been dispirited since their move to Kiruna. It was good to see her happy. Watching Kiruna burst into fragile bloom as its "summer" unfolded and the ice and snow mostly melted had briefly cheered Tyra, but letters from home always had the most positive affect.

"Erik and Nils will come for two weeks before Nils starts school! Mor says Nils has been doing odd jobs for farmers around Nykarleby, and carefully saved his fare, and Erik is keen to see what you're doing. They arrive on August three."

"That *will* be good. I'll see if I can get some good shifts then," responded Axel.

"Good shifts!" expostulated Tyra. "Don't talk such nonsense! You should take time off while they're here!" she chided. Axel pulled a face.

"I'm really serious," Tyra added.

"The men say the mine secretary is pretty tough about people wanting time off," pled Axel, lamely.

"At least try," insisted Tyra. Axel rolled his eyes.

"Ah, it'll be so good to see them," Tyra continued. "I've tried to be brave, but it *was* hard leaving Nils behind, very hard. And I've missed our Sabbath fellowship. Trying to worship on your own is lonely. Life here is lonely, despite the chatty efforts of our neighbors. Good thing the library has many interesting books, and Erik keeps us supplied with church news and newspapers." Tyra was silent for a few moments as she continued reading. Then she exclaimed, "Wow! Mor has more surprising news. In church last week they were told the government now allows people to choose their church! People won't have to pretend and go to the state church twice a year just to keep the authorities happy!"

"True? Are you sure?" said Axel, shaking his head. "No wonder that minister was so grumpy. How many people will choose his church? I tried to keep what happened to me quiet, but it was impossible. I couldn't tell a lie. Karl worked out why we were leaving, and he was angry. He told lots of people and they came and told me they were angry too. Some even wanted to set up a petition to the church, but I stopped that."

Tyra was silent. The shock of leaving Nykarleby, especially its cause, was still an open wound. She could not hide that her life felt empty. Caring for Roland and supporting Axel gave purpose, but she sorely missed her son and mother, Takla, her church fellowship, and her farm work. Often she had complained to herself about all the hard work the farm created for her, but now she longed for it. Mira and Greta were friendly, but she shared few common interests with them. They filled her time, but not her heart. Suddenly, she felt sorry for the church of her youth, derailed by politics from its purpose of supporting spiritual life. But, if the state was changing that relationship, perhaps the church could change. Maybe, she suddenly thought, surprised by the audacity of the idea, people should not rely on churches at all, but connect with God individually. Well, like it or not, she had to do just that in Kiruna. All her enquiries about a Sabbath-keeping fellowship had proved futile.

"Poor Pastor Järvinen," said Tyra, shaking herself out of her reverie. "I was angry with him, but now I feel sorry." Tyra paused thoughtfully, continued reading, and then suddenly exclaimed, "Oh, dear! Right at the end of the letter Mor has sad news she should have told us first! Mor Anna died peacefully in her sleep a week ago."

Axel was silent for a long time. Tyra was suddenly aware of the clock on the top shelf of the bookcase ticking loudly. "I wasn't close to her," he finally said, pensively, "but I did appreciate her. She didn't have an easy life. I'm glad Erik took good care of her. He was a very loving son. He'll miss her. I should write to him. But maybe on second thoughts you better do that for both of us, because no one understands my spelling! Mor Anna's death is probably the real reason he's coming to visit us. Anyway, we could take Erik and Nils to the Torneträsk, or the Torne River and do some salmon fishing. That would be nice for them, and get Erik's mind off his loss. We haven't done much exploring ourselves, but men at work have urged me to see the countryside. You can hire cars or trucks to go to the river."

"Great idea! But can you drive?" asked Tyra, anxiously.

"Don't be ridiculous!" retorted Axel. "I can drive a horse, and surely that's harder than a mere machine! I drove Karl's truck sometimes. It's easy!" Tyra looked doubtful. What she had seen of Axel's jerky driving attempts with Karl's truck, and bus drivers on trips into Kiruna, suggested coping with mere machines could be more difficult than Axel realized.

"It's strange," said Tyra. "I never wanted to go anywhere in Nykarleby, but here I feel restless. I guess I was just too busy there to even think of going somewhere else. But I *would* like to see more of this country. It's so pristine beautiful."

Axel nodded. "Yah, me too. Buried in the earth down that awful mine gives me a tremendous urge to get out and see places. When I'm down in all that blackness I force myself think about open country, or I'd go crazy. You have no idea how horrible it is." Tyra said nothing, but she could well imagine what being buried alive in the blackness of the mine felt like. It was too horrible to even think about.

With joy Tyra cooked vast quantities of food in honor of the visit. Axel did organize some days off, and suitable shifts so he could welcome his brother and son at the station. He admitted with relieved surprise that the mine secretary had been very helpful and friendly, more than willing to assist him. When the great day came and Nils and Erik arrived, Axel met them at the station, and next day Tyra showed them the sights of Kiruna, where they oohed and ahed just as she had done over the variety of goods in the shops. But shopping quickly lost its appeal for them, as for her.

To Tyra's relief Axel did not need to test his driving skills. Greta's husband got permission to use a mine vehicle, and the families made a party go to the Torne River. The landscape was breathtakingly beautiful, and Mira was right—the fishing was amazing. Everyone got a good fish, even Roland! Roland, however, was much more excited about finding a set of reindeer antlers on the river bank, and parading about with them on his head.

"I'm coming back!" declared Nils, as he and Erik boarded the train for home. "This place is magic!"

"Above ground," said Axel, wryly.

The departure of Nils and Erik was hard for Tyra. She missed them sorely. Mira's friendship, while filling a gap, was often rather domineering.

"What do you mean, you haven't taken Roland to the child health program?" Mira demanded, during one of her visits soon after Nils and Erik left. She often treated Tyra as though she were an ignorant child.

"I didn't know about it," said Tyra, trying hard not to sound irritated. "Where is it?"

Mira scribbled an address on a slip of paper. "It's free, you know. Make the most of it. All the mothers swap stories, drink free coffee, and generally have a good time. You don't take anything they say at the clinic too seriously, but it helps you feel good." Tyra was not sure about this clinic idea. Roland was fit and healthy, and Nils grew tall and strong under her care despite the food deprivations during the war. But she decided to try the clinic, although Roland was well past four, and the new year no longer new, before she organized to book an appointment.

Mira was right—the clinic was a social event. Mothers chatted animatedly in one corner of an untidy room while their children ran wild. No one seemed to worry about the danger cups of boiling coffee posed. Unruly children pushed and shoved and jostled to reach a large pile of battered toys, their cries a bedlam of confusion. The babble of empty conversation about bargain shopping, film actors and actresses, and boastful child comparisons utterly bored Tyra. When Roland was finally called, she was clearly superfluous, the nurse obviously regarding her incapable of child rearing.

"Is Roland really *your* child?" the nurse began, studying her notes, and merely glancing at Tyra. "Aren't you his grandmother?"

Gentle Tyra was angry. "He's certainly my child!" she retorted defiantly. "My second son. Our eldest is doing his last year of high school before beginning teacher training."

"A huge age difference," said the nurse, still determinedly examining notes. "Why did you wait so long?" Tyra ignored her.

Roland was weighed, measured, scrutinized, poked, sounded, tweaked, and finally declared normal except for a "slight" tendency to rickets. Tyra had never heard of this disease, and declared stoutly Roland never coughed, the coughing disease being the only condition she was afraid of. The nurse made a grunting noise, and did not explain that all children living in the arctic circle, without sunlight for much of the year, bundled up in layers to protect from the ever present severe cold, even in summer, were in danger of rickets.

"Make sure he gets plenty of fish liver and he has half a banana every day!" was the final advice, to which Roland exclaimed cheerfully, "Wow, that's good, Mor! Golden fruit every day!" before his mother hustled him out of the room. She hurried through the messy waiting room as quickly as possible, but not fast enough to avoid the young receptionist, who sported a mop of frizzy blond hair but had no a wedding band, loudly demanding why she was not making another appointment. "No need," called Tyra over the general din, and let the door slam noisily shut behind her.

Along the snow-dusted street on the way to the bus Roland danced happily, chanting, "Half a banana a day-ay! Half a banana a day-ay!" till Tyra could stand it no more. "Stop your noise!" she scolded. Roland's face fell, and suddenly Tyra felt very bad. He was a quiet, well-behaved child, and his banana chant was not noisy. Of course, she knew he loved bananas. It was not his song but the nurse's attitude that irked her. She gently took her son's hand. "You can have a whole banana as soon as we get home," she said kindly, and was rewarded by a beaming smile.

The Östrings celebrated their second Christmas in Kiruna, as awed by the brilliance of the northern lights as at their first. The Finnish families joined together for the usual Finnish treats, but they also sampled the amazing variety of food in the Kiruna shops, things Tyra never dreamed existed, like pumpkin pie from the USA, a cake made of dried fruits from Britain, German apple strudel, a cake with almond icing mixed through it, and of course, bananas.

Spring was just beginning to lighten their lives when another welcome letter from Anna arrived.

> *You will be pleased to know Nils' last school report was as good as ever. He did especially well in English. Strange, you learned German at school but now he learns English. Must be that war! He's such a help around the house, fixing little things I need, and if he can't do the job, he gets Karl or Erik and stays with them to learn how to do it. He's been doing quite a lot of woodwork with Erik, and the two of them have a lot of fun making all sorts of things.*
>
> *This year he began skriftskola. I advised him to take the class to avoid any fuss, just not take the confirmation communion. I'm not sure why, but Pastor Järvinen is a meticulous person. He consulted the church records and discovered Nils had not been christened in the Lutheran church, so he said Nils could not take skriftskola unless he was. When Nils' teachers heard this they were angry, and talked to both Nils and Pastor Järvinen to try to work things out. Apparently unless Nils is a confirmed member of the Lutheran Church he cannot undertake teacher training available here. The law about choosing your church does not seem to be*

properly applied, or at least not around here. Nils explained he was a Christian, and believed in God and Jesus Christ the Son of God, but that was not enough. Nils was adamant that he would not join the Lutheran Church just to get a job, even though his teachers tried to convince him it was just a formality.

As you can imagine, Nils was very upset by this. Erik has been wonderful, a tremendous support. He discovered Nils is interested in science, especially electricity, and so he's making enquiries about Nils training in Sweden to become an electrician. Nils is keen on this idea, but it rather changes the plans we had for him, and myself. Erik learned there's a good school for this training in Sala, Sweden, not far from Eskilstuna where Algot and Gunnel are. Erik tells me Sala was once famous for its silver mines.

One final thing, Nils declared that right now he doesn't want to join any church. He insists he believes in God, but says all this fuss about skriftskola and joining the Lutheran church has made him wonder about the value of any church. He's been faithfully attending Sabbath fellowship with Erik and me, and we are disappointed, but you can understand why he is not happy about churches at the moment. Maybe he'll change his mind later. He's still very young.

Tyra stared at the letter for a long time. She remembered her own teachers suggesting she consider teacher training. She did not regret her choice not to go ahead with that. But Nils had been very interested in teaching, and it was such an honorable profession. His teachers gave him glowing reports. She knew he would make a good teacher, and deserved the opportunity. Now it was suddenly dashed, once again because of the state church, or was it the government? She had no idea what an electrician was, although it seemed something that would be increasingly needed in society. She wasn't sure she wanted Nils clambering up ladders leaning against power poles, but maybe there was more to being an electrician than that. But why, oh why, did the state church control everything? If the church had been fair to her husband, she wouldn't be exiled in the strange arctic city of Kiruna. And if people could now choose which church to attend, why was Nils being discriminated against in his choice of profession? If Nils left Finland, who would care for her mother? Suddenly she felt a deep longing to go home, to talk to her mother, and comfort her son. No matter what Axel said, she must go home.

Roland was asleep, Axel away doing the evening shift. Axel usually arrived home exhausted, but Tyra decided to risk waiting up to show him

Anna's latter. She tried to read a book, but the words swam off on a life of their own. She was consumed by intense desire to see her son. Would Axel agree to her making the long journey to Nykarleby alone? Roland was now five, capable of carrying his own bag. She was sure she could manage the trip.

Finally, the door opened, and Axel walked in, fatigue etched deeply across his face. "Hello," he said, "You're still up? Something wrong?"

"Had a letter from Mor. Here, read it." she held it out, and intently watched his face. He began to frown, more and more as he read further.

With a snort of exasperation he looked up and said, "We should go to Nykarleby, as soon as possible."

Immense relief flooded Tyra. "Oh, Axel! That's exactly what I thought!"

"Talk in the morning," he responded. "I'm too tired to even think now."

Next morning, they had their serious discussion. The third and last of the Finnish wars had produced devastation in Lapland, and it had not been safe to drive there until very recently. But workmates had informed Axel that the undetonated explosives left by angry Germans had finally been removed, and the roads declared safe, although the railway in the extreme north was still being cleared. Axel joked that Germans had more bombs than brains, as they had left more than a million undetonated explosives in Lapland. Importantly for their plans, however, driving took less time than the train, because it was a shorter route.

"But, Axel, we don't have a car!" Tyra interrupted his enthusiastic planning.

"Coming to that! I've heard any vehicle brought from Sweden to Finland sells at a good price, and as a Finn living out of the country I'm allowed to bring one back free of tax. Wouldn't be good to go to Finland right now, not in winter. But how about I get leave, and a car, and we drive back in spring? Even if I can't sell the vehicle immediately, Erik would sell it for me. If it worked out, we could drive to Nykarleby and get back here, and it wouldn't cost us anything."

"Going in spring would be good. We'd be there for Nils' graduation. But is it safe, driving all that way on our own?"

Axel was hurt. "Don't you think I can drive?" he asked, plaintively. Tyra was silent. She dared not express her doubts. It was not just his driving, but those long, long, lonely roads on their own that concerned her. But Axel knew she was right, and began practicing driving, making impressive bunny hop starts at first, but soon mastering the skill. The search for a vehicle began.

Axel wisely decided he needed something sturdy to make the journey, a distance of about 750 kilometers on difficult, unpaved roads. When he heard some army ambulances were for sale, merely old trucks whose trays were covered to facilitate carrying the wounded, he went to look. He bought one immediately, although Tyra was not impressed when she saw what she had to ride to get to Finland.

When Axel applied for leave, the mine secretary grinned. "Off to see the Olympics, are you?" Neither Tyra nor Axel had any serious interest in sporting events, and had completely forgotten the Olympics. War had cancelled the scheduled Helsinki games in 1940, and because of collaboration with Germany, Finland was refused the right to host the 1948 games. But by 1952 the world had moved on, had forgiven both aggressors and collaborators, and Helsinki's moment had arrived. That evening he arrived home jubilant, assuring Tyra the Olympic games meant he could easily sell his ambulance truck, and make a tidy profit.

Because their route was southeast, Axel decided the journey should be made as much as possible at night, when he would not be blinded by the low lying sun. This dashed Tyra's ideas about seeing more of the country, although it did mean Roland slept most of the way. Tyra stayed in the back of the truck with Roland, and tried to transform the queasy misery in her stomach with the power of positive thoughts. Sustaining her as she bounced and swayed along was the thought that the return journey would mercifully be by train. Both Roland and Axel survived the journey without discomfort, but Axel had to stop many times for Tyra to empty her heaving stomach. The mighty Torne River, the border crossing, the excitement of coming home to Nykarleby, all were a nauseous blur.

The three weeks in Nykarleby were another blur, of faces, speeches, and memories. Tyra's heart was often too full to talk, but wherever she went, people wanted to talk, to show what they had been doing, ask her opinion. Rarely did they ask about her life in Kiruna. Reluctantly, when she watched Axel deep in conversation with his Nykarleby friends, she had to admit that while life in Kiruna was physically much easier for her it was not easier for Axel. The visit clearly showed just how much of a man of the soil he was. They had saved hard, now they searched hard, but there was still no land available, not anywhere. A conflicting array of voices bombarded her.

Roland complained, "Mor, why do they have funny toilets here? I don't like walking all the way to the barn every time, and they smell! Why can't we just pull a chain and make everything wash away like we do at home?" Tyra was shocked to realize her son didn't know where home really was.

Axel was clearly still looking for answers: "Went to look at what was my land. You know, they haven't even ploughed it yet! It's covered in weeds, like it was when I took it over. Someone told me it was supposed to farm pigs, but I didn't see any. Read in the paper that 63 per cent of arable land in Finland has been reallocated since the war, mainly because of those refugees from Karelia. Seems I wasn't the only one to lose my land. I feel for those poor beggars, having to leave everything or become Russians, but the government needs to improve its methods."

But he was delighted with his business acumen. "You won't believe what people are prepared to pay for our truck!" he exclaimed triumphantly. "I should have got you to learn to drive, and brought back two of them. Yah, we'll more than pay for our trip, by road and train!"

She was grateful Nils seemed content with the plans for his future. "Oh Mor! You know that Bible text you always quote? The one that says everything works out for good if we love God? Well, I think that's true for me. I thought teaching was such a fine, prestigious job, and I like helping people. But you know, I'm too much like Far. I like getting out and about. Now that I've had time to think, I'm not sure I'd want to be stuck in a classroom every day. This electrician thing will suit me fine. I can still help people."

Takla shared surprising news. "It's getting harder to get jobs if you don't speak Finnish. My two younger brothers decided to leave Finland to get work. No, they didn't go to Sweden, but all the way to Australia. Can you believe it, Australia on the other side of the world! I'll give you some of their letters. My, it's a weird world over there!"

The high school graduation was a highlight. The weather was perfect, and Nils proud in his white graduation cap. Tyra nodded and smiled to so many people (most of whom she barely knew) that she got a sore face. The most surprising event at the graduation was Pastor Järvinen's proffered friendliness. He thrust out his hand, congratulated Tyra on Nils' excellent performance, and commented on his courage in standing up for what he believed. Tyra was too surprised to reply, and merely shook his hand politely, noting, however, that the poor man was clearly ill at ease, and did not look her in the eye when he made his speech.

Exploring

But return they must to Kiruna. Although Nils was coming with them, she felt she was abandoning her mother. When Hjalmar hoisted Anna's bags on to his cart, helped her up (noting with concern that she struggled with the climb), and with a wave of his reins set off for Oxkangar, Tyra heart was too full to speak. Anna was her mother, she belonged to her, not to that family farm. Despite all the sensible arguments for the plan that her mother to go to Oxkangar, Tyra's heart felt as though it was being torn from her chest. She wished her mother had not been so brave and businesslike about the move to Oxkangar, and that they could have quietly shared some tears and heart thoughts.

Tyra waved till the cart had long disappeared, then finding herself alone in the familiar field beside the house, wandered down to the barn where she wept softly into a hay bale. Some time later Nils found her there, and urged she return to the cottage for a warm drink and some *griser* that Takla had brought over.

At dawn next day Karl once again drove them to the station. Takla, rubbing sleep from her eyes, ran across the dew-drenched field to say good bye, and thrust some papers into Tyra's hands. "My brothers' letters," she panted. "They're interesting. Send them back when you've finished." Tyra nodded politely and pushed them to the bottom of her handbag. She had other things on her mind.

Having Nils with them relieved the tedium of the journey. Roland took an interest in the trip which for him was new (he didn't remember the first, and slept through the second). Nils proved very patient at pointing out highlights along the way, as well as sharing basic science and geography with his young brother. As they came close to Kiruna Nils proudly pointed out the Kebnekaise to the west, the highest mountain in Sweden.

"Are there high mountains in Finland?" Roland asked, gazing at the snow-covered mass of land. "I haven't seen any."

"Yah, there are mountains in Lapland, but not as high as the Kebnekaise," said Nils. "But do you know what Finland has lots of? Lakes! There are about 188,000 lakes in Finland, and lots and lots of forest."

"Yah, I remember the forest around Nykarleby," nodded Roland. "There aren't many forests around Kiruna. Nothing to go blueberry picking in."

"No," responded Nils. "There's not enough sunlight there for things to grow."

It delighted Tyra to watch her sons enjoying each other's company, their age difference happily bridged. They continued having fun together in Kiruna, when Nils spent many hours in a makeshift dark room developing photos with his awe-struck little brother.

Axel proudly told the mine manager his son was a trainee electrician, and Nils was hired to check mine lighting. This was not exactly challenging work. Nils turned switches on and off, noting any light that did not work, so the mine electrician could attend to it. But there were benefits. Nils had well paid work for his holidays, and his experiences helped him appreciate his father's increasing aversion for mining. During their three weeks in Nykarleby Axel had gained weight and felt well, but as soon as he returned to the mine his irritating cough returned, and he once again began losing weight. Nils tried to convince his father that giving up smoking would solve the cough problem, but Axel could not believe there was any health issue with smoking.

Tyra's misery was acute when Nils boarded the train to Stockholm. She had struggled with grief over what she considered abandoning her mother, and having to farewell her son so soon after revived the pain. Life for Tyra now seemed a long series of sad farewells. In Stockholm Nils was met by Algot who assisted with the transfer to Sala, with Nils' accommodation there, and other needs. Algot was overjoyed to be involved, promising to bring Nils to Eskilstuna whenever possible, "to keep an eye on him".

Next year Nils again obtained summer holiday work in the Kiruna mine, work recognized as part of his training, and Erik came for another visit. When an unexpected dumping of snow fell both were delighted. They could go skiing in July! Erik spoke seriously about leaving Finland, but his brother's gruesome mining stories did not tempt him to follow his example. Tyra, missing both Nils and Erik when they returned to studies and work, felt the loss of Roland keenly when he started school a few weeks later. A change in mine manager meant she also lost her small part time domestic job. More than ever she felt her life was a series of goodbyes.

Roland brought home good school reports, but the only thing he talked about was the school's weekly sauna. "He's bound for the tropics, that kid!" laughed Axel. "Nils was keen to learn everything, but Roland lets it all flow over him."

After another visit from Nils, Tyra decided it was time to do what she had dreamed of doing ever since her arrival in Kiruna—take the train to Narvik, in Norway. Roland was now old enough to appreciate the trip. She had read of the spectacular scenery on the six-hour return journey, and knew Narvik was tragically impacted by the war, when Germany tried to gain control of the Kiruna iron ore mine, or at least confiscate its ore. She just had to talk Axel into the idea.

To her surprise, despite previous opposition, when Nils left for Sala Axel quickly agreed to visit Narvik. They would take the morning train, spend a few hours in the town, and be back in Kiruna that evening. For Tyra, the countryside around Kiruna had acquired a spiritual quality. In winter the vast vistas of pristine snow, the amazing spectacle of the northern lights, hinted at things much bigger and greater than mere humans and their feverish shopping. In summer, when the fragile arctic growth transformed everything, she could not help but think of an earth renewed.

She thought of a poem Erik had recently sent her. She appreciated his talent and spiritual insight. It was a pity, she thought, churches generally did not appreciate literature. There was a great deal of poetry in the Bible, she reflected, as she hunted for Erik's verse, which was finally found tucked into her Bible. *Last Days*, he called it. Tyra wasn't excited about last day discussions. She preferred to leave such things in the hands of God. But Erik's verse expressed her understanding of the importance of learning more about God himself, and the foolishness of science that dared claim to know everything.

Last Days
Many are saying we are
Living in the last days—
Nygård[1] smiles and asks
"You also believe in the last days?"
I try to answer and say, "Yes, let's see—
Must we believe only what we understand?"
"Soon we'll experience and understand
Everything in the world!"

"But"—Nygård wonders—
"Won't we eventually reach
"Heaven as we are taught
"Just by believing and knowing?
"So, what do you believe—and know—about salvation?"
"Perhaps," I say, "it is not enough just to believe
In the last days. We need more than to believe—
We must seek the God who gives
More to a praying soul."[2]

1. A common Swedish male given name, meaning "new land" or "new garden".
2. Translated from the Swedish by Roland Ostring

Tyra read the poem twice. She felt a deep longing for God. This yearning had been partly filled by her church fellowship in Nykarleby. But now she felt the deep need to get to know God himself, for herself. She had no idea how long she would remain in Kiruna, without a church fellowship. She must learn to connect directly with God by herself.

The spring day they left for Narvik was overcast, actually a blessing. A sunny day could result in blindness from reflections off the sun-drenched countryside. The softening affect of the cloud was welcome. Roland remembered the fishing trips they had made, and thought this trip would be much the same. But as they crossed into Norway, left the snowline, and descended into Narvik and Olfot Fjord, the sun broke through the clouds revealing azure blue sky, snowy mountains, and indigo waters, he was glued to the window, agog with wonder. Kiruna had magnificent broad, horizontal views of snow and beauty, but this scenery was vertical, the sea surrounded by breathtakingly beautiful snow-capped mountains.

They had ample time to explore Narvik, to take a boat trip on the fjord and ooh and ah over the spectacular scenery whose reflections in the fjord were sadly disturbed by their vessel's wake, to look at shops, and eat lunch at a local café. Tyra had never been on a ship before, and was a little apprehensive, but the fjord was so calm she relaxed, and enjoyed her meal afterwards.

They were strolling back to the train, with plenty of time to get there, when Tyra suddenly stopped and pointed to a sign. "Look!" she cried excitedly. "There are Adventists here!"

"What? Who? Where?" queried Axel, looking in all the wrong directions.

"Just think," said Tyra wistfully, "I've been feeling I was all alone, and just three hours' train ride away is a group of Adventists!"

"You're not thinking of coming to church here every week? Surely not!" said Axel in consternation, having finally found the signpost.

Tyra pondered the sign. "No, it's a bit far," she conceded, with a mischievous smile. "But what a lovely trip to get to church. Maybe I could do it once or twice!"

Axel frowned, not in antagonism, but because it seemed far too much effort just to go to church. Tyra never did go to church in Narvik, but the memory encouraged her. Kiruna taught her to value Christian fellowship, but it also demonstrated that church was not vital for her commitment to God. Someday she might have opportunity to once again fellowship with others, but, whatever happened, the trip through so much natural beauty had restored her restless heart. It was God, and God alone, that counted. Quietly, she hummed:

> Every day, the Lord Himself is near me
> With a special mercy for each hour;
> All my cares He fain would bear, and cheer me,
> He Whose Name is Counselor and Pow'r.
> The protection of His child and treasure
> Is a charge that on Himself He laid;
> "As thy days, thy strength shall be in measure,"
> This the pledge to me He made.

"I thought the whole world was like Kiruna and Nykarleby, sort of flat," said Roland, returning to his seat when the whistle blew after a scenic stop. "Are there any places nicer than Narvik?"

"There's beauty everywhere," smiled Tyra. "You just have to look. The only thing that makes places not beautiful are people who fight and hurt each other."

"Do people really do that?" asked Roland, wide-eyed.

"Yah, I'm afraid so. They'll teach you about war at school."

"At school they tell us Sweden is a good country because it hasn't had a war for ever so long. Was there ever war in Finland?"

Tyra sighed deeply. Should she laugh at his ignorance, or cry from her pain? How much should she tell this child of hers? She looked out the window as the pristine beauty of the Arctic Circle flowed beside them. Be honest, tell him truthfully, but as little as possible, she decided. "Yah, I'm afraid Finland has had war, very bad wars, but there's no war there now."

"That's good," said Roland, not understanding.

They watched the beautiful countryside flow past the train. "Look out the window," pointed Tyra. "You'll see a herd of reindeer! Some have antlers like those you found when we went fishing with Nils and Erik! Laplander people think having reindeer makes them rich! So you must never ask a Laplander how many reindeer he has, because that's very rude, like asking a person how much money he has in the bank."

Roland pulled a face. He didn't know what a bank was, but it didn't sound interesting. He tried to count the reindeer, thousands of them plodding through the snow, because he had finally discovered saunas were not the only interesting things about school. Numbers were very exciting. But the reindeer moved and straggled and crossed each others' paths, till he finally gave up.

"What fun to be a moose, hiking through that snow!" said Roland wistfully. "They have so many friends!"

"Do you remember the lemming we found on the snow?" asked his mother.

"The one that got left behind when all the others went running into the lake? There were so many of them, so pretty. But most of them didn't look as though they could swim very well. Were they having a war?"

"For food, maybe," said Tyra, and Roland nodded sleepily.

"Beautiful trip!" said Axel, when they arrived back at Kiruna. "So glad you made me do it! We need to do things like that more often!"

Hmm, thought Tyra, maybe I can get used to this arctic world, after all. Maybe, if only Axel could find other work here.

Chapter 17

Takla's Letters

Tyra was surprised to discover she had not only accepted, but was now enjoying her life in Kiruna. Although not her choosing, she had confidence it was where she was meant to be. Whilst the trip to Nykarleby was unsettling but revealing, the excursion to Narvik was healing. She was at peace with herself, had a library nearby, and contentedly watched Roland taking an interest in school. The only cloud in her sky was Axel, who was still struggling to cope with work in the mine. Not even excellent wages gave him satisfaction. But Tyra's new-found contentment encouraged her to think that maybe he could find other work in this strange arctic town, and after almost four years their lives could move on from the shock of his losing his farm.

Each evening Axel poured over newspapers, Finnish and Swedish, looking not for news, but for farms. Tyra never told him she had already done the same, and knew there was nothing available. Their bank balance was healthy, and they could seriously consider buying a small property, but land reallocation had gobbled up all available arable land in Finland. Axel thought wildly about harvesting his forest, and turning it into farm, but that would not only require protracted legal battles, which may or may not be successful, but he knew it was foolish to cut his trees when they would eventually be a fine investment.

On a beautiful Kiruna summer day (that is, sky blue, but wind icy), Axel was at work, and Roland playing with Greta's boy. Tyra decided she would clean her handbag of accumulated unwanted sundries from their recent trip to Narvik. She pulled out colored rocks Roland had collected at various train stations and arranged them on a saucer to grace the center of their table. Children love collecting things, she knew. A map of Narvik that Axel had wanted was placed on the bookshelf. She wondered if the map indicated he was thinking of finding work on the Narvik wharves. Wrappings from a few sweets Roland had persuaded her to buy were discarded. At the bottom of her bag she found some crumpled papers, at first puzzled what they were. Suddenly she realized they were the letters Takla had given her when they left Nykarleby more than twelve months before. She was flooded with guilt, realizing Takla must have wondered why she had never commented on them, or sent them back as requested.

"Well, better late than never!" she decided with a wry smile, as she spread them out to read.

They were cheerful letters, brimming with optimism, fun, and hard work. The brothers had pooled their slender resources, and, to Tyra's amusement, bought into a small banana plantation. The memories of their first taste of banana, and Roland's excitement at eating "golden fruit" came flooding back. How ironic that Takla's brothers should be growing these tropical fruit! The brothers described a small colony of Swedish-speaking Finns who had bought into banana plantations, and lived in an area called Main Arm, located in beautiful Australian rain forest which the locals called "bush". The bird life in this forest was amazing, they said, and they waxed eloquent describing some of the vividly colored birds they had seen. They admitted the name of the area where they lived was strange, and even locals did not seem to be sure what it meant, but "Main Arm" probably had something to do with the branch of a river. People in the district called the village "The Finns" because of its inhabitants. Bananas, they explained, grew on the sunny sides of hills, so it was hard work clambering to the plantations to get the fruit. Main Arm was near a small town (with shops and other facilities) with a really strange name, Mullumbimby. That name was an Aboriginal one, they explained, Aborigines being the native people who had inhabited Australia for centuries, maybe millennia, before the British came at the end of the eighteenth century. The brothers had not seen many Aborigines as they were shy people, and had mostly retreated to the interior of Australia. The brothers expressed disappointment about this.

One of the things they frequently mentioned was the weather. According to them, Mullumbimby had no winter. There was never any snow! Could you believe that! No snow at all! These Australians, or Aussies as they called themselves, even kept Christmas in hot sunny weather! What local people called "summer" was very hot and a bit unpleasant with a lot of rain and dampness, but the brothers still insisted the weather was wonderful. If it did get too hot, you just went to the nearby beach, only a short distance away, and cooled off in the water. Everyone had cars in Australia, good ones, and getting to the beach was easy. They had heard reports of sharks in the sea, but none of the local people were bothered by this, and certainly neither of them had seen one.

They sent pictures of bananas, in case Takla had not yet discovered this luscious fruit, and amazing pictures of trains, whole trains, with numerous trucks loaded with bananas! These trains, they assured their sister, went all over Australia delivering their produce. It was the crop of the future, the industry that would make them rich. And all the time they could live and have fun in this tropical paradise!

Tyra sat back and tried to imagine the type of place the brothers described. With her life experience limited to northern Finland and Swedish Lapland, she could hardly imagine what Takla's brothers wrote about. Dramatic changes in the seasons were a major feature of her life, and although she did not like the darkness of winter, she did appreciate the seasonal variety. It certainly sounded delightful in this Main Arm-Mullumbimby place, and she was sure Axel would enjoy the letters when he returned from his shift in the mine. She could hardly wait to show him.

But nothing prepared her for his reaction.

She considerately waited until after their evening meal, when she thought he would be rested and could enjoy the letters. She did not admit they had been in her handbag for months.

As he read, the hard lines of weariness and care on Axel's face slowly softened, and by the time he came to the end he was smiling. "What these boys describe is amazing! Sounds like working in paradise!"

"I'm not sure I'd like nothing but summer, but it certainly sounds interesting. Fancy having Christmas when it's hot! Christmas and snow just belong together. I guess that's because it's on the other side of the world, and everything is upside down there! What a strange place to live!"

Axel did not respond. He sat, his blue eyes gazing into space, a dreamy, faraway expression on his face. Idly he smoothed out the paper of one of the letters in front of him, and then leaned back in his chair and read it again.

Suddenly he sat forward, and his blue eyes bored into Tyra's face. "Tyra!" he almost shouted, "Tyra! Do you realize, we could do that!" He folded the letters hurriedly and handed them back to her. "Yes, we could do it!"

She smiled, eyebrows raised quizzically. "Sounds fun, doesn't it?"

"Not sure about fun, but that it's a chance. We could do it! No, I'm serious, so don't shake your head. Really serious! We've been saving furiously to buy land, the whole point of coming here. I've studied those papers till I'm blind looking for a farm, but there isn't one. Finnish land reform has tied up everything there, and Swedish prices are too high. But I simply can't cope with mining any longer. I've stuck it out for four long years, longer than most men. Every day I feel ten years older. I ache everywhere, and lately I've had trouble breathing and getting to sleep."

"Yes, it's hard on you. But coming here wasn't my idea! You surely don't want me to go mining!"

"Don't be ridiculous! Of course not! And I never asked you to! You know, after that Narvik trip I've even thought of going there, but it must be pretty tough on the wharves in winter. But, don't you understand, we could do this! We could go to Australia and buy a banana plantation. We'd have the chance to live again—independently—and with no snow, no winter! The boys would love it!"

Tyra was stunned. The letters were no longer a source of idle amusement. "But—but—it's on the other side of the world!" she stammered. "We can't possibly go there, so don't even think about it! What about Nils? Coming here caused a lot of changes in his life. Going to Australia would be crazy for him! He's trained to work in Sweden, not over there! And what about Mor? We can't leave them! I'd never agree to that!"

Axel didn't hear. He had caught a vision of a new life that sounded like paradise. His agile mind quickly thought through all the issues. "You know, while we were visiting in Brännon Karl mentioned those boys to me. He told me how much money they had when they left Finland, and he was surprised they could buy land for the little they had. He thought they must live far from civilization, but clearly they're near a town. It must be a reasonable place, and notice they describe a whole colony of Finns there."

"They don't say how many Finns," said Tyra, desperately trying to make him think logically.

"Don't be so silly about little unimportant things! Doesn't matter whether there are six or twenty-six families in the village they're talking about," retorted Axel. "Just one other family would be enough. Now, write to Takla, and get the address of those lads, and we'll write to them and see what we need to do to get there."

"Axel, you can't be serious, surely? I mean, would you *really* consider going to Australia, on the other side of the world? It's a ridiculous idea! Absolutely stupid! How would Roland get on in school when he can't speak the language? How could I go shopping when I can't talk to anyone? Please, Axel, be reasonable. I came to this outlandish place for you. It's taken me years to get used to it. At first I hated it, everything about Kiruna. I'm just getting used to it here. This Australia thing would be pure torture. I simply won't go. And I'm serious! Really serious!" Tyra pushed her chair back angrily, stood, and began noisily collecting dishes to wash. But her clatter did not distract Axel.

"And I've never been more serious either. Don't you realize people told me the same thing when I set out to court you? They said, 'Look, she's educated and lives in a big city. She'd never consider a country bumpkin like you! Don't be ridiculous!' But I tried, and I won. Nothing could be worse than mining. Nothing. You can't believe how dreadful it is! I can't take any more of it! Please write for me."

Tyra smiled, in spite of herself. "So I was a good catch, was I? You never told me that before! So with how many people did you discuss the great conquer-Tyra plan? You make me sound like a good heifer! But this old cow is not moving to another pasture, so forget it!"

"Well, put it this way, you're the best heifer I've ever come across! I haven't changed my mind on that. If you're worried, I didn't talk about you to the whole world, just a couple of army buddies like Algot, and my family. Now please, put all that education you've got to good use, and write to Takla!"

"I won't!" declared Tyra, tossing her dark hair angrily, and swishing her tea towel.

"I'll just keep asking," said Axel, shrugging and rolling his eyes at her. "It took me three years to win you. I hope this doesn't take as long, or I might be dead in that mine. If you won't write, I'll write myself."

"Has your spelling improved since you wrote to me?" challenged Tyra provocatively.

"No!"

"And just when did you set out on that great conquer-Tyra plan?"

"The day I first saw you. Your dark hair made you stand out from the crowd, and those grey eyes of yours are irresistible. Then of course, there was your reputation."

"Really?" said Tyra, but softly, and Axel knew he had won, at least about writing the letter, just as surely as she had won his heart a quarter of a century earlier.

Tyra wrote to Takla, apologizing for her delay in response, and included the brothers' letters. She down-played Axel's interest, and presented the request for the brothers' address as just general interest. But in her heart she knew, knew with an appalling, fearful certainty, that Axel was deadly serious, that he believed he had at last found a way out of the imprisoning mine that was slowly strangling life from him. He had always been positive, very committed to any course of action he considered right, and never had she seen him more committed than he was to this plan. But the thought of travelling to the other side of the world, to a place whose language she couldn't speak, a place shockingly without seasons, despite its colorful birds, appalled her. She had struggled hard, so very hard, to adjust and be contented in Kiruna, and now this! Ever since she had committed her life to God there had been one difficulty after another to face. She had managed to bury the enormous pain and anxiety of the war years under a blanket of forgetfulness, but now it all came flooding back with terrifying intensity. Axel was asking her to do what she was absolutely sure was utterly beyond her limits. She could only pray fervently that something would intervene, that something would block Axel's plans.

Takla responded promptly, confident her brothers would be delighted to correspond as they sometimes said they missed their homeland. She gave general information about Brännon, enquired about the health and welfare of Nils, Roland, and Anna, and asked when they would be visiting her again. Tyra took days to pluck up the courage to pass the addresses on to Axel. As she feared, she was immediately commissioned to write to the brothers and ask about the prospects of buying a banana plantation in the area they were working. Before she wrote, she went down to her much-loved, much-used library, and looked up every book she could find on Australia. Her only knowledge was that Australia was one of the two countries that had given women the vote before Finland. From the library she learned about kangaroos, koalas, gaudily colored parrots, and sheep and cattle farms so large that, unbelievably, it took days on horseback to ride around them. She learned the names of the main cities, and that only about one hundred kilometers from Mullumbimby town was the large city of Brisbane. Yes, beaches were certainly the number one attraction of Australia, according to all reports, and there was one close to Mullumbimby. This was all very interesting, but did nothing to relieve her anxiety.

Letters between sundrenched Australia and the frozen expanses of the Arctic Circle did not pass quickly, and it was late autumn before she received a reply. With a trembling heart, Tyra tore open the envelope. It was Axel's dream come true, she realized, but for her it was a living nightmare. How could she express her turmoil of emotion? Where was the prayed-for blockage of Axel's wild ideas?

> Your enquiry has come at a very opportune time. My brother and I have loved working here. Björn[1] returned to Finland for a holiday three months ago, but unfortunately has developed some health problem and doesn't think he will be able to return to banana growing. He would be very happy to sell you his portion of the banana plantation that we work. We rent the land, but we do own the bananas on it. I love it here, and have decided to settle permanently. So permanently, in fact, that I have married an Australian girl, and we live in the village. It's a nice little village, and we all get on well. Yes, there are several Swedish-speaking Finns here, but we are a bit of a United Nations, with an Italian family, and Aussies too. It's a bit primitive, and a few families working the plantations prefer to live in town rather than out here, but I would say life here in Main Arm is no worse than that Brännon village Takla lives in, and I understand where you lived too, at least for a time. When I've visited Takla I thought it was a pretty tough life that she had, but she seemed happy. Let me know as soon as possible if you are interested in this offer, and we won't put the plantation on the market but keep it for you. By the way, everyone here calls me Harry, so you can too. Harry Nylund

She had no choice, no honest choice, but to give the letter to Axel. But it took her several days to bring herself to do so. When she finally did, he was over the moon with joy.

"Write back immediately and tell them we'll buy it! Then find out how to get down there to Australia as soon as possible. There's a place in Kiruna that arranges travel, isn't there? They should be able to tell us what to do. We've got good passports, and by the sound of it getting into Australia is not difficult. We'll be there before Christmas!" Axel, suddenly noting the stricken look on Tyra's face, added, "Well, we'll be there soon. Oh, and write and tell Nils. He'll love this adventure!"

---

1. A pseudonym for a real person

Tyra decided to write to Nils first, as a litmus test. If he reacted negatively she would have her "sign," the blockage that they were not meant to go to this outlandish MullaBimba place, and she would put pressure on Axel to think of some other way to leave Kiruna and the dreaded mine. She was sure Nils would not be interested. He was about to finish his training, and no doubt would be keen to get on with his work as an electrician.

But to her horror Nils was delighted with the idea. He said he'd always wanted to travel, and this would be just what he had dreamed about. He admitted working on a banana plantation was not his idea of lifelong bliss, but if that's what it took to get to Australia, he was willing to give it a go. He included a helpful suggestion. After he finished his electrician training, by late spring the following year, he would be willing to go ahead to Australia and get things ready for his parents and Roland. His English was good, good enough for him to get around and work things out for all of them. Then the family could follow and settling in would be easy for them. Tyra's throat tightened at his suggestion; Nils understood her anxiety about the scheme, and was trying to reassure her. He knew, as she did, that once his father made up his mind, it was hard to divert him. He wanted to make things as easy as possible for his mother.

Well, at least they would not leave before Christmas! Tyra decided it would be Christmas as usual, and only then would she write to Harry, and go to the travel agent for information about travelling to Australia.

Tyra made sure she had all the traditional Christmas food, and many of those interesting foreign items that Kiruna shops sold. She invited Mira and Greta and their families, and did everything possible to make Kiruna festive. Whilst never close to Mira and Greta, she had learned to appreciate both of them. She extracted a promise from Axel and Nils that they would not mention Australia to anyone until she had definite information about travel plans, and even more amazing, they kept their promise! But in her heart she knew it was a farewell feast, and she struggled to maintain a cheerful face.

On New Year's day Axel asked if she had written to Harry. When she made a noncommittal noise, he reminded her that he had kept his promise to keep quiet about Australia during the Christmas celebrations, and now she must keep hers. The letter was reluctantly sent.

A few days later, with snow thickly on the ground, she went to Kiruna township. "Australia!" exclaimed the astonished travel agent, when Tyra explained her needs. "I'm not sure that I've ever had anyone want to go there! Do you realize how far away it is? Why, its on the other side of the world, honest! But I'll find out for you. Give me a couple of weeks, at least, and I'll see what I can discover for you."

Three weeks later Tyra left the agent's office loaded with shipping information, bus information, airline information, rail information, in fact so much information that Tyra almost expected hiking and biking information was tucked in as well! But no matter what she read, there was no disguising the fact that Australia was a very, very long way from Swedish Kiruna. She spread the brochures across the table, spent hours studying them, and when Axel came home he did the same.

"Ship," they both said, after their long inspections. "It has to be by ship." Tyra had never been on a ship, except for the placid Narvik ferry ride, and the thought terrified her.

"But from where?" she asked, anything to avoid facing the horrible facts of the journey.

Axel scratched his head. "All this shipping information says everything goes to Australia from London, so we have to get to London. That's not too hard. It just means we should go over to the west coast of Sweden and get across the North Sea to London from there."

"But we have to go back to Brännon, and I must see see Mor before we leave. How do we get from Finland to London?"

"Nah," said Axel, pulling a face. "Going to Finland would take far too much time, and money! What's the point? Your Mor is happy and well cared for, and we'll be back to see her, no doubt about that. Going back now would only upset you both, I know! It's not a good idea."

"Axel! I must say goodbye to Mor. Even if you don't want to go, I will! It would be a terrible thing not to do that. Roland and I can visit her on our own, if you won't come."

"Don't be silly! Waste of time, and money!" retorted Axel, then he shrugged. "Well, if you want, write and ask her what she thinks, and if she wants you to, then go. But I'm sure she'd agree with me and say it wasn't necessary. Your mother is a sensible woman. We saw her about a year ago, remember, and she was very well. It's not as though anything is likely to happen to her in the near future. Going back would be time consuming, money consuming, and no one better off because of it. I'm just going to write Erik a letter to say good bye. He'll understand. That should be enough for your Mor."

Tyra, too upset to reply, turned angrily away. Her mother would never push her own needs, but it was utterly callous, terribly callous, not say good bye to her own mother. This boat trip was going to take six weeks. That was an awfully long trip, an awfully long way. Well, at least she had Axel's promise they would return. That was something. But how often could she make a six-week ocean journey? The mere thought of doing it once was terrifying. A return journey meant three months of travel! It was unthinkable! She must find a way of seeing her mother before she left.

Tyra wrote to Nils giving him a broad outline of their plans, and to her surprise he replied that he was not happy about the shipping idea, at least for him. If he took a ship after he finished his course he would not have time to do the preparatory work he had promised. So, he planned to fly to Australia. The only problem with flying was cost, but he was confident he could cope with that without causing stress to his parents. As a senior student he had opportunity for paid-work assignments, and he was saving carefully.

Tyra laid aside his letter, horrified by Nils' plans. Her mind was flooded by terrifying memories. Fly! Her heart almost stopped beating at the thought. One thing only she knew about planes—war. Flying was . . . well, it was a fearful, dangerous, horrible thing to do! Planes either dropped bombs to kill other people, or they dropped out of the sky in terrifying crashes that killed themselves and all inside them. She knew nothing good about planes!

She went back to the brochures strewn over the table, and found that sure enough there was information about flying. Her thoughts were spinning so much she decided to write to Nils and find what exactly he had in mind. She dared not say "don't fly"; that would make him want to do it more than ever. Nils replied, advising he planned to take something called a Qantas Kangaroo Route that took only four days to get from London to Australia, a dramatic improvement on the two months he would take to go by boat. It cost more, but it was worth it in his opinion. As the plane "hopped" from airport to airport he would get the chance to see interesting places in the world, like Tripoli, Cairo, Karachi, Calcutta, Singapore, Darwin in the far north of Australia, and finally, Sydney. From there he would take a train to Mullumbimby, which meant he would know how to guide his family when they reached Sydney in their ship. His letter finished with a thoughtful note clearly guessing her concerns. "Mor, I won't be flying in one of those little planes you know from the war. I'll be flying in a wonderful new plane called a Lockheed Super Constellation. It'll be super safe! You know, they're the planes President Eisenhower flies in!"

Tyra had no interest in what planes an American president flew in, but she admitted Nils' idea, at least in theory, made sense. Still she dared not think of him travelling to such exotic places entirely on his own in any plane, presidential or otherwise. For a few minutes she thought of their road trip to Nykarleby, and wondered if he could buy a truck or other sturdy vehicle and drive himself to Australia. But then there was the ocean, the huge ocean that surrounded Australia and separated it from the rest of the world. Nils seemed far too young to make this enormous trip on his own. Why, he was only 20! However, the first step in all their plans must be confirmation from Takla's brother in Australia. Until she had that, there was no point in booking tickets anywhere. With Axel asking daily how arrangements were going it was hard to wait, but wait she did. Never before had the words of her favorite hymn meant so much, and never before had she needed their comfort so urgently. The situation was so terrifying that she had no idea what to pray for. It had become impossible to meet her husband's needs and her own. But she had coped, with the help of God, all through the terrible war years, so she could cope again now.

When the letter from Mullumbimby finally came it confirmed Axel's dreams and her worst fears. She was almost fifty, far too old to be learning a new language, to cope with a new country. Takla's brother, however, was delighted they were planning the move to Australia. He mentioned the slightly worrying fact that banana prices had dropped that season, but Axel was unfazed, and simply delighted when Björn reduced his price accordingly. It was reassuring that there were people like Björn, honest, kind, and not out to benefit from the difficulties of others. His brother Harry was optimistic, believing the price drop was simply from an extra good crop that year, and a swamped market. Axel sent off his check to Björn in the next post, and with cheerful triumph handed in his resignation to the mine manager.

Tyra went back to the pleasant travel agent and made firm bookings to Australia. It was easy booking a ship from London to Sydney. Connecting up with that ship was more problematic. But finally trains from Kiruna to Gävle, then across Sweden to Göteborg on the western coast were arranged. From there a ferry across the notorious North Sea would take them to London. The agent found an inexpensive hotel for their two-day stay in London.

Hardest of all was writing the goodbye letter to Anna. Tyra agonized over it, but finally told the truth. Axel found working in the mines extremely miserable, was convinced his health could not take more, and was overjoyed at the possibility that he could do something else. He had been looking for land ever since they got to Kiruna, but none had become available. This was the best chance he had. Tyra admitted her concerns, but assured her mother they would someday return and settle back in Nykarleby. She assured her mother she had prayed earnestly about the venture, and as everything seemed to be falling into place, it looked as though it was God's plan. She told of Nils' generous offer to go ahead and prepare, and did not stress her mother with details about how he was travelling.

As expected, Anna wrote encouraging her daughter, insisting she was well and would look forward to their visit when Axel felt able to make it. She promised to pray for them in their new adventure. Tyra suspected her mother confused Australia with Austria, and had no idea how far away it was. Anna talked about Hjalmar and his family, and gave news of Algot whom she was sure would like to see Tyra if their train happened to go past Eskilstuna.

And then, having done all she could, and paid for everything, Tyra was left to pack. It was not practical to take furniture. She had no idea what bedding they would need, not in a place that had no winter! Nils could purchase bedding for them when he got there.

What treasures, what mementoes, should she take? Suddenly she remembered the embroidery her mother brought when she came to Nykarleby during the war. It was worth nothing, but would be a link with her Mor, memories of the times they worked together. She would take it. Then there were her books. The healthy living books she had bought years before to make sure she did the right thing by her sons—these would still be necessary, as Roland was only eight. There was the precious book whose cover depicted a Finnish solider in prison, with his only hope a cross hanging above him. She could hardly bear to read that book, it brought back so many painful memories, but it did illustrate what they had both been through, and maybe some day she could talk to Roland about her experiences. He had often admired the cover of this precious book, but was too young to read the story. The pain of her war memories was so great she never spoke about them. But maybe when Roland was old enough, and she had both the time and the composure to do it, she would tell him and he could read about it. But it would not be easy. There were her favorite religious books, and of course her Swedish Bible. One of Harry's letters had mentioned rag carpets and woven runner mats were hard to find in Australia, so she would take as keep sakes one each of her mother's and Elin's creations. Finally, there was her big extravagance, the purchase that had shocked Axel soon after they arrived in Kiruna—the large tapestry bought in a well-stocked Kiruna shop. A beautiful picture of reindeer in a wild yet pristine Lapland landscape, it would pack easily, and be a constant reminder of where they came from. It would be nice for Roland too, reminding him of his heritage. She added a few favorite plates and serving dishes, favorite clothes for all of them, and was done.

Thus, with a trembling heart, Tyra was ready, but most certainly not willing, to leave. Why, oh why, she asked herself, had God not answered her earnest prayers to prevent this journey to the ends of the earth?

Chapter 18

Voyage

Listlessly, from the window of their dingy hotel room, Tyra peered at the thick yellow London smog that perfectly matched her mood. How could people live in such depressing conditions? she wondered. Despite her apparently placid compliance, she still felt resentful that Axel had insisted on this crazy trans-world venture. Winter in Finland was cold, crisp, and clear, black and white, not dirty and opaque. What had people said about London weather? Ah yes, pea soup fogs. Memories of the detested Finnish Thursday lunch food rushed back, and she thought how apt was the description—pea soup fog—thick, dirty, opaque!

She ran her finger along the sill, horrified by the heavy smudge of dust it collected. Surely, even in this small, low-cost hotel, people should have enough pride in their establishment to clean properly, she thought, angrily. Why, even as a country farmer's wife, managing alone during that dreadful Winter War, she took pride and pleasure in keeping a spotlessly clean house. The burnt smell of the fog puzzled her until she remembered a passenger on the North Sea crossing told her English people did not burn clean-smelling wood, but dirty black coal. They must burn an awful lot of it, she thought, to make the air smell so bad!

She remembered BBC stories of the heroic British King George and his family who stayed in London despite daily bombings and German terror, so he could lead his people. And then he died so prematurely, perhaps from the stress of it all, or maybe, Tyra now decided, from the foul weather. His youthful daughter was now Queen Elizabeth. Russian authority in Finland made her suspicious of royal rule, but Sweden had a king, a very popular one, and royalty had not done Britain any obvious harm. A visit to the Queen's Palace was planned, but the weather was so unpleasant she decided they would stay indoors, out of the evil-smelling fog. And there was the language issue—Axel happily yelled at people in Swedish, as though by sheer volume of noise he could make them understand, while she stood by, mortified with embarrassment. Getting a taxi to their hotel had been a nightmare, but somehow, they got there.

The journey from Kiruna was a blur. The bad tempered Kiruna station master grumbled about their large trunk, which, with difficulty, they transferred unaided at Gävle station to the Göteborg-bound train. Göteborg was a shock, so confusingly, unexpectedly large. Buses, trams, traffic, all totally bewildering, especially when a small boy, agog with all things on wheels, required her constant attention. Fortunately, Roland was awed by the variety of food available on the North Sea ferry, with none of the queasiness that bothered her. They made it across that notoriously restless ocean, and got their offensive trunk and themselves to this small hotel, discovering Göteborg was nothing compared with the massive chaos of London. Did so many people (more than twice the total population of Finland!) actually *want* to live in London, such a dirty, dismal place! They still had to get to the ship tomorrow, then she would try to relax on the long voyage to Australia. She prayed fervently that it would be easier on her stomach than the North Sea crossing had been.

Suddenly, with a pang of guilt, she remembered it was October 31, 1955, Roland's ninth birthday! She had prepared two small gifts—a miniature board game, no bigger than the palm of her hand (played with tiny sticks and called "foxes and chickens"), and a number puzzle. She watched Axel and Roland stir, went to her handbag, and retrieved the birthday gifts.

"Morning Mor! What were you looking at?" asked Roland, rubbing his eyes as he climbed out of bed.

"Dirty fog," replied Tyra. "London is very dirty. I'm glad we aren't staying here!"

Roland giggled. "It's very dirty in this room, I know! Have you seen the dirt under the bed? Big balls of grey fluffy stuff, bits of paper, and even a couple of old socks!" Tyra shuddered.

She handed Roland her gifts. "Don't worry about dirt! We won't be here long. Anyway, happy birthday! It's special to have a birthday in such a famous place," she said, and listened with pleasure to his squeals of delight.

"Can we eat something special, Mor? For my birthday?"

"Sure." Tyra had no idea how to get anything special in the yellow-grey expanse of the mighty metropolis of London

The hotel provided breakfast, but so very different from their usual that the family wondered how people survived such strange food. Familiar rolled oats porridge looked good, but was served with milk and dirty brown sugar instead plain with cream, or with bright tasty berries! Axel decided to get his money's worth and try the offered main course of fried eggs, sausages and bacon, but it was so long since he had eaten either bacon or sausages (Tyra never cooked them) he felt unwell afterwards. Tyra and Roland confined themselves to something called "toast" which seemed to be bread half recooked so that it was neither bread nor *knäckerbröd*, and Roland described it very well as being like rubber. They were given no cheese, tasty tomatoes, or berry sauce for this bread, but strange, yellow, lumpy stuff called "marmalade" that seemed to be made from bitter, unripe oranges. Axel said the coffee was bearable, but Tyra and Roland chose glasses of milk.

They walked along the busy road, but the air smelt so bad, and they could see so little through the fog, they retreated inside shops. Finally, they found a small café where they hoped to locate something special for Roland. His eyes fell on large, round, puffy loaves filled with cream and liberally decorated with something very pink. To Roland they looked like giant *griser*. They ordered three by sign language, and sat down to the birthday treat. The pink topping was very sticky and very sweet, the cream more like butter than cream, but the bread . . . ! Roland had already described it perfectly—like eating rubber. Did no one in Britain know how to make good, solid bread?

That evening, feeling adventurous, they again left the confinement of the grubby hotel, walked to another café and tried something that was clearly popular with other customers, food wrapped in a thin greasy bread and called "pie". With the pies came welcome mounds of familiar mashed potato and green peas. Oh the joy of something familiar and edible! Tyra and Roland scraped out the contents of their pie, and ignored the crust, but again Axel decided he wanted his money's worth, and chewed his way through the strange, soggy shell.

"It's another version of rubber," he announced as he chewed manfully. "How do they manage to turn good wheat flour into such inedible food?"

"Will we have to eat food like this all the way to Australia?" asked Roland anxiously.

Voyage

"I hope not," said Tyra, wearily.

They slept fitfully, next morning ate more strange breakfast, although Axel skipped the sausages and bacon and confined himself to eggs. By showing their tickets to the pleasant hotel receptionist, they enlisted her help to engage a taxi cab to the wharf. They arrived at the ship without mishap, with relief found their cabin, and collapsed on their bunks.

"This boat's a good size," said Axel, waving his hands. "Shouldn't roll like that North Sea ferry." Tyra smiled wanly.

"Can I go on deck?" asked Roland excitedly.

"Sure," said Axel, and taking his son's hand they left Tyra to organize the cabin.

Tyra was busy inspecting the cupboards of the cabin when a woman with a clipboard knocked on the door, handed Tyra a collection of papers, and began talking rapidly. Tyra smiled pleasantly, waited patiently till the woman paused for breath, which took some time, and tried frantically to remember the word the hotel receptionist had impressed upon her. Ignoring the papers the woman thrust at her, Tyra took a deep breath, pointed at herself, and said slowly and carefully, "Swedish. Swedish."

The woman nodded vigorously, smiled faintly, and walked off, leaving Tyra holding wads of incomprehensible papers thrust into her hands. Roland and Axel, full of excitement about their explorations, had returned before the woman reappeared with a very young uniformed man. He explained he was crew, spoke Swedish, and would be available to help them. In a few minutes he explained meal times and places, and other essentials, writing information on the papers. The young man said there was another Swedish couple on the ship, and in due course they would be introduced. Smiling and nodding, the crew members left, reminding the family the ship would leave in an hour, and if they wanted to say farewell to London, be on deck.

"I've had enough fog!" declared Tyra. "I'm staying here."

"But the fog's gone! It's getting better all the time!" grinned Axel.

Axel proved correct about the ship's stability, and none of the family had seasickness issues during the entire six-week journey. Unfortunately, his optimism was not fulfilled in the ship's food. Axel ate his way manfully through proffered richly spiced menus, determined to "get his money's worth", but admitting it was an ordeal. Tyra tasted, but could not swallow the unfamiliar, heavily spiced foods. It seemed that only English rubbery bread was not spicy. Roland flatly refused to eat anything, even bread, until he discovered cornflakes. These, he decided, were a wonderful treat.

The staff indulged him with cornflakes whenever possible, and left his mother to wheedle him into eating mashed potato (peppered!), soggy cabbage (peppered!), and rubbery bread.

There was one aspect of ship life that Tyra definitely enjoyed: everything was very clean, a marked contrast to their London hotel. There was a young Englishman, barely more than a boy, who daily cleaned their cabin. Tyra was amazed when regularly ship's officers, immaculately dressed in white, would come and check on the work he was doing. They even shone a torch into the teacups he washed, to make sure there were no stains left in them! It was a relief for her to discover that not all English people were dirty and careless in their behavior.

There was much excitement after a few days of sailing when those promenading the deck frequently mentioned "Gibraltar." The young Swedish crew member came and seemed to say the ship would stop at Gibraltar, and they could look around the famous rock. Tyra did not want to do this because of language, and Axel was arguing about wasted opportunity, when a middle-aged couple approached them.

"So you're Swedish?" the man asked.

Tyra was embarrassed their argument had been overheard, but Axel nodded vigorously.

"We're the Nilssons[1]," smiled the man. "I'm Fredrik, and this is my wife Kristin. The captain told us about you after we boarded, but my wife hasn't been well, and we weren't able to contact you until she was better."

Axel introduced himself and family, adding "I want to look at Gibraltar, but my wife is scared to get off the ship."

Fredrik Nilsson laughed. "I'm afraid your wife must win! The ship doesn't stop at Gibraltar, but does go close, so you'll get a good look."

"Thank you," smiled Tyra. "Neither of us speak English, and knowing what's happening is difficult. That's why I didn't want to get off the ship. I'd like to see Gibraltar, but it's exhausting when you can't make anyone understand you!"

"I understand how you feel," responded Kristin. "My English is limited. In fact, my Sinhalese is better. Fredrik and I will be delighted to help all we can. I'm sorry I wasn't able to talk to anyone for a few days, but I'm fine now."

"I'll show you a good place to watch Gibraltar as we sail by," offered Fredrik, and they followed his lead. The Rock, jutting from the narrow

---

1. Pseudonyms for actual people.

stretch of sea between Spain and Africa, was impressive, and Roland enjoyed watching sea birds swirl around it. Before they parted they exchanged cabin numbers, Fredrik organized meal times together, and Tyra felt greatly relieved.

"Those people speak beautiful Swedish," she said. "They sound well educated."

That evening, as the families ate their meal, Fredrik Nilsson asked Roland what he enjoyed doing. Roland proudly told about his ninth birthday in London, and the gifts he received. Immediately Fredrik promised to partner him in games of foxes and chickens. His patience was enormous, and they spent countless hours playing and talking together. Fredrik told them about nightly film programs, and showed Roland a vantage point on deck where he could watch the *Tom and Jerry* cartoon trailers that accompanied feature films. Roland became addicted to these cat and mouse cartoons, and watched them every night. Axel made no protest about his son's free entertainment!

"What other games do you play?" Fredrik asked after the zillionth game of foxes and chickens.

"Playing with cars, but they're all in our trunk."

"Yah, all boys like playing cars! What about toy soldiers?"

Roland shook his head firmly. "No, I'm not allowed to have those. Once in Kiruna I asked Mor and Far if I could have a toy tank. It had wonderful tires that walked like a caterpillar. It wasn't the tank but the tires I wanted, but Far absolutely refused. He got angry with me when I begged for it. Later Mor told me Far had been in the war, and seen what real tanks do to people, and they both hated anything to do with war."

Fredrik Nilsson looked up, very surprised. "Really? Sweden didn't have any war, so what war was your Far in?"

"I don't know," said Roland, shrugging. "We don't talk about war. But we aren't from Sweden, you know. We come from Finland."

"Finland? Ah, that explains everything, it really does!" exclaimed Fredrik, nodding his head with a deep sigh. "Yah, that explains everything. The Finns had a terrible time in that war. Well, let's go for a walk and find the others."

"You know, there's something else I like to do," said Roland cheerfully as he trotted beside Fredrik. "When my big brother is home we make photos together, in a very dark room."

"Really? That sounds fun. And where's your big brother now?"

"In Australia. He went there by airplane, and he's getting everything ready for Mor when she arrives. His airplane took only four days to get to Australia. I wish I was on a plane, instead of this slow old boat!"

"Your brother sounds like a nice young man. How old it he?"

"He's twenty, nearly twenty-one. Yah, he's wonderful. He learned to be an electrician in Sala, in Sweden. But I think he's going to help Far grow bananas." Fredrik Nilsson nodded thoughtfully.

"Your son is very persistent and determined," commented Fredrik, when they met up with Axel. "He plays that game of his with dogged determination."

Axel beamed with pride. "That's good to hear. I've often thought he had *sisu*. Finns think it's the most noble character trait. I hope he'll be successful in life. Thanks so much for playing with him. Tyra and I are a bit exhausted with all the trouble of leaving Kiruna and getting ready for this trip."

Although it was late autumn, sailing through the Mediterranean proved very pleasant. Everyone looked forward to the first port of call, Port Said in Egypt, where they could get off the ship and hopefully stretch their legs. Fredrik warned they would not see the famous pyramids, but walking on land still sounded good. "Trust me, keep very close together when we get to Port Said. You'll see what I mean when we arrive," he advised.

Fredrik was right; even getting off the ship proved almost impossible. Jostling, shoving, pushing to clamber up the gangway, held back only by burly crew, were hundreds of incredibly persistent hawkers. They thrust, heaved, elbowed, cried, screamed, until Tyra, already stressed about the trip, and used to well-ordered Finnish behavior, completely lost her composure. Normally most self-controlled, this undisciplined crowd unleashed her pent up emotions, and made her suddenly very angry.

"Get away! Get away! Get Away!" she yelled, waving her hands as people pressed colored glass beads, supposed antiques, spices, breads, cotton clothing, and models of Nile *felucca* boats at her.

Axel laughed heartily at her distress (to deflect his own) but Fredrik realized how distraught she was, and with shouts and gestures successfully commanded the hawkers to move away from her. Roland clung to his mother, frightened by people who pushed and poked him. They were happy to retreat to the safety of the ship, leaving souvenirs behind.

"Are those people desperate for money, or just rude?" asked Axel, as they sank on deck chairs and waited for lunch.

Fredrik shrugged. "Probably both!"

"It was worse than London!" sighed Tyra wearily. She was glad to enjoy the peace of the ship's deck, and had no regrets when she saw passengers returning clutching parcels bulging with souvenirs.

"Do you know about the Statue of Liberty?" Fredrik suddenly asked Roland as their ship sailed from Port Said. Roland shook his head.

"Ah well, you will some day. Anyway, it was given to America by France, but the man who made it really wanted it to be here in Port Said! American people think it's their special statue, but that isn't quite true!"

Port Said was challenging, but sailing down the Suez Canal proved fun. Although they did not see the Great Pyramid or the Sphinx, because the canal consisted of two channels ships coming in the opposite direction appeared floating on sand. This fascinated Roland, especially the strange sailed Arabic *dhows* and Egyptian *feluccas*. And safely away from the crowds, Tyra also enjoyed watching.

By the time they sailed through the Gulf of Suez, the Red Sea, the Gulf of Aden, and out into the Arabian Sea, the Nilsson and Östring families felt at ease with each other. Axel shared with Fredrik the increasing horror he felt for mining, his fears for his health while working underground, the reasons for venturing into mining, and his dreams of being an independent banana grower in Australia. Fredrik revealed that he and his wife were Lutheran missionaries returning to Ceylon (Sri Lanka).

While Axel and Fredrik kept their conversation to farming and political topics, Tyra discussed with Kristin the anguish she felt leaving Finland. It proved a healing time, as she discovered the genuine, caring attitude of this dedicated Swedish woman. She dared to reveal the deeply hurtful things that had happened to her as a member of the Finnish Lutheran Church, and Kristin admitted what Tyra had already decided, that God and Church were not the same thing, and confusing the two was one of the most common and tragic mistakes people make. Kristin knew of the work of Adventists in Ceylon, especially the Lakpahana College near Kandy. She admired its emphasis on both academic studies and practical crafts, and that students could work to earn their tuition.

When Tyra timidly expressed resentment towards Axel for compelling her to uproot from her homeland and mother, Kristin sympathized, but then surprised her. "I don't know whether God wants you to go to Australia or not, but I'm sure he can work out something good for you despite the pain of this experience."

This immediately reminded Tyra of words in her favorite hymn, "As thy days, thy strength shall be in measure, This the pledge to me He made." Why had she not thought of this before, instead of indulging feelings of self-pity, feelings that made her a helpless victim, she wondered.

One day when they were sitting alone in a secluded part of the deck Kristin asked, "Does your church fellowship sing the great Martin Luther hymn?"

Tyra looked up, "You mean *A Mighty Fortress*? Of course we do!"

Kristin nodded, Tyra began humming, and Kristin, in a beautiful contralto voice, burst into song:

> "A mighty Fortress is our God,
> A Bulwark never failing;
> Our Helper He amid the flood
> Of mortal ills prevailing:
> For still our ancient foe
> Doth seek to work us woe;
> His craft and power are great,
> And, armed with cruel hate,
> On earth is not his equal.
>
> "Did we in our own strength confide,
> Our striving would be losing;
> Were not the right Man on our side,
> The Man of God's own choosing:
> Dost ask who that may be?
> Christ Jesus, it is He;
> Lord Sabaoth His Name,
> From age to age the same,
> And He must win the battle.

"Ah, I love that hymn," said Kristin. "It's so God-focused, it stirs my soul!"

"Mine too!" exclaimed Tyra. "Thank you for reminding me of it. I need something inspiring, because I confess this Australia adventure is daunting. I pled with Axel not to make me go, but he was sure this was his only chance to get out of the mines. As I shared the other day, I've been feeling a real victim about it all. I'm not sure how I'm going to cope in a country I can't even speak the language. But I have a favorite Swedish hymn. It's been a big comfort to me, especially during the wars, and times of stress, like now. I'm sure you'll know it!" She sang the first verse softly:

> Day by day, and with each passing moment,
> Strength I find, to meet my trials here;
> Trusting in my Father's wise bestowment,
> I've no cause for worry or for fear.
> He Whose heart is kind beyond all measure
> Gives unto each day what He deems best—
> Lovingly, its part of pain and pleasure,
> Mingling toil with peace and rest.

"Ah, yes," responded Kristin, "beautiful song! It's Lina Sandell-Berg's lovely hymn, isn't it?" Tyra nodded.

"By the way," Kristin continued, a small, challenging frown across her face, "do you Adventists *really* not believe in hell?"

Tyra broke into a cold sweat. Memories of her *skriftskola* ordeals flooded back. This woman, she thought with wild panic, is an experienced teacher of Lutheran doctrine. She's a missionary, used to making theological explanations. But how could she, Tyra, naturally quiet and taciturn, even begin to respond? Why, in her isolation in Kiruna, it was almost five years since she had attended any church or heard any sermon. Somehow she had to get this right. The silence seemed to last forever, but she must respond. She sent a quick prayer heavenward. Suddenly she noticed Kristin was not glaring at her, but watching with eager expectation.

"I'm not a Bible expert," Tyra began, "but if you mean an eternally burning, tormenting hell, no we don't. But of course we know God has to deal with evil. He gives everyone a chance to choose, time to do it, and even sends the Holy Spirit to help them make the right choice. Accepting Jesus Christ by faith we have the chance to live a new life, if we repent and follow God's ways. But eventually, at the end of the world, those who choose their own selfish way instead of God's loving way must be destroyed, because God has promised to make everything new, and get rid of all sadness and suffering. We'll all be judged by God, and he knows the truth of the real heart inside us, so won't make any mistakes. The destruction of those who are evil will take just as long as needed to make everything pure and clean again, to rid the whole universe of evil. So, that's what I think hell really is. A tormenting, everlastingly burning hell where people burn in agony forever would be an evil, a sadness and a suffering that God promised to destroy, now wouldn't it? How horrible for God's people to watch such a thing! So it won't last forever, perhaps just a few minutes, but anyway, it'll burn just long enough to clean things up and get rid of those who are wicked, once and for all."

Tyra was a little breathless as she finished her monologue. Kristin nodded thoughtfully.

Tyra, still flustered, paused to catch her breath. But bravely she added, "I remember when I first saw an electric light. I was amazed that by just turning a switch the darkness disappeared, was destroyed. I imagine it's going to be like that when Jesus, who said he's the light of the world, will come again and destroy evil. Evil just can't exist in the presence of God."

Kristin listened thoughtfully. "What you've said makes sense, good sense," she responded. "So you believe in hell, but not an eternally burning one? Yah, as I said, it makes sense. I'll think about it. By the way, do you Adventists think you get to heaven by being good and keeping all God's rules, or do you understand the great teaching of Luther, that it's only through what Jesus Christ has done for us that we have the hope of heaven?"

Tyra smiled, encouraged by Kristin's positive response to her little monologue about hell. A trickle of anxious sweat ran down her forehead, but this time she was not concerned. "Our church regards Luther as one of the great Christians of all history. His understanding of the importance of faith in Jesus is basic to our teachings about salvation. But it isn't our faith that saves us, it's Jesus!"

"Ah, that's wonderful!" exclaimed Kristin, suddenly smiling. "You're a real Christian!"

Tyra looked thoughtful, was silent for a few moments, then shared, "I have a cousin I'm very fond of. He made a terrible mistake once, really terrible. He went to prison for ten years for it. But I know that by God's grace he's been forgiven, and he's a new person now. Algot was a huge blessing to me during the war, and I know God has changed him. He's living proof."

"How wonderful!" responded Kristin. She remained silent for several minutes then added pensively, "There's a Swedish hymn I love, and I'm sure you would too. It's become very popular recently, and been translated into many languages. It's by the Swedish poet Carl Boberg, and is set to an old Swedish folk tune. Perhaps you've heard it, or know it. I'm sure you'd love it." She began singing softly, in Swedish,

> "O Lord my God, When I in awesome wonder,
> Consider all the worlds Thy Hands have made;
> I see the stars, I hear the rolling thunder,
> Thy power throughout the universe displayed.
> "Then sings my soul, My Savior God, to Thee,
> How great Thou art, How great Thou art.
> Then sings my soul, My Savior God, to Thee,
> How great Thou art, How great Thou art!

"Why, yes! I know that! *O Store Gud!*" exclaimed Tyra. "I heard it on the radio sometimes in Kiruna, and thought the words fitted Sweden beautifully. When I saw the Kebnekaise, the northern lights, those vast snowfields of Lapland, and the mighty Torne River, the hymn was just perfect! It helped me thank God for his universe, all the wonderful things God has made, and remember how great God really is!"

Tyra paused thoughtfully. "There's another verse, isn't there, a gentle one about forests and birds singing?"

"Yah, there is," responded Kristin. "I'll sing it, as best I can remember."

> When through the woods, and forest glades I wander,
> And hear the birds, sing sweetly in the trees,
> When I look down, from lofty mountain grandeur,
> And see the brook, and feel the gentle breeze,
>
> Then sings my soul, My Savior God, to Thee,
> How great Thou art, How great Thou art.
> Then sings my soul, My Savior God, to Thee,
> How great Thou art, How great Thou art!"

"Beautiful," murmured Tyra.

"Yah, knowing the greatness of God is the most important Christian idea. But since Boberg wrote that hymn it's been translated into several languages, and at least two verses have been added to the English version. While we've been on furlough I heard about those extra verses written by a British minister working in the Ukraine, a man named Stuart Hine. You mightn't like that Russian connection, but the words are beautiful. One verse tells about the reactions of Ukrainian people when they first heard what Jesus had done for them. Hine added another verse when he met Polish refugees in England who were longing to return to their homeland after the Second World War. They told him how often they thought of the importance of Jesus' second coming. I wish I had a copy of those English additions, so perhaps when you get to Australia you might find one, and send it to me. There's a young American evangelist called Billy Graham. He works with a singer called George Beverley Shea who's made this hymn very popular. If you get a chance to hear him, you'd enjoy it."

Tyra reached over, touched Kristin's hands, and smiled. "You know, Axel and I like Russians! Honestly! We had some Russian prisoners of war helping on our farm in Nykarleby, between the wars Finland fought with Russia. They were lovely lads. I wish I knew what happened to them. We'll never forget them. I'll remember your story about the hymn, and if I get the chance I'll send you the English version." Tyra was thoughtful for a few minutes, and then added, "Isn't it wonderful how hymns bind Christians together!"

By the time they reached Bombay (Mumbai) Tyra had accepted Kristin's invitation to spend a night with the Nilssons at their Lutheran mission when the ship docked in Colombo, Ceylon. Unfortunately, a dock strike in Bombay meant they were unable to get off the ship at the scheduled port stop there. Watching the crowds from the safety of the deck, however, convinced Tyra and Axel that the chaotic crush in India was worse than the hawkers in Port Said. Somehow the captain marshalled the ingenuities of his crew and got essential supplies to the ship, and within a few hours they were on their way south to Colombo.

Tyra looked forward to getting off the ship, but when she walked off the gangplank she discovered her sea legs had developed so well she now felt unsteady walking on land! The ship made its own breeze as it travelled through the Indian Ocean, but once Tyra was off the ship she found Colombo was unbearably hot and sticky. She was very grateful of the transport and support of the Nilssons, as they negotiated the confusion of this strange new city.

The compound of the Lutheran mission was beautiful, and there were large cooling electric fans in the ceilings of the rooms. Tyra was overwhelmed by the generosity of the Nilssons, newly arrived back themselves, yet willing to make strangers welcome. They had noticed the Östrings struggled with spicy food on the ship, and with great kindness instructed the young woman who helped them to make a very bland meal. Roland was delighted with the unlimited plain rice available, and all of them enjoyed the mild fish curry that accompanied it. That evening Fredrik Nilsson conducted a simple prayer service, with favorite Swedish hymns, and all went to bed happy.

Next morning Kristin suggested they visit the nearby zoo. Tyra would have preferred to stay under the fans, but knew it would do them good to get out. To everyone's surprise, Roland showed little interest in the large mammals at the zoo, but his eyes were glued to the seething mass of snakes in the reptile corner. With difficulty his parents dragged him away from the slithering creatures. He was delighted when Axel told him there were lots of snakes in Australia, but Tyra shuddered!

Re-boarding the ship was a bittersweet experience. Although both families promised to write (and they did) they knew that meeting again would be unlikely. For Tyra, Kristin was not only a lingual link with the strange new world she daily experienced, but a spiritual anchor. Kristin had bridged the painful divide between her distressing childhood religious experiences, and her current growing faith. Kristin had restored her confidence in the message of Luther, despite the shortcomings of the organized church. Roland missed his ever-patient play-mate. But Axel thrived to once again become the leader of his family, and began playing games of foxes and chickens with his son. He varied this by encouraging Roland to solve the math puzzle, and the two of them spent hours trying to get the numbers in proper sequence. What joy when Roland finally succeeded!

From Ceylon the ship steamed steadily southeast towards Australia. The equator was crossed, but by keeping to the cabin the Östrings escaped the traditional tomfoolery that accompanied this event. With the equatorial sun shining directly overhead, it was many days before Axel noticed his shadow pointed in a different direction. Although somewhere to the east were the islands of Indonesia, they never saw land until someone shouted "Australia!" and a low lying smudge appeared against the eastern horizon.

To her immense surprise and embarrassment, Tyra felt a surge of emotion as the ship finally turned into Fremantle Harbor, their first contact with Australia. She thought, "This is it, and it's so far from anything!" Fremantle is indeed the most isolated harbor in the world. Her second thought, as she watched from the rail of the ship, was "How wonderful! No crowds here!" In fact, the town appeared empty.

They, along with most of the passengers eager to see the land of their journey's end, stood near the prow of the ship as it turned eastwards into the harbor.

"Look Mor!" cried Roland. "Two lighthouses, a green one over there." and he waved his left hand, "and a red one!" and he waved his right. The mooring process fascinated Roland, and he was reluctant to leave the deck until the last rope was secured.

Axel was keen to set foot on Australian soil, but what he saw did not inspire his farming instincts. The town was built on sand, and trees were not conspicuous. Tyra noted with relief the weather was pleasant, but the sun did burn down from a cloudless sky.

Leaving the precincts of the ship and struggling with sea legs again, they wandered along the streets of Fremantle. Some buildings were clearly old, made of beautiful pale gold-colored stone. A strange round building dominated the low skyline. Other passengers pointed to it, saying "very old" and "prison." Amazingly, this prison was open for the public to walk right in and look around as they liked! Only later did they learn this was the oldest building in Western Australia, the prison built for convicts in the days when Australia was a vast penal settlement, the repository of all the social outcasts of Britain.

"You couldn't grow bananas here," said Axel disdainfully, scuffing the sandy soil with his shoes. "I've no idea what you could grow in this sand!"

"Well, Australia's a big country," said Tyra wisely. "They probably grow other things here. We need to wait till we've got to the other side to see where bananas grow." How strange, she suddenly thought, that when they first walked on Australian soil she should be the one encouraging Axel, and not the other way around!

"You're right," admitted Axel sheepishly. "But let's get back to the ship. I can't see where to change money, so we can't do anything except walk around." With the hot sun burning down, Tyra and Roland were more than happy to comply.

From Fremantle the ship steamed south, then east across the south of Australia, sometimes sighting land to the north, but more often merely feeling icy winds from Antarctica to the south. Sitting on deck was no longer a pleasure, and they confined themselves to brisk walks to keep physically active. The days spent steaming under Australia emphasized how large the country was. When they got to Melbourne the weather was still very cold. The cabin had been pleasantly cool during the long voyage, but now they shivered in a draught of icy air, despite the fact that it was supposed to be the famous Australian summer. No amount of hunting could locate a way of turning off the icy blast, and the city of Melbourne lying in the distance was a dreary blur of low cloud. They huddled under blankets, content not to battle the cold drizzling rain that faded the city from their sight.

"This is supposed to be their summer!" said Axel with disgust. "What does that Harry mean that there's no winter and only summer here!"

"I thought you said we're going to a place where it's always warm!" Roland added, shivering.

"Well, don't blame me!" said Tyra, grimly. "This was *not* my idea!"

No one was unhappy when the ship left harbor and headed east, rounded the southern tip of eastern Australia, and travelled north. Steadily the weather improved, and by the time they reached Sydney Harbor, it was balmy Mediterranean conditions again. With shock they realized they were finally at the end of their long voyage. Going through Sydney Heads gave Tyra her only dose of queasiness of the whole trip, but that soon passed as they sailed into the wide and impressive harbor.

"It's beautiful," she said, looking around as the ship steamed through smooth waters.

"Wow! Look at that enormous bridge!" exclaimed Roland. "Will we go under it?"

"Don't know, son. Haven't been here before."

"That bridge is special," said Tyra. "I read about it in the library in Kiruna."

"What didn't you read about in that library!" teased Axel.

"Not much," admitted Tyra. "But, Roland, that bridge was built in 1932, just one year after Far and I got married. That makes it only two or three years older than Nils. You know, they talked about building that bridge for more than one hundred years before they finally got around to doing it. But after thinking about it for so long they have made a very nice bridge, don't you think?"

"Hmm, so you and I have been married longer than that bridge has been here! Wow! That's impressive. A bit of a shock, actually. This country really is very young! But yah, it does look nice," said Axel. "What else did you read about in that library of yours?"

"They got their ideas for the bridge design from somewhere in America. But that bridge isn't famous, whereas this one is! Now I didn't read about everything in Australia, but I knew we'd be seeing this bridge, so I found it interesting."

As it neared the bridge the ship veered left, to Roland's disappointment, and instead of going underneath it, headed straight for the city.

"I see him! I see him!" shouted Roland, pointing excitedly to a figure waving on the shore. "It's Nils, I know it is!"

"It's him all right," said Axel. "No mistake, it's him. He's come!"

Talk about bridges had distracted her, but now reality hit Tyra. They had arrived, halfway round the world to where everything, everything, was utterly different. And standing slightly away from the crowd of people meeting the ship Tyra saw her son, her tall, healthy, and surprisingly sun-browned firstborn son, cheerfully waving a white hat. For a few moments emotion choked her and she could not speak. Even Axel was strangely silent. They had made it, to the other side of the world, as far from Finland as they could possibly get, but there was Nils to meet them. Maybe everything would be alright, after all.

Tears poured down Tyra's face. Just as well Nils can't see, she thought, as she hastily brushed them away.

Chapter 19

Ape Land Battles

THE FAMILY REUNION, OUTWARDLY subdued in typical Finnish fashion, was joyous. Nils shook hands with his parents, riffled Roland's hair, and asked about their luggage.

"You look well, son," said Tyra, her tears safely brushed away, but voice slightly tremulous. "Seems Australia's been good for you."

"It's great, Mor. Growing bananas is hard work, but it's healthy. Now, I've booked us into a hotel called the Peoples' Palace for the night. Harry recommended it. It's very cheap, Far, so don't worry! It's run by a church called the Salvation Army, Sallies they call them here. It's in the middle of Sydney, close to this wharf and the train."

"Have you seen any snakes?" asked Roland, with hopeful eagerness. "I saw lots in Colombo zoo!"

Nils laughed. "I have, but there aren't many."

Once the outsize trunk was located, they found a tiny shop, more a stall, selling snack food on Circular Quay. Nils ordered egg sandwiches and bottled orange juice, and they ate hungrily.

"Strange putting the egg in the middle of the bread," said Axel chewing thoughtfully, "but it does make it easy to eat. Australians eat rubber bread like the English, I note."

"Can I have orange juice every day?" asked Roland, eagerly. He remained addicted to orange juice for the rest of his life.

The ungainly trunk prompted Nils to order a taxi. To Tyra's relief the room in the Peoples' Palace was clean, but other hotel clientele disturbed her. "They all look like drunks and criminals!" she declared anxiously. Tyra insisted they barricade their door with the large trunk, and the people lounging in the "Palace" made her reluctant to explore the city. Neither Nils nor Axel were disturbed by this, as they had plenty of news and activities to spend the rest of the day talking about. While the three "boys" went looking for food for their evening meal, Tyra rested. They returned with a huge newspaper-wrapped parcel, which, when cautiously opened, contained long rectangles of fried potato, and chunks of fried fish. "Fish and chips are very popular here," explained Nils proudly, as he extracted a bottle of something called tomato sauce from his back pocket. "I get some whenever I go into Mullumbimby town. They're cheap and taste pretty good." Somewhat reluctantly, Tyra, who always loved fish, agreed with him.

But despite her concerns about the hotel occupants, next morning Nils persuaded Tyra to walk back to Circular Quay, where they found a path along the waterfront leading to a large, grassy area with gardens. Tyra was thankful to sit on grass, feel it tickle her bare legs, and watch yachts sailing the harbor beneath the mighty bridge. She noticed several strange birds with huge bills in the area, but Nils had no idea what they were. He asked a boy running past, who informed him they were pelicans. Nils and Axel went looking for food, and returned with—egg sandwiches and orange juice! Tyra decided egg sandwiches were the Australian version of barley porridge, food you just ate. After a pleasant time on the harbor shore, late in the afternoon they returned to the hotel for their luggage, and headed for the station.

Sydney Central Station was vast, a grimy, cavernous confusion of soot, tenth-rate food stalls, ticket booths, money changers, and travelers. The Brisbane Limited was finally located, and Tyra and Axel were surprised to discover it was a steam train belching billows of black smoke. Finland had steam trains, but all trains they had encountered in Sweden were diesel.

"There are small cabins along a corridor," explained Nils, as they clambered on to the train. "Six people can sit in one, but if we're lucky we'll have a cabin to ourselves." And lucky they were. Whilst not a luxury sleeper, by taking turns they could stretch out. High on the wall near the window was a large bottle of water with cups, which fascinated Roland. He insisted on having frequent draughts from the bottle, which then resulted in many trips down the corridor to the toilet.

With a jerk and a toot, a few relaxed minutes after the scheduled departure of 8:00pm, they were off. Since it was already dark there was little to see except the flash of city lights. Nils, with difficulty, warned his father to keep the window shut because there were several tunnels along the rail track coming out of Sydney. "When we get to Gosford, Far, then you can open the windows, that is, if you don't mind the smoke."

Axel protested. He liked fresh air, he claimed. But there was nothing fresh about the black sulfuric-smelling fumes from the engine! Just when the window discussion got more than a little bothersome, Nils produced food. Tyra laughed, in spite of herself—egg sandwiches and orange juice! But this time Nils had bananas as well, at their peak of golden perfection.

"What are potatoes like here, son?" asked Axel, his mouth full of banana. "I don't feel well unless I eat them twice a day."

"They're great, Far. Cheap and plentiful." Axel gave a sigh of contented relief.

"Do they have *knäckerbröd* and good cheese?" asked Tyra wistfully.

"Plenty of cheese Mor, and Harry's given me *knäckerbröd* so you must be able to buy it somewhere."

"Can you write to Mormor and ask her to send us *plattar*?" asked Roland, plaintively. "I *really* miss that."

Tyra patted his hand reassuringly. "Don't worry, son," she said. "I'll make all the *plattar* you want once we get to our new home."

Roland's eyes grew round with delight. "Really? Oh, I'm so glad! When we left Sweden I though I'd never eat *plattar* again!" He sat staring at the blackness flashing past. "Mor, can you make them as soon as we get there? Please! The food on that boat was horrible!"

"It will be Christmas in a few days," said Nils. "The village plans a welcome for you. We'll have plenty of Swedish and Finnish food then."

After sleeping fitfully through the night by morning they arrived at the town of Casino; bright sun poured through the window, and they were glad to stretch their legs and transfer to the branch line to Mullumbimby. Tyra was too tired to take much interest in the surrounding countryside. Axel, however, was wide awake, eagerly scanning the landscape. He looked at the fresh-green, morning-glinted scenery flashing past his window and became more and more horrified. "Look at all that good land, and no one's using it!" he exclaimed, repeatedly. "What a waste! What a terrible waste! Just think what I could do with it!"

Nils laughed. "They do a lot of dairy farming around here, Far. Australia has heaps of land, and farmers don't need to work it as densely as you did in Finland."

"Terrible waste!" muttered Axel. "What a terrible waste of good land! Wasted land!"

"Here we are!" cried Nils. The slowing train chugged into a small town. With eager eyes they all looked out to see where they would be living. They could see a few small houses, but no shops. Nils, however, assured them they were not far away.

As Tyra climbed wearily off the train the heat of Australian summer sun felt like a sauna. Her cotton dress clung limply to her tired, sweaty body.

Introductions were made to Harry Nylund and his friend Karl Häger, who were walking up to meet them. None of the men noticed Tyra wilting in the heat. Harry had a car for passengers, Karl a small truck for luggage. Down the sleepy main street of Mullumbimby (where there were indeed some shops) they drove, and a dog, asleep in the middle of the road, did not bother to move as Harry's car swerved around it. Axel made more oohs and ahs about the countryside, but Tyra was silent, exhausted by heat, too tired to make sense of this strange place she had worried about for a year. The further they drove from the town, the richer and more beautiful became the tropical forested areas. But oh, so different from home! Finally, they turned up a steep, bumpy road into a tiny village nestled among hills covered in luscious banana trees. They had arrived at "The Finns" in Main Arm, Mullumbimby.

"Can we look at the plantation now?" asked Axel eagerly, jumping out of the car.

Tyra, rivulets of sweat pouring down her face, stood gazing at him, aghast. "What! Now? At least help me unpack before you go!" she demanded, her eyes flashing. The men laughed, except Axel, who was astonished. They had come to grow bananas, and surely looking at bananas was the most important thing to do first! He carried the trunk and suitcases into the house Nils indicated, unlocked the luggage, and immediately left with Harry to inspect his "property".

Forlorn, drowning in sweat, and gasping for breath in the heat, Tyra sank on a kitchen stool.

Nils walked in. He had done a great job preparing for his family, and the little house was spotlessly clean. His mother's relief at the state of her new home was obvious. "Mor," he said, awkwardly, "you'll find things here are more primitive than we'd been told. I don't know how much you and Far knew about Main Arm. First, there's no electricity, although they say we might get some in the next twelve months. We've got plenty of kerosene lamps, which makes reading manageable. The toilet is down the back yard; you'll get used to it, I hope! But it's not clean like the one in

Brännon. There is running water, you'll be pleased to know, so you don't need to haul water from a well in the heat. We have a sort of food box, called a refrigerator, that runs on kerosene. Because it's so hot here you really need this machine or butter is just grease, milk goes sour before lunch, and you can't keep any food more than a day. This fridge thing is pretty important."

Tyra shook her head wearily, trying to fathom such a strange machine.

Two woman arrived at the door. "Hello," said one, in Swedish. "I'm Margaret Liljeström, from the house across the road. And this is June Nylund, Harry's wife. She's an Australian, so can't talk to us much, but she's a good person. We've brought you some food to get you started. That train from Sydney is very tiring."

"Train from Sydney!" thought Tyra. "Don't they realize I've come half a world away!" She smiled politely and introduced herself and Roland. Axel was nowhere to be seen.

But when she saw the women place on the table two loaves of crusty bread, two packets of *knäckerbröd*, a large pat of butter, a big square of cheese, a roast chicken, a bowl of something called potato salad, a large "bunch" of bananas (which she latter learned was not a bunch but merely a "hand"), tomatoes, oranges, and some strange fruit called mangoes that the women strongly recommended, she was overwhelmed. Her muttered thanks were sincere, and a little emotional.

"Except for the bread and bananas, put the rest of food in the fridge, Mor," advised Nils. "It's going to be a hot day. Things go bad really fast here, trust me."

"This is a very strange country, but I need to use the toilet, now!" said Tyra, urgently, as her visitors left. "Can you show me where it is?" Nils took her to the door, and pointed to a tiny shack a few yards down an overgrown path. "They call them dunnies here, not sure why," said Nils, shrugging.

Tyra carefully picked her way down the rough track, but within a minute Nils heard a scream and she shot back into the kitchen, her face contorted with horror. "I can't use that place!" she exclaimed. "There's a huge, ghastly spider-like creature on the wall right beside the seat! It's bigger than both my hands!"

"I'll get rid of it for you, Mor," said Nils, and hastened to keep his promise. Tyra trailed behind, urgently needing the toilet, wondering how she could manage coping with such ghastly creatures. Nils emerged from the shanty with an enormous spider dangling from a long stick. "I've checked the whole place, and there aren't any more there, now." Tyra never relieved herself so quickly, and was back up the irregular path before she had time to think about mammoth spiders, straight from a horror movie, which she had never read about in her sedate library searches in Kiruna.

"There are lots of spiders here, Mor, so try to get used to them," Nils advised. "Those big ones aren't poisonous. Most of them aren't nearly as big as the one you saw. They can bite, but it's rare they do, and never fatal. People don't mind them because they keep down insects which are a nuisance with the bananas. I'll look out for them until you get used to the idea that they're not a problem. No worse than rats."

Tyra shuddered. "That thing could eat a rat! How could anyone get used to creatures like that? Rats look normal! What else do I have to get used to?" she groaned.

Just then Axel walked in, beaming with joy. "Ah, you should see my trees! They're such a goodly lot, they really are!" he announced triumphantly. "Huge bunches of bananas hang from them! This place is great!"

"Now, don't forget what I told you," admonished Harry, his banana plantation guide. Axel raised his eyebrows. "Look I'm serious!" persisted Harry. "Every time you get home check to make sure you have no leeches or ticks on you."

"Really?" scoffed Axel, pulling a face.

Harry bent down and pulled up Axel's trouser leg. "Ah ha!" he said triumphantly. "Look at that leech!" He pointed to a tiny slug-like thing on Axel's shin. "Got some salt, Nils?"

Nils produced a salt shaker, and Harry dosed the creature liberally. It fell off Axel's leg, and a thin trickle of blood ran down. "They're everywhere," said Harry. "If you aren't vigilant you can lose significant blood and get anemic. Check yourself every day." Axel looked suitably contrite. "By the way," said Harry, "you better get yourself some shorts as soon as possible. Much cooler to work in."

"I'm sure we'll all need more suitable clothes," commented Tyra.

Harry peered down at his own arm and gave a low whistle. "Looks like you're getting the full lesson today," he grinned, nudging Axel. "I've got a tick on my arm." Axel and Nils crowded around to look. Tyra felt sick at the thought of these hideous wild Australian creatures and had no interest to see another. She had yet to meet bull ants with bites like fire, flies that covered everything like a black carpet, huge cockroaches that scuttled and rustled in her pantry day and night, and overfed mosquitoes that zizzed and zinged all night.

"Have we come to Ape Land?" she moaned bitterly. "I had no idea this place had so many nasty beasts! At least tigers and monkeys are nice to look at!"

"You get used to it," said Harry, shrugging his shoulders nonchalantly. "Now, Nils do you have some tweezers?" Nils shook his head, so Harry hastened across the road, returning triumphantly from his home with the required tweezers, and two of his three children eager to observe the removal operation. "Now watch this," he commanded. "You grab the tick by its head as close to your skin as you can, and just pull gently until it comes out. Make sure you get the head! Then squash it. Get some tweezers, Axel, next time you go to town. In the meantime, you can use ours if you need to."

"Where do these creatures hide?" asked Axel.

"Ticks like long grass. Most are harmless, but they can sometimes cause very serious disease, and paralyze dogs. Don't be hopeful. Get rid of any as soon as you find them. Leeches like damp places. Keep an eye on that young kid of yours, Tyra. They run around in all sorts of places, and are liable to meet up with anything."

Tyra's eyes opened wide, and she shook her head in dismay. "Ape Land, like I said," she groaned. "How will I ever get used to this!" The men laughed, but Tyra was flooded with quiet desperation.

"I'm hungry!" complained Roland.

Tyra rose and placed the gifted English-style bread, *knäckerbröd*, and bananas on the table. When she opened the fridge to get the butter, cheese, tomatoes, and the strange new fruit, its icy air enveloped her. If only she could crawl into this strange box, she thought, to cool off! The family sat down gratefully to eat real food. No more egg sandwiches! The strange new fruit, mangoes, were delicious, and they all agreed they must find more.

Later that afternoon Roland came running in excitedly, something precious cupped in his hands. "Look what I found, Mor!" He opened his hand, and something leapt at Tyra's face! She screamed, shamefully aware that she had never, ever, screamed until she arrived in this Australian jungle.

"Oh, you've lost it!" cried Roland in dismay. "Ah, there it is!" he exclaimed cheerfully. He leaned forward and grabbed something from Tyra's shoulder. This time he opened his hand only a tiny bit, revealing a small bright green frog with bulging yellow eyes. "They say 'ribbit, ribbit' Mor," he informed. "Aren't they nice?"

Tyra sat down quickly and fanned herself with her damp handkerchief. The frog *was* pretty, but these strange creatures were simply too much to cope with.

Over the next few days Finnish members of the village made themselves known, and insisted there were several others living in the town of Mullumbimby. Karl Häger brought his brother Bill and his wife; Margaret Liljeström brought her husband Karl, their two boys, along with her younger sister and her husband, the Lillthors; next door to the Östring's house were two smiling and laughing Italian families, the Palazzaris, and the Naclerios. They waved and shouted cheerfully whenever they saw Tyra, and did not appear to mind whether she understood them or not. Two Australian families in the village came to visit on Friday evening. They arrived asking awkwardly, "Nils? Nils?" Clearly they needed a translator.

Nils was located at the banana packing shed, and soon engaged. There was a good deal of to and fro English chatter, and finally Nils beamed broadly. "Mor, these people are the Thompson brothers and their wives. They're offering to take you to church tomorrow, down in Mullumbimby town."

"An Adventist church, in this outlandish place!" exclaimed Tyra in utter disbelief.

"That's what they say. Harry Nyland told them his sister in Finland knows you and said you are an Adventist. They insist they have plenty of room in their cars. I've promised Bill to do something tomorrow, but you and Roland and Far should go."

"What an incredible surprise! I never expected this!" answered the stunned Tyra. "After years worshipping alone in Kiruna I hardly know what church is like any more. But yes, thank them and say Roland and I will go, and maybe Far too."

When Tyra told Axel of her plans to attend church he shocked her. "Ah, yah, those Thompsons are nice men. I'll come too."

Ape Land was full of surprises! Axel had never wanted to go to church before! They had few clothes suitable for church in hot weather. Tyra ironed her best cotton dress (she borrowed the iron from June), noting sadly she had no suitable hat, pressed Axel's best (woolen) suit and shirt, found a pair of very Finnish bibbed shorts for Roland, and hoped for the best.

"It's a real church!" exclaimed Axel, loudly, as Alan Thompson parked the car outside an attractive solid brick building. "I didn't expect that!" The Thompsons guided them inside, making introductions, explaining their guests spoke no English. By the time the service started Tyra calculated there were at least one hundred people in the church, but Axel insisted there were twice that many.

Hymns surmounted language barriers. Occasionally during the sermon, Tyra caught what sounded like the name of a biblical book. But when at the end of the service the congregation stood and sang enthusiastically *A Mighty Fortress is Our God,* her emotion swelled alarmingly. She glanced furtively at Axel, and saw he was singing the familiar hymn lustily in Swedish.

Christmas, a few days after their arrival, was a cheerful time, with traditional foods produced by the village women. They insisted Tyra be a "guest" and enjoy the celebration. But it was impossible to get into the mood of Christmas when the sun blazed like a furnace, and sweat ran in rivers down all parts of her body. She wondered what her mother and cousins were doing, if they missed her. Joining the celebrations was another Finnish couple from Mullumbimby town, Edit and Uno Söderholm. Uno was also a banana grower, but he and his wife preferred the amenities in the town to the primitive conditions in the village. Tom Mott, himself a banana grower but also the village landlord, also joined the festivities. He was respected, appreciated, and welcomed by the villagers.

While everyone around her was clearly having a good time, Tyra's mind refused to concentrate on her strange surroundings. She remembered the happy Christmases of her childhood, the day she sang in church, and Algot tried to ruin her top. She even remembered, with an urgent wondering, the terrible Christmases she had endured during the horrific war years. If she could survive that, maybe she could survive what felt like a Christmas in hell, and a tiny smile deep inside her cheered her wilting spirit.

A few days later Tyra carried a large basket of washing to the clothesline. Standing over the boiling copper in Australian heat was exhausting work, but with no electricity she had no choice. Suddenly a huge dragon-like creature, about two meters in length, ran across the yard straight towards her. She suppressed another scream of fear, just as Margaret Liljeström carried out her own basket of clothes.

"Did you see that?" gasped Tyra, pointing to the huge creature that had turned and was disappearing into some low bushes. "It was horrendous!"

"Oh, that!" laughed Margaret. "That's just a big lizard! They call it a goanna."

"I don't care what they call it, this place will be the death of me," sighed Tyra. "There are just too many ghastly creatures! I'm frightened all the time! I can cope with primitive conditions, like no electricity and no flush toilet, but these creatures will kill me! It's as terrifying as living through the wars in Finland!"

"So you went through those wars, too? I daren't think about those times, they were so bad. But don't worry about goannas," reassured Margaret. "Honestly, they're more scared of you than you are of them. They will never harm you."

"I doubt that!" declared Tyra, still shaking. "I wonder what's happened to all those nice animals I read about in the library in Kiruna, things like kangaroos and koalas. How come we don't see any of them around here?"

"I've seen them," admitted Margaret, thoughtfully, "but not around here. Koalas are sleepy things, and they only like certain gum trees, whose leaves they eat. I've seen a kangaroo hit by a car on the road to Brisbane. That was sad. Strange, Aussies don't seem to have much interest in their animals."

Towards the end of January, 1956, a little over one month after their arrival, when sweat ran permanently in rivers down her exhausted body, Tyra was sitting in the shade at her back door, futilely fanning herself to get cool, when her cheerful Italian neighbor Mario Naclerio walked over, waving the day's letters.

"Finland! Finland!" he grinned broadly, and handed her a letter.

Tyra eagerly tore open the envelope, joyfully noting the letter was from Lisa. Two letters from Oxkangar had been waiting when they arrived. How good to get an update now, when the heat was so unbearable!

> *Hello Tyra, it is with deep sadness that I write to let you know your mother died on December 30th, after a very brief illness. The last thing she said was to tell you she loved you, and then she fell asleep. The funeral . . .*

The words misted and swam away. The heat went from the sun. The world grew grey and fuzzy. Her mother, who gave her physical life, who shared her spiritual life, dead. Buried. Gone. Forever.

Tyra had no idea how long she sat paralyzed on the steps, but finally she rose, entered the sweltering heat of her house, and lay on the bed. For the first time ever, she could not cope with making her family a meal. Axel and Nils found her on the bed a few hours later.

"Are you sick? Do you have a tick?" cried Axel in alarm.

"Shall I get you a drink?" asked Nils.

"Bad news," said Tyra, pointing to the letter beside her, and turned away.

Her men read the letter, and did their male best to comfort her. Words like "she didn't suffer," "who would have thought that could happen," "rest a bit and you'll feel fine," floated over her head. She heard them bustling in the kitchen getting food, then Axel was at the door with a plate of his favorite potatoes and a piece of chicken, enticing her to eat. She shook her head, but did accept a glass of tepid water. Next day Tyra refused to attend church. Axel became worried.

News of Tyra's tragic and unexpected bereavement quickly spread around the community. But what could they do? There was no funeral to prepare for, no service to attend, no wake to bake for; and none of them had any idea who Anna Lall was.

Edit Söderholm provided Tyra's best support. A trained nurse, she invited Axel to bring Tyra to her home after their weekly trips into Mullumbimby to buy provisions, where Tyra could spend the day under the cooling balm of her electric fan. Edit encouraged Tyra to talk about her mother. As Tyra's words and occasional tears flowed gently, the black hole in her life began to shrink. Edit gently softened, and finally removed, Tyra's guilt about leaving her mother without saying goodbye. With true kindness she listened to stories of Anna's virtues and her deep spiritual convictions. Edit and Tyra had diverse theological ideas on death, but they discussed their differences freely, and Edit's kindness allowed Tyra to regain the assurance of her own understanding. Tyra's tragedy bound the two women in close friendship. They had much in common. Both loved literature, and pretty clothes. Edit introduced Tyra to the local fabric shop and dressmaker. As she slowly recovered from her grief, Tyra was able to indulge her delight in bright, cheerful, floral-patterned fabrics made into billowing cool cotton dresses.

Late one Friday afternoon Axel arrived home, smelly, sweaty, his clothes disagreeably stained with banana sap. How Tyra hated that sap! She could wash out the dirt of soil, the stench of manure, and the stains of blood, but banana sap defied all her efforts, and no one in the village had any answers for erasing its permanent stains. The sight of Axel's ruined clothes was one more depressing reminder that she was far, far from home.

"Did you cope with the heat, today?" he asked, gently.

"Axel, I'll never cope with this place! Why did you ever think of coming here? It's torture!"

"I know it's hard for you."

"Hard! Is that what you call it? Hard! All those dreadful creatures that lurk everywhere! And now Mor's dead. And who's fault is it, tell me! Who wouldn't let me say goodbye to my mother! This village is incredibly primitive, much worse than anything in Finland or Sweden. It's an impossible place! Don't talk to me about things being hard!"

"Tyra, I came to ask a favor of you. I'd like to go to your church tomorrow. Will you come with me?"

Tyra was too shocked to reply. She attacked the potatoes she was peeling with savage intensity, then turned and looked at her husband. In his dirty, sap-stained clothes and sweat-covered body he was not a pretty picture. He reached up and pulled off his stained cloth hat, and his tousled blond hair suddenly glinted in a shaft of sunlight from the window. With a spasm of pain, Tyra realized his hair was streaked with grey, and his forehead deeply furrowed with lines.

"I'll try," she whispered.

"Good," said Axel, and he suddenly reached across and gave her a pat on the shoulder. "I know it'll do you good." Then he walked off to have the favorite Australian way of bathing, a shower. Tyra longed for a properly cleansing bath or sauna, something she could immerse herself in and feel truly clean, but splashing yourself with a trickle of tepid water from a pipe was all Australians knew.

Axel's request was as unexpected as it was abiding. From that day he never failed to accompany Tyra to church. He did it for her, she was sure, because he gave no sign that he was personally interested.

Chapter 20

Choices

FEBRUARY CAME, AND ROLAND started at the local one-teacher country school, situated a few miles down the road. He joined other village children at the school bus pick-up at the bottom of the hill.

"And how was it?" Tyra asked, when Roland arrived home after his first day.

"Good."

"What did you do?"

"Oh, mowed the lawn."

A month later, her son, the special gift from God, the one who had shown scholastic promise in Sweden, was still pushing a hand mower around the extensive school grounds and admitting to doing little else. Tyra was worried, until she remembered his lack of interest in anything but sauna baths in the Kiruna school. Mowing laws would certainly be a novelty after his arctic life, and she could only hope he would eventually learn something else. His teacher, Mr. Clifford, soon discovered that although Roland could speak no English, he was interested in math, and gave him plenty of sums to do. But money questions stumped him. Sweden had decimal-based *kronor*, but Australia, at that time, had complicated British-style pounds, shillings, and pence. Applying decimal logic did not work on these unruly pounds, or shillings, or pence! The rest of the family had been forced to learn the vagaries of the Australian monetary system, and Roland was quickly brought up to speed. Nils drummed into him that twelve pennies made one shilling, and twenty shillings made one pound. It mightn't make sense, but was manageable just as long as you remembered. Roland's math reputation was saved!

The Söderholms introduced the family to Brunswick Heads, where the Tasman Sea touched the New South Wales coast near Mullumbimby. Beach life was a new but soon favorite experience for everyone in the Östring family. While Nils and Roland happily rode breakers, Tyra contentedly wet her feet in quiet pools near the river, and cooled off under the shade of a tree. But even beaches had nasty Ape Land creatures! Nils knew about sharks, but much more common, with an extremely painful sting, were blue bottle jellyfish, whose extremely long tentacles meant watching out for their tell-tale blob-like bodies was not sufficient to avoid their stingers.

Meanwhile Axel loved every aspect of the process of banana growing. He loved the variety, caring for the trees, chopping out spent ones, culling weeds, and watching bananas fill out till the huge bunches were ready to cut down. He was delighted bananas grew all year round, although he also experimented with growing vegetables which he took to the town market to earn pocket money. He did not like spraying weeds with an evil arsenic weed killer, but he enjoyed making boxes to pack bananas ready for shipping around Australia. Fussy carpentering was not his forte, but hammering a box was fun. At that time bananas were individually packed tight into boxes, which were collected weekly by a national distribution company. Axel, fond of the adage "women work inside and men work outside" classified packing bananas as an inside woman's job, and pressed Tyra into service. At first the horrendous huntsman spiders infesting the packing sheds made her shudder, even squeal with horror, but eventually she closed her eyes and brushed them away.

Yes, they were all beginning to settle in Australia, but even Axel's heart was still in Finland. Australian newspapers had virtually no news from Finland, or anywhere in Europe except Britain. In fact, it would seem that the only thing worth reporting was Aussie rules football, and trade with England! Occasionally there was a snippet about those little islands to the east of Australia, New Zealand, but not much else from the rest of the world. It took months for the news Erik regularly sent from Finland to arrive in Mullumbimby. The villagers were shocked to learn that early in 1956 Urho Kekkenen had been voted in as president of Finland, with the unbelievable majority of 151 votes to 149!

"Who cast that last magic vote?" sniffed Axel disparagingly. "Don't trust that guy Kekkenen! We all know he drinks heavily, and is a womanizer!" But whatever his faults, Kekkonen survived decades of political jostling, and certainly stabilized relationships between Finland and the Soviet Union.

A little later that same year Tyra and Axel were again shocked to learn of the massive general strike that had occurred in Finland in March. It involved half a million workers, and brought the country to a standstill for almost three weeks. Amazingly, the issue received not a mention in Australian papers! But for the Finns growing Aussie bananas it was a major concern.

"Yah, I thought those so-called price reforms last year would cause trouble," said Axel, as he examined the crinkled paper. "Look, it says here that even milk and rents have gone up by seven percent!"

"Poor Erik, he'll be extra keen to leave Finland now," commented Tyra. "It would've been very tough for us if we'd stayed there."

Axel nodded, grateful that his Australian finances were stable. They were so good, in fact, that he soon decided he could afford a car. This was a momentous decision, and he and Nils scrutinized newspapers for weeks. Finally, the big day came, and Axel took possession of his first car, an old Chevrolet.

"Got a license?" asked Harry Nylund casually, as the men peered into the bowels of the engine.

"Eh? What's that?" asked Axel, standing up and hitting his head on the hood.

"Look, you better get one. If you don't have a license, they fine you a lot of money."

The thought of losing his hard earned cash made Axel decide to comply with licensing regulations. Mullumbimby policemen were not too fussy about driving technique, so Axel passed his practical test, with or without flying colors. But the oral test for road rules was another challenging problem. Axel's shout-and-make-them-understand English technique was not quite suitable for discussing the intricacies of road rules. The policeman agreed Nils could translate. Nils was known as a responsible young man who could be trusted.

"Now, remember Far, no talking in your Swenglish," stipulated Nils as they arrived at the police station in Mullumbimby. "Leave it to me!"

"Yah, yah, yah!" grinned Axel. "I know."

"Hello, Nils," smiled the smartly uniformed officer. "Your Dad's ready?" Nils nodded.

"Now, which side of the road do we drive on here in Australia?" the officer asked, using a simple question to put his client at ease.

"'Whatever works," said Axel.

"The left," translated Nils.

"When is it compulsory to stop?" asked the officer, continuing his easy-question style.

"When you're going to hit something!" said Axel.

"At red lights, stop signs, and when asked by the police," translated Nils.

"My, your father has a good grasp of the rules," said the officer, impressed. "You'd be amazed what some new Australians say when I test them! What a relief to have someone who knows what he's doing."

To the officer's surprise, Nils blushed brilliantly. "What a nice, modest, young man," he thought. "Well, just a few more questions will do, as your father clearly knows the rules. Now, what should you do when you come to a train level crossing?"

"Put your foot down and go for your life!" said Axel.

"Stop if bells are ringing and lights flashing," said Nils, "and always slow down and look both ways very carefully at any time."

With a few more questions and answers in this vein, the offer was satisfied.

"Great!" he said. "That will do. The license will get posted out to you, Mr. O'string, but here's an interim one just in case you need to drive out of the district."

"Thanks!" said Nils, perspiring profusely.

Axel thrust out his hand, and shook the young officer's vigorously. "Tak you!" he grinned.

"How did it go?" asked Tyra when they returned home.

"If that officer knew the truth, I'd be up for perjury!" laughed Nils. "It was incredible what Far said. He knew nothing, absolutely nothing, despite those hours and hours I spent drilling him about road rules. I'll have to make him learn again or it won't be safe for any of us to go out with him."

"You didn't drive with him from Kiruna to Nykarleby. I could have told you what he's like!" said Tyra, and laughed till her sides ached as Nils shared his translating ordeal.

Edit Söderholm had contacted a Swedish-speaking Lutheran pastor in Brisbane. Convincing him that there was a significant group of Swedish-speaking Finns in Mullumbimby, she invited him to visit every few months and lead simple Lutheran services in her home. She invited Tyra and Axel to join the group. Memories of kind Fredrik and Kristin

Nilsson on the ship made Tyra quickly agree. Tyra enjoyed weekly Sabbath services, but her lack of English was isolating. The Lutheran pastor led a simple program. He asked people to read from their Swedish Bibles, Axel and Roland included. But when the first hymn he announced was Tyra's old favorite, tears pricked her eyes. How that hymn had encouraged her despite everything life had thrown at her!

These simple home gatherings brought complete healing to Tyra after the pain of her experiences in the Lutheran church. But better still, she noticed that Axel, at first very guarded, gradually softened his attitude to the church that he believed had caused him such misery. "I guess we can't blame them all for the mistakes of some," he commented.

Early in 1959 Edit discovered a unique program was coming to Brisbane, and invited Tyra to attend with her. Billy Graham? Where had Tyra heard that name? Ah, of course, from Kristin Nilsson on the ship! Buses were organized to take interested people from Mullumbimby to Brisbane. Axel refused to go, reminding Tyra he got a bad migraine after every one of their rare shopping trips to Brisbane.

"And you," he asked surprised, "are you sure you want to do this? Don't you remember how bus sick you used to get in Finland?"

"They tell me buses are better now," Tyra replied. "And anyway, I think God will help me do this. It will be good for Roland, if he'll come with me."

Axel shrugged. "I hope you like it," he said, doubtfully.

Twelve-year-old Roland did decide to accompany his mother, and the experience had a very positive impact on him. The crusade took place in May, when the weather was mercifully cooler, and the trip proved fun. Crowds at the venue were huge, but well-mannered, and whilst Tyra would have preferred a more sedate style of preaching, she recognized the sincerity of the evangelist, Billy Graham himself.

However, for Tyra, music was the highlight of the event. Hearing George Beverley Shea sing the full version of the hymn she had first heard in Kiruna, then from Kristin Nilsson, stirred her heart. She enlisted help from Nils and the Thompsons and got the full English version to send Kristin.

> O Lord my God, When I in awesome wonder,
> Consider all the worlds Thy Hands have made;
> I see the stars, I hear the rolling thunder,
> Thy power throughout the universe displayed.

Chorus:
Then sings my soul, My Savior God, to Thee,
How great Thou art, How great Thou art.
Then sings my soul, My Savior God, to Thee,
How great Thou art, How great Thou art!

When through the woods, and forest glades I wander,
And hear the birds sing sweetly in the trees.
When I look down, from lofty mountain grandeur
And see the brook, and feel the gentle breeze.

And when I think, that God, His Son not sparing;
Sent Him to die, I scarce can take it in;
That on a Cross, my burdens gladly bearing,
He bled and died to take away my sin.

When Christ shall come, with shout of acclamation,
And take me home, what joy shall fill my heart.
Then I shall bow, in humble adoration,
And then proclaim: "My God, how great Thou art!"

Tyra loved this Swedish hymn, and knew that whatever might happen in the future, she could exclaim, "*O store Gud!*" (O Great God!) although the English was still merely noise. She was very grateful Edit had invited her to attend the program.

One evening Tyra was washing dishes after the meal, and Axel was sitting on the back steps having his customary cigarette. Tyra hated smoking, but despite her pleading, Axel still puffed, and this even in spite of his regular attendance at Adventist church services where he had heard many times of the health hazards of smoking. Although he was ashamed to admit it, he was addicted. Suddenly a small explosion startled Tyra and a few sulfur crested cockatoos resting on a nearby tree rose screeching into the air. A few minutes later there was another explosion, more squawking birds, and Axel appeared in the doorway, guiltily holding two shattered cigarettes.

"You know anything about this?" he asked, waggling his blasted cigarettes. Tyra shook her head. "Where are those boys?" Axel demanded, and stomped into the bedroom to find his sons.

"You did this?" he asked holding out the ruined cigarettes.

Nils shrugged, but Roland grinned mischievously. "Far, we've talked to you for years, but nothing happens. It's smelly and unhealthy. We thought an Aussie fright might encourage you!" admitted Roland. In fact, Nils had decided drastic measures were needed to stop his father smoking, and found a willing accomplice in Roland. Lying around the village were toy gun caps. Carefully the brothers had teased tobacco from individual cigarettes in a pack, tamped a cap down each paper tube, replaced the tobacco shavings, and waited for the reaction.

"You rascals!" exclaimed Axel, grinning. Then looking thoughtful he admitted, "Smoking is a bit expensive," but went off to enjoy a smoke from another pack.

But it must have got him thinking. In several of Erik's regularly sent papers were news items about tobacco causing serious health problems, including cancer. Shortly after the explosions Axel gave up the habit, permanently, much to his family's joy. Once he made up his mind, he found quitting was much easier than he had expected. Cheerfully he announced how much his decision had benefitted him financially, as though it was all his own initiative. Tyra wisely refrained from saying, "I told you so!"

Tyra and Axel were close friends with June and Harry Nylund, bonded by Tyra's regular correspondence with Takla Höglund. With her own children away most of the day, Tyra took great interest in the Nylund children, especially Lloyd, the elder boy. She decided to teach him Swedish, and he was a willing student. Soon he was chatting happily in excellent Swedish, much to his mother's amusement, and his father's delight. Lloyd lost most of his ability to speak Swedish once he started school, but he remembered with great fondness the woman who taught him when he was a small child.

The independent attitude of Australians puzzled Tyra. When neighbors borrowed a cup of flour or sugar because they had run out and the nearest shop was 15 kilometers away, she was shocked and horrified that they always insisted on returning her gift. These neighbors considered her unnecessarily kind. Life as a farmer's wife in war-torn Finland encouraged her to have a well-stocked cupboard and share it, but apparently her neighbors were not experienced in country living. Would she ever get to understand these people? she wondered.

When Nils announced he wanted to become a naturalized Australian, Tyra was surprised and Axel shocked. They were Finns! They had no intention of permanently belonging to this strange new country. But Nils had discovered he could have dual citizenship, and persuaded his parents to follow his lead. However, even Nils was startled to discover when he went through the naturalization ceremony that he was no longer Nils

Östring, but Nils Ostring. The niceties and complexities of elegant Swedish spelling were too much for Australian administrators. Axel, Tyra and Roland all received the same odd surname. The fact that the family was left to endlessly explain that their surname was spelled with an "O" and not "Au," as in Australia, was of little concern to the bureaucrats.

"It's worse than that," grumbled Axel, with a mischievous grin. "Instead of being people from eastern Sweden, we've become people from cheese!" He chuckled.

"Oh no!" exclaimed Tyra. "You're right! I forgot about ost! Just as well I like cheese!"

Axel suddenly frowned, a faraway, puzzled look on his face. "You know, Finns forced me to change my name to become one of them. It took a long, long time for me to get used to being Axel Östring instead of Axel Hendriksson. Now the Aussies have done the same, without even realizing what they've done. Makes a man wonder who he really is."

But Nils' choice to become an Australian citizen did not shock his parents as much as his decision to leave the family banana business, and move to Mount Isa in northwestern Queensland where he began work as an electrician in the copper mines.

"But my business is called A. Ostring and Son!" moaned a deeply distressed Axel. "How can he possibly go off and work in a mine? In a mine, did you hear? A mine, of all places! I mean, that's why we came here, for me to get out of a mine!"

"Well, he trained as an electrician, remember," consoled Tyra, who by now was used to her men making strange decisions. "Perhaps he just wants to get experience and then he'll come back to Mullumbimby."

"What, and work as an electrician?" snorted Axel. "He's needed on this plantation, not running around fixing lights and easy jobs like that!" For several days he grumbled loudly to anyone who would listen, and then decided Nils merely needed to stretch his wings, and would come back and do a little electrician work for a hobby while he helped with the real work of banana growing.

Tyra sympathized with Nils, but his departure tore her mother's heart. He had smoothed things for her when she arrived in Australia, and she missed him sorely.

Nils' departure for Mount Isa had significant consequences for Roland. He early learned frugality from his mother, who cut up worn, torn bed sheets and turned the pieces into handkerchiefs on the ancient Singer treadle sewing machine Axel found in the Mullumbimby secondhand shop. Axel's penchant for finding secondhand goods once again impacted Roland; even in the opulence of Kiruna he found a bike in the dump, enthusiastically restored it, and presented it to his son. But with Nils absent Roland took over the serious responsibility as family translator. Thus while still very young he learned to fill out tax returns and other official documents for his parents.

Predictably, Nils did not enjoy Mount Isa. Mullumbimby is lush and green, but Mount Isa is in the dusty red desert heart of Australia. The glossy advertising brochures never mentioned the endless dust or the wind! Red dust infiltrated everything, and nothing, not tightly closed windows, nor doors, nor mouths, could keep it out. The heat was relentless in summer, but winter was bitterly cold in the mornings but by noon unbearably hot again. He began dreaming of more pleasant places to work.

With satisfaction Tyra watched Roland progress from lawn-mowing the one-teacher primary school to the high school in Mullumbimby. Mr. Clifford, his kindly primary teacher, gently nurtured Roland's talents and he arrived at high school with an excellent knowledge of math. There, to his delight, he discovered his new math teacher, Neville Leeson, was a member of his local Adventist church. Roland admired his math teacher, and excelled in all subjects, except English. When Tyra asked what he would like to do when he left school he invariably replied, "An electrician, like Nils." Axel was not impressed. It was bad enough having one son spurn his bananas, but not two! But by the time Roland entered senior high school, and was assigned a routine interview with the school vocation guidance officer, he had made another choice—he would become a scientist, and work for the CSIRO, Australia's national science agency. Roland did not bother to shock his parents with this change in plans.

"How's it going, son?" Axel asked on one of Nils' trips home from Mount Isa. "Ready to get back into business?"

With sinking heart Tyra overheard, "I've been thinking Far," replied Nils. "Australia's a great country with a great future. But I want to go home for a holiday, to Sweden and Finland."

"What!"

"They pay well in those mines, as you know Far," continued Nils. "I can easily afford to go for a trip, have a look around, and get the feel of things before I come back and settle."

Axel was angry, but Tyra deeply grieved. "I slaved for years in Finland, and Sweden, and never got anywhere, but now my bank balance is growing encouragingly. Why do you want to go back? It's a ridiculous idea!" Axel declared.

"Far, it's just something I have to do."

Suddenly Axel had an idea that cheered him. "Yah, I understand! Go back! Find a nice girl and bring her here. Your mother and I want someone we can talk to, not some Aussie we can't understand. Remember that. We don't want an Aussie in the family. No foreigners, did you hear?"

Nils blushed scarlet. "Far," he said, "I'm going back to meet my friends."

"Yah, but look around while you're at it. You're heading up close to thirty, aren't you? I was a father well and truly by then! Yah, that's the idea. Find a good girl and marry her. I don't feel so bad about your going, when I think of that."

But Tyra, despite the pain of losing Nils, understood. Her own heart was still in Finland. She listened to his speech and quietly said, "Son, I'll miss you, very much. Don't forget to visit Takla and Aunt Lisa and of course Algot in Sweden. And as Far says, bring a nice girl back."

Alone with his parents, Roland attended church regularly, a silent teenager who listened hard but rarely joined in with youth activities. Then one day he told his mother he had decided to be baptized. "Oh Roland! How wonderful! You'll never regret your decision! When did you decide?" Roland explained that several months earlier the church pastor had approached him, and started him thinking. When Pastor Duffy again broached the topic, Roland realized the kindest, wisest, best person he knew was his mother, and she was baptized. Yes, he told her as she beamed with joy, he believed everything she had taught him, everything she was.

Some time later a visiting speaker at church spoke of the huge need for medical help in mission fields around the world. He showed slides of primitive hospitals in New Guinea, across the Pacific Islands, in Africa and India. Roland's interest was deeply stirred. As the family ate their meal that evening, Roland casually announced, "Mor, I've been thinking. After that talk on medical missions at church today I'd like to become a doctor."

There was absolute silence. Neither Tyra nor Axel had ever dreamed of such a ridiculous possibility.

"But—the plantation!" wailed Axel, finally breaking the hush. "What about my bananas!"

"Son, if that's what God wants you to do, you should do it," said Tyra quietly. "Where do you have to go to learn to be a doctor?"

"I don't know. I'll ask at school." Mullumbimby was in the state of New South Wales, and both medical schools in that state were in Sydney. Nearby Brisbane was in the state of Queensland, with its own separate educational system. If he wanted to study medicine, Roland would need to go to Sydney. It was a long way from home.

Tyra pondered Roland's ideas in her heart. She was not surprised her son planned to do something different. She would support him, especially a decision that appeared so God-focused. But she recognized that if he went ahead with this plan she would be losing her son, probably forever, to who knew where. Axel might dream, but doctors don't work banana plantations in their spare time. But she firmly believed that mothers did not have sons merely to serve their own needs. Children were a gift from God, a trust from heaven.

Roland filled out the application forms, sat his exams, and waited. Tyra talked to Edit Söderholm who had a Swedish friend in Sydney, and after correspondence the friend offered Roland board if he were accepted for medical school. And he was. Tyra was proud of his accomplishment, but Axel remained perturbed. "Why," he expostulated, "doctors don't do real men's work! They work inside all the time!" Tyra merely smiled. Roland went to Sydney. It was a big change for a seventeen-year-old boy.

The departure of Roland goaded Axel to make two decisions. The first fulfilled a dream of his own: he bought land, his very own land, in a neighboring area called The Pocket, and planted it with his own banana trees, even adding some avocado saplings whose fruit promised to be a crop of the future. Tom Mott was a most reasonable landlord, but there was the niggling insecurity that if he ever chose to sell out, or give his land to his family for their own purposes, Axel might lose his land, a nightmare from the past he was not willing to repeat.

The second decision, although clearly related to the first, delighted Tyra. They bought a block of land in Mullumbimby township, and had their Main Arm house transported to it. Their neighbors, the ebullient Italian Nacherios, had moved their house to Mullumbimby, so Axel knew it could be done. The house was cut in two, hoisted on to huge trucks, taken down the road, then reassembled on the new block. Joy of joys, the final house was extended, and now included a modernized kitchen, bigger lounge room, a proper flush toilet, and space for an amazing apparatus—a washing machine! Tyra could hardly believe how easy this made life for her. The house was now very close to both Edit Söderholm's home and the Adventist church, which added to Tyra's enjoyment of life, both physically and socially. Axel planted his quarter acre town section in strawberries, while Tyra willingly watered them. They produced well, and sold profitably from a stall at the corner of the street.

Within months of reaching Sweden Nils wrote about a young woman called Ethel, and a year later they were married. He sent photos of his bride, but Tyra was unhappy that she had neither met her daughter-in-law, nor attended her son's wedding. Nils found work in Eskilstuna, where Algot had settled. Soon Nils was the proud father of two children, Rita and Anders, whom Tyra longed to see. But then a letter bearing good news arrived. Nils planned to bring his wife and children to visit his parents. When Tyra thought of the enormous journey she had made to come to Australia she found it hard to imagine that coming so far, with two small children, for a visit of merely a few weeks, would be anything other than exhausting.

Perhaps it was pure excitement, perhaps it was worry about the long trip her family was making, but shortly before Nils and Ethel arrived, with little Rita and baby Anders, Tyra was admitted to hospital with a heart condition called atrial fibrillation. For the first week of their precious visit she was sedated, had to rest in bed, and was unable to enjoy them. The heavy stresses of her life were taking their toll. But eventually she improved, and seeing Australia through the eyes of her small granddaughter was a delight. Ape Land creatures like leeches and ticks were rare around the "new" town house, nor need Tyra worry about small children falling down the terrible "dunny" hole toilet. As she showed Rita colorful birds, beautiful beaches, and enjoyed warm sunny days when baby Anders could play outdoors all he liked, she began to see beauty in Australia that she had never seen before. It was not easy to say goodbye to her family when they returned to Sweden, but the visit had been a blessing.

Axel's dedication to his bananas grew as fast as they did. Often Tyra, to quell loneliness, went with him while he worked at The Pocket. She sat in his old truck, and remembering her grandchildren, wrote long letters to Ethel, or read books. Axel parked the truck in the shade for her comfort, and under the trees she had ample opportunity to watch the beautiful birds of the bush. The noisy laughing kookaburras, screeching parrots, and caroling magpies were easy to see. But hiding in the canopy were delightful small birds, birds only seen with patient quietness, when they had the courage to come close by.

Roland graduated from medical school, and chose to work in Newcastle, still almost 600 kilometers from Mullumbimby. Tyra was overjoyed when she learned he planned a weekend visit. She made a celebratory apple cake, and remembered Roland had become a vegetarian while at medical school. This was a new idea to her, so she waited to learn what he liked to eat. Because of work commitments he could leave Newcastle for Mullumbimby only after he finished work on Friday. Both Tyra and Axel were relaxed about time, so quietly rested until their son got home. It was almost 3am before they heard a car pull into the driveway, but both were immediately wide awake, overjoyed with anticipation to meet their boy. They raced to the door, and stopped short. Walking in with their quiet son was a young woman!

"Ah! Ha! Who's this you've brought!" demanded a beaming Axel. "You're getting into the romance a bit faster than Nils did!"

"She's welcome," said Tyra awkwardly. "Will she like Finnish cooking? Does she know we don't speak English?"

"We're just friends," declared Roland firmly. "Elizabeth's a doctor at the hospital, and she knows you speak Swedish." He didn't bother to explain that he had told her this important fact only as they drove up the driveway!

The weekend passed quickly, and despite communication difficulties, went remarkably smoothly. Axel used his shout-and-understand English technique, but Roland's friend showed no talent for speed learning a language. She sat with a fixed half smile on her face, and understood nothing. After the meal the deaf young woman tried to show she was at least useful. With smiles and arm-waving sign language she indicated that she and Roland would do the dishes. Tyra was delighted, but Axel horrified.

"Vot!" He shouted in his you-understand-Swenglish-or-else voice. "Vot! Men vork outside, but vomen vork inside!" Roland was forced to translate, and for the first time that weekend Elizabeth burst into laughter. Tyra was more than happy to let someone else do her dishes. It was a most pleasant novelty.

Shortly after, Roland announced that he and his "friend" were getting married in early January, 1972. Please, Mor, will you and Far come? he wrote. Of course Tyra wanted to be there. She had missed Nils' wedding, she had missed Roland's graduation. Axel might be totally dedicated to his bananas, but this time she was determined, determined with every ounce of Finnish *sisu* that she could muster.

"Axel," she announced, "I'm going to Roland's wedding. It's somewhere near Newcastle."

"Don't be silly! I'd have to be away from The Pocket for at least two days! Some bananas might ripen and I wouldn't be here to pick them! Impossible!"

"That's fine. I'll go by myself."

Axel went.

Tyra, and especially Axel, could not believe how complicated weddings had become since their own, forty years earlier, although in fact their son's wedding was a small and subdued one. Flowers filled the church, the organist played majestic music. The minister was a friend of the bride. There were endless photos taken. The food, at the banquet afterwards, was vegetarian, like nothing Tyra had ever eaten, though the dessert, mainly strawberries, brought sweet memories. But Tyra felt a deep sense of sadness as she and Axel chugged back to Mullumbimby on the old Brisbane Limited. Axel might be in love with his Pocket and bananas, but there were times when she was lonely, very lonely. She could write frequent letters to Ethel in Sweden, but how could she ever communicate with this new daughter-in-law? Whilst Roland's spelling was considerably better than his father's, he had not proved to be a very frequent communicator during his medical school days. As the train clattered north Axel could not but notice her silence, extreme even for her.

"I've been thinking," he said, as he and Tyra ate their first meal in Mullumbimby after returning from the wedding. "I've been thinking we could afford to take a holiday back to Finland, like I promised you when we left."

Tyra, in the process of raising a fork to her mouth, dropped it. She stared silently at her husband.

"Don't you want to go?" he said, his voice full of disappointment. "I thought it would make you happy."

Tyra picked up her fork, put the food in her mouth, and chewed thoughtfully. Suddenly she smiled, radiantly. "What do you say when all your dreams come true?" she asked, her grey eyes twinkling.

Chapter 21

Home

"Welcome home!" cried Florence Nichols, bursting through Tyra's back door. Florence, a widow, and sister of June Nyland, was Tyra's Mullumbimby neighbor. "I've missed you so much!" Florence smiled, placed a platter cradling a magnificent cream sponge on the table, and beside it a punnet of luscious strawberries. "I hope your trip to Finland went well, and the flights weren't too tiring. I thought these strawberries might remind you of Finland." Two days earlier Tyra and Axel had returned from their long-delayed, but finally-made, Scandinavian holiday.

Tyra was speechless. Florence's kindness, and her words of welcome were comforting. But shockingly, Florence called Mullumbimby home, and even more amazingly, Tyra suddenly realized it was. Yes, she was pleased to be home, very pleased, back in her Australian home. Home was not a place but a concept.

"P'ease, stay. Eat!" Tyra's English was very limited, but Florence was one person who completely understood her. "Trip good," she added.

"Good, I'd like to stay. I'll just pop across the road and ring June and tell her to come over, and that friend of yours, Edit. We'll make a party of this, us girls!" Florence bustled off to make her phone calls, the Ostrings having no phone of their own because Axel couldn't see the point of such a contraption.

While waiting for her friends, Tyra remembered the bitter sweet of the Finland visit, but with warm gratitude the fun of her grandchildren in Sweden.

• • •

The clock cannot be turned back, Tyra now finally understood. For twenty years she had dreamed of returning to Finland. But the trip was confusing, and now, where was home? She honestly didn't know, but after more than 20 years in Australia the country was certainly becoming the new norm. During their visit Finland, now a prosperous and confident country, had sparkled in its summer sun, but for all those intervening 20 years she'd had endless summer sun. Once she dreaded the snows of winter, now she longed for them, deeply, passionately. Snow. So clean, so pure, so bright, so Finnish! Sleigh rides, bells tinkling, the fun of returning to blazing wood fires. But, suddenly, unwanted, buried subconscious deep, memories of snow brought images of horror—war; Tobbe killed; Axel a fugitive; nothing to eat but barley; the deep yearning to know what life was all about. Winter was beautiful, but cruel. The new Finland was propserous and handsome, and she was very proud of it, but it wasn't the Finland she remembered.

Spring, that's what she'd longed for. How could she ever explain to Ape Landers the wonder, the marvel, the pure joy of a Finnish spring? Trees—bare, blackened, ice-bound arms lifted heavenward in mute appeal, awakened to new life. Tiny buds of promise bursting along the twigs; in less than a week brilliant green leaves unfurling in riotous joy. Birds, winter-absent in the silent blanketing snow, escaped from southern sanctuaries, returned, and sang with joy. Flowers, every color, pushed through imprisoning earth, sent feet scrambling for golden buttercups and scarlet poppies. Oh, how she loved the Finnish spring! How she loved her native land! Then, with nostalgia unexpected, the memory of brilliantly colored birds in the Ape Land bush suddenly intruded.

They had returned to their old Finnish home. The rock on which her boys loved to play rose high in the Brännon field, but gone was the fencing and the much-loved animals it corralled—good sheep with thick woolly fleeces; essential cows with creamy milk; but oh, how she loved the horses! A flood of happy equine memories enveloped her. But these joyous thoughts were shattered as she looked out the window and watched Takla walk stiffly across the field. Takla, like everyone on this nostalgic trip, was old, her arthritis troublesome.

"My, Tyra, but it does my heart good to see you!" Takla hollered as she approached, voice deaf-strident. "I should borrow a cup of flour like I did in the old days!" she laughed. "But my cooking days here are done. Never mind, when I get to Björn's, I'll try my hand again. I don't think I could survive without stirring something in a pot!"

"Seeing you walk across the field reminds me of the good old days!" responded Tyra, smiling. Memory had Takla striding the meadow in purposeful, confident exuberance, not lumbering along in the unfamiliar gait of this shuffling old woman.

"Yah, we had good times, didn't we?" Takla was silent for a moment. "You said I was walking, but hobble's the truth. Couldn't run after those boys of yours like I used to, not if I tried my darnedest! But you, you're still so nimble! God's been good to you. Ah well, better get on with my packing. Now don't forget to come and say a proper good bye when those men get back." Tyra nodded. Takla plodded painfully back. She was packing to leave Brännon. Her husband Karl had passed away, coping alone was hard. She would move to the city she hated, close to her younger brother. Which city Tyra couldn't remember, but the address was safely in her handbag.

Many had moved away. The once busy village seemed now almost empty. The Öhling family had long gone, their land now a mink farm, the owner reputed very rich. But the farm's nauseous stench was overpowering, the poor creatures confined in miniscule compartments in long, inhumane cages, snarling and hissing menacingly at each other and those gawking at them. Wild mink hunt fish, small mammals and birds. These farmed mink, fed slaughterhouse waste and dairy products deemed unfit for human consumption, stank. Was their suffering justified to provide luxury fur for rich, coddled women? The idea, the smell, made Tyra feel sick. Finns were grateful for winter-warming fur garments; coats treasured, preserved for years, passed down the generations, never mere fashion statements!

In her familiar yet now strange home the stoves, into which Axel had put much so much thought and money, still faithfully did their job. But an unfamiliar faucet hung over a tub in the kitchen, the village well long since filled in. The faucet made cooking and cleaning easier, but how much village chatting, laughing, and sharing occurred around that well!

Tyra wandered across to the barn, down the old track, to the toilet trio unchanged since Axel made it, still clean and decent. The barn roof was in good condition, testimony to the quality work of Nils and Axel. But the barn's emptiness felt ominous, and the sight of her mother's loom lying broken in a corner brought sudden tears. Gone were the sheep, gone were the cows, no ghosts of horses ran for sweet apple treats. The old barn, reminder of months of fearful agony, now a vast emptiness.

When Axel and Nils returned from visiting friends, Tyra faithfully made the farewell visit to Takla. Finnish restraint outwardly removed emotion. They discussed general topics, like the much-debated hijacking of the Aeroflot Tupolev Tu-134 jet to Helsinki airport, an event that had shocked modern peace-loving Finns. After the chatter, Tyra presented her friend with a clock, of beautiful workmanship, made from highly polished native Australian woods, crafted as a map of the country. Takla stroked the polished wood appreciatively, and then pressed into Tyra's hands two small parcels.

"I thought the birch wood platter would be nice for Harry's June," Takla explained, "and I want you to have my old cheese cutter with the carved handle. You always admired it. I've been planning to send it to you for years. Now you've saved me postage, aren't you good!" Takla beamed with satisfaction.

Tyra swallowed hard, word-choked. She fingered the wheat and poppies on the carved handle. Takla had given the best she had. Tyra coughed, found her voice, said a banal thank you. Then impulsively she wrapped Takla in a very un-Finnish bear hug, and hastily walked away before she could witness Takla's shocking tears.

Halfway back to the cottage the world swam wildly. Tyra vomited before she reached the stairs, which she climbed with difficulty. Nils helped her to a bed that swayed in a mist of instability. If she closed her eyes and lay perfectly still the heaving world steadied, but the slightest movement set everything in nauseus motion again. The men packed the car, tidied the cottage, man-fashion. She let them, without a word of protest, then on Nils' arm she hobbled across the field to lie on the back seat of Nils' old red van, as they drove carefully away, away from a life rich and full, and to which she could never return. For the legendarily placid Tyra the emotion of homecoming had proved too much. The rattling red van took them safely to Vasa, where she had already walked in the busy central market square, and down to her old home on Rådhusgatan. The town was lively and prosperous, no hint of the misery of civil, winter, or continuation wars. She felt great pride for the contemporary, progressive version of her country, but its sparkling newness and prosperity were a little shocking, and jarred against her memories.

Axel's tenderness as he led her to their ferry cabin, helped her undress, and laid her gently on the lower bunk, surprised her. "Will you be alright if I go get food?" he asked, idly tucking a blanket around her.

"Sure," she responded, flatly, with a glimmer of a smile. "I'm better alone." He nodded, gave her a gentle pat, and left, while she tried to make sense of her troubled memories.

By the time Tyra had crossed the Baltic Sea and returned to Eskilstuna she was physically better. The distressing vomiting had gone. Probably a virus, Nils had muttered, but in her own heart she knew it was the the emotional pain of leaving forever her much loved Finnish home. She recalled that instead of the six-week sea voyage that took Axel and her to Australia, this time she had flown to Sweden. Not in her wildest nightmares had she ever expected to go anywhere in a plane, those dreadful bomb-dropping inventions! Instead of relaxing on a majestic ship, reading books, watching seabirds dive the waves, chatting with new friends, she flew across the world in a little over 24 hours, but saw nothing. The kindly travel agent in Mullumbimby arranged for "airport assistance", meaning she and Axel were guided through the Singapore and Frankfurt stopovers by helpful airport personnel. But the journey was hurried, bustled, pressured, and dreadfully, dreadfully uncomfortable, sitting cramped in that huge metal tube for so many hours. Flying was supposed to be progress, but Tyra thought nostalgically of the leisurely sea voyage. When she and Axel were finally disgorged from the third plane into Arlanda Airport outside Stockholm, she was very grateful to see Nils in the crowded arrivals room. The 90 kilometer drive to Eskilstuna, through beautiful but unfamiliar Swedish countryside was a bewildered blur, and when she reached Nils' home she discovered her days had become nights, her nights days, and she was introduced to a new disease called jetlag.

But the return to Finland was worth the effort. The threads of her life, some light with hope, bright with understanding, some dark with pain and fear, she now understood wove together into a pattern of love and meaning. God *had* fulfilled her dearest dream, and Axel *had* chosen to accept God's love. Life was not just about her, her understanding, her needs. Slowly, somewhat fretfully, she had learned to trust God, to give and receive love, and that made everything worthwhile.

Ah, and there were the happy memories of her grandchildren! They were the trip's pinnacle of delight! Rita was now ten, Anders seven, and little Mia four years old. Tyra's jetlag reduced her energies for an energetic young boy who loved outdoor activities and a little girl barely out of toddlerhood. But Rita was quiet, enjoyed being read to, went on gentle walks, showing her Farmor her school not far from her home, the shortcut through the cemetery, and where the park and river met beside the big, old, red, double-towered church on the corner. Rita showed Tyra the place near her *folkskola* where a statue to Saint Eskil would soon be erected. Rita learned this important fact at school, knew her city took his name, but was unsure what he had done that made him important. So Tyra accompanied Rita to the local library, and they searched for information on the saint.

"Look at this!" exclaimed Tyra to Rita. "Eskil was an Anglo-Saxon! That means he came across the sea from England, all that way to tell blood thirsty Vikings about God, and they murdered him. He was a brave man because he came to Sweden about one thousand years ago, when travelling was very difficult. Your town used to be called Tuna. But now it's called Eskil's Tuna!"

Rita listened, wide-eyed, apparently little comprehending.

"I went to England once," said Tyra, "on the way to Australia. It was foggy and miserable, and I didn't like it. It's a long way from Sweden, and hundreds of years ago they didn't have strong ships."

"My Mor went to England, too," said Rita, pensively. And then she skipped out the library door to catch a butterfly. Tyra sighed, thinking her granddaughter had no interest in history.

But when they got home Rita set to work with pencils and paper, and drew a most artistic picture of a saintly figure with a bright yellow halo being speared by a mob of wild stick men. "That's Eskil," she said. Then pointing to a cluster of houses behind the saint she added, "And that's his Tuna! I put a butterfly in to make him happy."

"That's very good! Why, Rita, you're very artistic!" exclaimed Tyra.

"Yah, Farmor. I want to be an artist when I grow up!"

"I'm sure you'll do very well," encouraged Tyra.

When jetlag finally subsided, Tyra did outdoor things with Anders, and romped with Mia. They played croquet under the apple trees, and Anders showed her, after she most solemnly promised to keep his secret, where a fieldfare's and starling's nest hid.

"I've seen a great tit in the apples trees," he told her proudly, "and a spotted flycatcher! But I haven't been able to find their nests yet."

"You do like birds, don't you!" exclaimed Tyra happily. Anders threw her a cheeky grin, and raced off to play with his mates. He *did* like birds, but he wasn't going to get caught by his friends discussing such things with his grandmother!

∴

Tyra was still wrapped in her reminiscences when June, Florence and Edit joined her. She was surprised how much she enjoyed the afternoon. It was as much fun, she suddenly realized, as the reunion she so much enjoyed with dear Algot and brother Erik. Ah, Erik, dear brother Erik, who so faithfully supplied her, like Nils, with Swedish reading material, books and magazines, including his own original poetry. He also kept Axel up to date with newspapers and the political situation in Finland. The brothers met as brothers do, with jokes about loss of hair and other inconsequentials, but it was so good to see Erik again. She couldn't remember what words were spoken when she and Algot met after thirty years, it was so deeply emotional. What a shock to discover he was old and shrunk, and realize she too was old! Algot talked about working with Nils on big Eskilstuna construction projects, and Gunnel chatted about food prices, and changes in Eskilstuna while she did beautiful embroidery. Only after several visits did Tyra remember with disbelief that Algot was once a hunted criminal. She was glad her Mullumbimby guests didn't know what she was thinking about as they chatted animatedly about things Australian, the usual political issues—the "new" Prime Minister Malcolm Fraser, the shock (and amusement) of Prime Minister Gough Whitlam's dismissal, the unsolved puzzle of Prime Minister Harold Holt's disappearance while swimming, and especially fond memories of the stability of Sir Robert Menzies' leadership, with, of course, ubiquitous discussions of the weather and banana prices.

Tyra never expected returning to Finland would be painful, but the changes she found there, she now realized, were just as difficult to accept as Australia had initially been. It took time before she identified what was missing from her birthplace, Vasa, the fondly remembered childhood home, now an attractive, bustling, modern city. Yes, the old house on Rådhusgatan was still there, well-preserved and clearly appreciated. The central market was a hive of activity, just as remembered. In Australia strawberries were sold in tiny packages called punnets, but in Vasa they were scooped up generously and sold by the kilogram. The market still traded hand-loomed carpets, and rag mats. There were stalls offering classic Finnish knives in fancy leather sheaths. Like the old days, tapestry nets and embroidery kits were available. The market was busy, an oasis of surprisingly cheerful calm away from traffic, extra noisy on the cobblestones.

"I felt so proud of my country!" Tyra blurted out. "It's beautiful and prosperous now. You know, it's more than 20 years since we lived there, almost thirty, in fact! Yes, it's a lovely country. But you know what was hardest about the trip?" she asked, suddenly remembering that noisy traffic. Edit, June, and Florence, deep in a discussion of the pros and cons of Australian Prime Minister Whitlam's dismissal, looked up in surprise. "It made me really sad. Because, you know—well—there were no horses and carts, not one, not anywhere in Vasa. The core of my childhood has gone, forever!"

"The clock can't be turned back," said Edit, kindly, and translated Tyra's speech for for Florence and June.

"Just enjoy us now," advised Florence, uncomprehending, but pushing the bowl of scarlet strawberries towards Tyra in kindly gesture.

June took another piece of strawberry sponge, and gave Tyra's arm a warm and friendly squeeze.

A few days later Tyra and Axel attended Mullumbimby Adventist church, and were overwhelmed by the warmth and sincerity of their welcome. The Thompsons, the Parmenters, the Cummings, the Winters, the Kemps, the Whites—so many people that Tyra lost track of names, but not of their kindness, all of them saying, "Welcome home!"

Shortly after their return Roland and family visited on their way back from Hong Kong where he and Elizabeth had been working in Tsuen Wan Adventist Hospital. He told stories of a Hong Kong world as different from Australia as Finland. Tyra met two more grandchildren, the twins Sven and Genevieve, about the same age as Mia. The visit was much too short, before Roland moved south to Newcastle then back to Hong Kong, and once again Tyra and Axel settled into the routine of bananas and avocados.

A few weeks later, one glorious Australian spring day Tyra sat, as she so often did, in the cab of Axel's old truck, parked at The Pocket under the shade of eucalyptus trees, watching red-breasted mistletoe birds, a pair of rufus fantails, and a cheeky yellow robin dart in the branches. It was peaceful, the birds beautiful. She could hear, but not see, Axel working nearby on his bananas. She put down her book and suddenly felt a surge of enormous gratitude to God. While she could no longer identify where her earthly home really was, she was content. She knew her ultimate home was heaven, and despite terrible heartaches in life, she realized God had been very kind to her, and that what she had least wanted to do, that is, come to Australia, had proved a real blessing. Suddenly, with luminous clarity, she remembered a special event, one that occurred soon after Roland's and Elizabeth's marriage, and the painful experiences of her life knit together as a completed puzzle.

She and Axel had sat on the front seat of Mullumbimby Adventist church. The Thompson families sat companionably beside them as on their first day at the church so many years before. Outwardly Tyra looked a quiet, placid woman modestly dressed in the pastel colors she always chose for church. People admired her faithful attendance, especially given her lack of English. They smiled politely and assumed life had been simple and easy for her, the obvious explanation for her serene and tranquil exterior.

But while the organ played softly, she suddenly remembered the Algot tragedy, the terrifying nocturnal encounter with him, the intense shame of the situation. And yet, inexplicably, that wretched experience allowed her to get to know Axel. Her mind flicked to her mother, the unbearable shock of her death so soon after arriving in Australia, but Anna had helped her find peace from the fear of death and hell. Then, blocked from her memory for years, came the unspeakable terrors of war, war that went on and on, not one war, not two wars, but three. Those dark, terrifying years of not knowing exactly where the man, then a once-imprisoned, public pariah, now sitting so tranquilly, triumphantly, beside her, even was. Her heart beat a wild gallop. But Algot, the criminal Algot, what a lifesaver he proved to be during those horrifying times of war! God certainly works in mysterious ways, she thought. The shock of Axel losing his land, and their desperate move to Kiruna, to its hated mine, loomed dark in her mind. But the beauty of Kiruna gave unexpected opportunity for recovery from the deep traumas of war, fearful traumas that still sometimes overwhelmed her and made it hard to function. But everything was worth it when she saw that it led to this moment in the church.

Recently Mullumbimby church had hosted evening meetings by a visiting evangelist. Axel, who had never shown obvious interest in spiritual things, accepted Tyra's invitation to accompany her. Night meetings allowed him to still check his precious bananas and avocados.

As Tyra and Axel were leaving the meeting one evening, the speaker approached them and asked Axel what he thought of the lectures. "Good," Axel said. 'Really good."

"Would you like to join this church?"

"I'm a Christian already you know. Supposed to be a Lutheran, actually. Learnt the theory in my youth. But Christianity and Jesus Christ, well, it's my wife who's shown me the real meaning of that. That's all I need, isn't it?"

"You believe the teachings?"

"Sure. Doctrines are fine for the head. But you have to see that head stuff turned into life stuff. My wife has done that for me. I've watched her and listened here in church. I want to follow God like she does. You know, I'm sure if it hadn't been for her prayers and her food and everything she did I would never have survived the war. It was a terrible experience, unspeakably terrible in those frozen forests, and that Karelia. Yes, I owe Tyra a lot. Yes, I'd like to join her church."

The minister was surprised that Axel clearly identified the church with his wife, but did understand why. "Then may I come and talk to you about baptism?"

"Sure," responded Axel, unhesitatingly. "You know, in Finland I never had time to think much about God. I put everything I had into the farm. Here, at first I came to church just to please Tyra, because I knew she had language problems, and, well, she had come to Australia just for me. But more and more I can see that God has looked after us, and brought me here. I'm very glad we came to Australia; very grateful to God."

As she listened, Tyra realized with a grateful shock that coming to Ape Land, which she had done purely from love for Axel, had given her a rich reward.

Axel's baptism was Tyra's dearest dream come true. Maintaining her trademark tranquility was almost impossible. She wished her sons were present, to see their father confirm his choice to serve God, and yes, dear brother Erik and the little Sabbath fellowship in Nykarleby. Her life had been obscure, filled with the blood, sweat, and tears of her own suffering. But that misery had meaning, purpose.

And now, as she sat under the trees watching colorful Australian birds, the beautiful Swedish melody heard in Kiruna, words learned from Kristin Nilsson on the ship to Australia, fully heard at the Billy Graham Crusade in Brisbane, and sung at Axel's baptism, filled her mind. With a surge of deep gratitude she understood the strange English words that now made sense, as did all the strange events of her life, and she could sing with heartfelt understanding and appreciation. Quietly, she hummed to herself,

> O Lord my God, When I in awesome wonder,
> Consider all the worlds Thy hands have made;
> I see the stars, I hear the rolling thunder,
> Thy power throughout the universe displayed.

Chorus:
Then sings my soul, My Savior God, to Thee,
How great Thou art, How great Thou art.
Then sings my soul, My Savior God, to Thee,
How great Thou art, How great Thou art!

When through the woods, and forest glades I wander,
And hear the birds sing sweetly in the trees.
When I look down, from lofty mountain grandeur
And see the brook, and feel the gentle breeze.

And when I think, that God, His Son not sparing;
Sent Him to die, I scarce can take it in;
That on a Cross, my burdens gladly bearing,
He bled and died to take away my sin.

When Christ shall come, with shout of acclamation,
And take me home, what joy shall fill my heart.
Then I shall bow, in humble adoration,
And then proclaim, "My God, how great Thou art!"

Suddenly, Axel opened the truck door and broke her reverie. "Where's lunch? Wow, you aren't writing to Ethel, or even reading?" he observed, looking at her quizzically. "You look as though you've just seen a vision!"

"Yah, I have." Tyra paused, awkwardly. "Life, all the good and the bad times, it all makes sense now. God is good."

"It hasn't always been easy for you," he said, not quite understanding. "But—well—I'm so glad I've got you."

Tyra nodded, a tiny smile brightening her eyes. "Things could have been very different for us, you know."

"Yah! If I'd been a good Finnish citizen and fought for that Hitlerish Germany, the Russians might have taken me to Siberia! Or I mightn't have survived that Swedish mine. I don't know how I survived those wastes in Karelia. Only your prayers, I'm sure."

"Yah, so many things could've happened. Imagine what would have happened if I had forced you not to come to Australia! I think you'd have to say God's been very good to us!"

"Yah. They sing a song at church, something about Jesus leading all the way. That describes both of us."

"That's exactly what I've been thinking!" Tyra smiled, surprised. "That was my vision! Yah, oh, yah! *O Store Gud.* Our God really is great! I just wish I'd trusted him more instead of complaining."

"Yah, how much time have we both wasted doing that!" agreed Axel, with a grin. "Me much worse than you. I've hardly ever heard you complain, though you've had plenty to moan about, especially me."

Tyra laughed good-naturedly. "I may not have said much, but I've thought plenty of silly things! Just as well God is so forgiving and merciful. But we have good sons, and a pleasant place to live, although I still have trouble with the creepy-crawly creatures here! Lots to thank God for, really, haven't we?"

"Absolutely!" grinned Axel. "But I'm hungry!"

"What's new? Food and work, that's your life! Shall we have egg sandwiches and orange juice?" responded Tyra with a mischievous twinkle in her grey eyes as she spread out *knäckerbröd*, cheese, tomatoes and half an apple cake.

"Nah! I'm not that Australian yet! Nothing but good Finnish fare will suit me!" said Axel, pulling a face. "But here's a couple of perfect Aussie bananas, straight from the tree. And, you won't believe this, but I do appreciate more than just work and food. So I give these bananas to the best woman I know!"

• • •

Sabbath May 9, 1982, was a beautiful day, Australia at its autumnal best. In church that morning Tyra enjoyed the hymns, and understood much of the sermon. They visited Edit, and then Charlie (Karl) Hägar in the afternoon. After their evening meal, Tyra settled on the couch for a time of of quiet reading.

She picked up a copy of the Swedish *Signs of the Times,* one of many Nils sent regularly, and glanced through its headlines. Suddenly an unbearable pain rushed through her head, she cried out, then all went black as she fell senseless to the floor.

In horror, Axel pushed a cushion under her head, and raced across the road to Florence Nichols' house to phone first a doctor, then Roland in Hong Kong, and Nils in Sweden. Roland was able to get a flight back to Brisbane that night, but his mother died of her massive stroke before he reached Mullumbimby. Nils was sadly prevented from returning for his mother's funeral by an inadvertently expired passport.

One word dominated the eulogies made at Tyra's simple funeral—faithfulness.

"She never missed church," one friend exclaimed in admiration. "She was amazingly faithful."

"True, but she was so placid, and very kind," said another. "So very kind. My idea of a really truly faithful Christian."

But most importantly, as Roland stood by the graveside, moist-eyed beside his shocked, devastated father, he knew they were both living testimony to the godly power of Tyra's life. She had shared with them, she had lived before them, as a loving and lovable Christian, the demonstrable reality of a great and loving God and the saving power of Jesus Christ. Hers was not only a life well lived. It was a Christian life well shared.

Axel lived another five yeas, a lonely old man, but still dedicated to his bananas, and faithfully attending church. He died after a very short battle with leukemia. Both his sons were present for his funeral, grateful for a father they could be proud of.

Bibliography

Oral History from:
    Nils Östring (1935–2012)
    Ethel Östring (wife of Nils, 1934–)
    Roland Ostring (1946–)

Hundreds of internet articles on Finland: its geography, history, religion, culture, food, and economy.

Campbell, David. *Finnish Soldier Versus Soviet Soldier*. Oxford UK: Osprey, 2016.
Goss, Glenda Dawn. *Sibelius—a Composer's Life and the Awakening of Finland*. University of Chicago Press, 2009.
Johansen, Claes. *Hitler's Nordic Allies?—Finland and the Total War 1939–1945*. Barnsley, South Yorkshire: Pen and Sword Military, 2016.
Linna, Vainö. *Under the North Star* Trilogy (Translated by Richard Impola), 1959, 1960, 1963.
Meinander, Henrik. *A History of Finland*. Translated from Swedish by Tom Geddes. New York: Oxford University Press, 2013.
Nenye, Vesa, Munter, Peter, and Wirtanene, Toni. *Finland at War: The Winter War 1939–1940*. Oxford: Osprey, 2015.
Singmaster, Elsie. *The Story of Lutheran Missions*. A Project Gutenburg ebook 2017.
Weigert, Ursula. *A Great Song: Biography of Herbert Blomstedt world-renowned conductor of the San Francisco Symphony Orchestra*. Nampa ID: Pacific Press, 2017.

www.ingramcontent.com/pod-product-compliance
Lightning Source LLC
Chambersburg PA
CBHW050612300426
44112CB00012B/1467